Long Life,
Honey in the Heart

A Story of Initiation
and Eloquence
from the Shores
of a Mayan Lake

Jeremy P. Tarcher • *Putnam*
a member of
Penguin Putnam Inc.
New York

LONG LIFE,
HONEY IN THE HEART

MARTÍN PRECHTEL

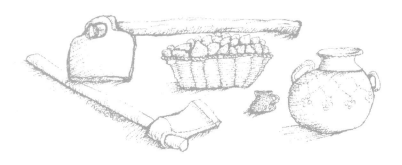

Most Tarcher/Putnam books are available at special quantity discounts for bulk purchases for sales promotions, premiums, fundraising, and educational needs. Special books or book excerpts also can be created to fit specific needs. For details write Putnam Special Markets, 375 Hudson Street, New York, NY 10014.

Jeremy P. Tarcher/Putnam
a member of
Penguin Putnam Inc.
375 Hudson Street
New York, NY 10014
www.penguinputnam.com

Library of Congress Cataloging-in-Publication Data

Prechtel, Martín
    Long life, honey in the heart: a story of initiation and eloquence from the shores of a Mayan lake / Martín Prechtel.
      p.   cm.
     ISBN 0-87477-994-4
     1. Prechtel, Martín.   2. Shamans—United States—Biography.   3. Shamans—Guatemala—Santiago Atitlan—Biography.   4. Tzutuhil Indians—Religion—Miscellanea.
    5. Santiago Atitlan (Guatemala)—Description and travel.
    I. Title.
    BF1679.8.P73   A3   1999   99-27247 CIP
    299'.784152'092—dc21

Printed in the United States of America
10 9 8 7 6 5 4 3 2 1
This book is printed on acid-free paper. ∞

BOOK DESIGN BY DEBORAH KERNER
JACKET ART AND INTERIOR ILLUSTRATIONS
BY MARTÍN PRECHTEL

ACKNOWLEDGMENTS

The fruit of any tree, no matter how delicious or beautiful, shiny or enticing, no matter how much it outshines its unsung origins, the tree's scarred and crusty bark, or its branches twisted by the rigors of life and the hungry teeth of change, the life of the entire tree along with its fruited flower is ultimately fed and kept erect by a tangled net of unseen roots that valiantly endure and stretch in a heroic search for water and food, dedicated in that mission to the point of cracking implacable boulders and heaving up the earth itself.

This strange little book, *Long Life, Honey in the Heart,* like that fruit has flowered out of the meandering branch of my own life story, which in turn grows on our collective ancestral trunk into the earth where this whole tree, this book, and all my life is rooted, nourished, and supported by many unseen courageous people both alive and gone. These inspiring humans struggle inside the earth, through the legacy of cultural humus, in search of beauty, imagination, and the furtherance of spiritual intelligence. In their slow and determined way each cracks open the lazy boulders of literalism and narrowmindedness and heaves up the earth in an unabashed revolution of possibility.

Of all these people I have to tell you that there is one who is the most courageous of all. Neither I nor this book would exist without the inexhaustible effort and dedicated love of the most beautiful woman in the world, Johanna Prechtel, my wife. After all my years in Guatemala, and the very, very hard years back in the States, trying to raise children and retain the tribal cultural vision, after being exploited, criticized, excluded, slandered, and misunderstood for my refusal to allow that vision to be dissolved or digested back into the unbelieving flatness of modernity, my soul was reduced to a hard little hollow form like a dried-up tube. But one day beautiful Johanna, like a steady, angelic breeze, came rushing over the end of my hollowness and turned me into a flute whose songs are these books. I love her.

Then there are Robert and Ruth Bly who, like two sandhill cranes, flew in here from the hills of possibility to become the best friends that I've ever known. They blessed my writing from the onset and showed me that there is a place in today's world for a strange creature such as myself. I thank them, bless them, and defend them for this.

And Miguel Rivera, my brother, friend, and comrade whose great comforting friendship comes from a heart that's too big for the world.

And Gioia Timponelli and Kenneth Baraclaw for all their love and defense of story.

And for the kind support of friend and poet Coleman Barks, who agrees it's hard to be very wise when you use a dictionary written by spirits who are drunk with longing.

And I don't forget or abandon poet Thomas Smith for his literary support, friendship, and marathon typing skills in the first drafts of this book and my first book, *Secrets of the Talking Jaguar*.

Mil gracias to Dr. Clarissa Pinkola Estés for her endorsement and her struggle to further Story.

To my friends and colleagues Robert Moore, John Lee, and Malidoma Somé for their sense of humor, generous hearts, and guidance.

I would like to acknowledge poet, teacher, and community leader Haki Mahdabuti, who, besides bestowing his encouragement, has helped me to relearn that it's not enough to have vision and speak it, that one has to try to make something worth seeing by eyes that have yet to be conceived, something that inspires community and life.

I want to let it be known that I acknowledge senior editor Wendy Hubbert for all her risk taking and demon wrestling on every side to allow my books to stand as they are written and to Joy Parker for her poignant suggestions and putting up with my long, Victorian sentences, medieval alliterations, and diatribal harangues.

Thanks as well to Mr. Ned Leavitt and Libby Stevens for their kind fielding and chasing of publishing details of which I am ignorant, which allows my brand of ignorance the freedom to be itself.

Thanks again to Jeremy Tarcher for his initial desire to publish my story.

My friend R.P., Jeff Harbor, for his true, friendly heart and support of my work and writing.

And Dr. Bob Roberts, Rosie Mum, and everyone at Project Return and the New Orleans crowd for their continued support.

Thanks to Richard Sideman and Rachel Resch for their faith and appreciation in hard times, which led to happiness.

To Marilyn Bacon for her loyalty, organizing, secretarial skills, driving, fetching, filing, and especially for feeding our old ponies.

To all the Vermont crowd, especially Marianne Lust and Deborah Luber, both bold and gracious women in a dark time, as well as Tom Vernor and Mira for the magic hospitality and affection.

To the Minnesota friends as well, in particular Wick Fisher, Craig Ungerman, Dominic Howse, and many others too numerous to list with the proper attention. To all of them, I thank you for the fine caring and support you've shown my books and work over the years.

To my friend from the village, Lenard Coriz, whose renewal of our childhood friendship is such a heartfelt relief.

And my Mongolian friends Enktur Ayush and Sas.

To all the fine hearts and minds from the conferences in Utah, Oregon, New Mexico, Michigan, Alabama, California, Louisiana, Massachusetts, Maine, Washington, British Columbia, Colorado, Wisconsin, Washington State, New York, Illinois, and the United Kingdom, France, Ireland, Italy, and Spain.

In England I would like to acknowledge the fine teas and intelligent consideration shown me in every district, in particular the strong understanding and generosity of Marc Rylance and Claire van Kampen. And as always I want to acknowledge the enormous generosity of Marc Goodwin and family. The untiring support and friendship of poet William Ayot and Richard Olivier.

Thanks to the people of the Chelsea Physic.

To Shivam O'Brien and Erica Indra, who no matter how difficult the climb will charge at any enemy of Beauty with curls flying to inspire the fire of origination with their kind hordes of images from Ireland and Hungary, for their tireless support.

To my father-in-law, Tom Keller, who holds up some big corner of the world like a quiet cliff of sanctuary, for his friendship and support.

With fond memory, I acknowledge Mintor Wood, who as William Faulkner's first cousin, dressed in white shiny shoes, bow ties, and houndstooth check suits, shuffled daily into our literature class on the reservation.

His unlikely presence introduced all us rough-and-tumble reservation kids to the written word as a possibility for cultural respect and self-expression. He also taught us how to make beer.

To artists Roberto Alire and Lezlie King. Without their firewood and friendship life would be too cold to finish a book.

Thanks to my father, George, and brother John whose curiousness about the world and admirable literateness gave me permission to write and forced me to put my imagistic ideas into words.

To my sons, Jorge and Santiago, for their unexpected love of my writing and appreciative respect of who we were and what we've become. To their courage and love.

To all the traditionalists of Santiago Atitlan, Guatemala, old and young, past and present, there will never be thanks or acknowledgment deep or large enough to encompass all that life they gave me, in particular Nicolas Chiviliu Tacaxoy, Diego Sisay, Ya Chep Ski', Ya Piskát, Ya Lur Ratzaan, Ya Merced, nbaluk, wxnam, jie taq aii, Ma Tacaxoy, Ma Teq QoQuix, Ma Pe', Ma Ki', Ma Buy, Ma Sosof, Ma Culan, A Lip, A Maash, Ya Li, Ma Pioum, Ma Lushpar, Ma Mooro, and thousands more.

To all those Atitecos and Guatemalans who died horribly and violently during the 1970s, '80s and '90s.

For Doña Julia Esquivel and Don Diego Tiney for their freindship and example of survival and grace for all of us who experienced that hard era.

For my ancestors, in particular my mother, who died before her flower could truly fruit but whose principled insistence on originality, authenticity, learning, and art as natural human obligations gave me an opening to pursue the only life possible for me.

There are innumerable people who I must thank and remember. Please know that you are not forgotten or abandoned.

Like trees, authors can't worry too much about what gets done with their fruit. They can only try to make fruit that inspires. Where their peaches end up is none of their business.

Some end slowly savored by lovers of life, while others are rudely consumed by greedy flocks of wild geese who chomp it all down, forget it, and look for more elsewhere. The remainder usually rots into humus that feeds the old tree again to make more fruit. But a very few reseed themselves and grow into flowering trees in their own right.

My hope is that out of each bud of imagination, a previously unknown flower will explode that inspires more stories and life than all the world of nihilistic insects can ever destroy by chewing down the hopeful buds. After all, the spirit feeds everyone, even the ungrateful, the unconscious, and those who hate the spirit.

God's imagination is the world, and out of that exuberant and terrifying mystery every food is produced for everything and everybody, yet it is our own imaginations that feed God as well. In the force field that is then created between the two imaginations of Gods and humans, Beauty lay in eternal suffering, giving constant birth to her child called Life.

It is Beauty's suffering to the joy of living, that I give my blessing and acknowledgment for all the mercy I have received.

Kiil, Utziil, Sac bey, Sac Coló, Qán bey, Qán coló, Nimlaj taq Kaslimal, Majun Loulo' nkokutuj, Choqá, Chajalniel, Nimlaj Matioshiil, Oxlajuj Matioshiil.

This book is dedicated
to the youth of the world
who are continually refused initiation

and

to all indigenous peoples
who have had to watch their
cultures dismantled,
attacked from without and within,
by other unfortunate peoples whose consciousness has been
scrambled by infinite dynasties
of greed-sanctioned violence and territorialism

and

to the memory of all my teachers and initiators
both living and passed on, in particular:
Nicolas Chiviliu Tacaxoy, Diego Sisay,
Juan Pancho, Ramón Montoya,
and Jimmy Weahkee.

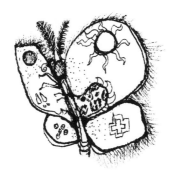

CONTENTS

Introduction ◇ **LOOKING FOR HOME** 1

One ◇ **THROUGH THE REED DOORWAY** 15

Two ◇ **THEIR FACES LIKE COPPER AXES**
First Glimpse of Initiation 34

Three ◇ **COURTING THE GODS, MARRYING OFF THE SAINTS**
Life in the Hierarchy 41

Four ◇ **DEER DANCERS, JAGUAR DANCERS, HATCHING THE VILLAGE HEART**
Going the Route to Initiation 61

Five ◇ **COURTING YA MACHETE** 75

Six ◇ **WORD WARRIORS AND DELICIOUS WORDS**
Tasks and Marriage 86

Seven ◇ **BY THE EYE OF NIGHT**
My Initiation 104

Eight ◇ **THE WATERS OF CONFIDENCE**
Birth in the Canyon Village 123

Nine ◇ **THE THROAT OF THE UNIVERSE**
Naming, Playing, Learning to Speak, the Life of a Child 145

Ten ◇ **GUARDING THE SACRED HOLE** 165

Eleven ◇ **HUSBAND OF THE VILLAGE**
Becoming Chief 186

Twelve   ❖   **COURTING THE CHIEFS**
             Mentors, Lords, Ladies, and Widows   207

Thirteen   ❖   **RAINBOYS AND SHIMMERING GIRLS**
             Gathering the Initiates   220

Fourteen   ❖   **ROBBING MOTHER, DRINKING TO**
             THE GODDESS   235

Fifteen   ❖   **THE ENFORCEMENT OF ELOQUENCE**
             The Heart of Initiation   255

Sixteen   ❖   **FEMALE EARTH, MALE EARTH**
             The Boys Go Down to Fight Death   271

Seventeen   ❖   **EMPTY AGAIN FOR GOD**
             Going Broke and Getting Full   286

Eighteen   ❖   **RETURN FROM THE UNDERWORLD**
             Reassembling the Goddess   306

Nineteen   ❖   **TRYING TO BURY OLD MAN EARS**
             The Zany Elder   322

Twenty   ❖   **BULLETS AND BUTTERFLIES**
             The Beginning of the Violence   328

Epilogue   ❖   **MY FATHER'S EYES ARE BEES**
             Becoming a Village Man   341

Note on the Language   ❖   351

Appendix   ❖   **A TADPOLE'S TAIL**
             An Essay on Initiation Versus Tribalism   355

❖

LONG LIFE,
HONEY IN THE HEART

INTRODUCTION:

LOOKING FOR HOME

Like a Mayan girl caught by surprise out on a well-worn village path, Guatemala is small and beguiling with a soul larger than most big powerful countries. Short and shiny, neatly coiffed with frangipani flowers, she stares back at the rest of the world with suspicious and hopeful eyes.

Located at the top of Central America, south of Yucatan, east of Chiapas, west of Honduras and San Salvador, Guatemala is a treasure hoard of cultural diversity. Fashioned by centuries of isolation, external and internal exploitation, misunderstanding, violence and suffering, her people are many and mixed, unique, and full of human beauty. Though the Western world categorizes Guatemala as a Latin American country, over 80 percent of her population of 11 million is comprised of Native Mayan peoples. Guatemala is a Native American country.

The landscape is even more diverse than her people: she has dry climates, wet places, surging giant rivers, little creeks, high-altitude cloud forests, lowland jungles, savannas, lakes, marshes, swamps, black sand beaches, talc-fine white sand beaches, hard crashing oceans, calm shallow gulf bays, mossy waterfalls, a tangled underground world of caverns, underground streams and tunnels, cultivated land, cities, villages, hamlets, wilderness, snowy peaks, tropical piedmont, and on and on.

In the southwestern highlands a great gathering of tall heavily forested volcanic mountains, molarlike ridges, and mouthlike craters hold up a brilliant turquoise sky that every fall throws a hurricane down upon the earth. The volcanoes answer with a trembling series of eruptions that turn the sky red with the cinders. Every spring when the rainy season begins, the earth quakes and a multitude of landslides come crashing down to the bottom of the hills, rerouting roads, rivers, burying villages, changing lives. Up in these dramatic mountains lies a large crater filled with some ancient jade-colored water, called Lake Atitlan. This crater's edge consists of a pile of still more volcanoes. Rising above the lake, these peaks mark the territorial boundary of a people called Tzutujil Maya.

Resting right on Atitlan's southern shores, at the mouth of the world's most magnificent freshwater bay, this large Tzutujil village was named Santiago Atitlan, by invading Spaniards four hundred eighty years ago. The villagers, however, called this place Rumuxux Ruchiuleu, the "Umbilicus of the Universe." They were a proud Mayan nation; open-eyed, mistrusting, jealous, funny, and magical—a people whose language had a future tense that was the imperative of its past tense, whose concept of Today was a place where yesterday, tomorrow, and all creation could be kept alive by feeding it the beautiful way people did everyday village things like walking down the street, arguing, working, or sleeping.

The men farmed the sides of these great volcanic hills by hand using axes, hoes, ropes, and machetes, to coax five varieties of corn, thirty varieties of beans, multiple kinds of squashes, three colors of cotton, infinite types of fruits, avocados, and greens from the templelike steepness of the rich volcanic slopes. Others fished on the lake in canoes. These canoes were hollowed out by hand in the jungle from the trunks of enormous wild avocado trees by specialists who had made the village famous. There were other men who braided tule reed mats, wove women's head ornaments, and a multitude of other creative activities, while every man cut and carried firewood neatly arranged on his back. They sometimes trotted twenty miles up and down steep hills with a hundred pounds of squeaking wood into the smoky compounds where the women carefully used the dearly obtained fuel to cook what the men brought home to the cooking huts.

It was there that the women ground the corn, tomatoes, beans, squash seeds, fish, and greens the men cultivated in the hills. After returning from the legendary open-air markets of Atitlan, the women hauled water from the lake. Balancing fifty pounds of water on their heads, they had to struggle as much as a mile to their compound of huts. Everyone's clothing was of a specific cut and ornamentation depending on one's age and gender, and it was the women who masterfully worried an ornery pile of native cotton bolls into tight threads and handwoven lengths of luxurious fabric. The cloth had to be tight to survive the washings of the women who formed long chattering files on the edge of the lake at their traditionally inherited *chjembal,* washing stones. There the beautiful clothing of their families was thwacked and twisted with Herculean force to get the dirt out. The women were very, very strong and the clothing they wore had to be as strong as they were.

The people of Santiago Atitlan had no concept of their town being part of somebody else's country. As far as they were concerned, everything real in the world was inside their territory.

Their land was the world to them. Guatemala as a country was a mythological spirit realm distant and unfamiliar to most Tzutujil people and categorized by them no differently than Japan, Jerusalem, Germany, or the United States. These strange spirit realms could be visited, but you had to return "Home" to the real Tzutujil land to be truly alive. There was no possible way of saying "leaving home" in the Tzutujil language. The people called the placement of their own town the Canyon Village. The surrounding land that was their world, the land that fed them, they affectionately called the Flowering Mountain Earth. This was their homeland. The village itself was known to all Tzutujil as Ch'jay, meaning literally "At Home."

This Homeland was bound and embraced on all sides but one by three forested volcanic peaks, and on the remaining side by the Mother Lake herself. Named for parts of the human body, this land was concentrically circumscribed by still more forested ridges, valleys, and bluffs radiating out some ten to fifteen miles on either side.

Though appearing relatively small on a modern map, this land of the Tzutujil was the world of the Canyon Village people and to them it was enormous.

The Canyon Village was subject to an ancient way of understanding I call Internal Bigness. This way of being and seeing permeated every aspect of Tzutujil life. In the same way little children can magically turn the ten-by-ten area of a sandbox play area into the farthest reaches of the Universe, the Canyon Village understood the internal bigness of their world. Because every rock, trail, mountain, stump, spring, and incline was either the backbone of a dead giant in an old story, or a rock placed there by a Goddess who in her grief could go no farther, the land opened up into an internal immensity that was known only to the people whose world it was. The road map to this internal Tzutujil kingdom were the myriad of stories, mythologies, legends, and histories taught to them during ritual meetings and village initiations.

This sandbox knowledge was not held by one or two children but handed down and added to by the twenty-eight thousand individuals of all ages who lived in this landscape of ancient Tzutujil story dream.

Because of this, their land was so big and magnificent that no human could comprehend it all. Only the Gods knew how to measure it. Its tiny physical size was simply an abbreviation of a cultural enormity that was carried inside each Tzutujil. Though it appeared to outsiders that the people lived off of and inside their land, the entire earth lived inside each villager.

This internal universe was set like a jewel of sparkling infinity into the finite matrix of the external world.

The external world called the people of the Canyon Village by the name Tzutujil. Linguists like to distinguish them from the numerous other Mayan linguistic tribes that surrounded the Canyon Village such as the Qekchi Maya, Quiche Maya, Cakchiquel Maya, Pokomam Maya, Ixil Maya, Mam Maya, Chorti Maya, Pokonchi Maya, Rabinal Maya, to name only a few. The people of the Canyon Village did not call themselves the Tzutujil. They call themselves what all Guatemalan Mayans call themselves: *Vinaaq*, which means a "Named Being." This also stood for the word "twenty" because humans have ten toes and ten fingers. Both the terms "twenty" and "named being" signify to the Tzutujil the concept of being completed, which refers to being an adult. They also call themselves the *Nim Vinaaq*, "Big People" or the "Magnificent Adults."

When a Tzutujil was born he or she was not automatically human. Babies' lives belong to the Moon and the spirit worlds. It took years to become human. This was accomplished by the efforts of one's family and, later, the extended family and, later still, at adolescence by the village as a whole, who came and removed you from the family nest to *cook* you out of your raw, unripe state into a "mature fruit," as they called it. Initiation was mandatory in those days and constituted the beginning of adulthood. This rite of passage, however, was not what made you into an adult. This first initiation only made you ripe enough to continue on in a lifelong pursuit of turning yourself into an adult, on through the next three layers of service to the village. By the time you were in your old age you became a *Nim Vinaaq,* "Magnificent Adult."

You carried yourself from one layer to the next on the shoulders of your ability to speak as an adult, which for the Tzutujil was defined by an archaic language that belonged to the Spirits themselves. This oral literacy was considered what magically kept the Universe glued together, running on a mysterious plasma of sound, song, and delicious speech.

According to the old people's understanding, being a Tzutujil was not a matter of race, it was a matter of memory. To them all people in the world at birth had forgotten this original multilayered spirit language. They had originally known how to speak it in the other worlds they lived in before this one. They simply had to be jolted by initiation rituals into remembering again in this world. These initiation rituals were presided over by people who'd already been initiated into the speaking and remembering ability of the layer they were teaching.

There were five main layers of initiation into becoming a Magnificent Adult. These were called:

Birth—Dawn Sprouting
Birth to Adolescence—Flowers and Sprouts
Adolescence to Child Rearing—Rainboys and Shimmerers
Child Rearing to Grandchild Rearing—Fruited Branches
Grandchild Rearing to Adult—Big Trees, Big Vines, or the Bark People
Adult to Death—Echo Person

Each of these layers corresponded to a ring in creation's tree and in the village matrix. They were not arranged in a strict ascending order or ranked in the style of the military. They were more like the cumulative rings and tiers of growth on a deer's antler as the deer got older.

Each of these layers or stages had an intact ritual that consolidated their passage over the threshold into the next part of the journey. You did not discard any of the previous eras you'd passed through when you entered the next phase. You didn't give up your youth to become a child-rearing adult. You added each layer onto the next like an old-time telescope with all its collapsible sections.

As a person went through each segment of his or her life, that segment was "earned" and fitted nicely inside the new one until in one's old age a spyglass at least five sections long had been constructed.

Like a spyglass when collapsed down for easy keeping, it appeared that every person, no matter how many life sections they had re-membered or added on, seemed to be composed of only one section. It always appears to the very young or to teenagers that old people are only a little wiser than the youth, but when questioned by the young, the old can metaphorically open up their "life" telescope to see. Their vision would be five times as long as the youth's. The highly initiated old-timer tended to have more compassion for the youth than other people did because the elders had a greater memory and vision. They saw by their combined abilities and vision of old age, middle age, teenage, child, and echo age, which all together gave them the accrued vision needed by the rest of us to find our own sections. In the village, then, these people were our mentors.

When a teenager got her or his "second section" of vision, it was so much more ample and different than the first eyepiece of childhood that they thought they were seeing everything there was to see. They thought they knew everything. These youth had to be pushed by more adult people into the next stage and the next to keep them safe from living out their lives with too short a spiritual vision.

There was no public pressure to be initiated into any of these layers, the only exception being the initiation in and out of adolescence. To the traditionalist Tzutujil this was absolutely essential. Besides, given the nature of adolescents, initiation would never be pursued voluntarily.

In this book not all of the details of young women's struggle for adulthood are included in deference to the women of Santiago Atitlan. In Tzutujil etiquette men are not supposed to know what goes on in women's rituals, and, if we do, we are supposed to act like we don't. In these pages, I hedge a little and tell a bit. I hope they will forgive me.

What is presented to us today as an adult in the modern world has little resemblance to those deeply veined faces of zany old Tzutujil women and men who spoke a complex magical language to rivers, mountains, trees, and the sun to make those things live. However, the uninitiated adolescent Tzutujil had a lot in common with the aggressive, freedom-oriented inhabitants of our modern cities whose bodies get old, but whose souls never volunteer for initiation.

Initiation rituals were not done for the initiate's benefit. They were done to keep the Universe alive for all of us. It was believed that in initiation by learning the ways and language of each layer, and then doing the rituals of each, the world as a Deity would stay flowering and flowing, greased on the beauty of the rituals.

One main reason individuals had for seeking initiation was to avoid becoming a ghost after they died. Ghosts are the spirits of people who at death could not get into the next layer of existence. This happened for two reasons. The Tzutujil believed that the dead rowed themselves to the other world in "a canoe made of our tears, with oars made of delicious old songs." Our grief energized the soul of the deceased so that it could arrive intact onto the Beach of Stars where the dead go to the other side of the ocean, the salty Grandmother Ocean who tossed and surged between us and the next world. On this beach of star souls our dead were well received by the "last happy ancestor" and then initiated further in that world into the next layer of life. After four hundred days of initiation into the next layer, these dead would graduate into the status of ancestors. In their new form they could help us here in this world, when they ritually fed our souls from their world just as we living here in this layer fed the beings we'd left behind in the previous layers of life.

Therefore, when a person was buried and not enough tears were shed and when truly felt grief was absent, the soul of the dead person could not make it to the next world and would be forced to turn back. Scared and invisible, it took up residence in the body of the tenderest and most familiar person it could find. To give themselves a feeling of physical substance, in desperation, the ghost would eat the life of that person. For this reason ghosts usually devoured their relatives, especially their grandchildren, jumping into their bodies and eating them from the inside out, consuming the little child's spirit also. Then the ghost went on to the next grandchild or some other relative of the next generation. Alcoholism, substance addiction, most depression, homicide, suicide, untimely deaths, accidents, and the addiction to argument were caused by the endless hungers of such ghosts. This kind of ghost consumed soul after soul until a whole series of generations had been destroyed.

The second way a ghost came about was if a person hadn't become initiated, or suitably layered, while alive. In that case, one didn't really exist and upon death there wasn't enough of him or her, as a person, for them to row to the next shore. Each layer of initiation, each layer of remembering and its language ability, was very literally represented by a layer of special clothing that the people wore. This thickened a person into a spiritual substantiality, making a person into a full human. At death each of these layers of clothing were considered a language and the body was dressed in them like husks on an ear of seed corn. When you went to the other world you were recognized by these husks, by your layers of clothing representing the other worlds that you had re-membered through initiation. It was only then that the custodial spirit of the other world allowed you to pass into that layer. Without this clothing you were invisible to the beings in the other world and your only recourse was to return bodiless back to this world, devouring the future of your people instead of becoming an initiated adult soul that could help our world from the next. This ghost problem, of course, is what makes the uninitiated world of modern times so scary. There are ways for shamans to deal with the ravages of ghosts, the epidemic destruction of lives through depression and addictions. But Tzutujil thinking said it was better to have initiations and avoid the ghost problem altogether.

When I left the United States in the early 1970s and crossed the border from my native New Mexico to Old Mexico, I was fleeing ghosts. I wasn't headed toward Guatemala, but away from what seemed to be destroying my people and the beauty of the Native New Mexican cultures I'd grown up with.

Like a proud battered horse who could still recollect what freedom meant, I was fleeing from what had caused me pain. At first I ended up in Mexico, bouncing from place to place, reveling in that new world of marvels, harsh realities, and mystery. I wondered if there were any chance of finding a welcome for me somewhere on this earth in my lifetime.

That winter before I'd commenced this wandering, I'd dreamt a series of powerful and vivid dreams, one each night for eleven consecutive sleeps, during a legendary blizzard in northern New Mexico. During this barrage of visions, a world unknown to me had presented itself in such a way as to seem deeply familiar. These dreams consolidated my longing for tribe and home, a longing I'd felt since before I could speak. Leaving behind the haunting memories of my mother's death, my failed marriage, my rejection by the world, and native village of my youth, I drifted despite myself, with these dreams stored in my heart in hairsplitting detail. Then, after a year of adventures and foolhardiness in Mexico, the Spirits nudged me with what appeared to some as chance, across the Chiapas border into Guatemala, right into the waiting arms of a hardheaded village of handsome Mayan people: the Tzutujil. It was here in Santiago Atitlan, in Guatemala, in Central America, that my teacher-to-be, Nicolas Chiviliu, took me under his wing, up the hill to Panul' and into the sanctuary of his home. I'd recognized him from the dreams, dreams he'd claimed he created to bring me to him. He complained about how slow I was in finally coming home to him.

Nicolas Chiviliu Tacaxoy was the most legendary and powerful Mayan shaman in the highlands of southwestern Guatemala throughout the twentieth century until his death at ninety-seven on April 21, 1980. He died dancing his bundle. It was this bundle that I caught before it hit the ground that day, thereby giving me a responsibility to take over where old Chiv left off.

In the beginning old Chiv had kept me by his side, like a little packhorse, slowly and osmotically shaping me into a good assistant, where I learned to speak Tzutujil, make prayers in Sacred Speech, call wild animals, hunt disease, make offerings and ceremonies. After three years he deemed me ready, and I went through a grueling shaman's initiation that almost killed me—and did kill two of his other students.

Shamanic initiation, as described in my first book, *Secrets of the Talking Jaguar,* was a rare thing, happening to less than one hundred Tzutujil in a century. A very different kind of initiation took place for everybody else in the village, an initiation into adulthood and not to be confused with shamanic initiation.

Old Chiv's compound was practically a village unto itself, larger than most and thickly populated with all his progeny, adopted orphans, ex-wives, their children, and his children's children's children. My eleven dreams were no longer part of a distant nostalgic memory of a forbidden, unobtainable life. Here at the heels of eighty-seven-year-old shaman Nicolas Chiviliu, and then later with the help of my advisor A Sisay and the whole village, I grew into a useful, happy man living in the matrix of an adaptive and ancient culture.

When I arrived none of the people of Atitlan had even heard of the word *Mayan*—that was an invention of Europeans. Nobody there wanted me to become a "Mayan," they wanted me to become a person. All the Tzutujil youth were fighting their way out of the spiritual amnesia we were all born with. My own struggle to become a part of the village was not understood as me trying to become a Mayan. It was fully understood as what everybody else was doing: trying to become a *Vinaaq,* a Human.

To begin to do this, I first had to give my ancestry a home and some due. My Irish, Swiss, and Native North American forebears were not judged, examined or understood by the people but rather invited to live right there along with everybody else's Tzutujil ancestors. There they were all feasted and made drunk while the ancestors told lies to each other about their living descendants, just like the living do about the dead; about how magnificent we were as we kept sending the dead all this ritual food and drink. My ancestors found themselves at home in the Mayan ancestral shrines, just as I did in the village compounds of their living descendants.

I didn't decide to stay in Atitlan with the intention of studying or writing books on the Maya. The Tzutujil were not known for their sincere acceptance of outsiders, though hordes had come and all had left. Though Chiv had called me here, I was also spiritually adrift, ready to find a home. What the traditionalists in the Canyon Village saw in me and valued was the very part of me that the modern world thought superfluous. My intrinsic way of being was not only accepted in the village but eventually called into community service for its usefulness to the people and the Spirits they served.

In the United States, when I ventured off the reservation of my youth, most of what was really me, my true nature, the indigenous part of my soul, had to be hidden behind a germane grimace of conformity or held back unexpressed in a flat silence of invisibility in order to keep my heart safe. I learned early on that spiritual intelligence should not be naively exposed to subscribers of a dog-eat-dog money-oriented environment. I had an inborn comprehension of that archaic instinct that all people have somewhere in their bones of wanting to give back a little something to the world of spirits that feeds them. This understanding of mine would be trivialized, mocked, and misunderstood. In the worst cases I was brutally punished by representatives of the modern machine-age culture who were proud of the fact that they had the power to blow up the whole world. At that early age I already knew that the consciousness that comes with a true spiritual initiation should be a required credential for those people whose decisions affect the rest of the world.

Other, more sympathetic people—some of my teachers, my friends, and my parents—felt that I was too idealistic, unrealistic, and naïve, because of my demand that people live with imagination.

My insistence on spiritual and social accountability were seen as unreasonable and anachronistic. Schoolteachers in those days considered anything spiritual to be a flamboyance of the mind. They told me I would never get a job with things like that running around my brain.

But I did.

In the "inner bigness" of Santiago Atitlan I became a shaman much in demand, and my compound was filled to overflowing by village clients looking for cures. Simultaneously in the mid 1970s I was discovered as an artist by the outside world, and it was through the sale of paintings to Europeans, Asians, Africans, South Americans, and Guatemalans that I was able to make a living while living in the village. Life was rich, good, strong, and real. Though I was loved by many, tolerated by most, and hated by some outsiders, I was deeply in love with the village and life itself. Those days are long gone, but these books grow off a vine rooted in that love.

Originally, *Long Life, Honey in the Heart,* and *Secrets of the Talking Jaguar* were both fragments of a very large autobiography. It became apparent, however, that I was telling at least two simultaneous stories. One story was about my initiation as a shaman. The other was the story of how I became a member of the Spiritual Gathering of Elders called the Scat Mulaj, which was a very different career than that of a shaman. I did both things at the same time, in the same period, with some of the same people. To avoid confusion I kept both stories separate from each other. Shamans were healers of individuals and families while the theocracy of elders were in charge of public ceremonies to maintain the health of the whole village. The modern world has no similar institutions and readers seemed to confuse these two dedications. For this reason, *Secrets of the Talking Jaguar* deals only with my life as a shaman and the year I spent in Mexico before I arrived in Santiago Atitlan.

The telling of the other story in *Long Life, Honey in the Heart* begins after I'd already been living in the village for over a year in old Chiv's compound. Though Chiv does not play a large part in the second book, you can feel him always looking on from a distance to make sure I was all right. Here the true story is told of my immersion into the everyday village life of courtship, marriage, childbirth, and childhood, while navigating the dangerous political obstacles of the time. Above all, it describes the initiations and rites of passage of the Canyon Village youth and myself.

For centuries on end, the old people of Santiago Atitlan re-created their culture over and over again every spring by remaking the human being during the annual initiations. The whole village was involved, everybody was renewed and blessed, and the culture itself was brought back to life. This was a slow, graceful, organic, archaic, and durable way of life until faced with the incomprehensible violence of certain very powerful uninitiated forces from without.

I was blessed to have been caught, corralled, mentored, remade, and absorbed into this brave, ecstatic culture who held their collective spiritual life to be a sacred particle of a divine brick laid into that wall of beauty the Spirits maintained against the oblivion of spiritual forgetfulness.

Though some may not agree, this book is not just about the Maya, nor is it, in the final analysis, mostly about myself. It is about young people wanting to live past twenty. It is about old people being useful, about community, about hope, about being willing to fail. *Long Life, Honey in the Heart* is about all people. It is about the capacity of the human spirit to retain its magic, dignity, love of folly, humor, and imagination in the face of imminent devastation from overwhelming, soul-crushing odds.

Above all else, *Long Life, Honey in the Heart* is my gift to the memory of hundreds of generations of Tzutujil people and the extraordinary spiritual intelligence of their initiations of all age sets, initiations that can no longer be seen.

And, last of all, it is my letter of gratitude to those men and women, ancient, old, middle-aged, young, and younger of Santiago Atitlan and the Canyon Village, who tried to teach me how to feed the spirit worlds and who transformed a bitter, shy, North American boy into a human being. Into a jumping, crawling, walking, flying, swimming, singing, praying drinker of liquids, eater of foods, day-carrying, struggling man willing to defend the sacred Hole, the Bride of Life, the roots of the Flowering Mountain Jade Water Earth Navel kind of man who just couldn't let all we did together fade away into the dust of Death's Amnesia. And for them, I give this book to you, as a gift.

T H R O U G H   T H E   R E E D   D O O R W A Y

A bold and sassy voice called me out of my end of Chiviliu's compound before the Father Sun cracked his way out of the seed of Dawn, sprouting into Day. Staggering half-awake toward this formal-sounding challenge, I found its author facing me in line with four other impressive black-blanketed *Cofradia* men whose short striped pants and long colored sashes swayed in the cold lake breeze.

Barely visible in the dim light, these emissaries had their heads bound up in deep red and purple headcloths called *xcajcoj,* worn only by Sacred House officials. Each tied his distinctly from the others, one with the knot in back, another on the side, or tied crossways, all according to the nature of the service they were installed to fulfill in the complicated system of thirteen sacred houses and village chiefs, known as the hierarchy.

The youngest, beardless envoy stepped forward brandishing a full bottle of cloudy brandy called *psiwanya,* canyon water, and commenced to give me a courteous and florid harangue. His weary seniors stood back in file, staring at the ground, nodding as he spoke, their hands folded over their sash knots on their bellies.

Exhausted and hammered by the stress of no sleep and the harsh bite of the cloudy liquor, ever present in the ceremonies, this fifth-position *Cofrade,* with great finesse, his eyes hardly open, proceeded to order me to present myself that very afternoon at the Sacred House of A Clash, whose chief was Ma Ziis, Coati Mundi, in the Pchibak, By the Mud, district of the village. I was to be very certain to bring along my *shool,* my cane flute!

The cloudy, fuel-like booze was trickled into an elegant shot glass filled clear to the top and ceremonially proffered to me, both as a traditional gift and to ratify my having received and understood the official message. This was like signing for certified mail. The Tzutujil felt that the message would be better understood if you "drank it into your belly."

Before drinking, one prayed to the spirits and saluted each official in turn, according to his rank of spiritual accomplishments, if you knew how to read his position by how he wore his ceremonial clothing. Then you waited for their flowery, enthusiastic response before addressing the Sun Father and the Grandmother Moon. After trickling a drop on the ground for the earth, down went the liquor burning just like the rising sun peeking over the volcanoes reflected in the breeze-rippled lake.

"*Titjala. Titjaga.*"

"Partake, son, please receive this one."

In turn, each official received as much as I did, according to rank and knowledge, from the same cup, always one cup for all. With slightly altered phrasing we tossed our acknowledgments to each other in order. The speaker went last, in this way fulfilling his initiatory role. Mayans like to teach by putting untutored novices in charge, under the scrutiny and supervision of those who know. Of course, when you're in charge, you always go last.

My "drinking in" of the message signified my intended compliance with the request, a kind of oath, though in reality there was no adult way to turn down a ceremonial drink of this type and still be respected, so everyone always complied.

One did not just sip this liquor, as drinking it had nothing to do with taste or preference. It was downed all at once, and the little drops left in the bottom of the glass were rained onto the thirsty ground while you solemnly spoke the words *"Ay Ruachuleu,"* Earth Fruit. By remembering the world, the world was fed and we little humans along with it.

Their mission accomplished and my compliance assured, the message drunk and delivered, we shook hands enthusiastically. The envoys yelled out formal greetings to the crowd of sleepy-headed kids, old ladies, and all of Chiv's people who had gathered there. Respectfully, all of us returned the required responses, each of us according to our age and gender. Then out of the compound the men sailed off in a tired but majestic roll, adjusting their blankets in the wind, intent on the next mission of their morning course set for them by the old chiefs.

❖

As old Chiviliu, my friend and teacher, was still out in the mountains harvesting coffee berries, I searched elsewhere for some comfort and advice regarding the nature of this "call to court."

One of Chiv's younger great-granddaughters in her twenties was fanning the morning fire under her clay tortilla griddle. She spoke to me as I hugged myself by the flames. In a formal, melodic way she explained how these messengers were lower-ranking members of a powerful and mystical group of village sacred leaders who formed a large theocracy of men and women dedicated to the making of ritual and public decisions for the village welfare. These were the Chiefs, the Scat Mulaj.

They dressed differently from the rest of the village, using only the most ancient forms. Every aspect of how their clothing was worn, the knots tied, the blankets folded, had special meanings. Old Chiv had served the Scat Mulaj in over fifteen capacities in forty years, including top headman of the village for three terms.

The villagers were in awe of these monklike officials, and an unexpected visit from them inspired in the villagers what it inspired in me: a combination of excitement, mystery, and dread. What these officials knew and did was held in a secret trust, and it was in this trust that the Village Heart was kept. They *were* the inner sanctum of Atitlan. What could they want with me?

As gossip is the neurosystem of a Mayan village, word of this visit from the chiefs had traveled among the twenty-eight thousand villagers before I could tie up the sash on my *scav,* or "Indian pants." Before the hour was gone, even the smallest child in the village knew more about my situation than I did.

Young friends of my own age set found me before I had gone sixty paces on the winding, knobby basaltic chasms of the village paths to search them out. Excited and anxious, each of them besieged me with questions and speculations, like a flock of noisy parrots on a cornfield.

Every member of our band had relatives in the hierarchy, but because these friends of mine had refused initiation, none had ever been called to the meetings of chiefs. Before I could say even a word, A Leep gestured nervously with his fat, uncallused hands as he spoke: "Those old people will kill you with that canyon water. A lot of them have died from it, you know. What did it taste like?"

And before I could respond, handsome A Maash, our turtle shell player, added, "What could they want with you? Is it true that they asked you to bring your cane whistle?"

On and on they went until, like uninitiated men the world over who begin to joke with a great proficient lewdness when they get scared, we tried to jostle and amuse ourselves back into a feeling of normalcy and the familiar.

But when we finally stopped poking and laughing, our hats cocked against "our Father's teeth," the sun's heat, the question still remained: What *did* an entire heretofore uninterested group of powerful village chiefs and ladies want with an uninitiated outsider and his ten-inch cane flute?

◇

One clear morning about a year earlier, after I first came to Atitlan, I was beguiled by a melancholy sound made by a young Tzutujil man astride a boulder in the labyrinth of rock-walled compounds.

He was hammering out a strange song with an ingenious rhythm on a fragile five-stringed guitarlike instrument whose voice was a mixture of a cicada, a sitar, and a muted bronze bell.

Split from sweet-smelling cedar woods, and held together with a glue of boiled animal hooves, this completely hand-hewn sound maker had dried rattlesnake tails glued under the top plate to give her the required buzzy sound that so appealed to Tzutujil sensibilities.

Mayans love things that buzz. If a musical instrument didn't buzz or rattle, the highland Indians figured it must be broken or badly made.

The Tzutujil even stretched little patches of pig intestines over the ends of their flutes with rattlesnake tails glued inside of them to give the flutes kazoo-like overtones. In any village in Guatemala, beautiful handmade marimbas, both large and small, with gourd or thin wood resonators, buzzed and plinked old Mayan songs and other music, and were ever present in celebrations, ceremonies, and feasts. Guitars were not a Mayan preference. For that reason I was stunned when I came across A Leep and his Mayan guitar, playing songs from a four-century-old tradition that very few Guatemalans living outside of Santiago had ever heard of.

After the first European invasion of 1524, the Tzutujil had sixteenth-century Spanish Catholicism and culture forced down their throats. During this time the Atitecos were exposed to the music of the vihuela, an ancestor of the Spanish guitar that had five sets of double strings. The Tzutujil learned how to make and play these new instruments, adopting their own indigenous drum rhythms and flute melodies to them. The Spaniards, who by then had melted into a colonial complacency, were mostly unaware that the Maya were using their classic ability to keep their ancient traditions alive by hiding some of their ceremonial music right in the conquerors' pockets.

For this reason, the Tzutujil guitar, with still only five strings played against a drone note, was used for centuries by shamans and love sorcerers to court the Gods and young women. Most of these songs were magical, making whoever heard them unable to forget the musician.

By the 1940s and '50s, however, this music had fallen into great disgrace as a new wave of shaming priests, pastors, health-care workers, and political zealots came into the area, denouncing anything from the past, Spanish, Mayan, or otherwise. The old music was demonized as "pagan ignorance" and seen as a hindrance to the enlightened advance of so-called modern progress. Indians were told that they really were playing the guitar "incorrectly" because their guitars had only five strings instead of six.

In a culture with open faces and hearts to match, it takes a lot of maturity and courage for a people to keep their cultural vision alive under a reign of imposed shame.

Since very few Mayans could read, the churches set up their own radio stations. They distributed transistor radios to the villages to make sure everybody got the word. Music was an integral part of the Evangelical and Catholic services, and both employed quantities of young people who sang Spanish and Mayan adaptations of hymns from the American Bible Belt, played on six-string guitars that didn't buzz.

Where before Tzutujil boys had played five-string guitars to enchant and court their brides, many young women now refused to marry boys who could sing their grandfathers' songs to them. Basking in the praise of Church officials, many girls thought themselves "advanced" as they sat laughing at their own people's tradition while entranced by the exotic mewings of American and Latin music squealing out of Church-supplied radios.

Originally Tzutujil girls chose husbands from among the young men who were admired by the community as a whole for their village-preserving abilities, such as farming, fishing, and making things with their hands. Young men of this type were also admired for their willingness to keep the village spiritually renewed by successfully surviving a difficult year of male initiation in which they were exposed to the spiritual aspects of the Female for the first time. Only then could they marry.

These young men courted girls partly by singing these old songs. Some of them hired shaman guitarists, while others were musicians in their own right. This style of courtship was admirable.

But the ranks of these young traditional men were shrinking. When foreign missionaries, who were allied to outside business interests, came to the Lake Atitlan region, they mounted a campaign to show how much better and more powerful their New Ways were. One of their tactics was to extend cash loans to the as-yet uninitiated young men, provided the men accepted the new religion and denounced the old ways.

For the most part the boys who took these loans started their own businesses, carting village products to the bigger non-Indian centers in Guatemala, and returning with piles of cash and lots of sparkling things for their sweethearts. To the young uninitiated girls, these fellows seemed wealthy, able, and wildly free of the pressures of slow, boring, village ways.

The leaders of their newfound religions told them that the old songs, clothing, forms, and initiation rituals were the work of demons and ignorance and would keep them in poverty. Native things were said to be passé and unexciting. Jesus loved them and showed it by giving them money and power.

Boys began refusing initiation because converted girls wouldn't marry men who were initiated. Soon the standards of marriage for those girls were measured in cash, what church one belonged to, and things that sparkled, rather than in corn, fish, and the mysterious songs of a slow-moving villager. Instead of marrying a boy who would become a good family man, who had learned the old things from old people, the girls began to refuse initiation also. They wanted boys who would make them socially prominent with new things from a new place. They wanted lots of earrings, tinseled shawls, gold teeth, shoes, radios, watches, and plastic. Many of these things were sold by missionaries on the side, especially watches and radios.

Men who sang their grandfathers' songs were seen as backward. Since for uninitiated men, the desire to be loved is greater than their ability to inspire love, the young men abandoned the old songs in hopes of drawing the attentions of these young women and eventually marrying them.

At this point, the music and a large number of other Mayan cultural treasures that had been preserved against the previous onslaught of cultural attack between 1542 and 1950 had been driven even deeper into a kind of Tzutujil underground. By the time I arrived in Santiago Atitlan in the beginning of the 1970s, Tzutujil music, especially that of the five-string guitar, appeared to be near extinction.

According to A Leep, only seven men were left alive who could play these old songs, and he was trying to learn as many as he could from one old fellow, Ma Reant Co, before he passed away. Teaming up, A Leep and I began to search out the remaining old people who could still remember this ancient music, even though some of them hadn't played it in forty or fifty years. Before long, I was repairing old warped and soot-encrusted guitars and getting a lot of precious lessons in this rare indigenous guitar style.

I loved the sound, which was totally different from anything I'd ever heard on this earth. A pretty fair guitar player, I thought I could learn the music quickly, but the tunes were wonderfully clever and the rhythm a lot like the Tzutujil people, more complex than they seemed. After four months of diligent practice, I could barely play one recognizable tune. It was not until I could speak Tzutujil well that I really learned to play the sixty or so traditional songs. Music and speech went hand in hand, both carrying the same heart.

I noticed that though a great number of the songs were courting tunes with lyrics, others were instrumental. The latter were considered more powerful.

These old men were actually serenading what modern people might consider things. There was the Song of the Stone, the Song of the Corner, the Song of the Doorway, the Song of the Road, the Song of the Compound Threshold, and so on. It took me a while to realize that these were shaman songs and that by performing them in the right order, one could actually charm the spirits residing in the places named. One could magically reassemble the "House of the World," bringing it back to life in a spiritual dimension. Tree by tree, stone by stone, the old shamans sang the world back together. These old men could ride this music like a horse to visit the dead, or the Lords of the Mountains, and so on. The music was considered an inebriate for these places and things personified, and the world got drunk on its mysterious buzzy sound.

A Leep was more interested in digging up the old songs used in courting magic so he could seduce and enchant the girls than he was in preserving the old ways. I was definitely more interested in the shaman songs due to my intensive training and simultaneous exposure to the same shaman music through my old teacher Nicolas Chiviliu. But, of course, I wanted the girls to like me too.

Although American missionary religion had demonized this old Tzutujil music, my own interest in it seemed to bring it back to life. Because I was an American, albeit an atypical Indian half-breed, my endorsement of this old music gave some of the youth permission to love their old ways again. No matter what anyone tried to tell them, there was always something lurking in the boys' bones that didn't want to throw away these ancient songs of courting, pain, and prayer.

It wasn't long before eleven of us young men had formed a music group, an indigenous band. We were dedicated to playing the old songs A Leep and I had uncovered while searching out the old guitarists who knew them.

This was a new idea. Never before had a "band" played sacred music like this, and the youth hadn't been interested in it for generations. People had become accustomed to one lonely expert on a five-string rattlesnake guitar, or a sad little cane flute player with a wizened drummer, or an old man or old woman fitfully tapping on a slit log drum. But all of a sudden we had three boys on guitars, snake tails and all, two slit log drums played with antlers, turtle shells, cane flutes, clay whistles, a skin drum, gourd rattles, and eleven good voices, all lifting at once from sincere uninitiated men under twenty. We were all trying as hard as possible to be the most old-time we could imagine.

Because none of the youth could transpose the guitar songs onto the cane flute, I became the flute player of the band. This was ironic, as the guitar songs had originally been taken from the little cane flute music of the old days. Now I was taking it back the other way.

When our little troupe began to chug and play, large crowds of noble-faced Mayan youth would huddle up around us, smiling and chirping salutations, pushing and shoving to get a good spot around us, scrambling like nursing puppies to drink in what the young called our new old sound!

Since the coolest boys were there, unmarried girls, on the pretext of errands, dragged their courting shawls past us, craning their suave and coppery necks to get a look at us young fools chugging away at the old people's music. Every evening after the work was done, we boys would gather, the music would start, and the girls would pass by, alternately admiring and heckling us to make sure we knew they were there. That was all it took. As soon as the young women noticed us playing the old tunes, *all* the guys wanted to learn. Within a few months nine teenage bands had sprung up all over the village, each competing to be the most "traditional." Every adolescent in the village knew a couple of songs. Even the girls started to sing them while they ground corn and sat weaving. Where a year before only a handful of old white-haired men could play this music, there now stood a whole generation humming the old tunes, even in their sleep. The young men finally began creating their own songs, using traditional guidelines, and the music was saved. This was the first proud thing I'd ever done.

Chiv said nothing good could ever survive unless it had tradition, but he also knew no tradition could survive unless it included change as one of its traditions. He was highly pleased with our proud little band. He'd flap and dance, pumping his shinbones up and down, spinning to our old-time rhythms, his coat and sashes flying in the breeze, bellowing to the *Nawales* at the top of his ninety-year-old lungs straight through our ecstatic ruckus!

Chiv loved the deviousness of it all, and his respect for me increased even more. My part in maneuvering the traditional music back into the forefront of Atiteco awareness corroborated the community-held notion that the spirit of the old *Nawal Achi*, the original keepers of the Village Heart, had jumped into me for a while and were using me to do their work. Chiv laughed with tears in his mischievous old eyes to see young men, who a year before would have spit on the old ways, now competing to be the best at their ancestors' music because the girls endorsed it. He admired their passionate faces, bawling out the old tunes, hammering at their old grandpas' strumming style with their youthful beauty.

As the originators of this renaissance, my little group became like youth elders, strange little subversive celebrities among the youth, defending the old with our newness. Our heads really swelled up. Like musical revolutionaries, we walked the streets all puffed up, feeling like a combination of a Mayan Elvis and Geronimo. What were we to do? Like all youth we wanted to shine, and this shine came from the ancestors.

⬦

Little Brother of Nettles was our slit log drum player in the band. His older brother, Nettles, had married the quiet niece of a man whose sister-in-law was married to Ma Ziis, this chief to whose house I'd been summoned to appear that very day.

After practice that afternoon, Little Brother of Nettles and the band decided we should all go and scout out the house, both to show me where it was and to find out what the old people were doing there. My flute still in my sash, we hiked to the northwest cliff of the village to a hut-covered slope overlooking the Mud. Sitting up a ways out of view, Little Brother of Nettles pointed out a long stone hall with a recently nailed-on tin roof that had replaced the century-old grass thatch.

Fragrant copal smoke mixed with tobacco wafted out of the old short doorway, which was framed top and sides by a thick layer of well-laid tule shafts, tied and trimmed in such a way as to give the door bangs and sidehair. Called *Tzokin* in Mayan, this reed doorway insignia was the universal emblem used to show that holy things lay within.

I liked seeing this because I recognized the motif from several Mayan ruins I'd visited earlier in my travels. This identical shape had been carved in the stone around the doors and over the lintels on top of the abandoned temples.

We stared down at the sacred place, but we couldn't see any people. Like little kids on a hunt, we figured that if we didn't see anyone, then they couldn't see us.

Little Brother of Nettles suggested that I'd be better off if I just fled the village altogether and waited a couple of months until this old hierarchy lost interest in me and got tied up with something else. These blanketed, cigar-smoking old chiefs and sacred women could be strict and unpredictable and sometimes cruel. A Maash figured they wouldn't have sent out a special patrol of underlings to fetch me if it meant anything good.

My little band of uninitiated men generally agreed that I was probably being set up to be censured or punished for something. Maybe some jealous rivals of Chiviliu had decided to get back at him by driving me out of the village in his absence.

With his hat cocked and showing us his famous big teeth, A Leep postulated through his grin that most likely these old people were secretly enraged at and envious of Chiv for having so much fun with us leisure-oriented, unscarred boys in his official retirement. Chiv, who had served the Sacred House system for over forty years, would inevitably have had to make a lot of hard decisions as Head Man long ago. This must have left him with more than one enemy carrying a grudge against his determined impish style.

Just as I was preparing to creep off a ways to consider the logistics of my flight out and away from Atitlan without disgracing old Chiviliu, my friends scattered past me like quail, squealing out an alarm as they bolted. As I turned to look at what it was they were fleeing, I was grabbed by the elbows and courteously but firmly dragged down the hill to the reed-covered doorway by the same officials who'd been to my quarters earlier that morning. We knelt in front before entering, chirping, "*Ex kola nuta, nutie?*" Are you present, My Fathers, My Mothers? A large, resounding response echoed from the deep dark belly of that sacred place. Only then did we step together over the threshold.

Copal smoke from several billowing burners choked the murky darkness. As my eyes adjusted to the crowded hall, it was evident that I stood surrounded on four sides by beings greater than myself.

To my right, behind hundreds of shimmering, dripping, smoking tallow candles, stood a row of life-size sixteenth-century Spanish Catholic saints dressed as Atitecos, and Mayanized beyond the conquerors' imagination. These were accompanied by the householder's personal spirits and "throne beings," and two rawhide boxes full of sacred ropes, obsidian blades, and spines.

Bright armloads of flowers encrusted the reed frame of the saints' "home." The ceiling was thick with fragrant portulaca flowers, and the holy images were covered in little orchids. To my left, on hundreds of braided reed mats sat at least a hundred red-halo-bedecked women of the sacred, dressed in ground-length white gowns. They were all holding fat candles that glowed inside of large lance-shaped jungle leaves, which illuminated the room in a beautiful green light

Directly facing me, extending down the south wall, over three hundred old eyes stared at me out of the heads of more than one hundred fifty official men in black tailored wool blanket tunics with unused sleeves, their luxurious red headcloths tied up pirate fashion or loosely draped over their shoulders. When I said my meek little greeting, "*Ex kola nuta, nutie?*" the whole room thundered with replies of various degrees depending on rank, gender, age, and relation to my lack of age and knowledge.

A stooped-over, grinning, chunky old Tzutujil fellow stood up behind the barrel of an old deerskin drum where he'd been hiding and asked the three main chiefs to bring me a stool. Before his initiates could do so, I'd dropped to the ground firmly and presented myself to the deities there first. Then I shook hands with all the hierarchy, one at a time, as old Chiv had told me they did at their meetings. I was a little unsure of the ranking among the women, since they sat in bunches instead of files, but then they were more forgiving than the men.

I felt very nervous, as if a trial were about to begin. As I sat down, I saw that the older chiefs didn't seem very sympathetic toward me. There were three main chiefs, an older Head Man, a slightly younger Little Brother, and a *Chp,* Last Child.

The driving force and executive chief was the second of this group, the Little Brother. He rose, magnificent in his deep blue *jaspeado* shirt and white streaked mustache, and asked me very pointedly with a flurry of tobacco-stained fingers, "Son! Why have you been playing sacred music with uninitiated youth in nonsacred places and nonsacred ways?"

I was devastated. It hadn't occurred to me that the Hierarchy was watching our young band, or much less cared. On top of all that, I had assumed that the old-timers would've been more than happy at the revival of an old dying tradition.

Having quite a bit of my old Irish grandmother's ornate tongue still curling in my cheeks, which is only a little less beguiling than Mayan in a fix, I broke out my best Tzutujil and replied: "Your words jump inside my ears and bite my heart. I feel pain when I hear these words spoken by the magnificent Lord and through him all you Lords and Women Lords, our Mothers, our Fathers, in front of wood, in front of stone. Do me the goodness of pardoning my lack of humility, but I was simply trying to keep the youth interested in the old words and the old ways!"

The crowd loved my words. I felt like I was in the hard, dark Mayan underworld from which all life itself emerges, being tested by the resident Lords of Death and Nature, who peppered me with riddles and kept a kind of abstract score for each of my responses. On that first round, I probably received a positive score for style and no credibility for content, as I was too young for such big words. The first chief stood sort of trembling, no doubt feeling the sacred liquor a little more than his "little brother" because he was much older and more frail. His face small under his ancient red silk turban, peeking out at me from under his white eyebrows, he quizzed me:

"Do you know, if you play those songs incorrectly bad things begin to happen? You're over there playing our music badly, and we're in here correcting the results of your self-aggrandizing blundering. Those children you play with know nothing; they just want to feel big instead of useful. We're over here trying to take care of the Gods and they're over there forgetting who takes care of them. Our Gods are starving and you guys are eating their food!"

I was defeated. No doubt about that, I reckoned. Tears of humiliation came to my eyes. They were right: By stumbling upon what, from my point of view, seemed like a dying form, I had assumed I had a right to it. Instead, it was a secret form. Among Mayans, great things had to be earned by "going the route," and these things weren't meant for mass consumption or public display. Profound discoveries were quiet, life-giving events, kept, fed, and maintained, and the fruit of such discoveries was distributed in a discriminating way. What I'd discovered was a sacred and secret form of music, not altogether dead but ailing—still attached to a very alive understanding. So impressed had I been with the power and uniqueness of the music, I'd overlooked asking permission to play it, unaware, because of its secrecy, of how many supporters the old music really had. Sure my welcome had deteriorated in the most complete way, the child in me finally spoke up in a martyred tone:

"Forgive me, my mothers, my fathers, but I'd not heard that our music wasn't sweetly heard by you. We meant no harm to the village at all, and, if you so prefer, we'll quit playing and not do it anymore."

Though a few old ladies were chuckling it seemed that maybe I'd won another round, since most of the hierarchy liked the humanness of my response. The throng was rumbling and discussing it all when out of the crowd a stout, well-made forty-year-old chief stood and yelled above the murmur, "Let's see if he really knows how to play at all. Maybe this talk is all for nothing. Venerable Ma Set the flute player was my uncle, you all know, dead now for one year."

The crowd agreed and the hierarchy's old drummer, grinning in approval, leaned across to me and murmured, "Do you know the Song of the Holy Boy?" Utterly silent, the royal gathering strained to hear.

"You mean all three?" I sheepishly asked.

The crowd roared.

There were three inseparable tunes and rhythms that had to be played in an unending sequence for Holy Boy. It was supposed that if they were played any other way or separately, the musicians would die within the year, having insulted the spirit of Holy Boy and messed up the order of the world. I'd learned this from some of the older guitarists, but still it was "inside" knowledge, even for them. The old people were amazed.

Pulling my little *shool* cane whistle from my sash, the room went silent as I began the first song of the trilogy. Ma QoQuix, the drummer, jumped in right on the beat, thundering away on the immense village drum whose ancient skin and cedar trunk groaned and buzzed under the flailing assault of his two ironwood beaters.

When I changed over to the second part, he stayed right with me, catching on to the new cadence as tightly as a flea on a running horse.

The room rustled with muttering and whispers of *"Rutkin oqa,"* He does know it, or *"Ki' nuna ruqa',"* His hand feels delicious to him.

When we'd finished the third part, an inspired crew of really old shoulder-blanketed ex–head chiefs huddled in an animated ball around the active chiefs. At some point in their secret banter, the head chief shot out of the crowd to his feet and ordered me to play "the Song of the Road, please!"

"I don't know that one."

A collective gulp of disbelief coursed through the smoky room.

"Then," he forged on, "play the Song of the Chiefs Walking."

"I don't know that one, either."

"How about the one for the Flowers on the Shrines?"

"I've never heard that one."

"How about the song for the young initiate boys when they come rowing in on the big canoes at night with branches for the Gods and Shrines?"

"Nope."

The crowd laughed and stared, captivated by the incongruity of my rousing rendition of one of the most secret, sacred, and difficult tunes while claiming ignorance of the more commonly used flute songs in public rituals.

Finally, the head chief interrupted the commentary and chatter and proposed to the men and women of the hierarchy, "Maybe, Brother Parents and Our Mothers, in light of his abilities, it would be good to give the post of head flute player to this big old orphan as punishment for past crimes. What do you say?"

The old women said yes all around, I think mostly because they liked my curly yellow head, but they held out their right hands, palms up, showing their calluses from grinding corn, in the universal sign of acceptance and pleading used by Tzutujil women to accentuate their vote.

The men seemed agreeable too, except for two who were sure I'd fail.

"Then it's good, son. Learn all the flute songs and in ten days please appear at the house of Ma Tec Sojuel and Ma Stev Tzapalu. Accompany the drummer here to come get us so that we may receive the initiates in all there is to do in their rituals for the five days that follow. Notify your relatives!"

Though I didn't know it then, this was a challenge beyond a human's capacity. As the price of my continued stay in the village, these old *Ajaua,* chiefs, required me to learn how to become a full-fledged village flute player in ten days flat. I would not only have to learn a large body of flute songs that, in fact, were practically extinct, but I would also need to know how to act in processions and in ceremonial context. I was being initiated into the village hierarchy in a very atypical way. That strange day was not over yet and the old folks weren't ready to release me back to the world yet.

The head chief Ma Wanit continued: "Now we have work to do today, and you should be our guest as we walk. This way our Flowers and Sprouts of the

Canyon Village, the people, will know you're one of us now, not just a boy making noise in the streets. Let's go to the challenge, Brother Parents, my Venerable Mothers."

Up they rose, standing like a congregation of large ornate water birds moving off their rows of nests, ready to flock together through the village paths and alleys. The drum and flute players always headed the majestic column. Although I played no tunes that day, as I didn't know them yet, I was asked to walk by the drummer's side, my flute unused, tucked inside my belt as he rumbled away.

An orchid-covered image of a saint concealing a deified obsidian blade was carried on four younger men's shoulders, while low-ranking *Cofrades* swung copal burners alongside, raising clouds of pungent smoke.

Dense crowds of villagers converged from all sides and followed us. People asked each other, "Why is Martín walking with them?"

Keeping watch at a healthy distance, my young friends who had fled earlier were scared, mesmerized, and jealous. Since they felt abandoned by my acceptance into the old folks' ranks, I lost them as my friends. The distance between us widened as I came closer to what they feared to enter, the road to initiation.

❖

It seemed as if nobody in the village knew the real way all those flute songs were meant to be played. Everybody had strong opinions about the matter, though, and they would whistle what they thought was this song or that, but it would all end up so birdlike and off the wall that I couldn't find a song in it. When I tried doing what they did, they'd always say, "No, no, no, that's not it. You're not doing it right!" Nobody really knew.

Even Chiv kept acting as if he knew. Puckering up his old lips, pushing his eyeballs to the side, he'd blow a toothless whistle, more breath than tune, emitting a series of incomprehensible tweets and whispered moans that rose and fell like sand in a windstorm, so abstract I couldn't get a handle on it.

The truth was, the last official flute player and the only person who really knew the songs, an old fellow named Ma Zet, had been so cantankerous that he had refused to teach them to anyone. His songs went with him into the grave, along with his technique for making his flutes. For this reason, the Tzutujil didn't like to give any one person full control over any one thing.

There was another man who was rumored to know most of the songs, but he'd gone missing and, even so, was an alcoholic who didn't believe in the spirits or the rituals the songs were for, and wanted pay to play in the ceremonies. I couldn't find him anyway.

One broiling afternoon, as I was dragging myself home up the steep basaltic thoroughfare out of Panaj after bathing in the lake, I heard a toothless lady's voice off behind me to the left, hissing out of a clump of small huts:

"*Sh la.*" Hey, your mother's son.

"*Ma il ye.*" Mr. Sir.

"Hey, your mother's son, come here."

"Hey, your mother's son, don't let them see us together."

"Mr. Sir, hurry up, come in here." Turning and looking, I felt my arm taken by a bent-over, ancient woman dressed with a raggedy elegance, in the late nineteenth-century Tzutujil style. Bustling me into a tiny hut no wider than I was tall, she sat me down on a finely carved wooden man's stool about the shape and size of a small skunk with a stubby tail.

Speaking softly through the three overworked teeth she still had, this old-time woman gradually generated the whispered understanding that she was the widow of the very same Ma Set, the late, grumpy sacred flutist who wouldn't teach anybody the songs I now searched for in vain.

Secretly and carefully, she spoke to me as if we were two lovers having an affair. Though she was all wrinkles and her clothes more patches than cloth, she had the smile of a little precocious girl, with the intense unblinking eyes of an anaconda.

She, of course, knew all the songs by heart, but no one seemed to know she did. Women didn't play flute songs, and technically weren't supposed to know them. Flutes were male things, but the voice of the flute is female. She told me, this old-time woman, that the flute song in the ceremonies was the voice of Nature in tears. It was the weeping of every Female life form, animal and plant, who wept as her children grew and were harvested by life, eaten or replanted. The voice of the primordial mournfulness of the Female lived in the flute, she said, and women didn't need the penislike flute to sing the tears of their own nature; they simply wept. Ritual, however, demanded it.

The flutes were alive, she said, they weren't just some means of making music. I should make sure to have at least ten or twelve flutes prepared at all times, as they broke easily and became jammed up with spit or humidity.

Given the extreme length of some ceremonials, she explained, one had to alternate flutes often to give each a chance to dry out while you played another. She said that to have an array of three-, four-, and six-holed flutes in the sash was a sign of a good flute man, an *aj shool*.

An old drummer had shown her dead husband how to "feed" his flutes and give them a special altar, just as drums were fed in private home rituals. She now passed this information on to me.

That lonely old whispering creature taught me how to make flutes, too. I'd cut three different types of cane in the mountains and secretly bring the segments to her miniature hut. There we'd size them, fit the mouthpieces and burn finger holes using hot pebbles from her cooking fires, until I had a fair little pile of attractive well-playing whistles and a good grasp of how to make more when those wore out.

To play the flute, the old woman said, you had to be able to drum the rhythm to all the songs, as each was distinct, and the flute tunes ran exactly with the drum cadence. To be a good drummer was necessary too, because occasionally the flute player got stuck filling in for the drummer when the drummer keeled over or disappeared into a trance or into the night due to the long stint of no food, heavy ceremonial alcohol, and all the effects of days of rituals.

She showed me how to play the flute with one hand, leaving the other free for the drum, just in case.

Every afternoon I'd sneak into her tiny little place, and she'd whistle in a whisper all the little flute songs for every ceremonial contingency. She made me follow and repeat them with her over and over and over, correcting and encouraging me very patiently. She did this until the fine nuances and animal-like tweets and moans were as natural to me as my own breath, and she was satisfied that her husband's sounds were faithfully restored, albeit without his help.

I brought her little gifts, though she'd make sure no one knew why or who they were for. No one had seen me practicing this music with Ya Sion, the old woman. Through her astounding method of teaching, I was now amazingly well versed in the crucial parts of the sacred flute music. When I showed up to assist the hierarchy during the initiation ceremony, it would be as if I'd been magically instructed by the spirits themselves for my having accomplished this impossible task. There were many mythologies about regular people being taken into the Mountain Kingdom of Gods or into the other world, returning a day or two later full of knowledge and talent that would have normally taken decades to learn.

To my flute teacher, I was her private soldier whom she groomed in traditionalism to launch against the Christians and adherents of modernism who hated the old ways. She wanted the people to see that despite the dusty layer of shame and skepticism the missionaries and businesspeople spread atop the village sense of wonder, the Gods could still make what had fallen dead rise back into flower.

The hierarchy, on the other hand, had utter faith that whatever spirit had given me the songs of Holy Boy in the first place would now give me the rest of the missing songs. To the old people it was all a test: If I was the one the Gods wanted as flute player, then their spirits would teach me. If not, the village was no worse off than before. The chiefs never pitied me, they just prayed we'd do good ceremonies and all get through them intact.

They needed the flute songs to keep the integrity of the village alive and to maintain a solid, well-done, year-long series of ritual spirit feedings to the Gods. Flute music was one of the many necessary ritual offerings the old people had been struggling without for a while.

The spirit did come to teach me. She came in the form of a bent old beauty of a white-haired lady in a small hut where, in a whisper, we whistled and laughed in a wheeze. Then I'd go home to my hut behind Chiv's and transfer the songs I'd learned onto the cane itself, my feet drumming the old woman's new rhythms until everything matched up.

Uninterested in this, my band chums left me alone to learn what I must while they cruised the village paths every evening, unattached, resentful, and uninitiated.

THEIR FACES LIKE COPPER AXES

FIRST GLIMPSE OF INITIATION

Their old eyes blinking and dreaming like a large herd of resting peccaries, the entire body of the hierarchy, both men and women, the royalty of the village, had been waiting in front of the long hut since dawn.

The town drummer, Ma QoQuix, and I, their new flute player, had "piped" them into this compound after our predawn meeting in front of the sixteenth-century church.

The rustling sound of their gnarled old feet, the swishing of their gowns, shawls, headcloths, sashes, and the clinking of their staffs in the cold pink light of dawn, over pebbles, cinder, sand, boulders, through throngs of dogs and turkeys, would be a familiar and homelike sound to me for years to come.

Each of these wrinkled creatures was a jewel of memory. Together with the younger middle-aged officials, they formed a treasure chest full of the memory synapses needed by the Tzutujil to keep themselves together as a culture. These royal spiritualists, who remembered the village back together every year, today went scrambling and giggling over the threshold into the compound to the rhythm of our songs, to sit and stand waiting for the initiate boys.

The old mustached men lit each other's cigars, smoked, spat, and discussed another ritual as they waited. The thirteen Sacred House chiefs leaned on their flowering staffs and insignias, their old salt-and-pepper heads tied up in bright red and purple headcloths. The *Xuoja'*, "Lady Chiefs," sank onto reed mats on the ground, moving elegantly, sitting well, holding long green jungle leaves with candles inside. Each of their hand-spun, ankle-length, white-and-purple gowns spread out sumptuously and tentlike around them, a twenty-four-foot-long ribbon headdress wound around their twisted hair like red halos, heavy and cocked to one side.

The hierarchy was good at waiting. All Tzutujil had to be good at waiting, but the hierarchy were the best there was because their waiting was sacred.

They knew after years of ritual that waiting beautifully and well was a major part of every ceremony. Each aspect of a well-done ritual was part of what they called food for the spirits. Because spirits ate mostly beauty, a body of ancient ritualists like these had to dress in the most delicious way and wait in such a manner that the beauty of their waiting could be feasted upon by the gods.

Today the image of the grand old chiefs and *Xuoja'* was irrefutably a feast for the spirits as they waited peacefully for the newly initiated boys.

The big initiation ceremonies for the youth were finally coming to a close but only after the boys had spent a year of separation from their families. These families now gathered off a ways beyond the mounded rock walls of the young chief's compound as it was the custom to continue the ritual separation and respect on this last day of the initiates' road out of childhood.

I was watching two butterflies playing on Yalen Botan's smallish headdress when a general murmur rippled through the assembled throng. Out of the cavelike darkness of their enormous thatched initiation house, from the village's spiritual underworld, the initiates began to emerge like newly fledged birds from a nest of tangled ritual smokes and smells.

Their faces the color of new copper ax heads, with billows of copal and to-bacco smoke rising off their backs like mist off a pond, each boy glowed from a source deeper than the ancestral pride that held up their exhausted bodies.

Reeking with a mysterious birthlike aroma of pine needles, tule reeds, jungle melons, wild cacao, dahlias, palm flowers, wild bananas, portulaca buds, orchids, and months of living together in the other world, they poked their way out of the darkness and smoke of their old nest, squinting in the bright April morning, finely dressed as Men for the first time. Fresh off the back-strap looms of their mothers and female relatives and out of the hands of their sweethearts, all their man-clothing was woven and embroidered specifically for this day.

Each novice man had his stiff white-and-purple cotton knee pants held tight up around his waist by the wrappings of a wide double-length sparkling sash. When they were yet boys before the initiation, the ends of their sashes were even more extravagant, worn wide and neatly tied in front so that they dangled in two- to three-foot sections of ends and finely knotted fringe. When they strutted around the village searching for girls to admire and be admired by, their sashes almost dragged on the ground in the appropriate al-luring exaggeration of both the youth and the unmarried girls who dragged their shawls the same way.

But today at the guidance of their middle-aged initiating chiefs and elders, these sashes were tied in a more ropelike, bunched-up way with a floppy knot in front. The remaining ends sparkled in the morning breezes, waving in uni-son well above their knees, as did the sashes of all the adult Tzutujil men pres-ent.

Trembling and tottering, they pulled into a line, face to face with the hier-archy, each shouldering a split cane basket from the Village of Humming-birds filled with a fish, an adorned cacao pod, a decorated jungle melon, and new plantains over which were piled flowers and honeycombs.

Only now could their initiating chiefs and old mentors to the chiefs stride out of the tule reed doorway of the other world into this one where Ma Qo-Quix and I stood facing the initiates along with two hundred men and women spiritual officers and related chiefs. The head chief of the initiates popped out last while adjusting his black tailored blanket, his *qu'*, around his left shoulder and over his right with the sleeves hanging in the rear. The sub-chiefs, with their white *anona* fruit staffs of office marking their swaggering stride, their hats cocked, and their sacred cloths hanging around their necks, also lined up behind their initiates.

The head young men's chief put his stout staff behind his shoulders like a six-foot club and rolled his arms in a dangling position over each end. His long exaggerated tasseled red headcloth was draped over his shoulders and reached to his midthigh past his incredibly ornate sash. He was shod in a six-colored Moroccan cutout set of bootlike sandals each with thick-soled Michelin tread, its straps bound with three buckles and covered with a prodigious quantity of colored stitches and brass eyelets.

Mayans are different from other peoples in that they guard and protect the spirits, the gods who gave them life. Like a hero, this village warrior, this year's young men's chief, was required to spiritually protect not only the youth in his charge but also the elders, the hierarchy of religious leaders, the widowed mothers of children and the spirits themselves whose otherworld homes were kept in the sacred houses.

Nine-tenths of that spiritual protection lay in this man's willingness to manifest a particular brand of male beauty. His duty was to maintain a constant unshakable stance, posture, and stride as he, well adorned as a spirit warrior, scared away evil by his animal presence and his mastery of an archaic eloquence when he spoke.

Most youth have bravado, but their initiatory leader had beauty, firmness, and a sense of direction, not to mention permission to wear the fanciest array of clothing in the known Mayan world.

That day, as he strode up and down gracefully, encouraging his subchiefs and kissing the ringed hands of all the old chiefs, he looked every bit the part.

Not a shaman or a leader exactly, the initiating chief, known as the *Najbey Mam,* Foremost Grandchild, was the man all boys wanted to be. He was a married hero who battled for beauty and whatever else was needed to keep the village alive.

Pacing in front of his tired initiates and subchiefs, he was misty-eyed for all the magical times they'd been through together in the last year, but he still bore the affected self-assurance, boldness, distance, and appropriate disdain that was the epitome of the arrogant pride his position required. The villagers felt safe and reassured when they saw him. Though nobody else in the village acted like that or would be tolerated for doing so, this behavior was expected of him. He'd learned it all from his elders, both men and women, who, having fulfilled this position in the past, had graduated to other spiritual pursuits.

He was an example to the young of something to aspire toward, then eventually move away from. He was something for the old to sweetly remember. Later, his reward for having been a fierce Mayan hero of beauty would be to become a regular man again, at home, farming, with his children and wife, knowing he had accomplished something wonderful and useful to the village, something he no longer had to be.

Today, however, he pulled out in front of the two lines facing each other, between the youth and the elders, and began an esoteric harangue in a Tzutujil ritual dialect I didn't understand. The hierarchy responded with rhythmic nods at certain pauses.

Standing behind the initiate boys the thirteen chiefs and subchiefs began to whisper in the initiates' ears. The basket-carrying boys repeated these words in unison out loud in a sacred form of male speech of such heart-piercing depth and majesty that the hierarchy began to weep. Men and women alike, mentors, all the parents and the relations of the boys who were held at a distance by the previous years' initiates, were touched.

At this point old Ma QoQuix, my companion the drummer, who always knew what came next in every ceremony, gestured to me to start playing the Song of Flowers. He did this in a matter-of-fact way, as if we'd been doing this together for a thousand years and I was just waiting for his signal.

At the squeal of the flute and the thundering of the drum, everyone, in an ancient involuntary habit, moved to adjust their blankets, shawls, headcloths, flowers, sashes, and baskets, readying themselves to process to the center of town where the village at large awaited the New Men.

Walking at a moderate speed, QoQuix and I, with the small official who carried the drum, headed out of the initiates' compound with the young men following us, two by two, at the head of the procession.

Pushing along behind them came the large body of hierarchy, wide and long. The clattering din and barbaric beauty of this majestic column was soon engulfed by hundreds and hundreds of relatives and neighbors who poured in on us as we oozed up the stone-and-cinder arteries of the village toward the plaza, the middle of their world. The initiating chiefs had arrived before us and had brought Holy Boy to his place on the plaza.

Shouldering their baskets of the fruits of the earth, which they had rescued from the Underworld, the initiates and their escorts came to a complete stop in front of more than twenty-five thousand Tzutujil and neighboring Mayan peoples.

When the initiating chiefs had quieted the crowd, the trembling youth began anew the ritual of speeches and prayers, so clear and loud that their words echoed off the old stone walls of the church and *cabildo,* the government house.

This time they spoke from their hearts, with no help from their teachers or elders. Many wept to hear them, and all the people's hearts were touched. Some were jealous, and others amazed, but none were left unaffected by their own courageous village youth speaking out their own big thoughts using ancient words in traditional forms in front of the whole world.

The New Men were incensed with copal by the initiators and then disappeared into the sanctuary of Holy Boy who, dressed like a chief himself, was waiting to fertilize their fruit in a secret ritual.

I'd never seen anything like this. Where else could you find a group of tired teenagers who actually desired to touch the hearts of their entire gathered tribe and elders?

You had to go through initiation yourself to really understand what was happening, and any Tzutujil over twenty had done so. They understood that no one could begin to explain it without having experienced it. You couldn't read a book about it and think that you understood it. It was as if initiation rewired you with a language ability that no one could acquire without it. This was part of the great incentive for youth to go through with a village initiation.

Though I was ignorant of what was taking place in its true depth, even though I spoke Tzutujil, anybody could see that what was done here this day was perfectly right and necessary for the village to stay alive. Now I was a part of all that.

I couldn't know yet that the fruit in those baskets was the boys' souls, nor was I aware that each of these boys' souls was a fragment of the Bride of the whole village and the world. It would take three more years before I'd be taught enough by doing what these tired shiny boys had done, literally risking life, limbs, and sanity to descend into the Underworld to face the Gods of

Death, to help retrieve the Goddess of Water and Growth back to her rightful throne here on this earth in our village, Santiago Atitlan, the Umbilicus of the Universe. All of these things and a thousand other necessary understandings were as yet missing from what I would need to know to become a full human being in the sense that the Tzutujil understood. But I, like hundreds of uninitiated Tzutujil boys that day, saw what these initiates had done and what they'd turned into, and we who witnessed this were aching with the desire to become just as visible, noble, flowering, able, courageous, and useful to the village.

In our hearts we didn't want to feel guilty about our heroic and animal natures, we didn't want to be declawed as boys. Like these initiates had done, we wanted to learn how to use our exaggerated naturalness, animalness, and heroic instincts for something that old women, young women, Gods and men could admire and endorse. To achieve that, to become useful village men, we'd be willing to be polished like pebbles in a stream of initiating fire.

The miracle of this first morning of my public flute playing and the praise I thought my having learned the songs in ten days would arouse was dwarfed by the immensity of the young men's ritual. That day, my service to the village became more important to me and to them than did the novelty of my unexpected ability to do it. The old people were right about the music, anyway. This was were it belonged. They had given me a gift.

After five more days and nights of ceremonies and marching, during which I was immersed in a blur of beauty, ecstasy, and an ancient intelligence, the initiations were over until the next year. Cradling large armloads of cacao pods, jungle melons, and orchids, ecstatic and babbling, old Ma QoQuix and I stumbled home through the maze of basaltic passages between the compounds at our end of the village, escorted like a couple of exhausted two-year-olds to our huts where we were ritually released back into our everyday lives. We were officially off duty until different public ceremonies would bring us back into village service.

Infected with ritual desire, I was saturated with a delirious comprehension of community and magic from which I've never recovered. Sinking into my pile of aromatic reed mats at dawn, I slept to the sounds of water birds and roosters, determined to serve this dusty flowering village until I too could become a village man.

THREE

COURTING THE GODS, MARRYING
OFF THE SAINTS
LIFE IN THE HIERARCHY

The longed-for rains had begun to gather. Thunder rumbled down from the deep volcanic folds, bouncing off our Mother Lake. Soon the dry, sad earth would "smile" again with popped-up green sprouts and the thick buds of the tropical spring. The flowering trees could now turn their hopeful dry-season blossoms into a myriad of rich and heavy fruits, and a deafening racket would echo off the canyons where they grew when clouds of little green hard-headed parrots descended to devour them. These parrots were the voice of the Mountain Woman Valley Woman, Ixoc Juyu Ixoc Taqaj, and they had a right to eat it all, as She herself had planted the world, the world we people nibbled at and depended on.

The wetness would sprout strange fungi; the rivers would swell, churn, and cut away whole mountainsides that would collide into the slosh, melting into silt. Springs would reappear and our beloved Mother Lake would rise. These were all signs that she of the "cattail-skirted voice of water birds at dawn, mother of fish, crabs and otters" had returned home. Our initiates seemed to have succeeded in bringing the Mother waters, the Goddess of life, back to our village.

Though the old woman had taught me the songs of the cane flute, Ma Qo-Quix, the town drummer, was my trainer in how to play each song, at what time, how long, how loud, and at what pace.

His old head bobbing, Ma QoQuix thrummed the double-skinned village drum with two ironwood beaters. The barrel of this ancient drum had come from an immense wild cedar tree in a canyon south of the lake by the Crossed Roads, which had figured prominently in the creation of the first human being long, long ago in the beginning of this fifth world. On one side of the drum was stretched a hairless jaguar skin, and the opposite end was covered with an equally hairless doeskin, both sides polished by long careful use.

Whenever the hierarchy had to stroll in a slow procession or march on a long brisk trek, this highly prized drum was carried on the back of an official called Ma Choot, Bee Stinger. Clubfooted, bent over, barrel-chested, with no neck and a face like a howler monkey, the inspired and long-suffering Bee Stinger carried the fifty-pound drum squarely on his spine by means of a rough handwoven maguey-fiber strap that ran over his forehead. Like most of us in the hierarchy, he knew that all discomfort was a gift of energy and food to the gods, a sacrifice for good.

At seventy years of age, Ma QoQuix, however, had banished the idea of discomfort. Dedicating his work as a drummer to the Gods, he could drum standing, sitting, marching, starving, full, drunk, asleep or awake, wet or dry for fourteen hours nonstop on a regular basis. There were times when we'd end up in rituals that lasted for six days, with breaks for food and liquid only once a day.

Under this man's tutelage I learned how to breathe a special way while playing, so that I would never run out of air when marching up and down steep hills out in the bush. I learned to focus on any change in the music yet still pace myself while measuring the expenditures of energy necessary to play a given flute song against my exhaustion and hunger.

Eventually, I would be able to effortlessly switch a spit-clogged cane whistle with another from the arsenal of flutes protruding from my red sash without losing a note in the middle of a tune.

Whenever I did this I was rewarded by a string of big gentle smiles from the drummer, the old matrons, and the priesthood. QoQuix was a very direct, uncomplicated instructor of this very subtle and complex ceremonial art. Whenever he saw the moment coming where we'd have to change songs and cadence, especially if we were in the middle of an entirely different song, QoQuix would whack me good and hard on my left arm with one of his ironwood drum mallets, flicking it at me between drumbeats, never losing his rhythm. He'd keep on pounding on me and the drum until I changed to the proper tune, and then he'd fall right into the new rhythm in perfect time with me.

After five days of that kind of clear emphasis, I knew all the changes really well and rarely lost my place during my next three years of flute playing to the sacred. By the end of that first week, my left arm was wonderfully bruised and blue. My elbow was so stiff that I couldn't even touch my chest.

One day, laughing but a little worried, old Chiv rolled up the ravine behind Panul' where we lived, returning with an armload of succulent rock plants called *tintaq' juyu,* thick mountain. After mashing them up between two stones, he buried the pulp inside a ball of chewed sticky wild tobacco leaves and rolled this mixture onto a big handlike *maxan* leaf. He tied the whole affair onto my elbow, bicep, and forearm, and then dragged me into his famous sweathouse, big enough for four, and steamed me while fanning my arm with a big shock of wild avocado leaves. Under the barrage of all this praying, smoking, and fanning, movement finally began to creep back into my poor limbs. A life dedicated to the spirit was more strenuous than most outsiders could ever know. This was only the beginning, of course. The constant renewal of rituals and offerings filled the lives of the hierarchy with daily rounds and procedures that required constant bodily resilience as well as a mental stability in the face of the ever-present ability for rituals to go haywire at the last minute.

These types of rituals were never meant for anyone's self-discovery. They were for the spirits themselves so that they would stay healthy and be inspired to continue providing themselves to us in the form of food, clothing, houses, lodging, and everyday life. But slowly and deeply I began to under-

stand the spirits' ways and the true magic of these old people as we proceeded with their time-honored obligations of giving their lives to the rituals
that made it possible for the spirits to give their lives to us and the earth. It
would take me a long time to understand the way this actually worked. But I
could see very well how effectively their subtle and complex ways of doing
things kept the Village Heart viable and the people together at a level of understanding corresponding to the knowledge of their own age set and level of
initiation.

The flute and drum were addressed as one unit and together Ma QoQuix
and I were called the *Ajshool Kajoum*. Once a public ceremony began, it was
hard to tell if we, the *Ajshool Kajoum*, ran the ritual like a little musical gener-
ator or if it was the ritual activities themselves that drove us into motion.
Every section of each rite had a specific cadence and melody sequence attached to it. After a while, when what we were doing together became pure
habit, it seemed as if the instruments were playing themselves. At times like
that, when the ritual ran concurrently with the music, I felt a freedom, a sensation of running fast on a many-legged horselike dragon of interdependent
excellence, my hands and heart connected to the rest of the hands and hearts
of the people in the ritual like branches on a trunk.

The old stones of the temples, shrines, and the church in the center of Atitlan were said to have been placed in their present positions after having been
charmed into motion by an ancient female music. Likewise, the old matri-
archs and patriarchs wouldn't even budge a rat's hairsbreadth to pray, eat,
dress, stand, walk, dance, or stop moving without hearing the proper song
from the flute and drum.

The earth and the world, the weather, the stars and moon, growth and decay—all things were powered, according to Tzutujil sacred knowledge, by a
sacred music, by the sounds of each thing being itself. And since humans,
just by being themselves, did so much damage to everything around them,
they must, by Mayan standards, send back an equal amount and quality of
beauty and deliciousness to the world of the spirits whose song we'd interrupted with our noisy experiment, which we called village living. For this reason, the carved stones, the images of these powers, the carved woods, the
images of those generous food-giving powers, the Holy Bundles and saints,
all had to be fed with offerings of products made by our fantastically inven-

tive human hands, the same hands that stole from the earth and spirits and gave to the people.

Because of this, the images also had to be infused with complex meaningful ritual words from the throats and inventive minds of we humans who disturbed the world with our strange wailings and wars. The masters of the making of these offerings and the remembering of complex ritual language were this hierarchy of men and women.

Above all, because of our human interruption of the symphonic song of all things being themselves, we had to literally dance with the carved stones, the carved wood, the bundles and the saints of those powers, holding them as if they were a beautiful friend, a spouse, or a precious child. This was done on the back of the Drum and Flute music, whose song was an offering in itself.

Every image of every power was majestically danced with in their respective feasts. It was this dance, these words spoken with tears, these offerings ingeniously made and given, that renewed the spirits behind the images, bringing them back to consciousness, reanimating them out of their swoon of exhaustion after having worked so hard for us humans here in the Umbilicus of the World.

Though not every member of the hierarchy was present during every ritual, some of them always had to be. The drum and flute, however, were always required to make their sounds during every ceremony of the sacred houses. On account of this, the *Ajshool Kajoum* had an atypically fixed position among the chiefs and *Xuoja'*, one of the main institutions that the old people relied on to remember how and when to go about making the yearly rituals happen in the traditional way.

The old people were full of contingency plans and used to change things as they saw fit while still conforming to the standards of the needs of the gods and tradition. But they relied on the drummer and the flute player to make sure all the rituals happened on time and to give them reports on what had happened in rituals that certain officials weren't required to attend.

After three years of this service, I became very good at ceremonies. I could speak like an old chief to matrons and chiefs. This training was separate from my shamanic training, with which I simultaneously struggled under the wing of old Chiv, who'd retired from the hierarchy long ago. This double training was difficult to do and not a typical way of going about things, but I was in love with the village and was trying to be as useful to those who desired my participation as I could be.

One day, at the top of the old temple steps, in front of the big stone colonial church, the old Head Man presented me with a *qu'* and the old chiefs' wives opened their shawls and gave me a wonderfully oversized (for my big American head) red, purple, black, and white checked handwoven headcloth made from natural cotton. These were the robes of a hierarchy member and the right to wear them came only after successfully completing several years of service to the spirits.

The *qu'* was originally a jaguar skin tunic in the olden days, and it was still called that. The front and back were named the head and the tail, respectively. Over the last four hundred years the *qu'* had become a thick, tightly woven, herringbone solid black wool tunic of the same cut.

Mine didn't have a hole cut for my head, and the sleeve holes weren't cut in yet either. This ensured that my *qu'* couldn't be worn as a chief would wear his, over the head, but had to be zigzagged over one shoulder and rolled on the opposite shoulder in a flashy way whereby the sleeves hung down in back. The "head" hung in front over the right shoulder and the "tail" draped over the left shoulder to the back.

This was the proper style for the hierarchy initiate who'd finished teenage initiation and had passed into the middle ranks of the hierarchy.

My headcloth or *xcajcoj* could not be worn on my head yet, only over my shoulders in a rectangular scarflike fashion until I became an active leader. I also wore it over the sash of my pants tied sideways to signify my active involvement during a ceremony.

This clothing signified the third layer of remembrance of the village, and anybody seeing me wear these regal garments would know where I stood in regard to my progress in the ritual theocracy. But I was not yet a chief or a headman.

❖

The real name for the active village hierarchy was *Scat Mulaj,* meaning the complete coming together, or the complete gathering. The Scat Mulaj consisted of a complex system of sacred houses tended by male and female chiefs, husband-and-wife teams for the most part, called *Ajau* and *Xuo,* respectively. The up-and-coming sacred house officers were called *ajsmajma,* meaning "farmers," if they were men, and *Tixel,* or "parent," if they were women.

Sometimes mistaken for a guild of shamans by outsiders, the Scat Mulaj did not have anything directly to do with shamans. Shamans and midwives were doctors to individuals and families, functioning pretty much as loners and never as a group. The Scat Mulaj, on the other hand, were concerned exclusively with the maintenance of the spirits who gave life to the village as a whole. They accomplished this through a set series of annually recurring ceremonies and ritual meetings, and worked only in groups. They were also a theocracy of priests and chiefs who, like a multigendered order of ecstatic monks, oversaw all village initiations. They were a kind of royalty whose former enormous political power had been reduced by the Guatemalan government after it had wrested its independence from Spain. The spiritual importance of their work, however, actually increased in the twentieth century.

Nobody actively campaigned to serve in the Scat Mulaj. That would have been antipathetic to what they were doing, and very bad form in Tzutujil etiquette. Each official was appointed to the position he or she would occupy by the very Spirit he or she would serve.

There was a very large body of old retired Scat Mulaj officials who paid great attention to their dreams and to the dreams of the villagers. If somebody dreamt that such and such a spirit wanted someone to serve her in the capacity of her sacred house, then the dreamer would casually report this to a retired Scat Mulaj, who was now a member of what was called the Trunk of the Village.

This Trunk member would talk about the dream to his peers in the retired circles and report it to one of the active chiefs. During the numerous meetings set up to determine new initiates for the specific sacred houses, the active chiefs would usually hear that there had been a concurrence of dreams endorsing the same person from other Scat Mulaj members. Once this had been affirmed, the headman of the Scat Mulaj would send a group of lower ranking officials bearing gifts, accompanied by a highly eloquent, senior ex-chief. When they arrived at the house of the candidate, who by now had heard through the grapevine about the possibility of such a visit, she would listen quietly to the request of the envoys, responding as best she could, refusing to accept the appointment for at least the first two visits, as is only right.

By the third visit, however, after having consulted with all of her extended family, the candidate might accept if all her people were in accord. If one of them or she herself had dreamt that she should accept, then the third time the envoys came, she would acquiesce. This acceptance is important so as not to insult the Gods. Such dreams are calls to service from the spirits, not messages from the dreamer. Then she would be escorted triumphantly into the presence of the Scat Mulaj and given a lot of tasks, introduced to her teacher, called a *teonel,* someone who was really just finishing up the same position in the same sacred house. These teachers advised the candidate on all they needed to know having them do the job the teachers had already carried out before they moved up to their new positions.

As the years went by, after entering the Scat Mulaj, one graduated from one sacred house to the next, going from sixth to fifth to fourth position until reaching one of two possible chiefs' positions after completing *Najbey Al,* First Child Position.

Members of different sacred houses had similar duties, which differed according to the idiosyncrasies and nature of the gods and powers each sacred house served. Each rank, including the chiefs, had distinct, well-defined responsibilities.

The *Rox Al* or "Third Child" had the responsibility in any sacred house of dancing the images, stone, wood, bundles, and Holy objects to the six songs of reception that Ma QoQuix and I played.

Women officials were exclusively in charge of ancient female bundles and female deities, especially anything having to do with water. These images were danced to the rhythm of the slit log drum called *cuncun.* Made from a gouged-out hardwood log with an *H* slit cut into it, these drums were played with a deer antler. Their sound suggested the call of the *poq,* a waterbird known as the pie-billed grebe. This was called the Voice of Female Water.

Like everything else in the village, where men and women even had their own distinct language dialects, the male and female members of each sacred house routinely did things in an entirely different fashion, according to what each gender saw as most useful to making the world come alive.

For instance, though appointed in the same way as men, women didn't sit or act according to rank, nor did they really like having ranks. They did not rise from position to position, they just rose. They observed who did what the best and, by common agreement, certain women just became experts at different ritual events. At their own discretion, each woman would maintain a position of expertise, adding another woman if they got the call to do so through a dream. Women were thus apprenticed to other experts. Women chiefs and men chiefs, however, served as couples and were almost always married. These chiefs were very powerful and had a lot of say-so.

No one in his right mind did more than one year of service in a row because of the terrible economic strain to his family. Spiritual service in the Scat Mulaj was not compensated. During a year's service, a member had to provide a lot of feasts and offerings, which put the official immediately into debt to the rest of his clan. This debt could take up to five years to recover from, not to mention the time it took to recover physically from the grueling service.

For this reason, in the most ideal of households, it would take a minimum of thirty years to fulfill the ten to twelve positions one usually had to serve to become a Sacred House Chief. When you retired from that position, you were retired into the prestigious Trunk of the Village Tree.

The Scat Mulaj were called the branches of this tree and the people were the fruit and leaves. The ancestors, of course, were called the roots.

Those chiefs who served as headmen and headwomen of the entire Scat Mulaj every year were chosen from among the retired old sacred house chiefs in the Trunk of the Village Tree. Some people fulfilled this role several times, as old Chiv had done.

As part of the ancient intelligence passed down from their spiritually practical ancestors and *Nawal Vinaaq,* each sacred house gradually rounded up an ordinary villager to sit and help each headman and headwoman decide things. These civilians had no ceremonial knowledge and did not wear the same kind of fancy clothing, but had just as much prestige as any other member of the Scat Mulaj. These ordinary men and women were necessary to keep the precious connections with the everydayness of the village, and their input was always listened to.

One of the three top chiefs of the entire Scat Mulaj was also an ordinary person. The first chief was an expert on tradition; the second chief was an expert on actually carrying out the various rituals; and the third chief, the civilian, was an expert on what the people needed or were thinking.

Outsiders and anthropologists who consider themselves experts on the Tzutujil hierarchy for the most part formed their opinions without having done much more than sit or drink with villagers and pass pleasantries in Spanish. Such interviews were usually pursued during the convenient break in the academic year between the spring and fall semesters, or during a generous paid stint to fulfill the guidelines of a book grant. But to really understand the Scat Mulaj took years, even for an initiated Tzutujil, and required that one have an enormous capacity with the Mayan language. This capacity extended far beyond ordinary speech. The Scat Mulaj spoke in a very high form of Tzutujil and prayed in an esoteric, archaic form. And they used kinship terms among themselves that differed from those used by normal villagers. There were no Tzutujil people, old or young, in the history of their tribe, who had experienced all seventy of the hierarchy positions and the hundreds of annual rituals that nurtured the village excellence, so how could a short-term visitor get more than a mere glimpse? And how could a glimpse be justification for all those authoritative books on what the Tzutujil knew about keeping the flowering earth jumping and living? Some of these outside experts did not even call the Scat Mulaj by its proper name, referring to it as the *Cofradía* system. They also claimed, inaccurately, that the Tzutujil spiritual hierarchy was just a crafty adaptation by victimized Mayans to sixteenth- and seventeenth-century Spanish Catholicism.

It was a great deal more than that. To understand the full magnificence with which the old Tzutujil Maya were able to keep their life-promoting ritual institutions during the horrible trauma of the European interruption of this culture, we have to first understand what happened to the Spanish before they invaded what is now called the Americas.

During the medieval period, in the Iberian Peninsula in what is now Spain and Portugal, several distinct cultures came to their flowering peaks side by side. Under the protection of the Spanish Muslim caliphate, literature, water technology, carving, cooking, goldsmithing, metallurgy, damascene steel technology, mathematics, medicine, agriculture, horse breeding, architecture, astronomy, building methods, alchemy, textile dyeing and weaving, library science, and, above all, a rare and fluid spirituality bubbled and cooked in a creative foment of curiosity and imagination of a kind never before seen in Europe.

Spain was not a country then. But in the south in Andalusia, a group of diverse city-states and districts, though officially under the domain of the Arab Muslims, eventually formed a loose confederation. Like Costa Rica and

Switzerland of the past, this area became a place where free-thinking people, artists, and mystics sought sanctuary. In these small and magical kingdoms ruled by powerful kings and queens, there was a minimum of organized violence. This was all the more astounding considering the violence that surrounded them in other parts of the world, and the atrocity-filled centuries of the Christian Crusades in Jerusalem against Islam and the Jews. Muslim Spain had miraculously escaped much of that horror and had actually been able to remain neutral to some degree.

A diversity of cultures such as the Gallego Celts, Andalusi Berber, Iberian Phoenicians, Italic culture, Muslim Arabs, the pre-Catholic primitive Christians, Gnostic Christians, Persians, Sephardic Jews, to name the better known, were permitted to flourish in city-states such as Granada, Córdova, Seville, Cadiz. These cultures freely added to one another without having to melt into each other except where they did so of their own accord. When this happened, there emerged far richer hybrids, and the little cities of the mountains and coasts became kingdoms of legend and imagination. It was here that the Grail stories were born. Writings of both distant and local tradition, religion, and language were cherished and translated into a mountain of interesting books, well tended by the Sephardic Jews, who had always been scholars. The Iberian Peninsula was the safest kingdom in the Western or Eastern Hemisphere of the time. Women could walk the streets at night in safety and foreign travelers didn't worry much when traveling from city to city because they could live on the hospitality of the curious princes and knowledge seekers they found there.

After Europe's last Middle Eastern Crusade failed and lost momentum, thousands and thousands of European men who for years had lived by violence and heroic crisis and who had a homeless existence returned to northern Visigoth Spain, France, Germany, Italy, and other Christian countries. Muslim Spain gave sanctuary to many dissident Crusaders who, having learned a great deal of wisdom and having grown accustomed to the civilized garden life of the Middle Eastern civilization, found it intolerable to continue living in the dog-eat-dog harshness of Catholic Europe.

Most Crusaders returning from a life of war, however, found no place for themselves, and lived landless and purposeless. The Catholic pope was quick to take advantage of the violence that had now become a part of the people, seeing these unemployed soldiers as a means to stamp out all of the enemies of the "true faith" and Rome's centralized kingdom. By reorganizing returning Crusaders into glorified goon squads, Rome set the frustrated defeated knights onto their own people, massacring millions of Cathars, troubadours, and many others. When they had finished this internal Crusade against the "heretics," the formerly flourishing earth and culture of southern France, from Provence to the Pyrenees, was a razed, smoldering, depopulated desolation, utterly devoid of resources.

Once Rome had reconsolidated its political and religious power base in this area, it was time to launch a new Crusade against Islam. This time the target would be Spain. Coming from a culture with no vision of personal or spiritual freedom, and having been traumatized for generations by a life of violence and emotional numbness in service to an angry God, the northern Visigoth Christians vented the fury of their inferiority complexes further and further south until two centuries later they'd rendered Spain a poor, ruined, raped land, united under one God and two Christian sovereigns.

Gone was pluralism, gone was free thinking, literacy, safety, abundance, and beauty. Gone was money, gone were the rich human resources of Andalusi culture.

By the 1400s, Spain was so far in debt that it had stretched out its fleets of ships all over the world, searching for peoples to overrun, enslave, and plunder to feed the monster of an unnaturally synthesized, top-heavy kingdom. England, France, Holland, and Portugal did the exact same thing.

In 1524 when the first Spaniards arrived in what is now Guatemala, they came in on a tornado of shame, hatred, and a numbness from centuries of wars with their own people, wars that had originated with other traumatized people like themselves. Generations ago they had forgotten what it meant to be truly at home in the natural earth.

Deranged and damaged from generations of violence and cultural misunderstandings in their own lands, with elders who couldn't remember life without the violating and mining mentality of war, these invaders of Native America were worse than blind to the excellence of the cultures that they found there. They could not understand the hearts, subtle beliefs, and strong tribal identities of the peoples they overran in search of Spain's artificially enforced identity.

As far as the Mayans were concerned, this was simply uninitiated behavior. Spain was a melancholy and depressed country that, like all conquering entities, was being eaten by all the ghosts it had created through all the killing wars waged on its own people. Essentially, Spain sought to export this kind of domestic depression and self-violence onto what they rationalized as "lesser" peoples. By taking the gold and abundance of these peoples and hollowing them out, just as they had done with the Spanish Moors and Jews, they sought to fill the empty hole in Spain caused by the erosion of their own nation's soul due to self-violence. Ironically, large groups of Spanish citizens, Jews, and dissidents emigrated to the "New World" to escape this repression, only to reestablish the same syndrome out of old habit. All those countries who wanted to be powerful by enslaving and conquering others were mostly one-God people. This imperial concept came from having no true parents, no true initiations for the young, and a culture that promoted an empty grandiosity that covered up a mass cultural depression that was only sometimes successfully exported to their subject colonies.

After the conquerors came the *ecomenderos* or landlords. These colonial families were given large tracts of Native land. These tracts were usually divided along the boundaries of the indigenous kingdoms who had inhabited the lands when the Spaniards arrived. The Mayan population living inside these boundaries were taxed by the *ecomenderos.*

Next came the Spanish clergy and the bureaucratic officials of Spain's civil governments. The Church levied a 10 percent tithe and land labor from the Indians in their diocese. The clergy and the *ecomenderos* were always at each other's throats and in competition over territory, each raising tribute for themselves and the Spanish throne from the conquered lands. Both the Church and the landlords had to pay taxes to the Mother Church and the monarch, respectively, keeping what was left for themselves. Sometimes they raised taxes illegally, misrepresenting the income on their rents, or reporting a census lower than reality.

Spanish landowners often allowed the political organization of a Native kingdom to remain intact if it hadn't been decimated during the conquest. Except for three famous Tzutujil leaders who were imprisoned in the Spanish capital in Guatemala, the local tribal hierarchy was left in working order as long as they made sure the tribute for the Spanish throne was levied by the chiefs and turned over to the *ecomenderos'* henchmen.

The Church, understanding that the spiritual organization of the tribe was identical to its political organization, levied tithes from the common populations inside the Church's domain instead of the Tzutujil Hierarchy. They also prohibited the hierarchies and shamans from practicing their "heathen rituals." Needless to say, the *ecomenderos* had a great deal more success getting their tribute than the Church did its tithe, as *ecomenderos* used the Native institutions to collect it. Nonetheless, the regular people, who had already been leveled to poverty by the conquest, were again taxed by the landowners who represented the Crown.

This competition between the Church and the landowners was so vicious that the strain of such double taxing on some tribes caused them to commit mass suicide. Whole villages would disappear overnight. Other villagers ran away into the bush in hopes of not being detected, and were thus forced to live a lonely, ostracized existence, something that was unbearable to most Mayan peoples.

Most of the Tzutujil did not kill themselves, flee, or give in to this overbearing dominance of these two feuding factions of European greed. The Atiteco hierarchy found a highly intelligent and crafty way to miraculously turn the whole Spanish system back on its purveyors. First off, they sent a whole group of village youth to study with the Church. These youth returned to the village literate in Latin and Castilian Spanish. The old people then developed a phonetic way of writing the Nahuat dialects of neighboring non-Mayan tribes.

With this weapon under their sashes, the hierarchy secretly indicted both the *ecomenderos* and the priests by drafting well-written reports in both Spanish and Latin. These reports described both parties' respective corruptions, explaining how much they were cheating the Crown and the Church of their "rightful" percentage. They paid a disgruntled Spanish overseer to sail to Spain and deliver these secret writs directly into the hands of the king and archbishop.

In the end the Atitecos were given an unprecedented degree of home rule. They also had their taxes and tribute lowered considerably, and were left alone as long as the tribute came in regularly.

To complicate the lives of the Mayans, the Spanish Church itself was divided up into feuding factions made up of powerful orders of clergy, monks, and ecclesiastical bureaucrats. They too fought among themselves, competing for authority over different areas of Mayan territory regardless of the boundaries of the landlords. Once jurisdictions had been assigned, the clergy often built complex churches, monasteries, and clerical quarters right smack on top of old Mayan temples, forcing the beautiful old temple stones, originally shaped with jade chisels and axes, into the form of European buildings. Having a great manipulative understanding of the Maya's reverence for sacred places, the Church fathers thought that by setting churches on top of temples that had been in use at the time of the Spanish invasion they could more easily coax the Maya to transfer their spiritual allegiances to the new god and his temple. You can always tell when this has been done. Even today in many villages one can see how the steps leading up to the atrium of a colonial church are fan shaped, mimicking the pre-European temple beneath.

One of the biggest and earliest Catholic churches ever built in a tribal town in Latin America was placed right on top of a small temple in a Tzutujil village called Siwan Tinamit, Canyon Village. Situating it just opposite the old Tzutujil capital of Chitinamit across the bay, Franciscan monks and priests used the original temple stones and forced labor to raise a very large colonial church complex. Though partly ruined, the church still stands in full use today. This was the beginning of Santiago Atitlan.

European Christians, Templars, Cabalists, Masons, Copts, Buddhists, Hindus, and almost every people in the world understand their temples to be a sacred architecture in which their own cultural vision of the whole world is represented in microcosm. But the Tzutujil, with no verb "to be," spoke about their temple as a nonrigid, fluid thing to be added to and fed with offerings. These offerings kept the world alive, like the fertilizing and watering of a tree, an ancient tree that continually bears the fruit of "now." The Spaniards of the sixteenth through the seventeenth centuries, however, saw their churches as static representations of heaven, of God's territory.

Every angle, corner, length of wall, step, layer, and direction in these old Tzutujil temples was the microcosmic home to a family of deities who represented a part of the House or temple of Time. Each of these deities came to the temple on roads of time radiating in from concentrically placed mountains, valleys, springs, rivers, cliffs, and so on, where they lived in concentric rings of temporal deity families.

This made the old temples into a kind of spiritual clock whose outer form represented the fifth layer of existence in which we live now, bound into a form called the Fruited Earth, held together by an architecture of deified Time Ropes. That is why the Tzutujil called life destiny *Bey* and *Colo,* Roads and Ropes.

Every part of the temple itself was holy, and the Deities of each of these Time sections were called by their calendar names as represented in the old Mayan calendar. Inside the temple structure, invisible to the eye, were secreted all the other layers of possible existence like the unblossomed petals of a flower. It was this inner possibility, maintained in a tension of withheld potentiality, that gave the spiritual force necessary for life to continue.

The temple's physical shape, composed of Deified Time and tangible form, was called the Earth Body. Every part of the temple Deified, called by its calendric appellation, was simultaneously understood to be a part of an anatomy of a spiritual body much like our own, containing at once a heart, lungs, liver, limbs, head, and so on: a body of calendric days, a body of named time.

Every part of this body was analogous to a part of the temple and a part of the world, but certain joints of this Body of Earth were considered to be places where Time could be actually fed. In others words, like a flowering tree, the temple sat between the four previous worlds and layers that had already flowered, and the other eight worlds that were held in perpetual possibility like a huge set of concentric buds of creation inside the temple's form. Time, in the form of hungry Deities, kept our present existence tacked down to a tangible reality, like the temple's form.

Because all the architectural aspects of the temple were also parts of the Earth's Body held together by Time, we humans could feed those individual places of time with our rituals to keep the Earth-Temple-Time-Body alive. Throughout the year in the old days, the whole universe, born and unborn, was kept alive by the hierarchical priests "feasting" time through ritual in different parts of the temple in the umbilicus of all reality.

Because this temple was called the House of the World, and Tzutujil houses collapse every year if not maintained, the House of the World had to be renewed every year, and the human being, along with the Earth, had to be remade. This remaking of all things was what the Tzutujil called initiation. Without initiation, renewal ceases and the flower withers. To understand all of this took years, and it was in the initiations that this knowledge was imbued into one's bones. It was this understanding of Time, Earth, and Temple that made one into an adult. What made one an elder, on the other hand, was understanding how to carry this knowledge and still go about a regular, hard-working life, knowing that the flow of everyday happenings in the village and the world were of that Holy Temple's Body.

I suspect that most of the European colonists didn't know much about any of this; their universe was in the hands of one distant God. They weren't trying to feed this world, the past, or the future; they were mining and wasting this "evil" material world to build a ladder to heaven, a happy world eternally suspended in an unattainable future.

When the Franciscan fathers came to Atitlan, they brought a great quantity of hand-carved images of particular Catholic saints in attitudes that were revered as part of the Franciscan cult ritual of this order. In those days, Spanish Catholic churches contained rows upon rows of amazingly carved images of all the Christian martyrs and saints, representations of the different stages of Jesus' life and death, Mary in all her difficult postures, the eternal Father, and a million other angels and ornate holy concepts.

To their credit, the old Tzutujil hierarchy paid great heed to where all their recycled temple stones ended up in the Catholic colonial church, as well as to where these Catholic images ended up being placed. Depending on where they stood in the church in relation to the original temple stones, these new saints became a code for the old Tzutujil Mayan deities of time and place. It was the same old Mayan Earth, the same Tzutujil Time, but in a strange foreign configuration.

Of course, there were saints, images who were the patrons of things the Tzutujil didn't have before the Spaniards came, like sheep, horses, wheat, cows, pigs, steel, glass, money, and so forth. But these were interpreted simply as a tribe of minor Time Gods from another Earth come to live in Atitlan with the sophisticated Mayan layered Gods. These new Gods were simply the Spaniards' old Gods. They had been the power behind the life lived in that other Earth just as these Mayan deities made life happen in the Mayan earth.

The Scat Mulaj spent a great amount of time and prayer feeding and incensing these holy places inside the central church. The European priests, like the American priests three hundred fifty years later, assumed that because the Tzutujil theocracy was in the church kneeling in passionate prayer, lighting candles, leaving flowers, liquor, and copal smoke in front of the specific Christian Iconography, that they were somehow participating in an erroneous folksy Catholicism.

In the 1600s Spaniards started becoming rare due to earthquakes, volcanic eruptions, and the mass plagues of yellow fever, cholera, malaria, typhoid, and typhus they had brought with them. These sicknesses killed off so many Indians, too, that there was little tribute to be had. The clergy quit the highlands for at least three decades.

By the time churchmen and Spaniards started reappearing later in the century, something disturbing had happened in their long absence. The old Tzutujil, who were in complete sympathy with the new priests, tried to explain it to them. "What happened," they patiently demonstrated, "is that when you Holy Fathers left our village all your saints got lonely. After all, even Jesus wasn't married, and God himself was pretty much on his own. So, they all fell in love with the local Gods and Goddesses for the most part, except for Maria Natividades there, who ran off with San Antonio, but what can you do? After a while babies were born to them, as often happens when beings get together. They in turn grew up and married the sons and daughters of other Gods and Saints. Now we have thirteen Jesuses, six of whom are girls, and the other six boys. We're pretty sure the thirteenth one is both. We have white Jesus, yellow Jesus, red Jesus, green Jesus, spotted Jesus, and sparkling Jesus. There are so many Saints and Gods now, there aren't enough of us to take care of them."

The church had filled to overflowing with so many little saints and little stone Gods that no one person knew all their names. Someone would have a dream about one, and explain His or Her name and what he or she liked to eat to the rest of the hierarchy. Then the people would know what to call him and the person who dreamt him would be responsible for his feasts. But, for the most part, the Tzutujil world was now overrun with nameless little Gods, all on account of the great promiscuity of the Spanish Saints and the beauty of the Mayan Goddesses. These little Gods, it turned out, were the Gods of a different kind of time, another earth with the strange new things that modernity would bring in a couple of centuries, things that neither the Maya nor the Spaniards knew anything about. The Tzutujil prophets did know, but that's another story.

Guatemala has always been rocked by one earthquake or another, and the

Earthtremors were particularly violent back then. Soon the village church was so damaged that by the late seventeenth century the Catholic priests thought it better to rehouse their "legitimate" Saints and carvings in the private homes of high-ranking Mayans for safekeeping where they could continue to be adored. In order to continue receiving their tithe, the priests eventually put into place a system intended to imitate a well-established Spanish institution called *La Fraternidad* or *La Cofradia,* both of which translate as "brotherhood." This system is still very much alive in Spain and Latin America today.

A *Cofradia* consisted of a lay brotherhood made up of appointed, unordained pious civilians, both men and women, dedicated to the maintenance of the cult, vestments, and fiestas of a given image of a Saint, or an aspect of Jesus or Mary. These organizations were responsible for any expenses incurred during their term of office, insuring that masses would be said at the appointed times and processions carried out. Above all, the *Cofradia* had to make certain that everybody in the village paid their *tasacion,* or tithe, to the priest, who usually skimmed it.

Besides giving homes to homeless Saints, the rationale of the Church was to put in place a system that would insure that the Indians paid closer attention to the finer points of seventeenth-century Catholic dogma without the constant need of a priest, while keeping the coffers filled.

The Tzutujil loved the idea, and mysteriously engineered it so that the official Saints (which were Gods of Time now) were kept in the *Cofradias,* or private huts, right in the same lodgings where certain prohibited Native Gods, bundles, and secret ceremonial relics that had craftily escaped the scrutiny of the *padres* and had been kept for centuries all along. Here, too, was where all the offspring of the Gods lived.

Soon the *Cofradias* simply became Sacred Houses, called *tzokin hai,* or *shutin hai,* where the families of the Gods and Saints of Time and the deities of the products of these seasons were housed and maintained as always. But now, with the added company of the Saints officially sanctioned by the Church, the Tzutujil were able to merge it all and keep what was best alive.

The Saints' celebrations would innocently take place in the home of the old gods, which they shared. Each Sacred House thus formed corresponded to one of the thirteen aspects of the powers anciently maintained by the old

Tzutujil in their constant efforts to keep the Flowering Mountain Earth alive and well.

Some of them housed:

Wild Animals and Plants, Winds, Blue Corn Woman
Domesticated Animals, Above-Water Animals and Plants, and Yellow
    Corn Woman
Cacao (Chocolate) Growth, Underwater Animals and Plants
Ancestors, Death, Underwater Dead
Three Corn Plantings

The Hierarchy maintained some of the medieval Christian aspects in their processions, while the language of the ritual and the rituals unseen by the priests kept what was truly Mayan alive.

Married into, eaten into, absorbed, or alone, what the conquerors of those days brought was made much more beautiful by the Tzutujil. The old Gods salivated in hunger alongside the new ones and their mutual offspring in expectation of the delicious recipe of faith and eloquence which fed them. What the Scat Mulaj fed with their prayers, processions, dances, songs, candles, copal, tobacco, flowers, liquors, turkeys, shrines, and offerings made life live in Atitlan. And now I was one of their new helpers.

D E E R   D A N C E R S ,   J A G U A R   D A N C E R S ,
H A T C H I N G   T H E   V I L L A G E   H E A R T
G O I N G   T H E   R O U T E   T O   I N I T I A T I O N

Up from the Big Road, a sound like a thousand adolescent coyotes bred to large moaning cats rustled in here on the chilly night breeze of November. Faint at first, then close, then far, churning in the sweet lake air, their screaming, hooting, howling, and cooing came creeping in on the wind, through the upper cornstalk walls of this Sacred House.

Here Axuan, the God of Mountain Wind, North Wind, Dry Wind, and all the wild animals, with his wife, Ya Xuan, the Mother of Blue Corn, stood majestically attired as mountain royalty, eating in the flickering flames of a thousand kidney-fat candles laid out for ten feet in front of them.

Ma QoQuix and I entered. We knelt praying, greeting Axuan and his wife between the hot flames and the images of the Gods and saints. The old hut was like a spiritual engine, fueled by a fluid archaic language and ancient pro-

cedures. Each member of the theocracy of Axuan and Ya Xuan was performing his or her diverse duties. Some were sitting on the bench in state as kings
and queens, while others swung ornate incense burners full of coals, which
released chokingly fragrant smoke trails directed skillfully to each deity and
holy direction that still other members of the Scat Mulaj who had returned
with us were praying to. We had all just returned from a mission to other sacred houses to retrieve more boughs of cedar, cigars, and sacred liquor.

Having finished saluting the spirits and the officials, the drummer and I
were boisterously greeted by the chiefs. Their heads were all covered with
beautifully tied headcloths and their backs with long black blanket robes
hanging to the ground.

Grabbing our arms, they graciously sat us, as always, in the very special
place at the main bench next to the chief of Axuan and his wife, the Xuo of Ya
Xuan. Ma QoQuix and I faced a covey of happy Tixelí, who waved their
hands at us sitting with their legs folded to the side on their finely woven little reed mats. These women officials of this Sacred House nestled comfort-
ably on the six-inch layer of fresh pine needles that covered the entire floor.

We yelled a greeting to them: "*Ex kola nutie?*" Are you there, My Mothers?

"*Jie oq kola joj nta.*" Yes, we're here, My Fathers. They waved their arms,
laughing, and rolling their eyes at us.

The *Xuo,* a dignified old matron with a skunk stripe of white running
through her black hair, presided at her place by the head of our bench next to
a rawhide box that was suspended with ropes like a baby's cradle from the
cross poles, allowing it to rock freely. Blackened with centuries of caresses
and copal soot, it held the *Nawal taq Alaniel,* the Holy Wombs of the Earth,
and the much adorned dried placentas of the first boy and first girl ever born
at the beginning of the Earth in this creation.

The *Xuo* was in charge of this powerful bundle, which no male could
touch, as it was a woman's territory. It contained all the spirit umbilical cords
of every living thing in the universe, which connected us here to the Big Thirteen Goddess. These included the ocean, moon, lake, hot springs, rivers,
plants and earth and every wild animal. This bundle was taken out and
danced only twice a year, once in June and once in November.

The chief of Axuan, the *Xuo's* husband, sat next to her. He was trying to
explain something to us about a prophet coming to visit the next day, but we

couldn't hear him well over the driving din of the marimba band chugging away in the corner.

Besides my official duties here as a flute player, I had apprenticed myself to a bundle in this Sacred House called *Rukux Way Ya,* the Heart of Food-Water, Heart of Earth. This grand bundle contained the supernatural male power to fertilize all living things of the earth. It was the male equivalent of the woman's umbilical bundle and was said to hold many powerful holy objects that were left to the tribe by the Gods at the beginning of the last creation. A twin bundle of the same type was cared for by the Gods themselves inside their sacred mountain house, *Q'alibal Juyu Taq'aj,* Mountain Valley Throne, where I'd received my jaguar whisker.

Though our male bundle was also taken out of its big ancient box and danced only two times a year, only a few highly initiated men had ever seen or touched the gifts that lived inside. Every time the bundle was danced the Gods in the inner bigness of the other layers danced theirs. Their bundles and ours were all married but kept in separate places. The force field of longing created between the faraway bundles gave life to the world. Tonight was one of those nights.

In this world, the Heart of Food-Water was cared for by a jealous and neurotic rain priest who wore a white-purple headcloth over his shoulders unlike the red, brown, and purple ones the rest of us had. This signified his celibacy and marriage to the Gods.

I'd fallen in love with the Heart of Food-Water ever since Chiv had brought me here five years earlier. But like anything you love, you have to first learn her language before you're allowed inside her heart.

The secrets of this carefully wrapped pre-Christian, Seed Heart of Abundance lived inside an archaic ritual Mayan language reserved for the priests and initiates of the Bundle itself. I'd have to become one of four students who would serve for four years, learning all the dances, origin stories, and ritual procedures of the bundle before I'd be allowed to really look inside. Though we had been promised great mystery and ceremonial vision, one whole year still remained until we'd be called on by Chiviliu, the Rain Priest, the Prophet, the Chief of Axuan and his *Xuo,* to ritually initiate us into the secrets of the Bundle of Food and Water.

Tonight, however, the Rain Priest readied the bundle, chiding the attending officials into doing everything just right as they spread it out. Because the

copal and tobacco smoke rose so thickly and the bodies of the officials intentionally obscured everyone's line of sight, it was impossible for anyone to see
what the priest was doing deep in the bundle box. This was a common technique used to maintain secrecy in all the sacred houses.

There were still a few deerskins left on the table, their antlers tied up in
colored ribbons. Soon any number of this year's new men, recently initiated
boys, would ooze through the reed doorway into the sweet smoke and mystery of this night and claim them, joining the wild band of Deer and Jaguar
Dancers.

The bundles could not be danced without a visit from the Jaguars and
Deer who danced out the story of the first human being who had received the
Bundles. This story was told only to new men initiates, and only they were allowed to dance under the skins. This was a serious part of male initiation and
anyone else not "cooked" enough could die, lose his mind, or, at the very
least, get very ill. Men with pregnant wives were ineligible to dance, as they
were past this stage, having already fertilized the earth, and were moving on
to other rituals more in line with family life.

All of a sudden the marimba was told to stop playing, and everyone went
silent. We strained to listen as the antique mystical speech of the *Najbey Quej*,
the First Deer, the Priest of the Hide Dances, seeped like a confident stream
of murmuring birds past the tule reed doorway into the Sacred House.

You couldn't quite see them all outside, the row of bobbing antlers upright
in the soft candlelight rising from a dark file of deer heads, while the hides
that completely covered their bodies clacked and rustled on the ground as
they knelt, praying and shifting to the directions. For all the world here were
sacred animals from the "Other World" at our door, kneeling in a long row in
the dark, asking permission in their ancient tongue to come into our world,
the world of people.

The stiff-eared Jaguar moved his head slowly back and forth as the huge
crowd of Deer followed his old words in prayer.

Finally, the praying stopped and, kissing the ground, the Jaguar popped
up to what seemed an enormous height, and all the Deer, yelling and whooping, leapt over the threshold into the Sacred House, madly dancing and
screaming.

As if it were our second nature, in love with this old semiannual ritual,
knowing the truth, that real spirits were here with us, the drummer and I

struck up the stirring Song of the Deer. When he felt the roar of the drum, the Jaguar went wild, whistling and yelling in a desperate loud mewing complaint, "Fall down cliffs, close up canyons, come into my clutches, I'll grab you, Uh ooo o ooo ou. . . ."

Swirling like an enraged tornado, his timeworn skin flying up, whipping his tail around, the big old Jaguar transformed into a monster cat who tried to maul all the Deer with the claws of a moss-stuffed ocelot he wielded skillfully on his frantic paws. Spinning furiously in on him with lowered heads and jabbing antlers, the herd of Deer tried to gore the angry old feline, dancing all the while. With their shields and rawhide aprons lowered, they fended off his blows, raising the dance to a frenzied battle of beauty: fur flying, animals screaming, Jaguar swearing vengeance.

We played louder and louder, then we switched into the next phase of songs. Twelve stanzas had to be completed in each of the three phases. When we finally finished the last one, the Jaguar and the Deer separated, panting, to opposite sides of the hut. The candles were flickering wildly while their wax gushed into grotesque forms from the wind the animals had raised in their furious dance. An official tied a blanket over the doorway. Villagers began rushing in, especially unmarried girls who wanted to see the initiates, but no pregnant girls or their husbands were allowed into this ritual, for fear of miscarriage from fright. Sacred guards were posted to keep out anyone who was not already there to begin to witness what followed.

Using two loose glossy antlers, the Sacred House chief played a big slit log drum that looked like a capsized wooden canoe: *blung, blung, chat', blung blung blung chat', blung blung chat', blung, blung, blung, chat'!*

From one end of the room, a strong, well-adorned Deer danced forward into the space in the middle of the Sacred House. The Jaguar started to dance toward him slowly and majestically from the opposite end until they faced each other, both smoking long ceremonial cigars. The fumes of the tobacco rose elegantly from under their hides.

Gradually, they worked their high-arched dusty bronze, bare feet toward opposite ends of the heavy canoe-bottomed table where I, the drummer, and the lords were sitting. This table weighed at least a hundred fifty pounds. Sinking into the pine needles beneath the ceiling of portulaca flowers, these two dancing spirits, without any pauses or rests, simultaneously bit their ends of the table with their teeth. Clamping down like beasts, their eyes bulging, without the use of their hands, they picked the table up into the air with just their clenched jaws. With the table in their teeth from opposite ends, they began to dance both the table and the Holy Bundle of Heart of Food-Water, which had been placed in the middle of it earlier by the rain priests. Picking up speed as the ancient sound of the *cuncun* quickened, they began to rotate the table, dancing and leaping all the while. The table still in their mouths, they kept this up until they had returned it back to its original place. Then, sinking to the floor in a reverent kneeling position, they released the old table. Leaping up, they began to dance frantically, the two of them sparring viciously, swirling and swirling until finally the Jaguar fell to the ground in a death trance, trembling. With the sound of the drum rolling, the Deer adversary pulled off the Jaguar's hide and placed it over the incense burner that had been kept smoking by the Fourth Brother of the Sacred House. The Jaguar's Skin was placed with reverent care on the altar in front of all of the Gods of this Sacred House, and the log drum ceased its old rhythm.

Jumping up from beside Ma QoQuix and me, the Third Brother and the sacred women, the Tixelí, grasped copal burners, and after thoroughly smoking and incensing the dancers, they carefully removed their skins one at a time. When the dancers had finished praying to the bundle, we all rose to greet them as young men, sitting them next to us on the benches with the chiefs. Though proud to see them as young human beings, we knew full well that these boys were still in the "bite," or trance, of their spinning dance. We didn't expect them to be totally human yet.

When the Jaguar Dancer finally got up, we greeted him roundly with fierce affection. He was and always had been the Master of the Dance, called *Najbey Quej*, First Deer, by everyone in the tribe.

I had danced this dance a couple times the year before. The air under these magical hides became wide and dreamlike as you spun. You actually became the First Man, the Deer, and it was hard to stop being the Deer even after the hide was gone. There were a lot of procedures for getting under the hides and into their magic, into the other world and back home, in one piece. *Najbey Quej* was the man who knew it all, and in our youth we all looked to him to help us get through the experience.

He always had his head tied up with a silk scarf and he had the powerful, playful face of a Jaguar in a man, if I ever saw one. *Najbey Quej* was considered a kind of prophet or visionary. This dance was a spinning dance that let you know things beyond the scope of humans, and *Najbey Quej* knew more than most. He had the air of a grudge about him, probably like nature itself: unhappy with humans but still tolerant of everyday human ignorance—only God knows why.

Najbey Quej and I were always friends, but his job this night was to remain a Jaguar, keeping the whole world alive by being the Great Wind Jaguar who danced out an old secret story that only the initiated understood. This way he simultaneously taught the fresh crop of village initiates how to go through their animal nature without losing their humanness.

When all the prerequisite prayers, salutations, gift giving, encouragement from the old ladies and lords, and the ever-present canyon water was distributed, the youth lined up and said their farewells to us one by one. They asked for our blessing to do well, and we gave them the best we had. Donning their deerskins, antlers up and ears poking out, they started to circle, walking backward, swaying their heads back and forth into a spiral trail back, back, back into the other world of the Gods and animals.

The *Najbey Quej* once again became the Jaguar, and he led the initiates now not as an antagonist but as their captain into the Holy World of the Wild Creatures.

Whistling and whining, growling and screaming, all the animals knelt to thirteen directions, raising and hooting, falling again and whistling, praying as animals now. When the marimba began to pulse again, they commenced dancing almost cutely in place. The shadows that fell over the cornstalk walls entranced the village back into the original world at the beginning of ancestral time.

Then at a given signal the dancers all shot out into the dark like startled swallows, faster than can be imagined, onto the paths, running and hooting, spinning and jumping, sparring and flying. The hides gave them an inhuman power everyone understood, and off they flew to another sacred house containing another bundle called The Herd and a different Baby Bundle. They would go on like this for two days until all the bundles had been danced.

As soon as the ceremonial dancers were gone, all the officials, men and women, inside our Sacred House jumped up and started dancing abstractly, some with their hands behind their backs like ice skaters. All of us were required to dance ecstatically, even to the point of fainting. Some of us would not wake till dawn.

At sunrise a feast was called and we, the holy wounded, were healed by the kind voices of our mothers, the Tixelí. They called us to eat the food given to us by the Heart of Food-Water, the Baby Bundle, through the Deer. We thanked everyone in order and feasted together, each of us eating the exact same things cooked in conformation to the old foods traditionally eaten at this time. These foods included the Foot of the Holy Children, a tamale the size of a child's foot in which the Road of the Sun Father was etched; *pulic'*, a stew made from turkeys sacrificed the day before; and wild mint, white corn, dried and ground mouse chilies, toasted squash seeds, small tomatoes, and salt from the mountains.

One at a time, each official thanked each deity, tribal ancestor, hierarchy official, and all of the sacred cooks. With such a large retinue, a feast "thanking" could take more than an hour. By then the food was usually cold, but the opportunity for gratitude was understood to be the main reason for a feast anyway. After all, it was the bundles, the Gods who danced as we danced, and the visiting animals who actually occasioned this feast. The ornateness and eloquence of the gratitude given during a morning feast of this kind was one of the things that caused the earth to come back alive again. Indeed, the Gods and ancestors were feasting right along with us in their world, only what they were eating were the things we'd sent them the night before—candles, liquor, flowers, tobacco, incense, songs, prayers, ritual, and dance. They too had fallen down in a trance of ecstasy and were now being revived by the delicious steam and aroma of our thanking them for what they'd given us.

The Gods sent us food and life, and the thanking made the feast delicious to the Gods. Everyone and everything was thanked and fed in every way.

The same thanking was repeated after everyone had finished eating. Each of us took our bowl to the cooks and showed them its emptiness, thanking them profusely in one of the many fine eloquent language forms used by initiated adults. These were not liturgies but well-made ancient speeches distilled from a rich horde of traditional images that expressed the excellence we felt in our full hearts and bellies. There is nothing more wonderful than being sacredly happy, fallible, full and hungover on God in a group of people dedicated to these activities, knowing that by doing so you were helping the world and the village.

When we had finished, we readied ourselves to reenter the sanctuary, the Sacred House where the Old Heart of Food-Water Bundle sat in state, unopened, feasting on the magnificence of all the flowers, smells, and fires.

Suddenly, old Chiv, accompanied by the Rain Priest, and two ex-chiefs thudded into the compound flanked by three tall white Guatemalan Ladinos in polyester shirts and slacks, cigarettes hanging out of their mouths. Two of them had fierce-looking machine guns in one hand and clip belts over their shoulders. They laughingly followed the old Tzutujil leaders, lining up to face the chief and *Xuo* of the Sacred House.

Old Chiv said they wanted to see the Heart of Food-Water and have a look inside of the bundle, as they'd heard it was very interesting.

The chief, old Chiv, and the Rain Priest's eyes locked in some kind of shock and unspoken recognition. The Chief and *Xuo,* with a regal flourish of hands and robes, invited the "visitors" in while sending word that the rest of us, the Scat Mulaj, should keep our distance.

A blanket was again hung over the doorway and copal smoke began curling out under the eaves of the Sacred House and through the roof thatch.

The crowd of officials who should have been inside were confused, doubtful, and uncharacteristically silent. Something very bad was happening and we all knew it. A political candidate and his bodyguards were "visiting" us traditionalists. It made us all nervous. Mocking laughter arose from the hut and finally the three short-haired, hatless, tall white men with guns strolled out of the hut making jokes in Spanish. Ignoring the village officials, they disappeared up the Big Road to their shiny car at the mouth of the village. The hut was closed to us for another hour, and then the old people emerged. Chiv explained nothing to me personally nor to anyone else, but said his polite and formal farewells to all present and then disappeared into the bush.

By the time we'd reentered the beautiful Sacred House it looked small and humble. We'd lost the ceremony; the happiness was gone.

We'd been violated by what didn't love us, or comprehend the delicateness of what it took to get to the common spiritual ground where what was human could feast with the divine. The beauty had been scared off like deer in front of sport hunters. The immenseness had been diminished and trivialized. How could Chiv have sold us out like that? How could the Rain Priest have let him? What was wrong with these old men?

I'd been Chiv's student for three years now. I'd been initiated as a shaman and knew him to be a strong defender of the traditions. Nevertheless, he had, with no warning, nonchalantly allowed a bunch of insensitive goons to come right into a sacred sanctuary with no procedure or ritual. These men had no respect or knowledge for what they wanted to see, and yet Chiv had allowed them to peer into the most significant Holy Bundle the village had. I and the other Bundle students weren't even allowed to see inside those multiple mystical wrappings until we had undergone the requisite four years of focused training that it took to mature us enough to understand what every shred and crumb of the Bundle meant.

Why hadn't the other officials stopped them? Why hadn't the village barred the way? It was like inviting some horrible men to sleep with your wife, daughter, sister, or mother while waiting outside for them to finish. To make it worse, these strange men made it all look as casual and trite as if they were in a *tiendita* to buy cigarettes. I was furious and so were the other young men with whom I'd been training.

We held our peace and completed the remaining rituals for the House of Axuan, all the while keeping silent about our anger. But the following day, after we'd all been released back into regular life, we were unable to contain our feelings of violation and disappointment. We were determined to confront someone, and so we confronted Chiv because he seemed like the guiltiest party.

When we arrived at his compound, the old shaman was sitting in his personal Sacred House, the one with the stuffed fish hanging overhead.

Trying not to enter surreptitiously, we boys yelled out the customary "*At kola Ta'?*" Are you there, Father?

"*Jie n kola anen ai'i.*" I'm here, little lords, Chiv bugled.

"*Kixjona.*" Come in, all of you.

"*Kixits be ga a i'i.*" Please, all of you sit, young lords.

Chiv had several freshly steamed duck *patíns* laid out in front of him. This kind of *patín* was made by taking a club-killed lake duck and smoking it over a hardwood fire, then cooking it in a paste of achiote, tomatoes, squash, seeds, and salt, with little chunks of *piech'*, wild banana-stalk hearts, and gourd tendrils sprinkled in. The duck was then wrapped in a plantain leaf, tied with *zibaque* fiber, and the package was steamed for an hour in a big clay pot made for just that purpose. It was as if he'd been expecting us at that very moment and had a feast laid out for us. You can be sure that was exactly true. He was a magician and a rascal.

"*Kixwa aii.*" Please, eat your fill, young lords!

"But, Father, we've come to speak to you about what happened yesterday morning in the compound of Axuan."

"Oh, yes, but first it's good to eat. Look—smoked duck!" old Chiv replied, grinning and salivating.

"How come you let those *Mosi'* see the Bundle?" I blurted out, ignoring the requisite Tzutujil etiquette of gradualness. "These men are uninitiated, they know nothing about the true meaning of the Bundle at all. How could you just open it like that without any of the respect and time it takes to do it right? How come you sold us out?" I wanted him to answer, to tell me he hadn't done it for money, as some suspected and had whispered about since yesterday.

But Chiv was hungry. "Well, maybe that's true," he said, "but the best thing, really, is to eat. Look, smoked ducks, five of them!"

The other boys couldn't take it anymore and began to eat, because this was a prized, rare, and delicious food made only by the Tzutujil. In the past, legend said, Tzutujil shamans and heroes had used *patín* to beguile monsters and bribe their Spanish overlords into letting the Tzutujil do what they liked without restriction.

"Father, you know it takes four hard years to learn the old words and dances to open that Bundle, and now these *Mosi'*, these laughing, mocking people, with no work and no culture, come ruin our sacred Bundle. When you let those people see what we boys are kept from seeing, the sacred ran away from the Bundle. These people just come to steal, they give nothing and have now ruined the most holy thing in the village, the Heart of Food-Water. How could you let that happen? Tell me how?" I was getting really worked up, and though the other boys had their mouths full of the delicious fare, they nodded in agreement. Chiv had his mouth full too and was nodding also, but mostly to help him chew because he only had about eight teeth.

Finally, swallowing his semichewed food, he spoke.

"Son, the duck is really delicious. Please eat, look—smoked duck! What can be so troublesome when you have smoked duck? Eat." Chiv was like a hawk on a sparrow, with no time for anything other than what he was focused on.

Disgusted, I rose up and, in the worst breach of Tzutujil etiquette imaginable, I had begun to exit without so much as a "Thanks" or "I'll return," when the *Najbey Quej,* the First Deer, the powerful Jaguar Dancer, strode through Chiv's door with his hierarchy wife. Dressed in his best blue-and-white handwoven striped shirt and bird-embroidered knee pants, his lined jaguarlike face grinned like a big cat when he saw me. He grabbed my hand, seeming to shake it in greeting, but he actually prevented me from leaving, making it all look as though I'd risen to go greet him.

He had a grip like a howler monkey and, winking, walked me together with his wife back to the smoked duck, everyone shaking hands, exchanging greetings, happy to see one another. Finally, we all started eating together. *Najbey Quej* was very happy about the smoked duck and his wife did a lot of damage to my *patín.* I gradually started eating too. Chiv and the jaguar man kind of smiled as they gnawed at the bones, crunching them like skunks eating mice, their heads bobbing, humming in delight. When it came to birds and smaller animals, the Tzutujil don't leave any bones. It was good, I had to admit.

Finally, after another hour of smoking pipes, belching, and storytelling, old Chiv told the old jaguar man about my complaint.

Najbey Quej just laughed, barely parting his lips. He and Chiv lit their funny, tiny stone pipes, sharing a half-penny cigar to fill them up.

"*Tdta',* Brother Father, I call you this because you are hierarchy, but you're acting like a spoiled baby monkey. This bundle is older then any of us, and was here on the earth before any humans were created. This bundle's holiness was not created by people physically, and, for the same reason, there are no people who can destroy it by taking it apart. When people take the holy apart, they take themselves apart.

"Don't you think the bundle must have its own protection? The power in that bundle makes us whole but we don't make that power. What you say is true; in order for that power of the great Heart of Food-Water to keep us whole, we must maintain the bundle properly. But does that make these disrespectful people so powerful that they can diminish the power of the bundle?"

Calmed a bit, I was listening, and I replied, "We have to wait four years to see what they demanded to see in the blink of an eye, and then they went off joking as if they'd just seen something unimpressive, something they already knew. Why do we have to wait if you just let anybody else treat it like a piece of junk?"

Chiv had digested enough to get in on the conversation by now. "Look, son, for years we people of the Canyon Village, the Temple of Birds, have had to deal with people from other countries, whites from the cities and all kinds of people who always wanted what we have. It's getting worse all the time, and up till now the spirits have protected themselves. People from the outside want to take apart our bundles to see what's in them. You can take one apart in a second, but you see nothing. The only way to "see" what's in the bundle is to learn slowly how to put it together and how to take care of it, like an egg, for instance. If you want to see why the mother bird thinks her eggs are so precious, like our village loves its bundles, then you could break the egg. All you would see is mucus and yolk. But if you initiates sit, hatch, maintain, and care for the egg without breaking it, you will see in the end what an egg is all about. An egg is really a bird, and a bird that can lay another egg. To hatch an egg and raise that hatchling so that it can fly takes time, care, and worry. That's initiation.

"By looking in the bundles those people saw 'nothing,' and, seeing nothing, they took nothing away with them. Like most of the greedy peoples of the earth, when they heard rumors about the most precious thing our village had, they assumed it must be gold, material wealth, or who knows what. They wanted to make sure we 'poor' little Indians didn't possess something that these big politicians didn't already have, something that had somehow missed the avaricious scrutiny of the previous oppressors.

"And mark this: If they had seen any worth in our bundle, they would have connived to own it or just stolen it at gunpoint. But since what is in the bundle cannot be seen without going the route of learning, they saw nothing.

"You have to go the route, boys. This means that by going the four years you learn how to see 'nothing' in a substantial way. What is in the bundle is in the seeing. We are not so primitive as to think that the bundle is the power, it is simply a home for the power to be seen. The bundle is a throne, and it takes four years for our poor human eyes to see the spirit sitting there.

"All of our bundles contain ordinary things that, when seen in ritual context, become the extraordinary things they really are. Our everyday human struggle for food and life tends to sprinkle a dust of commonness on the world. Our ceremonies 'repolish' the spirits, make it so we can see the holiness of what surrounds us every day. The Spirits are big and they've always made it so that we have to go the full route of learning to see what's really in there. Everybody else who takes the shortcut will not see. You will see in time, boys. Don't be scared off the nest by some clumsy hunters; be patient and courageous like mother birds and hatch the spirit."

What Chiv was saying was very beautiful and true, but part of me believed that this was just a quaint comeback to avoid telling us the truth. But old Chiv was right. The Old Jaguar man was right. The old men and women of the hierarchy were right, for when the time came for us to see what was in the bundle, it was so beautiful as to be undescribable. Like all those who came before me, I promised not to tell what I saw, and I won't.

"Besides," Chiv continued, "they had machine guns! You'd be out of a teacher if I hadn't gone along with it. So, did you get enough duck, lords?"

We sang songs and talked all night, waddling home as the morning star began to rise. I fed that star and slept.

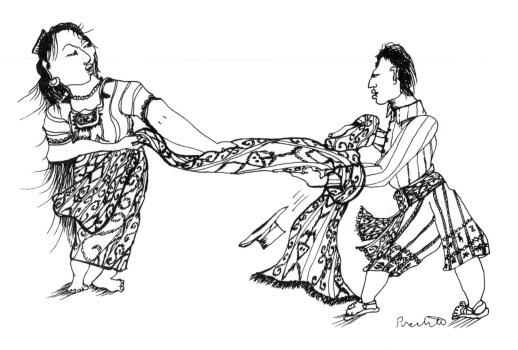

FIVE

COURTING YA MACHETE

Courting was everything to the Tzutujil; it permeated every aspect of life and every age set. When shamans made ceremonies, they were courting specific spirits with offerings and beautiful words. When the Scat Mulaj moved in their complex, interminable cycles of processions and Sacred House rituals, they were courting the Gods, hoping to beguile the Gods into continuing the abundance of this creation. When any person was to be appointed to a powerful or meaningful position, the village leaders were required to court their candidate slowly until he acquiesced. A village youth could not be eligible for initiation into adulthood until he or she was seen courting on the village streets, because that adolescent courting signaled the approach of the time when a young man and woman could begin to see and feel the physical presence of the divine in their longing for each other. Courting was the beginning of initiation, and the language of courting was the language of adults.

Though the village ran on courting, it was a learned thing, and it took the youth a while to get the hang of it. Boys and girls actually began by hunting each other. All assorted shapes and ages, the young women of the village were just like a surging herd of nervous, glistening deer.

Each girl worked for months weaving her courting shawls, intricately designed, full of intriguing knotwork and sparkling thread, only to drag the ends on the ground behind her in hopes a boy or two, finding her handsome, might grab the loose end behind her, to capture her into talking to him.

Girls never went anywhere alone. They were always seen in little flocks trolling the village streets for boys as they headed to this or that place on some pretext or other.

Because it was bad form to step on the ends of the dragging shawl, a boy all dressed up out on the village paths with his cronies, who were patrolling the village like ocelots for quail, would have to run up behind the girl, seize the end of the shawl, and wrap its luxurious length around his hand a couple times, then continue walking with her.

The young women would make a break for it in a run and either hit the end of the taut shawl or jerk it out of the hands of the boy, chattering complaints all the while, even if she liked him. This was protocol. She couldn't just stand there talking to a boy the first time he grabbed her shawl, no matter how much she admired him.

At the same time, by not letting go of the shawl right away until he had received a promise from the girl that he could catch her again the next day, the young man showed the girl that he was serious. The girls liked that. It was never an option, however, for a girl to return home without her courting shawl. If a girl hated a boy who insisted on ambushing her and holding her by her shawl against her will, she could always just let go of her end and he would be left without her.

This posed a problem for the girl, since village protocol demanded that the boy return the girl's shawl. If the young man was intent, in love and intelligent, he'd come to her hut some evening when the entire extended family of the girl was in their compound, winnowing beans, cooking, chopping wood, and stacking corn ears. By then he would have made a trip to the market or to his relatives to obtain carefully selected gifts for the girl's parents and the rest of her compound. Symbolizing a girl's soul and her artistic abilities, the shawls were so difficult to make, one of a kind and valuable, that most mothers didn't want their daughters to be seen without them. For this reason the mother usually allowed the guilty boy into the compound and fed him at the family fire to get back the shawl, but also to acknowledge that he had shown some respect to her family by giving good gifts.

A girl who let a boy take her shawl gave him a passport to her family's heart. Worse yet, if her relatives liked him then they might put pressure on her to marry him. All this for a boy the girl was probably trying to get as far away from as possible. That's why girls rarely let go of their shawls during the orchestrated madness of village courting.

The girls were fast runners and the boys highly predatorial in a kind of friendly way. In the afternoons you could see little bunches of beautiful teenage girls break into a run when a young man came trotting up to them from behind.

Teenage boys would sometimes engineer their routes to walk down the opposite direction that certain girls were heading. After they'd just gone past, one of the boys would turn and grab a shawl. Sometimes in the confusion he'd catch the wrong girl.

Some girls threw rocks, bit with their white teeth, or punched with their fists, driving off all pretenders until the right guy grabbed her shawl. Then she'd fake a tame kind of wiggling struggle, hissing and complaining like a drunk squirrel, raising a modest din to give a theatrical appearance of feigned distress but putting no real force behind trying to get her shawl back.

The next two or three times the boy approached, if she truly liked him, she'd actually drag her shawl right by him, slowing up as she cruised by, casting her shawl like a fisherman's line in hopes that he'd pick it up and walk with her, each of them holding the opposite ends loosely. Relaxed now, the boy and girl could stroll and chat, connected by the decency of the shawl. This was a common sight. True success occurred when, as the days went by, she just tossed the boy one end of her shawl as she sailed by where he, looking cool and well dressed, was leaning against somebody's house with all his teenage friends. When he grabbed her shawl, she'd hook him like a fish. Happy to be caught, she pulled him out of the pool of his friends, who then, like a bunch of disturbed crustaceans, snapped all kinds of mocking nonsense at the two of them as they strolled up the village paths out of sight into each other's hearts.

Some of the most beautiful or able girls had any number of suitors. Sometimes these girls were so swamped that young men competed in impromptu contests of beautiful speech in order to get their attention. It was during courting that young men and women actually began to try to say what they felt. This was where they began to do what the whole existence of the village depended on: the feeding of life with Beauty, keeping the universe tied together with a rope made of eloquent speech that touched the heart.

But some girls had hearts like the big hard buds on certain jungle trees that took extreme heat and the bite of an angry monkey to get them to flower. Once in a while a big flashy, black-eyed girl with hair down to the back of her knees, her smooth luxurious breasts wobbling inside her *pot,* blouse of her own excellent weaving, her hips waddling in the tight red wraparound, her high arched feet, still young and suedelike, not yet gnarled, her delicate elbows out above her, balancing a heavy clay jar on her well-postured head, her industry making her all the more alluring, would just seem to have no interest in a boy. Some boy might have stopped working and started trembling while standing and staring over his unused hoe and ax out in the mountains, mesmerized and thrilled by this young woman, hoping to get her attention and meeting with war instead.

There was one such girl named Machete Woman whose heart just wouldn't open no matter how well a boy spoke. And getting that close to her was the bravest thing any teenager would ever have to do. She was beautiful, unattainable, fierce, and good at everything girls had to be good at: weaving, grinding, cooking, embroidering, washing in the lake, tortilla making, selling her father's reed mats at market. She wasn't very good at speaking, however, especially to my friend A Coy, Spider Monkey. Above all, she was highly opinionated and strong, stronger than a whole village of unmarried boys. No one could figure out how to marry her because, when she went by, if you grabbed her shawl, she'd slug you so hard you'd go down like a hammered cow. And if you dodged that, she'd commence throwing stones at you, stones that never missed.

When she first started wearing a woman's sign of marriageability, the big red head ribbon and a maiden's *pot*, a number of boys could be seen limping around the village, holding bruises on their ribs with shiners on their faces, wondering why she advertised her marriageability when she was so uncordial and uninterested in the game of courting. Of course, her aunts and her mother were pushing her to take her place in the matrilineal succession of marriageable girls. Out of respect for her female relatives, she'd wear the clothes, but she wasn't going to be anybody but herself. That meant she liked to work hard, she liked to fight, and she didn't need marriage.

A Coy just wouldn't be stopped. He was in love with this demoness and had tried every con and dodge with her. Most of the tried-and-true tricks used by other boys wouldn't work with Machete because you couldn't get close enough to smooth-talk her. A Coy had knots on one side of his rib cage and one under his shoulder blade to prove it.

Some girls whose parents were strict and didn't approve of the boys they flipped their shawls to would generally resort to the time-honored courting procedure of assigning different birdcalls or whistled phrases to their suitors, along with the names of the vicious compound dogs. After everyone was asleep in the compound, the boy could sneak outside her hut, make friends with the dogs, and whistle in a low tone. The girl would stealthily make her way toward him by pretending she was going out to urinate, though she would not return for some time. Love affairs could be carried on in this way for a while.

Some girls actually assigned separate whistles to as many as five or six cow-eyed young men. That way she'd know who was waiting for her and decide whether he was worth risking her parents' wrath if she ever got caught. Occasionally a boy would even sell a girl's secret birdcall melody to another if a girl fell out of favor, or if he got jealous about the attentions other men gave to her.

A Coy came running in one day to the hut where I lived at the end of Chiv's villagelike compound. He whispered to me as I was carving flutes, letting the chips drop into the cooking fire.

"Ya Machete sent me a song and her dog's names! A Martín, let's go late tonight and see if she'll come out and talk. Good?"

"How true could this be, *ach*? She wouldn't give anybody a whistle song. The sound of your howling after she boxes your ears is the sound she likes to give."

In the end, though, I couldn't turn him down because he was my friend. Besides, it could turn out to be an adventure.

Somewhere in the neighborhood of two o'clock in the morning, A Coy whistled for me at my compound, the whistle of a boy going to work. This was like your friend honking a car horn to pick you up to take you to school. Nobody paid too much attention to that.

After I tied up my Indian pants, we trotted down the hillside, over the boulders, past the Big Road, down the next cliff, then turned left past the rotting reeds and God Rock, over the gardens of Box Head, and past the compound of old Ma Xkin, whose three little mean dogs knew A Coy and wagged their pitiful bottoms to see us. Then we tiptoed up the narrow path to the compound of Deer Cross, Machete's father. Though they were poor, their compound small and overcrowded, everything was beautifully made and the food and tools meticulously stacked and arranged.

With six or seven people sleeping in every hut, our chances of getting that girl to the wall to talk without being heard would be near to impossible, I thought. But A Coy was in love. Deer Cross was known for his instant reactions and straightforward thinking. He killed every snake, burned every stick, and punished every transgression. Ya Machete must have been his student. A Coy was crazy to want her.

Hurrying under the small hut wall we had been told she slept behind, we very, very quietly leaned up against it and A Coy began whistling three quaint, breathy, chortling bird sounds. We waited and then he tried again. We held our breath and a little sound of rustling about in the hut could be heard. Then we heard the shuffling of her bare feet on the smooth threshold stone in the wonderful gait of a girl whose hips are bound with a tight wraparound skirt which limits walking to a particular motion. Her whispering voice quieting the dogs came over the wall.

His heart thudding in excitement, A Coy whistled again, turning to look up at the compound wall three feet above us to see if she was there yet, when . . .

Bplaaang, rrauch . . . A shower of sparks shot into our naive hopeful faces, and in the millisecond of light they gave us, we could make out the face of Deer Cross and his powerful hand scraping his razor-sharp grass machete across the jumbled basaltic rocks of the compound's *koxtun*. He didn't say a word, and if he had, we couldn't have heard him because we started sprinting like a couple of scared weasels with every male member of Machete's house-hold hard on our heels. Luckily they were considerably slowed down by their untied Indian pants, which hobbled their legs so that we soon outstripped them, as we intentionally headed away from where A Coy and I lived so as not to be suspected. We hoped. . . .

But the night-watching patrol of new initiates was rounding the corner right below, headed toward where we were hurrying. We jumped uninvited into the compound of Round Tamale, a fat little guy and his sad wife who had no children and strangely enough no dogs, and who were sound asleep. A Coy dove into their sweathouse, pulling me down in there with him and the blanket over its doorway.

Thrilled and petrified, we crouched down in the little ovenlike house, hid-ing like a couple of shaking mice who'd tried to bite a herd of badgers. We could hear old Deer Cross and his sons running to catch up with the initiate patrol. Complaining and yelling, they tried to get these young men excited about two demonic men who'd been whistling and scaring his compound while they slept. (This was an unpardonable offense, worse than stealing a daughter, because at night peoples' souls are traveling in dreams and, if frightened out of their dreams, a soul can be damaged or killed by getting stuck in the dream world.)

The initiates, only a year removed from intense courting themselves, and fully aware that this was a courting antic, tended to be sympathetic with us. Assuring Machete's relatives that a mission of greater urgency awaited them elsewhere, they continued on toward their original destination. Disgusted, Deer Cross headed home, sputtering and cursing all the way.

We stayed put for two more hours then wandered home separately, A Coy heartbroken for having failed in his quest to hear the unknown voice of Ya Machete.

Most teenagers would have given up by now, but A Coy was so deeply in love with this hard-hearted, cloistered girl that his health began to suffer and his people began to worry.

If the longing for an unresponsive girl became too strong, making a boy so sick he didn't want to live anymore, the help of a love shaman was often peti-tioned by the family. Love rituals took a lot of resources and were highly frowned upon by most Tzutujil. However, this didn't explain why there were so many bad shamans getting rich off of them.

A Coy wasn't so rich as to find the gifts and demands of a love shaman within his means; and he was too impatient to have to court a shaman as well, not to mention the months it could take to gather up all those butterflies, hummingbird feathers, iridescent beetles and so forth that were necessary for the charm. Later on, I would know perfectly well how to do such charms, but I'd never use them, except on one occasion.

Rejecting the idea of a love shaman, A Coy decided as a last-ditch attempt to use the water jar method, which almost always backfired. He had me go with him to the open marketplace three days later when the makers of clay vessels arrived in Santiago.

We wandered though an impressive field of handmade pottery, jars, tubs, cooking pots, *comales,* lime pots, bean pots, tamale pots, chocolate pots, and *nixtamal* strainers, whose forms had not changed in the last two millennia. Using these same indigenous pottery styles, the Atitecos cooked today the same greens, fish, corn, meat, flowers, mushrooms, chocolates, and drinks in the same way they were cooked and eaten by their ancestors for thousands of years past.

Shards of red pottery going back forever were under our feet everywhere in the village. We, as fruits of that past, were about to add to that holy detritus of living and ancient dust within which the village life was rooted.

Courting made sure that life continued in that old humus of culture, and human ingenuity was what kept it fresh and alive. The dusts of tradition were bound together by the waters of desire and ingenuity, cooked hard in the ritual fires of the village nature into a solid vessel of community, capable of holding the spirits that kept all things alive. Just as the hollow part of a pot was its most useful aspect, that hollow place in A Coy's big heart was the driving force behind why we bought five fancy eight-gallon *Chinautla* water jars that day.

Always interested in girls, A Leep came along too, as it took three boys to carry the jars. We hid the jars under big dried castor bean leaves, beneath a low loose wall of rocks removed from Chij's, Cottonman's, grove of lime trees. We crouched down low behind this wall and waited to ambush Machete, on her daily errand to fetch water for her family. She would invariably come strutting and oozing luxuriously right through here, down to her grandmother's special water-gathering place at the lake.

I thought he was going to offer her the heavy pots as gifts. But as we crouched down to hide in our ambush, A Coy whispered, "When I tell you, start running to her mother's house with these water jugs." A Leep and I said we would.

Then down to the water she came, right past us as we hid under the little wall. She was with two of her cousins and a couple of neighbor girls. Gracefully, they moved like swans into the water, rolling up their skirts to just below their bottoms. Swishing around to clear the surface, they filled their pots to just below the flare at the jar's wide mouth. They helped each other raise fifty pounds of water and clay to their heads, and began their heavy swaying march back to their respective compounds.

We boys watched in admiration as the chattering beauties drifted past us. Then Coy stood, ran up as close as he dared and, with a slingshot, sped a smooth rock the size of a deer's eye smack into the belly of Machete's water jar. The pot collapsed, drenching the poor girl head to foot, the pottery chunks thudding to pieces on the ground.

A Coy gave us the signal as he commenced running in the opposite direction toward the water to divert the girl who had regained her wits amid the shrieks of "*Tiosh tali*" and "*Nakshubanga*" of her companions.

Running, screaming, crying, and bending to grab stones, Machete tried to pelt the crazy boy, but he dove underwater each time she pitched a rock and the stones lost their momentum in the deep lake water.

A Coy having swum out of range, Machete became enraged. In her humiliation she swore vengeance on his head at the top of her lungs, speaking in public for the first time as she marched and trotted back to her compound to rally her troops and lick her wounds.

Meanwhile, A Leep and I had each shouldered two of the clay water jars and had already made our way up toward her place where we were hiding behind an *amate* tree fifty yards down. It took A Coy half an hour to show up, but when he did he was carrying the remaining big pot, a new machete, and an armload of dyed weaving thread. He had also dried off and donned a finely embroidered young man's pants and a new courting sash, which was dragging on the ground in the best style.

Taking deep breaths, we stood behind A Coy who, in front of Machete's house, where just a few days before we'd been showered with sparks, began to make well-aimed arrows of beautiful words and apologies, which he yelled unabashedly toward the parents of the girl still cloistered in the compound.

Her sisters came running out and swore at us, shaking their open hands with their grinding calluses. Her brothers, though recently arrived home and fatigued from hauling firewood on their backs all day, looked very amused.

Finally Machete's mother came to the compound's threshold holding a shawl over her mouth because she didn't want anyone to see the shameful hilarity on her face, hoping her gesture would be interpreted as humility and rage.

A Coy, in love and with nothing left to lose, kept right on chirping about how he didn't know why he'd done such a horrible thing, especially to the wonderful, inspiring daughter whom he promised to love forever, the daughter of what must be the Moon herself standing on the threshold, and the daughter of the Sun who'd himself sent fiery sparks down on their heads, whose fierce loyalty to his daughter was so admirable, and to the sisters and brothers who were obviously stars who couldn't get back up into the Milky Way and got stuck in this the Umbilicus of the Universe, shining on this day where "I, A Coy, made the horrible mistake of drenching the Goddess of Water in herself." And so on and so forth, until he got to the point. "And because of my crime I've brought five jars of the best quality to replace the one I broke, and to fill a little of the hollowness I created. Please receive a little of this the Original Flowering Earth of the village where all of our ancestors here have struggled together to live since the beginning."

By now the brothers were actually laughing, and the irate sisters were holding their breath, their eyes bulging, waiting to see what their mother might do, when the mother burst out laughing and crying like one should when one's pride has been charmed by its own folly. And then a voice was heard from within the main hut. It was Papa Deer Cross: "What's wrong with you people, anyway? Invite the poor boy and his friends in for something to drink by our fire."

A Coy's eyes got misty, as did mine for pride of being part of such a fine people—so beautiful, so good at carrying out life in all its folly and finery, never refusing to participate in the drama of the village and the ritual of life.

Upon entering the hut, we noticed that Machete too had changed into her very best courting clothes covered in tiny embroidered birds, lightnings, and flowers. She sat open-faced, legs to the side, pouring out hot coffee into little clay cups. Her hands strong and smooth, the same hands that tossed stones and slugged us, handed each of us a warm little potbellied mug. In a voice like the child of a bell bred to water, she urged us to drink in the most demure fashion. Ya Machete, whose hair was well arranged but still wet, had the comb inserted into her hair, perching above her ear on one side according to fashion. She almost looked angry, but I caught her smiling as she looked A Coy over with sidelong glances. They are still married today.

W O R D   W A R R I O R S   A N D

D E L I C I O U S   W O R D S

T A S K S   A N D   M A R R I A G E

The antics of confused teenage hearts and the newly budded hungers of girls for boys, and boys for girls, kept the ancient Canyon Village stirred up like a favorite old cooking pot, still bubbling with youthful intrigue, the thudding sounds of bare feet running, cries, giggles, and shouts. The youth raised a dust off the village streets like the fertilizing tassel pollen hanging above the Mayan cornfields, rippling and rustling over the volcanic hills that formed edges of the cauldron of this our Mother the Lake.

The initial stages of courting had been a kind of flowering warfare, where those who lost their hearts were winners in a strange aching hunt where everyone was both hunted and a hunter, and each was simultaneously fed by being eaten. An ancient custom of radicalness, courting was a ritualized version of an involuntary event necessary for young Mayan women and men to chew their way out of the tough skin of the suffocating family egg.

The Tzutujil Maya called adolescence the "great swelling of the earth," or the "pollination of the cornfield," or the "holy illness."

Everything the Earth experienced, the people went through on a personal level. Everyone was an Earth, and as the Earth went through its annual period of "swelling," this corresponded to the adolescence of the year in the tropical springtime. Around the lake area the air in the spring literally turned yellow with pollen, and every mammal and human became temporarily achy and ill, sneezing, coughing, and most of all moody. We considered this normal, not a sickness, nothing to cure, just an irritating blessing. It was a part of the unfolding of one's life.

When a boy or girl began that era of their lives where, like the earth, plants, and animals, they began to swell and molt, producing pollen and flowers, they became moody, lovesick, single-minded, beautiful, and easily hurt. Like crabs shedding the shells of their childhood or birds losing baby feathers, they passed through a period of vulnerability before the hard shells and strong feathers of young adulthood sprouted and grew over their tender hearts. The young were so easily crushed and killed at this time called adolescence, because the madness of their holy pollinating illness made them run directly toward death and ruin. As all the initiated people knew, in adolescence death steals your soul, your heart, and only teenage heroism, romance, and love could drive adolescents toward life and give them courage enough to face death in order to retrieve their hearts. Courting was the first step toward molting. Initiation was the time spent sprouting new feathers.

Courting was an ancient tradition of antitraditionalism sanctioned by the traditionalist adults and parents who fully expected to be disobeyed and subverted. They supported courting as a form of change that would lead their young people into initiation. Without the hope of initiation, no adults could have allowed their children to court one another. Making love and babies without the maturation of initiation was too dangerous for the young, and unhealthy for the village.

Initiation could only begin the moment a sexually mature adolescent began to yearn and long for another. It was this longing of the heart that motivated youth away from their families and clans toward their lovers and eventually to the spirit. This movement away from obeying one's parents and away from the family and clan was always felt as a subversion by one's relatives, no matter how well they might understand the naturalness of it. It was natural for parents to detest children who wanted to leave them to go with their sweethearts. The village understood all sides of this.

In order to protect the youth from their parents, and the people and the parents from the disruption of the youth, and in order to ferry the young people through the churning rivers of adolescence, the village took it upon themselves to gather up the teenagers and begin initiating them into a bigger family: the village.

Initiation taught the youth how to navigate past the narrow-mindedness, prejudices, and survival opinions taught to them by their families. It gave boys and girls the hope that they would eventually be received into the welcoming arms of the tribe as a whole, into the community and away from the weight of family, parents, and compound. But they really had to work hard for this. It wasn't a lazy thing or an easy thing. It wasn't just given to them; they were put inside of initiation and under the guidance of their elders, they worked their way into the community.

The Tzutujil believed there was no such thing as a family who could function well for a fourteen-year-old girl or boy. Families whose children didn't go through initiation would feel they had failed their children, or, worse yet, their children would be held suspended in eternal childhood.

One of the greatest anxieties for the Mayans was to make sure their teenagers confronted death in a controlled way before they married. If the youth didn't confront death as teenagers, they remained dependent children throughout their lives, or confronted death arbitrarily, in an uncontrolled way. This was the all-consuming theme of Tzutujil initiation.

When uninitiated people grew old and died only their body actually melted back into the earth. The soul, however, for not having been "cooked" by its dealings with death in initiations as a young person, would not be solid enough or have the right shape to be able to enter the next world. In such cases it hung around its relations like a hungry dog. The soul of such a person was still dependent and needed taking care of. This bodiless soul became a ghost, and these kinds of ghosts could eat generations of descendants, turning them into greed mongers, addicts, drunks, backstabbers, sociopaths, or bullies, all unwilling to grow up. Suckling on the lives of its descendants like a large, invisible, demonic baby, such a soul would add onto itself the soul of each life destroyed until, after generations of sucking the life out of its people, it would become a monster, five souls wide, or worse.

A monster ghost like this led whole tribes to ruin or war, because an increasing quantity of people's lives had to be destroyed to "feed" its bottomless, dependent existence. Though catching and curing such a perverse thing was the specialty of certain brave shamans, the village preferred to keep it from occurring in the first place by enforcing initiation. The Scat Mulaj were in charge of this.

Courting and initiation went hand in hand and, at some point during the course of the adolescents' initiation into life, they became one and the same: an approach to the holy, an immersion into the spiritual sources of all life. Very few youth ever actually sought initiation consciously, much less desired the work and tasks that went with it. But almost all of them had the youthful fire, or the cool weirdness of adolescence, that motivated desire which could pull them right into their initiations and gave them the fuel to surge right through it. Only by passing through initiation motivated by the heroic and romantic could a young person survive to adulthood in a tribal village such as ours.

Most parents become inspired geniuses when dealing with other people's teenagers, but turn into judgmental imbeciles with their own kids. This was a law, a rule everybody knew in our village, and one everyone consistently forgot. This forgetfulness formed the basis of why, during initiation, only initiated adults from families and clans distant from the young person were put in charge as mentors and surrogate parents to the youth. The initiating chiefs who presided over the council of mentors gathered the village youth together at a certain time of year and set them to work communally "healing" the village as a whole through a year-long series of tasks. Before this could happen a young person had to be "indicted," so to speak, by a couple of older people who'd noticed that their young people were getting seriously involved with the other gender.

The youth always underestimated the slow, zany vision of the very oldest villagers; those bent-over ancient ladies who are more wrinkles than skin, more canyons than cliffs, not to mention these old-time, cane-walking men, shrunk down from years of overwork carrying loads twice their weight, who talked too slow for the youth. Crouched around village corners, these old people, like old turtles on a log, had glazed monkey eyes that saw only in visions.

Youth the world over chase the thought out of their minds that their juicy, well-inflated, unscarred bodies, rolling around the village in the euphoria of limited experience, will be led, by everything they do to avoid growing up, to wander directly into the open jaws of age and life until they too, with any luck, will be gnawed into one of these beautiful gnarled old creatures.

It was these prehistoric watchdogs who fooled the youth by their rocklike slowness, standing still at odd hours, long enough to see everything small and unnoticed that normally got lost in the bustle of the everyday pursuit of life. Having seen it all, these ancient villagers felt it their duty to betray the unsuspecting youth in love, reporting their "pollinating" behavior to the Scat Mulaj, who, in turn, kept it secretly in mind until the day they went to round up the youth, house to house, to begin the formal initiations.

A Coy had not been caught yet, but it wouldn't be long before the old people showed up to take him to his year-long challenge.

Meanwhile he and Ya Machete dressed up every day and paraded slowly, sparkling through the village streets doing what teenagers in love do the world over: they talked incessantly about themselves and their opinions, more in love with being talked with and listened to than with the actual content of their beautiful banter. Listening each to the other showed both of them how much the other loved him or her. By emptying out all of the personal ideas each had, they made a kind of nesting hole in their own hearts into which the other could climb and find the object of his or her desire in the sanctuary of the other's hollowed longing. Their private birdlike murmuring meant that the world was good as far as they were concerned; they knew everything they needed to know. They were kinglike and queenlike. The village admired them and allowed them this short time of respite from that hard everyday struggle for life in a place that broke backs, swelled up hands, and made people die young of malnutrition.

After a couple of months, when A Coy showed up at Ya Machete's compound to see his beloved, he was met by a younger sister who courteously informed him in a maidservant's tone, "Father, my sister wants to tell you in 'our words,' true words, that it's time for you to send your 'word warriors' against my people. The sooner you send them the sooner we'll be together again, but until then we can't see each other anymore!"

Though this was normal procedure, expected and totally traditional, young people were always caught off guard and angered by the need to go through the *kute,* or asking process, in order to be officially married.

The formal asking ritual didn't have so much to do with getting the parents' permission to marry as it did with the making of a ritual of words and gifts that gave the relatives of both sides enough honor. It also made the lovers' desire public enough to provide sufficient scrutiny of the young people's relatives to ensure that the marriage would not be destroyed by the intrigue of jealous families.

One of the most appealing aspects of modern life for Native people when they give up their old life is the freedom individuals have to live unbeholden and unaccountable to the world around them. But in a village your survival as a couple and as a people depends on a mutual interdependency. Being unaccepted and unwelcome in a village is the worst hell imaginable and kills the marriages of two individuals faster than frost on a flower.

To get married did not make you an adult, but it was an adult-making activity. You had to be able to use words as a hunter uses arrows or a farmer uses a hoe. You had to be able to pierce the heart, and plant and slowly cultivate the tree of your intentions. The ritual of asking for a bride was, for all intents, a medieval siege of the heart in an attempt to melt the various prides of the people in your bride's compound—her parents and their ancestors. This ritual was arranged by the boy's people with gifts, magical words, and music.

To become a true adult, however, also meant that you had to be able to use words the way a deer used the hunter's arrow, by allowing yourself to be deliciously wounded into becoming food for the village; or like the corn under the farmer's hoe, which patiently manifested so that it could be taken home and consumed as sustenance for the people.

One had to be initiated to even understand what any of this meant. The young didn't understand; all they wanted was their sweethearts in their arms. Until the youth could learn, through initiation, to touch the heart with magical words, they were forced to hire village experts, people who were very good at laying verbal siege to their fiancées' households.

These hirelings were called the *Ajkutlaj,* the "searchers of the mouth for delicious words," or the "word champions" or "warriors of words."

Always an older couple, a man and a woman, the *Ajkutlaj* were themselves courted by the parents of the boy on his behalf. Usually members of the Scat Mulaj, they'd been married a long time and had grandchildren, which gave them clout with both the spirits and the girl's people. Their knowledge of procedures and prayers was prodigious, but mostly they had a good record of beguiling families into permitting their young girls to marry a boy in the traditional way. They carried a horde of magical words, images, sacred references, and metaphors whose very sounds were considered irresistible.

The *Ajkutlaj* were required to devastate with beauty the sensibilities of the girl's household until everyone in the compound became drunk on their delicious words. Usually many repeated attempts or "sieges" were necessary since the parents of the girl and her household also hired a similar old couple to defend themselves. This opposing couple was known as the *Culoykute,* which meant "adversaries of the askers," or "word catchers" or "going to meet those who pretend to show us." Both the *Ajkutlaj* and the *Culoykute* fought back and forth for the upper hand in these magical battles of courteous words, mostly to raise the value and honor of their client. The whole event transformed itself into a mythological contest between cosmic powers.

In the end, everyone knew that this ritual game had to be played out to keep the marrying couple safe because the Gods needed to "eat" the beauty of it, the soul-honoring beauty of the *Kute.* For an event such as a marriage to take place—an event that aided the human situation in the world through the procreation of more humans and the happiness of the couple—for such an enormous event to succeed, the Gods would normally require the death of a person as a sacrifice to keep a balance against a spiritual quota of grief. This is what it took to make a marriage work! When a little baby was born, somebody, usually an old person, died to supply the spiritual replacement of energy required to make the new child survive, to create a spiritual space. Marriage was just the same.

To avoid this serious arbitrary loss of life to the village, the courting ritual went on in all its splendor, humor, mystery, romantic feats, and flowery argument. The ritual itself would be a sacrifice consumed by the Gods instead of the couple's marriage. Simultaneously, it would assuage the clannish jealousy of the relatives. The couple were then free to live happily, honored and protected by those very people who had stood in their way.

According to the natural rules of spirits, when children become adolescents, both Death and society sit up and take notice of such blatant, delicious, potentially happy, naive beings. Death especially wants to eat and consume young couples and society because it wants to kill in the youth what it might have lost, hoping to make them as bitter as they might have turned out to be.

Death usually finds a subversive, subtle way of jumping into people's thoughts and they become, for a time, Death's servants. This turns the village into a neighborhood of jealousy that tries to diminish or destroy the boy and girl, unconsciously making them into victims who are sacrificed to the village's own inadequacies.

No one saw this village tendency as irreparable or the work of witches, but it was a known fact and pretty much accepted as inevitable. Any woman or man who claimed to be above this impulse to ruin someone else's love was jealous, a liar, and the most likely candidate to become Death's servant, without knowing it.

By eating the Beauty of the asking ritual instead of the couple in love, Death's quota was filled for the time being. In fact, Death was made so drunk on the ritual's excellence that, in the end, Death actually helped the couple to flower so well that they bore fruit. The fruit of this became the marriage of the new couple, who were then allowed to proceed to the next layer of learning: how to live with each other and to begin to make babies.

To be married in a Tzutujil village in those traditionalist times meant being in love in the biggest sense, to be willing to feed the Gods with your beauty and carry the heavy load society would lay on your love.

Neither A Coy nor I knew much about all this in those wonderfully ignorant days of our youth, and neither did any of the other boys. They just knew that if they wanted their hearts' desires, they had to convince their relatives to allow them to go into debt by hiring word warriors and conspire with them to launch a delicate and well-aimed siege over the walls into the hearts of their sweethearts' parents. By the time all had been planned and paid for and the date was set for the first attempt, A Coy was deeply in debt to most of his relatives, and for a great deal more than the cost of five water jars.

When the day arrived, A Coy didn't even accompany the asking party on its first foray. According to custom, he was considered the "wordless prince child of a woman mountain" who must stay home while his emissaries sallied forth to be refused by the girl's people as always.

On the first attempt the party included A Coy's father and mother; the famous old word warriors, The Nose and his wife, Grinding Stone; and ten married relatives who carried covered gifts of rare impeccable fruits and woven goods.

Made at intervals ten days apart, the first two tries were courteously turned away from Machete's compound threshold. This, of course, was protocol. The parents of the girl were supposed to listen to the first words of the courting party with enormous feigned surprise, refusing the party entrance into the courtyard while expressing the inadequacy of their daughter, their reluctance to give her up, and how this was all so sudden, and so on. This fine theatrical exhibition was designed to raise the importance of the eventual marriage and to force the boy's people into yet greater effort to show their solidarity and how much of themselves they'd put into making sure the couple were not shuffled into misery and obscurity.

By the third attempt, however, the air of an excited pilgrimage permeated the courting party, which now included A Coy, myself, a lot more of his relatives, the word warriors, and even a shaman who'd been added to ensure success and magically open the way for the *Ajkutlaj* to get into the parents' hearts.

When we issued into the streets, the old women and old men took the lead while gift bearers, heavily burdened, formed a file back into the cindery trails behind us at an impressive distance.

Dressed in their best, everyone had to wait each time for the shaman who, buried in the smoke of his incense burner, knelt with his guitar, charming the very road we walked on with his songs and rituals.

As we neared the girl's home, the shaman would kneel, pray, then sing, addressing the earth itself as "the very earth the young lady walked on, which must be the path of the Moon her mother whose face reflected in the river was carried by her daughter on this Road of Water to the Lake" and so forth.

Relatives and friends of Ya Machete's family listened in the streets and periodically ran to report everything that was done and especially what the shaman, Turkey Eyes, was saying.

Stop by stop, step by step, song by song, the shaman turned the village into the universe. The huts and walled courtyards became the family kingdom of the mountain Gods. The roads to them became the paths of the morning star through the Milky Way, the twin stars, the grandparent stars, the northern wind, his little brothers, the southern lake winds, and so on.

By the time our gift-bearing courting party armed with delicious words arrived at the threshold of Deer Cross's compound, Ya Machete's home had become the House at the Center of the World. Its paltry courtyard had turned into the courtyard of the palace of the Fire God, "paved with polished jade bricks in the midst of which grew a cacao tree on whose trunk chocolate pods matured and from which drizzled a rain of cocoa beans of yellow abundance, cacao beans of red jumping life, green lightning, sudden youth and the clear white seeds of dawn."

Ya Machete's mother was now the original mournful mother of all life itself, none other than the Grandmother Moon, who lived with her ancient husband, the Grandfather Fire. Together they kept holy and isolated their daughter, Ya Machete, who was now known as Our Mother the Lake.

This humble little hut had become the palatial temple home of all these Gods who dwelled within and who were now being fed by themselves being courted. A Coy had become the young, shimmering, inexperienced, hopeful, longing red child of the foaming faraway Ocean. He was the Sun.

The steam at dawn would become their marriage. The Sun reflected in the Lake at sunrise was what they both wanted. But those other beings that had given birth to the Sun and the Water, the parents of these two, had not yet done their ritual battle of words, task assigning, and permission. Until that took place, Ya Machete, the Lake, and A Coy, the Sun, could only cast shy glances at each other, like water sparkling in the dawn's light.

Ya Tiney, Dahlia Woman, Machete's mother, now called the Moon, this time allowed the courting party to enter into a large hut filled with a row of well-dressed relatives and knowledgeable older folk from Ya Machete's people who had mysteriously known exactly when the courting party was coming.

For hours a polite, poignant battle issued between the two couples of word experts. Sagalike poems of ancient stories with cryptic allusions and mythological references were examined as lawyers do looking for a precedent, as if A Coy and Ya Machete were the first boy and girl in the whole world ever to fall in love and want to marry.

Ya Machete herself was not there at first, but somewhere in the middle of the palaver she was called in. Kneeling in front of the two old warring couples, she was interrogated about the truth of her marriage desires as if we were all involved in some big court case.

But the fate of the universe of course did hang in the balance. Wasn't she the daughter of Fire and Moon, who wanted to marry the child of Ocean and Thunder, the Sun? The marriage would have timeless consequences. Would the Earth be the better for it, would it make life live? After all, the girl had been living here with her parents and all was well. The boy had been living with his, and that had been fine. Why change now? Was change the secret to how things must be? If that were the case, the word warriors argued, then change had to be accomplished in an unchanging pattern.

A Coy's word handlers began *Nkut ruchi,* the searching of the mouths, of the youth. "Little mother, has any person yesterday or the day before forced you, convinced you, 'cotton-mouthed' you, or extorted you in any way on behalf of your beloved's people or your own people to accept this young man as your sweetheart, your husband, your father?"

"Not at all, old Mother, old Father," Machete replied.

"Did anyone tell you it would be easier or delicious or fun or beneficial to you?"

"No, old Father, old Mother," she replied, sweating under her red halo.

"Then is it true that you want him to marry you and you to marry him?"

"Yes, Father and old Mother."

Then her word catchers started to question A Coy the exact same way, and he replied with the same answers.

Another hour of beautiful speech ended by asking the parents what they thought. For the first time they were admitted into the circle of word makers, graduating from parents into a position of mutual loss and mutual gain, in which they expressed their thoughts as admirably as was possible, given their lack of experience.

A bride price was set through the word collectors and word warriors, who then decided on the tasks to be set for the young couple, tasks designed to slowly teach them how to function as man and wife, because in the arts of longing for and enjoying each other, they were already experts.

The relatives all had ideas about this. They chimed in with suggestions or refusals, defending their relatives against undue toil, compromising until finally, in each case, a task and countertask were set for the Lake and the Sun, who tried not to wince or look disgusted.

A lot of what we humans observe as weather and cyclic change on the earth and in the sky was, in reality, the Gods going about their courting tasks. A Coy was to bring a full load of dry split oak wood on his back to Ya Machete's people within the week, along with fifty pounds of the finest dried white corn. Ya Machete would grind this corn and make a ceremonial drink called *maatz,* cooking it with the firewood. This would be delivered in clay jars to her relatives and A Coy's people on the heads of Ya Machete's female relatives.

A Coy would bring twenty pounds of fresh red meat; grow and deliver five pounds of raw cotton, brown and white; make a set of spindles and a brand-new smooth set of loom sticks for weaving; and bring five pounds of purple and sparkling cotton thread made in Germany.

Ya Machete would make *pulic'* with the meat, having first dried and marinated it. Then she'd spin all the cotton into thread on the spindles, then weave four *stoys,* shawls, of an exact and matching design, one for her mother-in-law, one for her father-in-law, one for A Coy's initiation, and one for herself. She'd carry the *pulic'* stew in pots covered with the little shawls, delivering them to their respective recipients while speaking fine words.

A Coy would then work three days a week alongside Deer Cross making firewood from trees on his father's land for a few months, giving Ya Machete's family all the wood.

Ya Machete would grind corn and cook with A Coy's mother three days a week, giving all the food to his people.

Though the bride price was set in a quantity of cacao beans, it was actually paid in meat, firewood, and cash, which could be spread out over a couple of years. It was set high enough to put the boy deeply in debt to his own relatives and friends. This was to make sure he really wanted to marry, as he would be paying out on his desire for years to come. Ya Machete's father and mother would have to pay back the bride price if she resigned as a wife.

This was not so if the couple mutually consented to let go of each other, but that situation was very rare. If one courted in this way, being married became useful to the whole of creation. This experience was exalting and filled the couple with a kind of honor and hope that kept them together later on when their souls were rubbed thin in the tough everyday environment of the village. When the tasks were agreed upon, a ceremonial drink was passed around to seal it all and the raid was over. We "invaders" left all the pots, baskets, and clothes right where we'd sat. Then we returned as a group to the house of A Coy's parents where everyone rehashed the evening's events till dawn, when we dispersed. These tasks would take a year to accomplish.

The gradualness, ornate complexity, and the large expense of the resource were engineered in the most thorough way by the experience of the word warriors. The two old couples of mythological word slingers were no longer adversaries but became A Coy and Ya Machete's greatest supporters and advocates for the rest of their lives, often against the combined forces of their mutual families. Like love lawyers who worked for the young peoples' mutual affection, they realized that what made most couples hate each other was their trying to be what the world wanted them to be. The Tzutujil were smart, but they never let their intelligence get in the way of their natural emotions. One did not need to kill or repress every stupidity, because there was a village device waiting to deal with the inevitable shortcomings of us all.

People who come together out of desire and love and who are willing to feed the spiritual needs of the Gods through their courting become as affectionate as trees do with the ground they grow in. These elders who started out defending the separate clans and families ended up by joining to form the old humus out of which the new sapling of the young married couple could grow. Without this, the marriage would be imperiled. The old watched out for the young; the young gave the old a place to use their experience. But, more important, all parties involved fed God with their beauty and anxious desire.

After all was set and in the process of being carried out, A Coy was free to visit his sweet Machete anytime he or she chose, and they were essentially, though not officially, betrothed. The whole ritual of courting, drawn out in this way by using eloquence and gifts, made it so that a "foreign" man was slowly made familiar and welcomed into her people's kingdom of the heart. Each threshold of the compound through which the courting party passed was analogous to the many layers of a woman's heart. Refused at first, then gradually accepted when the honor, desire, and beauty of the ritual were increased, the family of the girl slowly and deliberately admitted the boy's family though the door of their own hut, and into the intimate part of their people's existence. Only then, after respectful permission was granted, could the boy come into his sweetheart's life.

Like the gradualness of being allowed to make love to her, the girl finally accepted him into her heart and body, let him come over her multiple thresholds into her heart, invited him into the village of her soul, into the secrets of her family's frailties. The honor of it all was maintained by the explicit respect represented by the tasks set to the couple by the aged marriage brokers. In exactly this same deliberate way, the shamans and the Scat Mulaj also courted a good relationship with the deities.

In the village everything was courting, gift giving, and an eloquence of words. Here a beautiful and long-lasting togetherness between the spirit and the human came about through mutual longing and need. This allowed for the tendency, so natural in humans, to waltz with the spirit, like a couple in love.

If the couple's relatives were unbending and didn't want the two young people to marry, then, like everywhere else in the world, the couple would elope. This was hard to accomplish in a crowded village, and elopement could end up being the source of generational feuds and ostracism.

Nevertheless, every twenty-third of July any couple that wanted to elope could do so with a minimum of quarreling if they could find an aunt, uncle, or cousin to give them sanctuary for a while, and if they were willing to brave the insults of their parents.

It was quite humorous to see the parents of just such a couple standing in the middle of the village attending the ceremonial processions and religious feasts, pretending not to look behind them while dozens of young men and women, taking all their clothing and belongings on their backs and heads, tiptoed anxiously together through the streets to their new hideouts.

The parents, upon returning to their huts, would break down ranting and wailing in deep grief as if someone had died, often staying drunk and not working for weeks, until the couple had gifted all parties concerned in such a "courting" way that they had gotten back into their parents' good graces.

In the end, eloping was still courting, and ended up being more trouble than normal, but what could they do? Besides, it was cheaper.

Irrepressibly curious, the villagers would jump to their compound walls, peering over deep-colored basaltic rock or out from under the leaning overhanging trees, interrupting their conversations or their courting or their dinners to get a little glimpse of A Coy proudly marching his squeaking load of perfectly split oak firewood to his in-laws. Raising dust, running to see, little kids and teenage girls would round a village corner to stand belly out, hand in mouth, to stare at beautiful Ya Machete, head swaying, waddling with a new style, her bundle of weaving in her tied-up shawl on her way to her in-laws to deliver her tasks.

All such sightings were brought around the evening cooking fires where, sitting on the ground, every chattering family digested, savored, and assimilated the excellence of A Coy and Ya Machete. The new couple were a comfort to the people and fed the Gods as they carried out the old conditions of marriage, made even better by their admirable style and willing visibility.

By the end of the year, the village knew just how close the couple had come to finishing the challenge set to them, and waited with expectation for the day Ya Machete would move herself permanently into A Coy's compound.

Once both had accomplished all their tasks, all of us who were friends or relatives in the hierarchy were politely and ceremoniously summoned to help witness the formal coming together of the couple and the mutual endorsement of the marriage by the clans and families. This was called *culbic.*

A large hut was chosen, adorned with fruit and studded with orchids and irises. Its floor was paved with pine needles upon which all the hierarchy and family members sat.

The parents of A Coy and Ya Machete sat like royalty at the end of the hall facing the doorway. To the left, in great rows, a crowd of high-ranking relatives and friends of Ya Machete's people sat elegantly attired facing a similar crowd of old people, chiefs and chieftesses from A Coy's clan, who sat on the ground opposite, leaving a great aisle between them down which the parents, *Ajkutlaj* and *Culoykute,* stared.

A Coy sat in the crowd of his people, facing toward the door, looking for all the world like someone who'd just sort of wandered in. Ya Machete sat opposite him with her crowd. Every shawl-wearing woman and black-jacketed man had a bottle of *psiwanya,* canyon water brandy.

Then the *Ajkutlaj* called things to order and began to speak the old language, making a lot of references to trees, fruit, and marriage, adding a lot of esoteric and eloquent details. But A Coy and Ya Machete were so stunned and nervous it was hard for them to focus on the fine words spoken on this day when they were finally marrying.

After the principal men and women had made their speeches, Machete and A Coy knelt in front of their parents, who interrogated them on their motives for marrying once again. Then Ya Machete was interrogated by her in-laws and A Coy by his.

"Has anybody forced you, convinced you, extorted you, or magically enticed you to marry this woman?"

"No, Fathers and Mothers," Coy replied, and Ya Machete said the same.

When their motives had been completely searched for the truth of their desire and love to the satisfaction of the *Ajkutlaj, Culoykute,* and the parents, the couple were told to "receive words."

This meant that Ya Machete and A Coy should kneel in front of each of their respective relatives, all one hundred and fifty of them, and receive their blessing and advice, one at a time. At the end of each blessing, a small sip of canyon water was shared with the relative, thereby drinking the blessing into their bellies.

When that had been accomplished, Ya Machete and A Coy knelt in front of their own parents, who blessed them and now sent them to the opposite side to receive blessing from their spouse's people. The whole kneeling and receiving was repeated with their in-laws' relatives until, a couple of hours later, they were once again in front of their parents and in-laws, who blessed them fully.

The parents of each gave A Coy and Ya Machete a little glass of canyon water and they both fed it to the other and spilled the rest on the ground to feed God.

Then they rose up and walked out to live for two days in one of their family's empty compounds, empty only because all their relations were here in the wedding hut. For a couple of days they had a honeymoon: no work, no tasks, no trouble, and no people. The relatives and friends stayed in the meeting place ceremoniously distributing the remaining liquor. If you added it up, everyone who came to that wedding brought a bottle of that strong brandy, which, when shared equally, would mean that each person present consumed the bare minimum of a full fifth of one hundred proof alcohol in less than four hours. A great deal of singing, dancing, talking, weeping, passing out, grieving, and laughing took place until everybody succumbed and slept. Then everything started up again on the following day.

By the second day everyone went home with enormous hangovers and, well feasted, tried to get back to normal home life.

The couple's honeymoon ended with the return of the staggering relatives. Ya Machete then returned to her mother's hut and put all her appurtenances into many handwoven cloths and tied them in very large packages with a big luxurious knot on top. These in turn were put on the heads of fifteen of her female relatives who, in a formal processional kind of way, followed Ya Machete out of her mother's house. Held back by her sons, her sister, and Deer Cross, Ya Machete's mother beat her chest, screamed, and wept to see her daughter go, yelling evil things about all men, and about A Coy especially. But a minute later, drunk on grief, she extolled the mighty worth of her son-in-law and the fineness of her daughter, then wept sitting on the ground like a little despairing child, repeating over and over things she meant and things she didn't mean.

Parents grieved like this every time a daughter married, and a lot of old people stayed around their compound to help the mothers and fathers to get through it. It was normal, expected, and necessary.

When Ya Machete arrived at her new home, half of that end of the village stood watching her sisters, cousins, and aunts as they unburdened their heads of all the clothing and implements they'd carried there.

At first, Ya Machete and A Coy tried to live like other married couples, cooking, going to the fields, eating with the in-laws, but it was a hard adjustment for everyone. All the members of the crowded compounds had to reconfigure their lives around the new couple. Sooner or later trouble would surface. A Tzutujil marriage usually only lasted for about six weeks before one of the husband's sisters or one of the wife's brothers started spreading bad rumors or making cruel traps. And in the end quarreling set in. The enormous pressure of having to work and function in a compound foreign to one's upbringing became so overwhelming that either the boy or the girl would flee back to their ancestral compound.

Unless something besides homesickness was at work, they were usually returned to their spouses, accompanied and defended by the old word warriors. No matter how hard the couple tried, eventually tensions grew again until a huge fight escalated into a feud, the proportions of which, if not dealt with, could become physically dangerous and last for generations. This is where the *Ajkutlaj* and *Culoykute* took over, along with all the outside witnesses to the wedding who, having no family association, could help take some of the sting out of the feud. A second wedding often took place at this time in the same hut with the same participants. When the couple was interrogated, it almost always turned out that they themselves were doing fine and still very much in love. But jealous adult relatives in their separate compounds were making it very hard for the couple, both at home and in the village.

The old *Ajkutlaj* and *Culoykute* now came to the rescue, publicly exposing the family and clans as the culprits. Being old, honorable, and respected, they were listened to as they blurted out blazing indictments of intrigue and jealousy against both sides of relatives and levied a kind of fine to be paid in feast food and firewood to the couple to compensate them for all the stupidity they'd had to endure. Then a second blessing time took place and the couple tried to get back together again, sometimes changing residence. All was as well as it could be until children were born, and then feuds became extremely rare. Babies were always the peacemakers because now everyone was related to the child. If the truth be known, no couple was really considered more than a beautiful irritation until they had children anyway, after which they began to become slowly accepted as adults with something to say, with a place solidly established in the everyday consciousness of the village.

When children were born, a married couple did not become relegated to a roll call of humdrum, shrinking gray people who faded into something nobody wanted to become. On the contrary, adults raising children became the fully feathered birds everyone desired to be: adults, people who could feed their nestlings.

SEVEN

BY THE EYE OF NIGHT

MY INITIATION

Once you'd gone through the trouble of courting and being courted, once you'd made beauty and spoken from the heart, once you'd accomplished the teenage ritual of longing, searching, grabbing, asking, tasking, living, loving, trying, arguing, failing, and trying again—then you were off the hook with the Gods as far as literal marriage went. In other words, if later you broke up with your spouse and were ready to remarry, you did not have to court again, at least not in that involved public way.

The Gods were not impressed with or particular about who was getting married to whom, they were impressed with the idea of marrying. They flourished on the ritual itself. Once the Gods were given what was theirs, the people were free to make their lives, that is, if both parties had married and divorced. Rare indeed was a remarriage of a previously married person with another who'd never been married.

When people were courting formally, it was the Goddess and the God who were being courted, not the individuals. Couples knew perfectly well what they wanted and how much they cared for one another. They didn't need a ritual for that, but the Gods did. To make sure that the boy or girl in love did not mistake the other person for a God or Goddess and expect god-like things from who and what they loved, the courting ritual had to be played out.

Since I had been married and divorced before I'd ever left the States, before I'd come to the land of the Maya, it was decided that I could be exempted from the courting procedure, even though, in all truthfulness, I never went through such a courting process the first time.

Living in the village as I was—in love with life and deeply involved in the complexities of the yearly flowering of the Village Heart of ritual and hardship—it was incomprehensible that I should not be married. The old matrons and officials were constantly badgering me to marry, giving me tips and whispering about the availability of such and so's daughter, or of their own daughters. Never for a moment, however, did they think that I hadn't been initiated as a man, as almost all young Tzutujil men had been in those times. They simply assumed I'd received some even better kind of ritual initiation in the land of my upbringing. For this reason, the old people never really bothered to question me about it at all.

When it came to light that I was an uninitiated man, though serving in a highly initiated position, the officials assumed that this was the reason I hadn't yet been married in the village. Tzutujil men traditionally didn't marry until after they had been initiated.

Now it remained to be seen how I could be initiated, in light of the fact that I was completely involved in serving the village in other ways and wouldn't be able to take the necessary year to go through the normal process.

Since I'd witnessed and participated in three years of initiation as a flute player, it was decided that I should simply fulfill my initiation responsibilities by serving as a "dog" to the third initiating chief in charge of the High Mountains. I would accompany one of the thirteen initiatory chiefs on all the initiation expeditions throughout the mountains and canyons, trotting at his heels and speaking for him, as chiefs of this type only speak to the village through their "dogs." This year, at the age of twenty-five, after having seen the initiation ritual so many times, I would finally participate on the inside as a young man, though it wouldn't happen until the following year.

I was happy about this as it meant I would get to go over our Mother the Lake at night on a canoe raid to find cedar branches to build the initiate's monument shrine called the House of the World.

⬦

Far away from the village earth we boys swayed in the high mountain breeze, hugging our trees like sleepy porcupines. Besides the constant popping of fires far beneath us, around which we'd heard the story of the Crooked Bow Boy, the night was very still. A glow appeared above the hills, and soon, like a perfect turtle's egg, our Grandmother Moon was squeezed out of the earth and laid into the sky; up she rolled into her sky road over the canyon rim trailed by a procession of celestial Scat Mulaj composed of planets, chiefs, and retired stars. Below us the darkness began to fill with the waterlike mutterings of the *purpäq,* pygmy owl, who, like the flute player in the village, was signaling the arrival of this retinue. We initiates, strapped to the trees, hung closer to the moon than the earth, as the friendly night birds, even more exuberant now in the moonlight, cooed far beneath us.

Out of each other's sight, we'd separately, at a sign from our initiator, shimmied up our chosen cedar tree in the pitch dark. Some of us tied ourselves to the main trunk with the ends of the thick coils of handmade rope that crisscrossed our bodies and chests, while others sat unattached on branches. All of us were very high up and invisible to everyone on the ground. Alone and together, the force of the breezes in the forest canyon could easily toss any of us to our death. It was treacherous, thrilling, and exquisite in the dark.

For hours we lurched and dreamed up high out of the canyon, poking up above its rim. Here in the smoke-spiced air, cradled in the rocking arms of the moonlit night, caught between wakening and dreams, our souls elaborated the story of the Goddess Remembered, putting ourselves into her legend as the guilty human who forgot. The air belonged to her up here next to her mother, the old Moon. What had happened in the story had happened right here. We boys had been shown the spot in the forest where she'd been left to die. It was an unsharable secret, but a secret known to all initiated Tzutujil.

Though drowsy, we tried to keep awake, knowing that if we slept we'd lose our grip and go crashing to our deaths, one hundred feet below into this canyon at the base of the mountain called Molar. We dangled all night, waiting and drifting. Dreaming, dreaming, dreaming, we remembered now, all of us together yet apart, how each in his own nature was really fruit hanging from the trees.

Our initiations had been showing us that the forms of all the things that we so innocently took for granted were really the Earth's face. Everything we touched, everything we could see, everything we could feel and taste; everything we could walk on, into or carry; everything we loved or grieved and missed when it left us or burnt up in a fire, even the fire itself, was the Earth's face.

The word *face* in Tzutujil is the same as the word for fruit. So, the Earth's face, this earth of form and taste, word and movement, was the fruit of the Earth. The spirit was a grand tree and all existence was a fruit hanging in her arms.

Each of us boys, whose heads were like the fruit, had within our thick, hopeful skulls the *atas q'or,* the remembering dough—our hardly used brains. This remembering dough was the flesh of our fruit, the inner part of us that sat behind our faces remembering us together every moment.

Pondering this as we hung up in our trees, the breeze pushed our thoughts further and further into the idea that every woman, man, and child on earth was an ancestral trunk, whose head was the fruit growing off these ancient, handed-down trunks. The unique form of our own faces sprouted out of the spiritual DNA of our inherited bodies, a form dangling on the tree of our bodies, born into this world of movement, hanging as we did tonight alone, together, swaying on trees in the canyon, young men thinking the thoughts of initiates.

Below, our initiators sat smoking with the old drummer. In a forest of tree-tops, beneath our grandmother, the Canyon Moon, the world below us was invisible. While swaying we became moonlit cedar clouds in the sky. For years I'd been down on the ground with them administering, wondering about what happened up here. Maybe the moon was the fruit of the night, maybe the sun was the fruit of the day; maybe together they were the two eyes of day and night, combined to make the dawn, both light and night, that in-between place. Was this canyon really the vagina of the earth, where all men longed to go, out which all people emerged born into dawn carrying our good new faces into the abundant foment of life and lost in that enchantment we would forget so easily and in such a friendly way who had given birth to it all and to everyone? It was She whose eye, like a newly made tortilla, re-minded us tonight of why we were called the canyon people. This canyon, the thirteen holy wombs, rocked us boys in the branching arms of her long cedar trees.

Silence, thought, dream, thrill, the old stories, our doubts, our focus, all of these swayed us into manhood, lurch by lurch. Suddenly, the groaning of the old skin-covered tree came thundering up through the branches—the village drum had been born from an old trunk a few feet up this canyon at the be-ginning of it all. We'd seen the old umbilical stump at a place under where that old cedar had taken down the Wind Jaguar.

All this I thought about, and then the signal came.

Grown men's voices yelled out to us before the dawn in high whoops and grieflike cries. We hidden tree boys shouted back down to them from way up high in voices mightily changed since the last evening when we'd all gathered in the sacred house of the *Najbey Mam,* First Grandchild, the initiating chief.

The drum's thick roaring drone echoed up the canyon over our black-blanketed initiators, who yelled an ancient sound up to us little brothers, the monkey boys, the animal boys.

We, the boys of the trees, of the mountains, were in charge of bringing home the arms of the beautiful Goddess who'd been dismembered in her struggle to help the humans. The other boys had gone to the underworld for her heart. As the flute player, I had come out of the underworld with them for three years. I was never the same. But this time I was with those who brought her arms back to the village. The branches of the spruce and cedars here in this secret canyon were her arms, lost and distributed in diversity when she'd been "forgotten" by us who were suckled by her diversity.

Every patrol of initiates went to a different part of the world to retrieve back to the Canyon Village the different part of Her so we could put Her back together again.

Our own souls hung on these trees, and each little part of Her was the whole soul of each of us. How we succeeded in bringing home what had left us empty and longing in our youth would tell how successful we'd be at re-assembling the Bride of Earth. Each of our own souls in love meant that a piece of us was missing, and that piece was part of the big dismembered Goddess. We as individuals could not live without our sweetheart-souls, and the village could not live without the Goddess remembered and reassembled.

Our initiators called for our ropes down below. Each of us tied our rope's spare end to the tree in which we sat and lowered the opposing end down through the branches to the yelling elders below us. From where they stood gaping up into the sky, our thick ropes became umbilical cords by which we boys were attached to the Earth Mother's gravity.

The initiators tied their own machetes onto the ends of the ropes with an expertise befitting the woods-born Tzutujil, and signaled with a tug. Still swaying in the dark, we carefully pulled the sharp-edged steel up to our towers of fragrant needles and pitchy bark.

Tiny flames appeared beneath us, casting large flickering shadows that returned the night back into an impenetrable thickness; and fifty murmuring prayers shuffled up to us through the branches.

The old men had lit tallow candles and ringed a place for our branches.

No one had to tell us how to cut the branches, or which ones to leave, or how to lower them down. We'd been taught too many times inside the secret stories of initiation how to make noninsulting moves toward the Goddess whose life gave us ours, especially as we took from it now to feed Her.

The nostalgic perfume of Her juices in Her canyon was on Her trees. We covered our hands with pitch as we cut the luxurious needle-covered branches, Her arms; and tying them to our umbilical ropes, we lowered them to our initiating fathers, who gently removed them from their knot. Tugging again, we pulled our line back up, each time lowering our own selves a bit farther down the tree's trunk so as not to take too many branches from one place.

We lowered ourselves from one set of limbs to the next, until we sat forty feet above our initiating fathers and our personal large pile of branches. Candles burned in front of each pile to feed the ceremonially taken limbs.

At each level we threw the ropes over the branches we were sitting on and tied the opposite end to our waists. Our initiators bid us hang freely as they lowered us, lower and lower, forcing us to trust them in the dark, while they prayed—until we had landed next to our pile of branches.

The ground seemed strange now, and we seemed taller. Like men whose animalness made them useful to the village Goddess, some part of us stayed up there in those trees of the Women, a natural part of us that She would look after and keep well. She loved that wild little animal in us boys. While we were gone, She wouldn't forget us. We in the village would most likely forget again She who made us live; but that part of us we had left there in the pitchy trees would call us back to this night so that we'd remember over and over how we boys tried to put the Lady back together again.

The older men smoked and mumbled things of beauty and archaic significance over the large fluffy piles of branches whose sacrifice and fresh smell was like youth itself. Then, kneeling in front of each pile of cedar boughs, we boys began our speeches to Her, our eloquence, while firmly and tenderly coaxing these uncooperative fanlike branches into a more transportable package.

Each initiator placed a bough at a time onto our package as we tied them, pushing our bare feet into the delicious mounds of elegant branches to hold them tightly while we strapped them in. Binding and sweating, cajoling the spirit of the tree, the arms of the Goddess, to come back home with us, the "great forgetters," we initiates tied and spoke and tied and spoke, talking Her into our arms as a midwife speaks a baby into this world, out of the womb.

Our faces sweaty and full of purpose, we tried to remember what our initiators had shown us, that every knot tied, footstep walked, tree climbed, canoe paddled, song sung, prayer whispered—that every part of everything we did inside these ritual days was not only holy but that all that was holy depended on us boys for its survival, according to how we moved and acted in these initiations. Our beauty, our resolve, and our clear movement toward making this six-week-long ritual part of initiation could magically restore our people's work-wounded bodies and brighten again the shores of our everyday lives where the spirits desired to beach their overloaded canoes unbalanced by the enormity of their gifts for us, to give us another year of life.

We boys, proud and hungry in the fragrant dark, deep in the origination canyon, bound our branchy bundles with ropes and words, binding our prayers down with knots. Our initiators' faces were deeply carved by life and ornamented by the dwindling flicker of fire and kidney-fat candles.

When the last of the branch bundles were made fast, all at once, like a line of cowboys done pig tying some supernatural calf of beauty, we leapt to our feet, triumphant, our hands in the air.

Then from our wide bulging sashes each of us produced a *ruq'a ejqan,* a new tump line, wide head strap, some made of rawhide with the hair on, others more humbly made of woven maguey fiber.

We handed these to our initiators, who prayed over them, and then began to ritually whip our calves and thighs. They took our hands in theirs and stung them with the stiff new head straps, then our arms, backs, shoulders, chests, butts, and heads, all the while blowing tobacco smoke over us and muttering phrases of encouragement, health, and strength:

"Tiya ruchoqa' ruqa'
xtit a k'as taja
tityiktaja a jahala'
xtasiil, xtayic
xtusiilila xtuyictaja
jic xtu pe a
jic xtu beyna
majun stcoptaja
majun xtupaja
xin nuná ruqa'
ja jala catie
xtu kwin nuriraj
atet ctit
ruman xin kastaj
kotsejal ruchiuleu. . . ."

Give force to his hands
Let his ember glow, his life be well lived
Let him jump back into life
Call his body back to movement
Make it jump and live

That he makes what we do here move
That his force makes it jump back to life
Erect and true he could stand
Erect and true he could travel the earth
Never coming untied
Never tripped as he walks
Never falling to be crushed
He carries you gliding over the earth
That which is you, Mother
Make it so he can bear weight
As he carries you (Goddess)
In order to bring back to life
The Flowering Earth. . . .

Returning our head straps, the initiators showed us where to bind the free ends: just under the juncture of the boughs and with a special knot friendly to the Goddess; a knot that could be easily undone but which held firm.

All the knots had to be ritually made so they could be undone by simply pulling on the rope. This way we men let the Goddess know we were think-ing about the women, so all that was female on the earth, every being that car-ried her young in her belly, should have easy births. During rituals, all hard-to-loosen knots made births difficult or killed the female. Men had to be aware of this. In the same way, girls wouldn't walk over our axes or poke the fire with metal, to ensure that we men didn't break our backs under our heavy loads. We watched out for each other that way magically.

The signal was given by the third subchief who sent his personal initiate, Tjoy Snic, Anteater, scurrying to scrape hot coals out of ashes of the main fire into the large copal burner that accompanied the chiefs and the drummer.

As the drum began thudding its song of flowers, all up and down the path in the candlelight fifty bundles of cedar boughs rose up in unison. Placed onto our heads and backs, the branches' long feathery hands bounced as much as three feet off either side of us, and trailed from our heads completely to the ground.

Very little of us was visible, buried as we were inside the bundles of the arms of the Goddess. Covered in heavy lilting vegetable fur, we began to dance, holding our head straps, our elbows jutting out, the branches bouncing and waving, rustling to the beat of the drum whose echoes came thudding back down to us from the canyon walls as if God were making a counter-rhythm.

The third chief, along with Anteater, came wafting the bright coals and delicious "white" copal fumes under our dancing branches, praying all the while. Then he broke into a rhythmic call for strength and enthusiasm. This raised goose bumps on our skin, and we boys responded to this signal by whooping, yelling, and crying out like birds and wild mammals as the clumps of dancing branches moved down the steep canyon on our hopeful backs.

There were no boys here anymore, just chiefs and the dancing Arms of Our Mother, the Bride of Earth. Our column of branch mounds danced all the way down the canyon to the beat of the village drum until we hit the lake shore. There our long dugout canoes still sat, firmly entrenched, this way and that, in the black volcanic sand that sparkled in the moonlight.

After pushing the canoes into the shallow water of the lake, the old chiefs loaded the boys one by one. They removed the first boy's branches, then placed the bundle in front of him; and then another boy in front of his branches and so on, the branches hanging over the canoes' edges. They did this until all twenty canoes were filled, each with a row of boys alternating with beautiful mounds of trailing branches. Nothing of the canoes could be seen. They were just big long lines of standing boys buried to their chests in fragrant moonlit cedar branches, their needled ends dragging in the water.

The big drum, without stopping its rhythm, was propped into the prow of the forty-man canoe of the third chief, where it sat right at the tip of the prow facing the stern and the boys. The drum wailed away, echoing and thundering over the volcano-lined lake, where we hoped our village and remaining chiefs stood waiting for us far away in the night.

After wheeling back the lead canoe, the third chief leapt into his canoe. With his staff in hand, his headcloth tied well to the side, his black *qu'* criss-crossed over his shoulders, he stood, facing backward, from the prow. He began to yell the old call and response to us. A hundred voices rang proudly back to him, excited to begin the journey back to the village. Yelling, digging in our oars, standing firm, off we sped, twenty canoes wide, our branches trailing in the sparkling Mother Waters. To the beat of the drum, we screamed and called out as in an old-time Tzutujil canoe raid, rowing like fiends, drunk on the moon, our discoveries, our togetherness. Delirious from our participation in such immensity, we were of the lake, the village, and filled with the useful fierceness of youth. We were young men going to war against death, going to fight what killed life, not with spears and guns but with eloquence, beauty, tree branches, and a willingness to make it all live.

For miles we sped, our oars crashing, the wind whistling in the branches, until we passed the bay where Holy Boy's clothing had been washed earlier by his priest. The water there had taken all the hardship, evil, jealousy, envy, warfare, and pain out of him who took it from us.

From our canoes, we'd seen the candles of Holy Boy's priests as we pushed our way toward the canyons. The priests had yelled out encouragements to us. But now, they'd already returned to their Sacred House with their heavy washing stones strapped onto their backs and tied over their foreheads. There was no sight of them now, just the Moon, the shore, and the water at the base of the volcanic rim where the lake met Holy Boy's springs.

On and on around the point of Panaj, past Tiosh Abaj, speeding farther and faster, and howling and hooting, we raised a barbaric din so inspired it made the drummer smile so you could see his teeth in the murky light. We crossed the point and slid into the shores of Chinimya' beside hundreds of canoes basking in the moonlight. It wasn't until then that we saw the crowd of five to six thousand people lining the lake's edge in the dark. All our twenty laden canoes were pulled by their many hands right onto the spongy ground.

Without losing the rhythm, the drummer had his drum unloaded and put onto the back of his little clubfooted drum carrier.

The crowd parted and we saw the *Najbey Mam,* the First Grandchild, the head initiating chief and most of his subchiefs, descend the hill toward the water, elegantly dressed in the robes of their distinct positions. Wasting no time, lining up at the edge of the lake, they leaned on their white moon-polished staffs, their fists over the ends, under their chins.

The initiators led us, one by one, out of the old wooden canoes to the shore. They helped position the feathery arms of the Goddess, the cedar boughs, over us until a dense bristling row of branches with legs stood in front of the hollow-log canoes. The lake shone silver under the moon, our faces hidden by the branches.

Our third chief, the chief of trees and mountain things, addressed his peers and his chief, the *Najbey Mam:*

"As seen before on the backs of young men now gone.
As seen before by a village those Flowers and Sprouts stand here.
To receive what the Holy Carriers,
These great-grandchildren of ancient people do here returned from
    the Holy Canyons,
Over our Mother to your feet, roots, and to your arms,
Branches who have come out of the wilds to our home,
Where all our natural ancestors paid with struggle
To give us our faces here today. . . ."

The head chief replied as loudly as he could:

"It is good to see your faces again
Good to feel your breath again,
Young lords,
You who came dancing with the generous arms of green,
Generous wood over the Mother Lake for the Bride of Earth,
You who tolerate cold,
You who risk death,
You who have forgotten comfort
Shielded by your desire to see Her face again.
Withstanding doubt, hunger, lack of sleep, you homeless boys,
The eight hundred shimmering boys,
Dance home with me.
It's good to see your faces,
Good to feel your breath again. . . ."

Twelve incense burners came forward in the hands of the initiating Lords' private assistants who, two by two, incensed our bodies and cargo with great thoroughness. The smoke percolated through the branches of the hidden boys, rising up through their tops like rain and mist on the forest mountains. The village dropped to its knees and prayed, saluting the Grandmother Moon.

Then rising, the drum rolling, we danced to the top of the first hill at Chinimya', the crowd pressing in, the branches bobbing above. We danced all the way to the middle of the village, where the very old people who'd chosen us for initiation met us in front of a fire and helped remove our heavy loads in front of the crowd. A long line of branch piles was made, reaching all the way across the plaza. Hugging us four different ways, blessing us, and looking into our faces, they gave us a ceremonial drink. Then we were taken away, escorted back into our vegetation-walled, flower-ceilinged hall of isolation to await the next challenge. While we were being led back to the plaza, some older Scat Mulaj men and the guild of canoe carvers had descended upon the arms of the Goddess to adorn and tie them into ornate bunches with the palm flowers retrieved from the hot coast by the bravest crew of initiates, who'd returned from the underworld earlier that day. The monumental flowering House of the World would be made tomorrow, and we would once again sally forth to carry the wooden parts. But for now we sank into the pine-needle and tule-reed-blanketed floor of our long initiation hut into a dawn's sleep, almost like men but more like half-grown puppies, exhausted, dirty, and proud.

The ritual of initiation would last eight more difficult and delirious days. Then, technically, we all had a year of service patrolling the village at night to keep her safe from unknown enemies. All initiates did that, but I was exempted from this by the chiefs as my duties as flute player were of greater service than my patrolling would have been. I wanted to patrol but I was put back into the Scat Mulaj.

❖

After seeing and experiencing what we did in our initiations, we boys realized that every human being's goal in the village was the eventual admission into the pursuit and maintenance of the sacred. The very position I'd achieved in the hierarchy as a flute player was precisely the kind of service men and women aspired to when the everyday struggle to earn a living and to take care of their families loosened up enough later in life, enough for them to make the attempt.

So, wherever possible, traditional full-grown Tzutujil men and women continued their education and dedication to the sacred by entering into services with the Scat Mulaj, learning more sacred language and gaining a greater memory and knowledge of God and how to maintain the earth. This was the furtherance of the next four layers of initiation.

The first initiation at adolescence was mandatory in the old days. The rest, after that, were undertaken by appointment, personal desire, and through the urgings of the unpredictable deity forces themselves. The fact that I'd entered into the sacred system already was an anomaly that conformed to the pattern of the rest of my crazy life. I was caught up now and could continue my life in the village in a more normal sequence.

I'd been blessed with a life of magical happenings and a painful ability to understand them in a different way than most people did during the fifties and sixties in America. My life would often bring me into grace with something that lay way ahead for most people while I was still very far behind in a lot of the knowledge that led up to what I'd already achieved. Becoming the village flute player before I'd been initiated was backwards, and, even then, for a regular villager the two events should have occurred forty years apart.

As a teenager growing up on a Pueblo Indian reservation in New Mexico, I also had a predilection for beginning at the beginning of the things I loved. I was preoccupied with what was authentic and original to such a point that other people couldn't understand why I went to such great lengths to ensure the authenticity of my actions. At an early age I had a keen sense of history and a strong belief in the value of what was hidden in the small, despised, and abandoned. Even then as a boy I found divinity in what other peoples had discarded.

At an early age I was resolved not to purchase any mass-produced item from a store. Like the older generation of Pueblo people with whom I'd been raised, I would grow all my own food out of the earth without the aid of fuel-burning machines. Everything else I would need to live, I'd make with my hands with the available raw materials from the wide unpopulated mountains and deserts that surrounded us in those times. People would laugh, amazed at how I untiringly tried to dig, cut, tie, carve, plant, hoe, hunt, tan, dry, and sweat my way back to the origination point of all life.

My fanatical teenage search for what was real and original was more than a personal code of aesthetics. For me it had been a life-or-death quest for the survival of my soul in the face of the modern world that was being forced on us in New Mexico. I had hoped that I was connecting myself to everything I touched and attempted, and that by doing so I would slowly find the divine nature, the Spirit that sat at the beginning of all things.

For example, I made saddles even before I could ride horses. I'd carve the saddle frame from a cottonwood tree beneath which horses had grazed and eaten its bark for a century before the old tree had fallen. I covered the saddle frame with rawhide from an ornery bull who'd been eating my Spanish peas, and who everyone wanted to kill. When he finally fell dead after totaling a pickup truck belonging to the Lieutenant Governor of the Pueblo village of my youth, I skinned him, and used the hide.

Only after I'd mastered saddle making did I study how to catch horses from a wild herd. Though failing dangerously at first, I eventually succeeded with the help of other reckless boys. But I'd do this only after I'd gone through the tedious and fascinating motions of learning the hard way what people had already learned thousands of years ago, like how to water-trap a herd instead of chasing it. Only after learning how to make ropes from rawhide was I willing to rope a single colt onto a dead tree trunk. Blowing dust into his nostrils from his own vestigial toe, the chestnut, I spiritually merged with the freedom-loving, herd-hearted, grass-preoccupied nature of this head-tossing, snorting, flighty child of the wind, whose cactus-knotted mane flew up a little as he stood staring, the little bristles around his mouth hung with tiny spectrum-filled drops of precious water. I loved the part of horses that only horses noticed. This gave me a certain way with them.

Likewise, when I first learned to play the guitar I made a primitive one from old pieces of pinewood that were lying about. It looked like a fat canoe paddle married to the child of a banjo and a balalaika. For strings I unstrung a discarded tennis racket I'd found in one of the trash piles that the whites from the cities used to dump on the reservation.

I took the cordage and strung it onto my creation, drew lines on the fret board with a pencil, and proceeded to invent tunes. I actually played songs on that guitar until everyone tired of its plinky wheeze.

Soon enough I was hemmed in by a thick clutter of homemade tools and instruments, piles of food I'd grown, beautiful buckskin jackets made from the hides of animals I'd killed or raised or eaten. Most important, however, I was surrounded by all the stories of how all these things had come to be.

I fit into these stories. For the first time in my life, I was attached to earth and human existence by the stories of my failures and the eventual successes of these products of my ingenuity and creative self-sufficiency. There was some satisfaction in my capability to live without being dependent on machines from a culture who'd hated its own origins, who disregarded its people's stories and tried to tell the rest of the world's cultures that the modern story was the only story worth having. But my satisfaction evaporated when I realized I was sitting in a miraculous nest of stories and meaningfulness that nobody wanted to hear. Like a mother bird who insists on hatching infertile eggs, my nest grew cold as the embrace of my zealous vision was unable to fill my longing for human affection.

Would I have to abandon all I believed and felt I'd discovered in order to be loved? Would I have to pretend to like the blatantly disconnected life of modern people just to receive a crumb of affection? How would my love be accepted? Or would it be accepted at all?

Since in the past every time I wanted to understand something I had to go the path that the originators took, the same trail that my ancestors might have traveled. I learned mostly by suffering. This kind of on-the-job, trial-and-error, self-schooling inspired me to wander in search of a life where the origination of life was understood, where I could live, love, and belong. When I finally ended up in Santiago Atitlan, I was immersed in a life where this kind of authentic existence was normal, where the people knew how to grow every seed and spin every string, where everything had stories and the people knew them all.

If you went into the market in the Canyon Village and bought tomatoes from the most wrinkled woman you saw, rather than from a smoother girl, you'd probably learn the story of how these tomatoes came from her grandfather. How having been the chief initiator long, long ago, he had received the seeds as a gift from a strange tall Indian from an unknown tribe and village who'd come wandering through one day and then disappeared. When this ex-chief, reduced to poverty by his ceremonial service, had planted the seeds, tomato plants came up and flourished in such a way as had never been seen before. The plants never really died and the tomatoes grew so thick and constant that this old woman's grandfather recuperated his losses within the year. Other people tried to grow the tomatoes but no one ever succeeded. The old man was the only one the Tomato Goddess graced with abundance from these seeds.

When you bought these tomatoes you were participating in his story. Every person and product in the village had a face behind it, and the stories about their existence and their continued struggle to exist were common knowledge. Even the basket in which the tomatoes were stacked was made by a Tzutujil Indian lady from farther around the lake who had . . . and so on.

When dinner was prepared, every ounce of it had an ancestry and origination point of which the diners were conscious. When we ate such a meal, as we did every day, we took these stories into our bellies. We became part of them by eating.

Thus, when I had arrived here in this village, that very part of me that in America had been seen as ineffectual, useless, comical, incomprehensible, backward, and fanatically concerned with the beauty of ancient connections all of a sudden found a home and a use. The initiations of the young in Santiago forced them to physically reexperience by actually doing the story of the ancient days of their ancestors, forcing them for a moment to become their own ancestors. Here young people faced the same tenuous situations their forebears had faced, and they learned how to physically do what they anciently had done to survive. They continued struggling, month by month, at every stage, to live all of their people's mythological history until it was all brought into the present. Then the youth would be admitted back into experiencing the everyday life of the village once again. Young people were changed by this hands-on spiritual education. People were linked personally not just to their families but to all of creation's history. After initiations the village of today was understood by the youth as another hair on the head of the deity called Life, another leaf on a tree bigger than their own families.

My initiator into manhood was called Chom, Fat Shrimp. He was a balding, obstreperous, solidly built man, who was highly feared. Chom was the husband of that sweet woman whose grandfather's tomatoes I used to buy in the market.

Chom was famous for knocking men out while he slept! I saw him do it once in a sacred house during my initiation, when the middle-aged son of the drummer who was drunk and full of himself wandered in and began mocking my initiator for snoozing when a crucial ritual was about to begin. I was the only one in the crowded hut who saw Chom's fist flash out from under his dozing head, and knock the young chief out cold. He sank into the cushioning layer of pine needles on the initiation house floor. Everyone thought he'd just passed out, as this was very common in ceremonial contexts.

Anyway, Chom was tough, but very steady and even with me—and he certainly loved his tomato-growing wife. After my initiation, his wife and all the other hierarchy matrons couldn't imagine how I could survive without a wife. They kidded me and prodded, pestered, and shoved me until finally, one day, a year after my initiation as a man, two years after my initiation as a shaman and four years after I began my flute playing in the hierarchy, I woke up and the air was filled with a strange aroma.

Some smells, I think, must determine the fate of some tribes or redirect the world, when people become intoxicated by the mysterious nostalgia of an aroma that takes them back to the day when they first walked, the new air of the green flowering earth filling their little tender lungs as they toddle ecstatically toward the flour-stained arms of their kneeling mothers, their smiling expectant mothers who thus coded their memories and future with the smells of some sweet substance baking.

God must be a smell, one of those delicious dreamy aromas that float into the soul on the warm hopeful days of spring. What is God must be one of those smells that beguiles and inebriates the mind, who like a fine drunken horse of water the heart can now ride, gallops wild like a river of possibility, right through the topsoil of your youth, cutting and eroding a groove that will be your life, a canyon sunk deep into the virgin plains and unsawn forests of your early days.

That ragged strata bared, the columns of ancestral stone poking through your silty shores of pain and wonder are the carvings of freedom and, eventually, the beauty and meaning of that gash people will say is you. Your children will complain about the directions that river took. Your parents will not understand the convoluted path you've taken around and past their old stone and will think they have failed.

But at those depths there are smells others could never read, because at your river, at the base of these beautiful cliffs of bared bone pain and ancestral memory, lies a beach where things wild and natural come to drink, and their footprints are the memory you have of how your canyon water smell brought them here.

Even the Big Picture of life comes here and bends down its head like an antelope to drink, sniffing the air for that smell. The footprint of God is here, the memory of having sniffed something at the spring, the memory of a myriad of smells cooked by desire into what moved you forward into the choices taken, decisions made, hearts broken, and Gods discovered. Because of this, no days are losses; each one becomes a gift, an adventure, a prayer and an obligation to live each of them fully. And I, upon that day, lifting from my sleep, smelled that smell like bread baking; but still, it was the mixture of clear lake air, the smell of some wild plants, flowers, pollens, fruits from the lowlands, and the sweet cedar smoke of someone's cooking fire. It was a morning of mystery run by nostalgic smells that gave me the grandiosity of a one-year-old child learning to walk, a child who would condescend to the public's general obeisance and assumed affection for me.

Drunk on smells such as these, the sunlight through the balmy trees, and the ancient bubbling heart of the village going along in its clackety old way were what had me married by the end of that week to a Tzutujil girl of sixteen who couldn't be loved because she hated all that men had done to her. I would try to love her for almost two decades and finally admit failure. She had some love in her, but it was maimed by events beyond her control and exploited by outsiders. Still, she gave birth to three beautiful sons, two of whom survive, and though at times they've doubted me—not having known the whole story—we love each other as tears and rain love to moisten the thirsty earth.

My wife was hard and small but lived up to everything loaded onto her. In the beginning we were married, two young people: I a traditionalist, her parents Catholic Christians. Together Ya Lur and I did what we could to be husband and wife, to keep alive what mattered in the Canyon Village.

EIGHT

THE WATERS OF CONFIDENCE
BIRTH IN THE CANYON VILLAGE

The sun was deep inside the earth at about three in the morning. There was no moon, and the lake was as dark as an unlit hole and waveless. Not one dog had whimpered or cried since the din they'd set up at sunset, and the claustrophobic silence of this night made even the squeak of my sandals sound as loud as a train wreck as I shuffled over the dark volcanic cinder to my end of the village.

The thatch of our hut's overhang barely caressed my already hatless head as I ducked into our commodious *pach jai,* our hut where I found Ya Lur sleeping on the pile of tule reed mats in the corner.

Like an eye of the water monster, the tidy remnant embers of the evening's cooking fire still glowed in the opposite corner where a tiny sporadic popping and bubbling tune sang in a clay pot still positioned in the pile of banked coals.

"*Shaht tool a' la'?*" Have you returned, little boy? she strained out, still facing away toward the wall. "There are two *quiscil* squashes in the ashes, a pile of warm *wai* and a pot of warm coffee if your stomach is gnawing at you."

After seeing eleven sick people in our hut that morning, I'd been absent from our in-laws' compound since early afternoon. I'd gone up on the Big Trail to a hut where last year's young chief's wife was prostrate from an excruciating pain in her ears. All her relatives had come to petition my help in my capacity as an *ajcun,* a shaman, to attempt to alleviate her distress and to address the Gods through divination, thereby determining the true spiritual reasons underlying her suffering.

Ya Par was a young queen, a first chief's wife and an initiating mother. Tall for a Tzutujil and swanlike when she walked, she was much loved by the young unmarried women in the village, as an example of who they wanted to become.

Like all sacred officials in Atitlan, reduced to poverty from the year-long administration of the initiation of the young men and women, Ya Par had become less pretty yet more deeply beautiful from the strain.

She had been "shot down" by a jealousy attack stemming from some residual negativity as a consequence of the ever-present envy of her majesticness and a job well done. Some people couldn't help hating what they couldn't be and this sort of problem came with all spiritual positions. Suffering and poverty were the expected side effects of being a leader.

By the time I had arrived at her home, she had collapsed and fluid was gushing from her ears. It took me several hours of plants, poultices, prayers, and songs before she had ceased vomiting and could stand again. By then I was exhausted and hungry. Shaking hands in the candlelight with the attending crowd of her ground-sitting men and women relatives, I shouldered my shaman bag and padded my way home in the chilly pre-tremor darkness. It was eerie but I was at home in my village, headed to my own hut to eat, sleep, and check on my wife, who was nearing her due date.

"How are you, little daughter?" I mumbled to her in my extreme fatigue as I sat tearing apart the perfectly cooked, tender-fleshed, one-seed squash, washing it down with fine smoky coffee.

"*Utz ninbanoum anen.*" I've been well. Go ahead and eat, she replied, but then moaned off to herself, fitfully thrashing somewhat on the mats.

Ready to sleep, I wandered over to where she lay in the warm glow of the fire's eye, when finally the earth tremored. A dull cannonlike thud, the shuddering of the three pine-covered volcanoes surrounding Santiago, moved the cups and machetes, setting them to rattling against the thin walls. There was a swimming of the ground, like walking on Jell-O, and then it was gone, echoing and rumbling underground like a monster mole tunneling into the northern mountains of Quiche.

"My water's broke."

"What, just now?" I said, overwrought.

"No, a couple of hours ago."

"Why didn't you send for me?" I replied.

"Wal' has gone to get Ya Kinoum, the midwife, but she's in another birth."

I gently turned Ya Lur face up and removed her worn handwoven skirt she was using as a blanket. I saw to my astonished eye that she was already prepared to crown, "to bring sunlight through the mouth of the temple," as they say in the village.

Panicked, I went to find all the relatives. They wandered in sleepily and sat around her, waiting for her and the midwives until we all fell asleep waiting.

When I awoke, my head was bobbing sideways. I was brought to consciousness by being kicked by my wife's knees, and the sounds of her short brave little grunts of birthing.

Arising from our dreams, I jumped up with everyone else and immediately noted that the baby's head was just moving into this world. I took it in my hands just as Ya Kinoum waddled through the doorway with her niece, the old woman's assistant. White Head, my mother-in-law, grabbed her checkered *jaspeado stoy* and trotted off, tears in her eyes, to announce the progress of the birth to her sisters down the path and to make sure the village women knew that her first grandchild was almost home.

Old Ya Kinoum took the little creature's head in her friendly leathery hands and politely scooted me first to the side, then eventually completely away as she began the cheerful bantering liturgy of a midwife addressing the deities. First, the Lady who wove our bodies together was kindly addressed with her husband The Great Tyer of Knots, who assembled what his wife wove. For two hundred sixty days a series of these Gods had woven and tied unborn children together with fibers made of holy words that manifested in this world at birth as a child. Babies were the echoes of previous creations sung into life from the other worlds. As babies all of us were songs woven and tied by the deities that our mothers pushed into this world.

Turning the baby's shoulders to the side, the midwife signaled to Ya Lur to strain and push. Struggling and biting down, she gave it all she had. Without a peep or groan, instinctively like a mother fox, quiet to make sure that which hunts out there would not have her child to feed its own.

The little kids of our compound were given whistles made of clay, and began to tweet them like birds to welcome the new child into a village of sounds. The earthquake over, the dogs began to bark and the roosters resumed their normal patrols of darkness and dawn light. The noise of life came back to the village.

Women started padding in, holding their callused palms out in greeting, sitting on little square mats, while Ya Lur began delivering our little son's funny legs and the rest of the fluids, which gushed onto her *uq,* her wraparound skirt. Her aunt fanned the fire until the room was softly illuminated and only slightly smoky. Half-dressed and worried, the menfolk of my compound, myself included, hung about the ancient doorless doorpost, respectfully tying up our sashes in front, the older men instructing the younger to wait for signals from the midwife as to what duties they might attend to.

Ya Kinoum called for my *pas,* a long man's sash without scratchy tinsel, a clean old used one; and I ran to get one that was slung over the crossbeams of the hut. Nervous, I stuck my foot into the corn-washing pot, cracking it, releasing its precious liquid onto the smooth mud floor of the hut. A chuckle of understanding and affection rippled through the crowd of forty women seated quietly there.

My old red colored *pas* was the first sash I'd ever worn in the village as a man. Like all first fathers here, I was proud to see it used to bind my child's arms and legs so he wouldn't feel so alone, unheld now by the womb in this colder, scarier place with so much unknown and a horrible dragging amount of gravity.

Whereas in the womb we floated and dreamt for what seemed like a complete lifetime while we were being assembled, coming into this world was almost unbearable and hard. To help with this, all the midwives used the father's working sash to bind the baby to make him feel that he was not going to fall, held securely in the binding and the arms of his people.

Losing the world of the womb was the hardest thing for a baby, especially losing the rhythm of the mother's heartbeat. We people, especially the men, spent the rest of our adult lives looking for that old familiar rhythm, listening to our wives' heartbeats, playing drums, making music. For this reason the midwife was always singing and talking to the unborn children right from the first days of conception, and on and on, way after the birth. Like a beacon of sound, this consoled their little sad hearts, and gave them a new road of familiar songs and welcoming chatter to follow out of the other world, away from the womb and into our huts out here in this cold, noisy world. The midwives constantly talked and cajoled both mother and child. But the loss of the kingdom of the womb, with its proximity to the Gods and to the drumbeat of our mother's heart, was overwhelming, nonetheless, and the first thing a child did was to cry out in a lonely little bugling of the purest expression of human grief.

Maya knew we were grief animals, and grief animals are speaking animals.

For what seemed to them like ages of steady sureness, babies having lived in water for nine months were thought to be water animals, like fish, crabs, and tadpoles. It was strange and mortifying to be fished out of the rhythmic ocean of the womb into these windy shores of life where we are asked, for the first time, to breathe air. To breathe air after centuries of essentially breathing water was the same as being asked, while we are in this world, to have the courage to breathe water.

The feeling of burning or being drowned rushes into our little lungs; and to the courage needed just to take that first breath, untutored and inexperienced, we had terror added to our grief. The first use to which we put our first breath is a sad and furious cry. So the greatest sound on earth is the grief-stricken cry of a brave baby, newly come into our world, hoping to be welcomed. As soon as that first cry was uttered, the women in the room spoke together in a beautiful jazzlike singsong cacophony of welcoming and congratulations, so touching that not an eye within earshot could be dry.

Soon the afterbirth, the husk of the old placenta, was pushed out. Ya Lur, sweating, glowing, and exhausted, finally got to rest with four ladies holding her gently.

The animal soul of my son was in the afterbirth, separated from him by the midwife's blade after she'd tied off the cord with a bright red boiled thread. Old-time midwives had three-inch thumbnails that were sharpened like little claw blades. These were used to cut the umbilical cords of the Tzutujil ancestors. This was the claw of the Old Mother of the Animals, Ixoc Juyú, Ixoc Taqáj, whose nonhuman essence was the heart of all nature and mammalian birth.

My little son was handed to me by his grandmother, and all the women were happy to see me so scared and willing, clumsily supporting his wrinkly head and squinting eyes.

My son looked as if he knew something very important from the other world. Like most of us, he would slowly forget the true world, the beautiful worlds of the Gods, which we all forget as our little fontanelles seal up. We spend the rest of our lives longing and searching for whatever it was that we can only remember a little, but which our hearts never forget.

Culture, according to the Tzutujil, consisted of keeping alive those rituals of remembrance that caused us to grow ourselves anew out of the fertile bed of amnesia and possibility into the memory of the earth before now.

My little son was the holiest in the village today because he could still remember. And you could tell this was so because this precious, weighty, tamalelike little package was smiling off and on as the Old Birth Goddess in the sky, the moon, tickled him from the other world.

Ya Kinoum was a type of shaman, a midwife shaman known as an *iyom*. Most shamans did some spiritual divining, but midwives excelled in making clear what a child's life might be and what talents or mysteries needed to be looked for as the little one grew. Illnesses and weaknesses could be perceived in hopes that the parents might remember to find shamans, *iyoma,* or others to help the child survive.

More often than not, the midwife told what she'd discovered only to the grandparents—aware, as we all were, that they had more experience with navigating life and were generally the memory of the family clan. These old grandparents sat around remembering necessary things. Another reason she told them specifically was that they were to be replaced by the grandchild, and a lot of what the *iyom* found to tell about a newborn was already up and running in the grandparents' lives. They'd recognize the signs more readily than the parents, who were otherwise occupied trying to feed and clothe their offspring, sometimes sacrificing their own health and appearance to do so.

Ya Kinoum blinked in the firelight, holding the long rope of life and the rubbery placenta, now pale and empty and waiting to go to the ground. She held it and pointed, turned it and spoke, reading my child's life in the umbilical cord and placenta as if it were a book. Waddling outside, she looked into the stars. Then she sent two old sisters with her niece to dig a hole inside our sweathouse where they buried the afterbirth. On top of its burial mound, its planting, they placed a little charm made of lightning-struck wood. This would be the home for my son's spirit for the next nine months.

His spirit heart was planted there in the sweathouse, which became his new womb for the next nine months until he could begin to talk and tear at food with new teeth and begin to walk. This new womb was called the Heart of Earth, the Earth Womb. Here his delicate baby soul would be protected by the Grandmother Moon and grow out of the sweathouse into the world, just as his body would grow in his parents' house at his mother's breast out into the village streets.

Our little son's head was examined along with his feet, his back, and his toes. Ya Kinoum sat the grandparents down and distilled what she'd learned from the placenta, the stars, and the whorls of hair on the little child's head, reeling it off like a message from the Gods.

At the next dawn, Ya Lur and her baby would go together into the hot sweathouse with Ya Kinoum. Only after eight days of dawn sweathouses would the boy receive his real name. It would take eight days for his animal soul to get here; meanwhile, he still belonged to the Moon Goddess.

Just before that first dawn, my old mother-in-law and old Ya Kinoum came over to me where I leaned against the inside of the hut with the men. They had a medium-sized clay water jar in their outstretched arms.

"La kamic caraja xtit jaura penaq cokin, nraj ruya' xinba nutakma' rumaq majun nxibej ri." Son, what happens now is that this tiniest one, who just arrived here with us all, desires that his father go to obtain the Waters of Confidence.

The old men instructed me as to what she meant. Alone, I would have to row my dugout canoe a couple of miles into the dawn-reddened misty Mother Lake, skimming unseen to a place in her middle. The lake was our Mother, the Mother of all, and we called her the Umbilicus of the Universe. I was to find the middle of her middle and fill up this water jar with the purest, freshest, most powerful lake water I could find. Ya Kinoum said this water would be used to make the "Waters of Confidence" to bathe the child for the first time. As the father, I was the only one who could do this well. I was, she said, to row out to the middle of the universe, bring the water, and come back again.

To make this magic liquid of the Mother waters into the Waters of Confidence, no one must see me going or coming. If someone should see me pulling water for this ceremonial washing of the baby, then my son would grow up feeling shy, ashamed, and unwelcome wherever he went. A warrior's stealth was necessary to go unseen through this village of twenty-eight thousand souls at dawn's rush hour.

Love is shown in a village so often in a nonverbal way. After hearing the news of our family's new addition, the paths around our end of the village and the trail leading to where we kept our canoes were virtually deserted in hopes that our child would grow up blessed by all the villagers to be confident and welcome. Many people sacrificed an early start to their fields for food and firewood in honor of the child.

Alone and unseen, I pushed my short cedar canoe into the flat morning lake and rowed to the center of the bay, the knocking of the oar oozing through the cold December mist like a wooden bucket kicked by a cow.

The foggy steam closed in on me like a pile of duck down, hovering an inch above the water. No one could see me and I could see no one; even the reflection of my face was missing. The water at the center of the universe swirled in alternating hot and cold eddies and as I pushed the heavy clay jar into the pure water, I prayed for my son to survive, to be well loved, and to always be welcome wherever he went.

Balancing the pot on the ever-present bed of dried tule reeds in the bottom of the canoe, I rowed slower and intermittently, not entirely certain where the shore lay, obscured by the thick fog. The silence was immense, but gradually the normal symphony of roosters, turkeys, grinding machines, laughter, and barking dogs gave me a beacon to pull toward. Soon I was rowing the old hollow log out of the steam into the shore from right where I'd departed.

I went the back way, hiding and creeping, trying to protect the water I balanced in my hand from the prying eyes of humans.

When I paced into our compound's threshold, having barely missed old Box Head rolling home drunk, four old ladies, Ya Kinoum, Ya Lur's great-aunt Ya Sosof, Ya Ros, and Ya Chirij, greeted me as if I were now a man, smiling and whispering so that no evil should be alerted: *"Xat tula ta?"* Did you come home, father?

"Jie ja jala nkutun chwa." Yes, here you have that which was asked of me to make apparent. And I handed the Waters of Confidence to the four women, careful not to spill any.

Those old ladies, being what we knew them to be, were already waiting with powerful plants in their hands and ancient prayers of beautiful protection in their heads. Each put sweet-smelling leaves and flowers into the pot and swished them around clockwise with a weaving stick, praying for the child's strength, cleverness, happiness, and for confidence, calling it all into the Mother Waters.

Then Ya Lur's mother brought our son to me and the old ladies taught me how to bathe the little child in the Waters of Confidence. All the men had to bathe their newborn children in the Waters of Confidence, that water brought by stealthy fathers past the hard envious eyes of humans, blessed by old women.

I bathed his little toes and tiny feet, like little tamales, his froglike legs, his little back, and his head, his eyes, and nose and ears and mouth, everywhere washing away any fright and despair, chanting the old prayers of confidence with the midwife who dried the child in a new soft handwoven child's cloth provided by the female relatives.

He opened one of his eyes and took a quick suspicious glance at me, then smiled for a split second as the moon tickled him from the other world. The crowd of ladies, young men, and old-timers shook their heads while laughing and commenting. Old Ya Kinoum hailed the Sun Our Father, thanking him for helping deliver into the day a "completely gathered, ten-fingered flower; completely gathered, ten-toed sprout; a first dawn light, a first sunlight," and so on until little mothers with babies at their breasts began meandering into our compound as we finished the washing of the child with the magic waters. The fine-smelling tree flowers and leaves the midwife had put in the water with her magic prayers were good for everyone, so the young mothers dipped their fingers in the jar and washed their little ones in confidence too.

At the midwife's bidding and Ya Lur's command, I placed the little bound-up nestling into the arms of Ya Tzimai, Corn Silk Woman, my first client as a shaman. She had been unable to have a baby, but after our ceremonies she was nursing my own boy, who suckled milk from her breasts brought down by the birth of her own child two months before.

Then he was passed to the next woman, and the next and the next and the next. Every woman who was lactating, who wanted to bless the new mother, my wife, came to let the newborn suckle so that he would never feel like a stranger in any compound of the village. In the minds of the Tzutujil, having suckled from the breasts of women from every clan in the village, my son would now be related to the whole village in the deepest way possible. This was the beginning of initiation because the Tzutujil knew that the smell of one's mother was strong, and that the sweet animal smell of all the village mothers huddled together lived in your memory like the house in the village where you were born. Once more this made you feel even more intensely received and at home in your village and welcome to come through every doorway.

Adults sometimes had to stop quarrels among their peers by reminding them how they had suckled from the other's mother or grandmother. This milk-giving was a peacemaking thing. Women were proud to come sit and talk to the mother, breast-feed the new child, then get to work fixing up something in the compound.

Every first-time mother knew she should visit each successful birthing mother, bringing with her a particular birthing soup. This would give good luck to the soup bringer when her own birth-giving day came around. Women went to get meat for the soup from the "cattle walker." Meat was rare and expensive, but it was an indispensable part of the delicious rich soup in which cabbage, stone-ground tomatoes, dried yellow corn and other plants were also ritually prepared.

At the bidding of their knowledgeable mothers, lines of red clay pots full of these soups were brought on the heads of excited expectant mothers. Besides, the Goddess demanded it. In this way, not one man or woman in the baby's compound had to fret about cooking or washing at all during the week-long birthing time.

No one could ever finish up all the soup or meat that the women brought. The new mother was now considered one of them, a kind of veteran chief among the younger married women, and under her direction the old ladies of the birthing compound would move the two- to five-pound chunks of tender meat from their broths and pots, and skewer them on wires or ropes to dry in the smoke or out in the sun for everyone to see.

Babies were not measured by how much they weighed but by how welcome they were made to feel. People didn't go around saying, "My child weighed seven pounds and six ounces," they went around saying, "My grandchild is a one-hundred-fifty pounder," referring to how much meat the child's birth had brought in, how many people had brought food.

My boy Jorge got over two hundred pounds of meat, and we exhibited it in front of our hut for all to see. People were not ashamed to be grandiose about how well they were loved. A lot of meat in front of the hut meant a lot of people wanted to participate in the blessing of your life and the birthing of your children.

Though archaic and barbaric, the beauty and wonder of the sight of one hundred women suckling your child and a hundred pregnant pretty ladies admiring the new addition to the village while elegantly swaying into the compound with food on their heads made you pity the isolation of modern birth. There you hear only the whirr of fans, the hum of fluorescent lights, the beeps and chirps of monitors, electronic static, and the squeak of bedsprings. It's a small wonder children born like that get numb and tough quick.

The old men of the village also came to see a newborn baby, blessing and pontificating with all the men in the compound while helping them with firewood and crops to keep life as unburdened as possible for everyone in the family.

We had to keep a fire going for eight days, especially the first night after the birth. Ya Kinoum made sure we did so to keep the Goddesses happy. Though there are thirteen Goddesses of childbirth, and all of them love children, the most powerful of all has no children of her own. She is extraordinarily jealous of all things female on the earth who do have young or give birth, and without any kids of her own, she steals from people who forget the suffering female earth and the children. Like a sad old barren mare, she robs other mares of their colts. She is called the Orphan Parent. It's for her that the fire is made, mostly as tribute, because if the fire goes out, the child could be stolen into the spirit world to live with the old Goddess, who keeps piles of stolen children at her grieving side. But it is she who also makes birth possible. Though we love her, we never know what she thinks of us. Only shamans and midwives understand her.

After a few days the crowds began to thin. Every night up till then, Ya Lur and I had slept together in a crowd of forty to fifty people. Ya Kinoum came to check on Ya Lur every day like an old herd mare checking to make sure everyone was doing what he or she should.

On the eighth day after the birth, the relatives had sacrificed a large male turkey and the blazing cooking fires were utterly obscured by a profusion of clay pots and griddles that bubbled and hissed, cooking up the required and much-loved feast of the baby's official naming.

Ya Kinoum returned to give the baby and mother a big sweat bath in the *touj* at dawn. Women are the only ones allowed to use the sweathouse in the daylight, everyone else sweats in the night. Ya Lur, the baby, and ponderous old Ya Kinoum squatted down to pass through the tiny entrance to our compound's undersized, ovenlike sweathouse. Every five minutes, between long shamanic women prayers and the great rustling of avocado leaves, a wild panting voice leapt out in a muffled kind of way to the waiting crowd of the compound.

"*Chinumaq chiwe*," she said, to which a volcanic reply of "*Ei*" and "*Bai*" was roused from every human being within earshot. This meant "For our cause, thanks be, forgive us." *Ei* was a women's word of all-out endorsement, and *bai* was the men's word for the same.

Finally, after half an hour, the midwife, baby, and mom issued forth from the Womb of the Moon as the *touj* was called in the secret language of the old people. We all rushed to help them to their reed mats and birthing bed and gave them handwoven towels to dry themselves with.

Once again, I washed the baby in a new batch of the Waters of Confidence into which were mixed the flowers from fruit-bearing trees. This time he complained in a very confident and defiant fashion, to the amusement and approval of all the clan. For the first time since he'd been born, the midwife dressed our son in one of the gorgeous hand-woven, skirtlike Tzutujil diapers, taken from a colorful pile woven especially for this birth by women who wanted children. These complex articles of clothing signified the fifth layer of remembrance and were kept hidden until a successful birth had been achieved. Then they were awarded to the mother.

A little cap had been fashioned out of one of my old work sashes made soft by use, and a shirt from an old handwoven shirt of mine was festooned over the blinking little creature. We all laughed and gave enormous attention to the newly adorned child and mother as they took their place in our midst, the mother's movement gradual due to her proud aching body.

Babies' souls are delicate and very loyal. For this reason the child's first clothing comes from the father's clean old clothing. The child's spirit might miss his father and follow his father to work in the wilds where the baby's spirit might get lost or damaged in the hard world. To help the child from feeling left behind, and to help the father not to worry for having left his beloved child at home, the women put the father's shirt under the child as he slept. The baby also wore certain articles of his father's clothing to reassure him of the presence of his father. This clothing also protects the child from evil in the father's absence until he returns from the mountains.

The old women bound up Ya Lur's belly with a long, wide sash in which a secret midwife object was hidden. With a loud pop this charm would magically find its way back into the shaman midwife's bag when the mother's womb and midriff had resumed their normal dimension. This usually happened in less than a month. In the harsh and natural world of the village, Mayan women were very resilient.

Ya Kinoum held the baby with Ya Lur and me by her side. Presenting him to the sun, she gave him the name of my father, which is the custom with a boy child. A girl child would have been named after Ya Lur's mother. We passed the baby from old couple to old couple who spoke long prayers to the child, to the Gods, and the deified ancestors to protect the child and let him grow.

Old Chiv surged and rolled in through the door, just in time, of course, bellowing his usual archaic Mayan greetings in the way only old living legends could. With venerable Ya Kix, his wife, striding in with him, the old chief and shaman took the little dog-headed stool proffered to him by my sister-in-law. Chiv, like the king that he was, had called to see my new son.

Caressing the wrinkled, well-dressed infant in his expressive old tobacco-dyed hands, Chiv inspected the little being, looking for all the world like a glazed, blue-eyed howler monkey sizing up a little piece of blinking, well-dressed, wrinkled fruit.

Old honest words from the days before people were on the earth flew through our compound like a flock of invisible bugling cranes, and this, in turn, called in more people to the feast from the street to see what crazy old Chiv was up to now.

The old man passed little Jorge to his wife, whose intense affected style of blessing with a great flourish of gnarled words was interrupted rudely by Chiv's nonchalant assertion, "I see that you two have been teaching each other by day again!"

The ladies flipped their finely woven tinsel shawls over their heads, horrified but with muffled laughter, hidden from view and in direct competition with the loud guffaws, hissing, and tongue clickings of light disapproval from the old men.

It was common knowledge that people should try to make love at night instead of the day, that they should rest when the sun rested and work when the sun worked. If the sun is present while a couple is in a delicious embrace that ends up sprouting a child, then the sun, being the male power of the earth, will give his own face to the child instead of the parents' face. This was Chiv's irreverent and grandiose way of telling us and everybody else that our child had the face of a God and was very beautiful.

When Ya Kix had finally stopped scolding old Chiv, the feast was handed out to all the people present. The old chiefs and their wives and the old people of the compound ate first and the rest of us last. Women with older babies chewed their food for them and, by kissing their little mouths, pushed the well-ground paste into their fat cheeks so that they could swallow it all. Without this stage of using your mother's teeth to grind your food, a child would grow up attached to themselves only, become insensitive to the people, and want everything for themselves. This way of receiving your food, graduating from umbilical cord, to the breast, to the mouth, to the mother's hand, to feeding oneself, all done in a gradual way, made babies feel welcome to all parts of the body.

Venerable Ya Kinoum was plied with canyon water until she was almost too drunk to make her own way through the cinder sand paths of the village to her tidy, medium-sized hut at Sour Point where she lived. This was protocol, of course, because no one should come home from a feast sober, hungry, or sane.

We had been sending large pots of babies' gift food to her faraway home on the heads of our young female cousins and relatives all week long, so that when Ya Kinoum arrived home after working so hard there would be food for her family and herself. But today, we sent twice as much.

Emerging from our granary hut with three ears of special white corn, my father-in-law thrust them into my hands and bid me gift them to the old woman. This was the time-honored, symbolic payment for a successful delivery.

Holding out the three perfectly formed cobs evenly pared in translucent ivory pearl kernels, I gave her the promise of three ears of corn every time we saw her for the rest of the baby's life. Ya Kinoum at first refused the gifts three times, as is only right and customary, to show her love for us and her unwillingness to seem too greedy. But in the end she tendered the corn in her arms like a baby itself and blessed the whole compound and our friends. Held gently by the arms of my sister-in-law's husband, the Red Banana, and Grackle, Ya Lur's little brother escorted the fine old lady to whom we owed so much to her home. The sun drew a long red road across his wife, the lake, Our Mother, and all was good.

For the first time in over a week, Ya Lur and I and the baby slept in our own hut more or less alone, with only aunts and great-uncles watching the world and our lives from outside our doorway. We drifted into the sleep of parents who were still children of the village.

◇

Old Ya Kinoum, whose name meant Jungle Plum, was always my friend after that. I in my capacity as a shaman attended many births with her over the years, always keeping our promise of three ears of fine corn. I never got to finish our debt to her because she was killed two years later by an angry shaman who blamed her for the stillbirth of his son.

By then I was a big man in the village and I certainly wanted my vengeance on that man for poisoning beautiful Ya Kinoum. But I held my hand in deference to her who always taught me to think of the children first, knowing full well that any action of bad intent I'd take against another villager, whether spiritual or literal, justified or not, would only make the village a worse place for all of us to live. I remember Ya Kinoum. I miss her and remember fully what she was for us all in that hard and beautiful place of cinder paths, sweat, death, waterbirds' songs and flowers, called Ch'jay, at home.

Being born was all about welcoming.

◇

Every woman in the Canyon Village called each of her children *Najbey Sac, Najbey Qij,* the First Dawn, the First Sun. It needn't matter if you were the first, third, or thirteenth child. It didn't make any difference if the child was a girl or a boy, or if siblings were all standing together, Tzutujil mothers always introduced each child as, "my First Dawn, my First Sun." All women knew that inside their bodies, hidden like genetic magic in the germ of a corn seed, lay an ocean that crashed in on the Beach of Stars from the outside, rocking in an infinite, hidden way and called the *Alaniel* or Baby Maker. The womb was an ocean that gave birth to the Sun every day, the Moon when it came, and everything else. Inside each woman lived a million beginnings, and possibility itself. If you walked far enough toward dawn, you'd eventually come to where you could see the dawn sun born from the steamy seas, its big orange head crowning in day.

Every woman knew that her womb, like the fresh spraying ocean, had given birth to Dawns and Suns. They were the givers and the hardworking mothers of light.

All children knew that they had sprung from the ocean-holding Earth and toddled over it, lighting up the toil-filled, aching days of their parents.

Their cold funny cheeks and big-eyed thoughts were the main reason adults were willing to live longer than their bodies told them they could, just to survive to be with their little ones.

Small-hearted, mean, visionless people are everywhere, and there were those who beat their children, their wives, their husbands. But, on the whole, children were more precious than the threads they were woven from, more adored than the jade they were carved from, more holy than the human conceit that claimed to have made them. And my son Jorge was one of these wonderfully spoiled little creations.

Babies' feet hardly ever even met the ground until they could walk, and it was dangerous down there. Jorge was always missing, in someone's arms, at a cousin's, or an aunt's, or a brother-in-law's, or gone off with my mother-in-law's sister to visit her husband's uncle, the canoe mogul, who owned one hundred ten canoes. Once he could walk, Jorge would eat at everybody's fires.

We all longed to carry his fat face around. It was an embarrassment to go to the market because all the ladies would fill Ya Lur's baskets and shawls to brimming with gifts for the little boy. He was a king and soon the little rascal learned to blow kisses for every gift, thereby increasing his haul when people wanted to see his endearing show of appreciation.

When he was born Jorge's umbilical cord had been cut over a little ear of white corn, Birth Corn. The juices of the old cable of life seeped into the seeds, which were then shelled and passed out to the male members of the clan, the extended family.

These they would plant in a special field for the baby at the next planting time, of which there were six possibilities each year. This corn took approximately two hundred sixty days before it could be harvested. This was both the cycle of our calendar in the divination bundles and the length of a woman's pregnancy, if you counted by the moon. More important, this time period represented the "second gestation" of the child after his birth, a gestation inside the womb of the village as a whole. At nine months or so, Jorge had sprouted teeth and begun to walk. Because of his new teeth he would want to eat food and, in particular, make sounds like a Tzutujil.

It was speech that would make him one of the people. As the birth corn plants grew, so the child grew in a parallel way. For this reason, we men took great care of the birth corn, as its fate was the legacy of the child's ancestors, having been passed for generations from birth to birth. This corn outlived the people, having been dutifully planted at every birth since the beginning.

In the meantime, a couple of weeks after his birth, Jorge's little umbilical stump fell off. The midwife and grandparents were invited over and together they wrapped the tiny little piece of dried skin with hand-spun cotton thread until it became a little ball the size of a marble.

Climbing onto a stool, Ya Lur's mother reached into the smoke-varnished, century-old plant-stalk rafters of her old hut, retrieving a sooty black bag with an embroidered flap a couple of hundred years old.

Into this bag she placed the little ball of cotton string containing the memory of my son's origins, his belly button stump. Inside this revered bundle thousands of similar little balls resided, each containing the belly button stump of Jorge's ancestors going back hundreds of years. Each had been wrapped by yet another ancient ancestor, going back in sequence forever. After they were placed in the bag, no one knew which pill was which or to whom they all belonged, each family member merging into a collective memory and the whole constituting the Seed Heart of the clan.

By the time the birth corn was ready to harvest, the baby had teeth, was laughing regularly, had started to walk, and wanted to speak. So we held a tooth feast in which this bundle was incensed thoroughly and danced with by all the people, held like a little baby alongside my son.

Every generation had its navel stumps in these holy bags. Like the corn, they too were what gave the family its spiritual DNA and ancestral force to continue carrying our lives from generation to generation.

By dancing the bundle, it was reanimated, refreshed, made new and alive with its myriad of umbilical seeds. Together, awash in a pile of your ancestors, your umbilical connection was protected, then made strong and reassured of its place in the social dream world of the household, forming together the family umbilical place of attachment for those babies yet to come, enabling them to latch on to a long line of this very moment repeated, beyond us here today.

Tied up in the middle of the rafters, representing the sky, the little bundle of belly buttons was also called the Umbilicus of the House. It was the seed bank from which babies' souls were kept. It was taken down and fed anytime something big happened in the family. The village as a whole had its own belly button bundle called Heart of Food-Water, *Rukux Way Ya*. This was the bundle I loved inside the sacred house of Axuan.

Having finally sprouted teeth, the day arrived for our son's birth into the extended family, and a feast was called.

All the men returned the new corn, bringing it in their string bags and adding it all up together until it formed a pretty large pile of dentless ivory corn, which shone just like fine teeth.

Except for twenty ears that they tucked away carefully, the women shelled the whole pile, then toasted it on clay griddles over a slow smokeless oak fire. They pulverized it by hand on their stone grinders, then poured water through it, over and over, until it took on the consistency and look of milk, making the liquid into a female substance.

Then with great muscle and teamwork they arranged large clay tubs on top of several fires, the very old ladies directing the ritual cooking, as they knew best, of course.

Cooking down the female corn milk by the addition of the male fire created a male liquid, a semenlike drink known as *maatz*. This pastelike liquid was served to all the guests at this feast of the teeth in elongated, bone-smooth, ceremonial tree gourds. Everybody came to my son's feast: all the new mothers, all the relatives, Scat Mulaj relations, friends, and old Ya Kinoum—everybody who'd come to the birth and then some. By drinking this ritual drink, a beverage made from corn that came from a long line of ancestors, Jorge was feeding his people while at the same time being drunk into the belly of the village.

Like semen, this drink spiritually fertilized the whole village. The bonelike patina of the gourds made them seem like skulls. Indeed, they represented the heads of deified ancestral seeds, the lineage of all life that had died by being planted in the earth. After struggling underground against death and disease, they returned back to this world, just like our babies and the corn seed. They had transformed into the sprouts. The Mayan word for dawn and the word for a sprouting cornfield are one and the same. That's why we called our babies the First Dawn; they were our ancestors' sprouting seeds returned to this world from the other wearing the funny new faces of our children.

The matured seeds that grew and fertilized themselves from the dawn sprouts, the corn sprouts, were returned to the village in greater quantity than when they left. This new seed was a renewed seed, and when ingested it kept the whole village full of life and gave it the ability to make more of itself. When a person died, the same corn, left over from his baby feast, grown over and over to preserve its viability, was once again shelled and made into *maatz*, and the dead person's "substance" was again drunk back into the mass of the village body. This way no part of the ancestral substance was dissipated or floated off to nothingness.

When a clan drank *maatz* at the teeth ceremony, they blessed the child with long life, a life long enough to eat well, and then be eaten back into life, and finally planted and resurrected as a dawn.

Eventually, after the drink had been gulped down and the gourds were all emptied, bottoms-up in the basket, signifying that everyone had drunk, Ya Kinoum took up Jorge and painted different protective symbols on his fat feet, his handsome forehead, his chest, all his joints, and his belly button with the pastelike drink. Then, releasing a little live lake crab from a long string of crabs tied with reeds, she deftly held the little crustacean up to the bare soles of our son's sturdy feet.

The crab hissed and flailed all her legs and pincers, tickling the baby's arches and toes and making him jump. Ya Kinoum all the while whispered prayers about how well the baby would walk, sure like a crab, and not fall down, would be quick and energetic like a crab, strong and nimble like a crab, and so on. Then the little crab was released onto the ground to go her way, and she headed toward the lake, moving sideways, complaining all the way.

Back in the corner of our big *pach jai,* our long thatched hut, Ya Lur prepared to dunk five strings of live crabs into a huge *ptix,* or pot full of water that bubbled furiously over our cooking fire.

The old ladies hushed the crowd as five dozen crabs went into the water. *Tup,* the Crab, was a holy animal and, like other fish, water snails, grebes, and all the lake animals, it was considered to be an incarnation of the Mother Waters herself. As such the crab had "skirts," a voice, stubborn attitude, and a reputation for imparting longevity to whoever ate her or let her go.

When crabs were cooked by being boiled to death, the people close by always kept silent out of respect and reverence until the little beings died. If people were oblivious to the little crabs' horrible demise, especially during a tooth feast, and continued to joke and gossip, then the offenders would lose all their teeth when they got old.

If the legs and pincers of the crabs had fallen from their torso when the pot was opened then it was thought someone had spoken or was not concentrating. Speaking and eating well came from having good teeth, and a tooth feast celebrated being able to speak and eat solid food. If the Goddess was insulted, you also lost the ability to eat and speak easily in old age. But today no one had to worry because this particular batch of little ornery red and brown crabs had no intention of being cooked. Ya Lur, in all the confusion of the feast, forgot to put a lid on the pot and left the hut to be with the people in the little plaza of our compound. Herds of little scuttling crabs were seen scuttling sideways all over our compound, looking at the people who were observing a respectful silence. Soon enough a happy ripple of feigned alarm and laughter took over the dignified gathering as every crab made a break for it, piling out at top speed from the pot of boiling water.

We laughed so hard we couldn't sit straight to see our feast running away, back to its beloved watery home, in every direction except ours. Jorge got mad and started crying because it wasn't him we were laughing about. Someone went and killed a turkey and we ate well after all.

That night a line of cute old ladies, two fat ones and a fidgety one, waited for the Grandmother Moon to rise. It was a full moon night. Grandmother Moon was the one in whose charge babies remained until they could speak, had teeth, were eating solid food, and began to walk.

A child's first words are best spoken to our collective Grandmother. That way the child will grow up to be a human being, a good speaker of Words of Deliciousness, as they say. As the phosphorescent glow of the old moon began to melt the darkness with a sliver of her silver face, the old women called for the child. Taking Jorge into her arms, the old midwife began to rattle gently on his chest with a small ornamented tin money box with corn inside.

The rhythm kept going while all the ladies kept singing and murmuring

"Wai tie, lo' tie,
Wai tie, lo' tie"

Tortilla Grandmother, eggs Grandmother,
Tortilla Grandmother, eggs Grandmother

over and over until the Moon rose and the little boy was staring straight at the old Goddess. The old ladies chanted and rattled until Jorge tried to grab the moon, blurting out

"Lo' tie,
lo'-, lo'-, lo'-, lo'-, lo'-, lo'-, lo'-, lo'."

Eggs, eggs, eggs, eggs.

And everybody laughed. Jorge's first words were to the Goddess and he would be blessed. The yellowness of the fire in the hut turned its little lair golden as the people said their long Mayan good-byes, hosts and guests chattering at the same time, receiving and giving until everyone, having gone, left Jorge fallen asleep on my shoulder and Ya Lur joking in the other huts with her sisters. The old Grandmother Moon had let us have our son; the village belly was full; the crabs had run away, and I was a man who could speak and be honored now. In the Canyon Village, without a child on your hip, no one thinks you know what you're talking about.

NINE

THE THROAT OF THE UNIVERSE

NAMING, PLAYING, LEARNING

TO SPEAK, THE LIFE OF A CHILD

A lot of the weather in and around the village was controlled by little children. The potbellied crews of saggy-pants, raggedy-sashed, droopy-skirted little kids were always playing some kind of game. Everybody knew of course that certain ancient kinds of games control the weather, big games and little games too. So all the games the little ones played in their yelling rambunctious way had their own time of year, and they never played them out of season. Unseasonable storms, hail, drought, or strange winds could be caused by playing certain games out of sequence. Kids knew this and they taught each other the rules.

I loved to play *xca'*, or "beeswax." Balls of black fragrant wax from wild honeybees in the forest were added to or diminished in the course of play and handed down in families for decades or more.

The little kids would find a flat rock or a space of hard dustless earth. Pinching off little dark chunks of wax from their big ball, they'd flatten them into discs. Holding them flat in their hands up to the Sun Father's face, they would let the discs soften in his heat. Then the first dusty boy, maybe seven years of age, would throw his disc down hard to make it stick to the stone. His adversary had to throw his disc so as to hit the other one and stick to it. If it stuck and flipped over he took both discs and added it to his ball of wax. If it missed they started over. But if it stuck and didn't flip, they got two more discs. Then they tried to stick and flip the other two, and on and on till somebody got into an argument and the other kid's wax ball got too big, and then they'd all go fishing.

By tearing apart an old discarded hat, the little people would get some strong thread out of it for the fishing line. Making hooks out of wood or old pieces of wire, or tying certain knots around the bait, kids would fish off the purple rocks that hung over the bay of Xechivoy where I used to paint pictures.

Sometimes they would run up to me, their undersized handwoven pink or blue shirts showing a belly button, with a string of silver-dollar-sized *culha* fish flashing like rainbows in the dreamy Atitlan sun. As a big Scat Mulaj official in the village, it was not so dignified for me to be buried in a herd of ragamuffins, but I loved to play wax discs, though most of the time I lost and ended up rolling in the dust with a pile of funny kids throwing themselves on top of me. The old people just laughed.

Once initiations and Easter had passed, wax playing was finished and it was time to fly beetles. Every spring when all the trees flowered, herds of big beetles flew into the village. They were very friendly and didn't fly too fast. Like polished chunks of black obsidian, they were called the Eyes of the Ancestors, and it was well known that you shouldn't ever kill them. Our Ancestors' Eyes came flying into our village to get a glimpse of their descendants and see if everything was going along as it should.

However, as everyone knew, the Ancestors' Eyes come principally to play games and have fun with their grandchildren, whom they missed. Some beetles were smaller and flew faster, but, for the most part, they were about the size of half an avocado pit, or a pigeon's head, or three bumblebees.

All the kids ran around trying to catch as many as they could. They kept them on their shirts or blouses. The beetles had bristly little feet, and once you stuck them somewhere, they stayed for a long time. You never had to feed them because they had already eaten as grubs before they came flying to us. They were the children's prized livestock, and because most kids didn't trust anybody with their beetles, they slept with as many as fifteen or twenty of these Ancestors' Eyes across their little chests at night.

Some parents didn't like it much, but when they thought back to when they were kids who insisted on sleeping with beetles, they gave in.

Since a whole family in the village slept like a big pile of puppies, it wasn't so much the bristly, crunchy nature of the little beasts there in bed with everybody that was problematic. It was the fact that these enormous beetles were very opinionated and liked to argue with each other—about what, we were never sure.

They hissed all night, emitting at times a sound somewhere between a whistle and a beep. Sometimes they'd all get going at once, and you couldn't get any sleep with such a racket going on. Of course the little kids, after running around all day barefoot, could sleep through a hurricane, so they were never bothered by the noise. The parents were constantly getting up to calm the beetles down by talking to them, which always worked. The Eyes of the Ancestors seemed to listen when you talked to them.

The best part was flying them! We took little threads about six feet long that the kids begged off their mothers from their warp strings and tied them just under the big beetle's helmet around its neck. Then we breathed on them and threw them into the air, holding on tightly to the other end of the string. Off they went like idiotic flying Volkswagens, around and around your head for half a minute or so. Then, plop, they dropped out of the sky right to the ground, tired but undamaged, with a kind of dizzy beetlelike smile on their faces. I used to fly three or four at once. They'd braid the strings and we'd all laugh.

Some of the beetles were shiny bright gold. My favorite was one that I'd traded for that was an iridescent sky blue with gold designs all over his back. Depending on how you held him to the light, you could see that he had a big iridescent red *V* on his funny old head.

Sometimes when the Scat Mulaj sent their initiates as messengers to fetch me to a ceremony, I would be engaged in flying the Ancestors' Eyes. It was comical to watch them as they tried in the most serious way to lay out their florid harangue of magnificent ancient words while I was busy getting my blue beetle to fly higher than seven other beetles flown in competition by screaming little kids. All our heads looked upward and even our dog was gyrating his head sideways, back and forth, watching the bugs go around.

Pretty soon, the hierarchy messengers were looking up too, their heads going around and around like the dog's. One early morning when a team of messengers came, one of the officials got engrossed in our beetle flying enough to criticize my method. It wasn't long before he started showing me how he used to do it. In the end both messengers became so involved in flying beetles that a second team of messengers of much higher rank had to be sent to find out what had happened to all of us.

On that particular day, they were calling me to come help with a disaster in the Sacred House of San Antonio where the Rkux Qán, or "Heart of Yellow Abundance," and the Muuc, or Herd, were kept. The bundle containing the Huur, or the "Throat of the World," had been accidentally dropped when old Ma Tzajpen had fallen during one of the daily dancings of the fetish.

Very tall for a Tzutujil, Ma Tzajpen was slimmer than a cattail leaf, which made him seem even more towering. In his eighties, he'd lost his footing during his ritual to feed the Throat of the World and it had broken inside its beautiful layers of wrapping.

No one alive today except Ma Tzajpen had ever seen what the Holy Throat actually looked like. Ma Tzajpen had inherited his lifetime position as *Najbey Siil* from the man before him, who had been the only one in his time to see it unwrapped.

It had been handed down for hundreds of years after being given to the people by the *Nawal Achi* and *Nawal Exqui* in the beginning of this fifth creation, the fifth layer.

In this bundle one could feed the whole universe. The Holy Throat received all the ritual gifts the initiated could muster. But also this was the larynx of God, the larynx of the Spirits. It was here we put our ritual foods to feed the other worlds, who were then energized into speaking us back into life.

The Throat of the World was a short umbilical cord of words and music, the place where this world and that world of Spirit connected, where both spoke and fed each other in the arterial and veinal back-and-forth effluvium of village ritual. Today it was broken and Ma Tzajpen was heartbroken. Tears washed his old sunken eyes, his immense nose leading his kind skinny face out from under his headcloth. Distraught with guilt and his inability to put the Throat back together, he called on me to help him.

I'd been repairing and renewing many saints, God rocks, and bundles for the past years. Because I was a member of the Scat Mulaj and could see the Gods, and because they were familiar with me, Ma Tzajpen felt I would be his best bet.

A blanket was fixed over the doorway, and guards were posted to make sure no one entered while we worked, especially children to keep them safe. When an anomaly in the normal spirit world occurred, there was usually a reason and lots of unpredictable powers could be called or released at such times.

We had to capture it all in the Sacred House to keep the village from being spiritually at risk. At the same time the sanctity of the Throat had to be maintained as it was being examined.

We filled the room with fat candles and copal smoke, prayed hard, and put down protective lines on all sides.

The wrappings of our beloved Throat were many and each had a procedure and a story. They read like Tzutujil spiritual history. In each layer the cloth and style of dressing the sacred had changed as it evolved into what it had become in the 1940s when this bundle has been given to tall Tzajpen.

The innermost layers, having been put there first before the 1500s, were tender like the innermost husks of a fresh ear of corn. They lay there fragile and embroidered with brightly colored wild bird feathers, most of which had rubbed off in the centuries of bundle dancing to keep open the conduit between this world and the other.

Buried in clouds of incense smoke, five officials stood around us, facing outward with their backs to us, while Ma Tzajpen and I gently opened the last layer to reveal the most beautiful Throat in the whole world. Weeping with high female voices, we spoke to it as a midwife does to coax a birthing child into this world. The Throat lived on strings of archaic words, each with many simultaneous meanings. Our words were like plasma, like electrolyte, like a blood transfusion that had to be fed to the bare vulnerable dying fetish as we like surgeons operated to piece it back together again. We kept her alive this way as we worked, never stopping the stream of images and old words.

Weighing at least twenty-five pounds, the poor little coral-colored beauty was cracked a few inches up from the side where she fit into the other world.

Working fast, I removed all the magic necklaces, ancient feathers, and other intricate word knots. Taking a mixture of boiled deer hooves mixed with copal resin and a red clay on the end of a burning *ocote* stick, I cemented the old Larynx of the Universe back together, holding it tightly as we sang until it cooled and held fast.

Lifting her into Ma Tzajpen's cradling arms, I noticed—as we sang and talked two different stories—that his face glowed through his lizardy skin and he smiled, swallowing hard as his old head bounced, dancing the bundle.

The slit log drum rang out and the bundle dance was continued at the point where it had left off when the bundle had broken. The Throat of the World had been attacked by something that attacked old Ma Tzajpen. Something in the world today wanted our friendship with the stream of deified speech to be blocked and wounded.

We wept, danced, and prayed until the beautiful Throat was safely back in her box. And as we knelt saying our good-byes and thanks, sending them back through the Throat itself, we could hear the bubbling world of the village being spoken into life by the Gods, coming into us from the Larynx of the Gods. Outside little kids giggled as their beetles flew around them higher and higher, around and around.

❖

Carrying my tools of repair and prayer, I drifted home the long way around the rocky inside shore of Panaj. The Sun setting behind the Elbow of the Earth volcano was laying down a burning pink road across his wife, the Lake, in whose tule-studded shallows young fishermen laid crab lines from their canoes, paddling with the oars in their armpits. A little gathering of eight-year-olds with no front teeth was looking up into the immense sky of Atitlan, yelling for teeth.

Purple martins and lake swallows were careening, doubling back, diving and hovering all about as they hunted evening bugs. Thousands upon thousands of them were there where the children and I stood at the edge of the lake. In the light breeze the little iridescent birds found it easy to hover, and eventually all lowered themselves into a static flying position without moving their wings, all facing the lake until a thousand martins and swallows covered the children and myself like a cloak of birds. Over the burning afternoon, this lake blanket of magical birds was unfrightened by the yelling children's petition to give them new teeth.

The purple martins were Gods, and the people called them *Xuy Qoum*, Stingy Medicine. The shiny iridescence on the swallows' backs was known to be the ephemeral magic of the birds that gave them the power to distribute new teeth. When the children began to lose their teeth they would yell at all kinds of shiny birds, especially the martins, then open their mouths and show them their missing teeth.

"Xuy Qoum, Xuy Qoum, tiyajuvie, majun tabant xuychwa." Stingy Medicine, Stingy Medicine, give me a tooth, don't be stingy with me.

It always worked. The kids would wake up one day and they'd have a new molar poking through their gums.

When I finally wandered home I interrupted a little flock of graceful young mothers with their fat, colorfully adorned babies on their swaying hips, queuing their way up the two stone steps of the narrow corridor into our compound. The ladies' birdlike twitters were tempered by the lower voices and the more professional calm of their mothers and mothers-in-law who had arrived before the younger women. Young women rarely went anywhere alone if they could help it, as most people liked to visit in groups.

After florid, salutary hellos, regards, and gifts had been exchanged, the visitors were given reed mats to sit on while the women of our compound rolled up their weaving and brought them something hot to drink from the clay pots heating in the embers of their cooking fires.

All the women and kids sat together and vigorously dove like pelicans into the waters of village gossip, pulling up a wordy fish or two until one of the older ladies, in a whispered tone of polite affection, would approach the truth of their visit. We already knew, of course, why they'd come.

"A Martín, utz arja nkima ba kitzij tsra' rilaj vinaaj." Martín, is it all right if we gather up a few mouthfuls of words from the old woman?

The "Old Woman" was, of course, our big green parrot.

In hopes of helping their little children to speak well, young women would feed their babies crumbs of food that an eloquent parrot had dropped. The girls would show their babies to the parrot, who eyeballed the children sideways and shuffled nervously back and forth on her smooth pole. Then they would utter phrases to the parrot, and the bird would begin to whistle a song or repeat something she'd heard earlier. Ideally, the baby might begin to converse with the ornery green beast, who would then reply back, and everything would be set.

After rewarding the bird with a set of well-made *pishton,* thick corn tortillas, the older women would stretch out their shawls under the birds as they greedily tore the tortillas to bits, eating only a few pieces.

The highly prized remains of the tortilla that rained into their shawls would be taken home to the mother's hut, toasted hard over a fire on a clay griddle, then ground to dust on the grinding stone.

The resulting flour was then mixed with the Waters of Confidence and cooked into a thin porridge. This was fed to the babies when they began to teethe in hopes that the child would magically ingest the parrot's enthusiasm, manifesting her ability with speech, enabling him to begin early making the sounds of the ancestral tongue.

Wild parrots out in the rain forest and the half-domesticated macaws, conures, and Amazon parrots of the village actually eat very little of whatever they try to sink their adamantine beaks into. This is not wasteful or neurotic behavior, this is how parrots are meant to be. Watching from the sky, these flashy birds follow the pattern of the maturing fruits and seeds from area to area, descending in earsplitting hordes upon the ripened sweet-smelling trees, violently devouring and dropping to the forest floor ten times more than they actually eat.

Because of this rain of fruit and seeds, other animals like tapirs, *tepeizcuintes,* deer, peccaries, and many ground birds follow the parrot flocks around, keeping one eye up and their ears alert for the mad raucous feasting of the birds. Once they have located the flock, they consume the seeds and broken fruits piled at the roots of the trees that the parrots have harvested for them from the otherwise inaccessible umbrella of the forest.

Some of the hard jungle seeds the parrots throw down are eaten by tapirs and peccaries and don't digest but just get broken or scarred enough to actually begin sprouting in piles of their manure distributed throughout the forest. Only in this way do certain of the biggest and most magnificent types of trees get their start.

The meat-eating jaguars, pumas, ocelots, weasels, margays, jaguarundies, owls, hawks, and tayras follow the parrots too, as they in turn stalk and harvest the fruit-eating vegetarian animals gathered in oblivious mobs at the base of trees, chomping glassy-eyed and delirious on the scattered piles of sweet debris. Then the vultures, coyotes, lizards, and other scavengers follow them for the meat left behind.

For this reason the parrot, the animal that speaks, was seen as a provider, a parent animal who teaches speech, feeds all the other animals, and instigates the replanting of the fruiting trees, all at one time. Really the old Hill Goddess, masked in the form of a parrot, it is She we address and give an offering to every time we eat any food that comes from the wilds. One of the main deities of things that are wild, She is also the first one who taught humans to speak beautifully, to dance, and to make ritual. Her name is Ixoc Juyu, Ixoc Taq'aj, Woman Hill, Woman Valley, and She is also known as the *Rilaj Vinaaq*, Venerable Being, i.e., old woman.

Human mothers wanted the Parrot Women and the Moon to teach their children speech. Speech came from nature, and to speak and express oneself was the nature of a human. Our compound had three parrots, which all belonged to me. The little redheaded one was a cringing irascible little ball of beautiful feathers who spent most of her days snuggled up with the yellow-headed parrot, a chubby sweet old beast. Neither the yellow one nor the redheaded one ever spoke more than a croak or a squawk, intimidated and dominated as they were by the size and genius of my big solid-green parrot, whose mean old black beak could sing, whistle, and speak with the clarity of a boarding school rector.

My mother-in-law loved the bird and named her after her oldest daughter, my wife, for reasons too cruel and extensive to explain. Ya Lur was famous far and wide, and highly coveted by the villagers for the astounding fact that, unlike most parrots, she was trilingual and had a memory like a recording machine.

In our compound she'd become invaluable, ending up as a kind of secretarial answering service or voice mail. If our compound had been left deserted for any time at all, Ya Lur the parrot could be counted on toward evening to replay all the conversations that had taken place inside our walls and without.

Whenever anyone came over while we were gone, they would just go up to the old bird and say what they'd come for, and sooner or later Ya Lur would sing it out, usually in the middle of our evening dinner. The message would be mixed in with playbacks of women walking past our compound arguing about the prices of tomatoes, complaining about their neighbors, the quality of a kind of rope, or the scarcity of fish. The parrot would repeat any gossip whatsoever, playing back conversations in their every detail, redoing the dialogue using different silly parrot voices for each person.

She delighted all of us bone-weary returnees from the mountains, lakes, markets, ceremonies, or from seeing a sick client as we ate our afternoon meal. She'd even imitate our laughter during her fine performances, repeating in turn even what we said about that. She was an auditory mirror.

Then as our Father the Sun disappeared behind the Elbow of the Earth volcano, she would sign off every night, in the voice of an old lady, with a brilliantly composed song synthesized from six or seven other songs, silly and heartwarming. She'd keep this up until the world was dark, which silences all parrots.

For several years she'd been my companion on the road, long before I'd come to Santiago. In a rowdy market on the coast I'd caught her as a ball of fluff, orphaned, starved, and half-stunned after having been whacked like a baseball through the air by a broom-swinging, aging prostitute who wanted to shut the poor hungry bird up.

Positive she was dead, I stuffed the little fluff ball in my shirt as I walked away from the insults of her drunken owner, only to find the sad parrot struggling for shelter into my armpit half an hour later. I raised her into adulthood and she grew to be an oversized plain green Guatemalan parrot with no fancy markings, a plain black beak and a big talkative ugly tongue.

A jade-feathered glutton, obstreperous and self-centered, she trusted no one except myself to pick her up without snipping off a finger or sinking her wicked hooked beak as deep as it would go, then backing off, flapping her wings, bobbing her head and dancing.

The heavy traffic of Scat Mulaj officials, shamans, and midwives in our compound meant that Ya Lur witnessed some significant rituals and had mastered some well spoken archaic prayers. Many famous speakers and important elders had sidled through the rock threshold of our stone walls into our family grouping of huts and they, in their great understanding of things, would address the amazing bird as they would a person. It wasn't long before Ya Lur, my parrot, could make replies according to age, gender, and village rank. This delighted many of my old mentors, the hierarchy members, and especially old Chiv, all of whom were great supporters of the belief that their tribal prophets and Holy People would often return to this world as certain animals.

These people came to regard Ya Lur's speech as meaningful, mysterious, and coming from the world of the Deities. Whenever old people came to visit, they would listen for any prophetic outpourings our parrot might reward them with; and before they'd leave many would ask the bird a question, hoping to receive an answer in their dreams. Many decisions were shaped by Ya Lur's verbosity and her dream appearances.

The old ruined temple village across the bay from Santiago was known anciently as Tziquin Jay or "Bird Temple," and by the villagers as Chitinamit, the "Place of the People." All our huts and homes were huddled on the edge of our Mother the Lake at the base of three steep volcanic mountains, known to have been the original trunks from the trees of life in the time before this creation. Through farming and gathering, these heavily forested "Thrones of the Clouds," these volcanic tree trunks, showered us with corn, pumpkins, squashes, melons, avocados, natural cotton, *jocotes, zapotes, zunzas, cuxin,* thirty varieties of beans, wild greens, *malanga, camotes,* yuca, a million types of medicinal plants, woods, fuel, wild meat, stone, minerals, flowers, and fibers.

Just like the herds of deer, peccaries and *tepeizcuintes* who huddled hungry at the deep spaghetti-veined bases of giant rain forest trees to receive the bounty that the parrots threw down to them, we too gathered at the base of our mountain's trunk for a similar bounty.

Like the jaguars and mountain lions who hunted the deer and peccaries, Death hunted the Tzutujil, taking people every week through sickness, drowning, farming accidents, snakebites, landslides and so on. But recently a new kind of predatory being had come among us, stalking and attacking though, mysteriously, not trying to kill us or steal our hard-earned goods. The people of the Canyon Village were being subjected to raids on their souls, raids by marauding bands of white missionaries who prowled around our village armed with poor Spanish and clumsier Mayan. These missionaries exploited the courteous inclusiveness and general respect the village had for anything sacred to get themselves invited into the matrix of a household.

Once there, they began to lay eggs of self-doubt and shame. By diminishing our ways and Gods, trivializing what to us was big and important, the missionaries tried to demoralize the villagers in hopes of scaring or coaxing them into the sticky addictive web of simplistic polarized Eurocentric thinking characteristic of certain missions from the outside, mostly the U.S. These invaders called themselves Christians.

Like shoe salesmen trying to sell shoes to people who traditionally go barefoot, in order to sell their God they had to create a need for it. This was not an easy job considering how the Tzutujil had married their old Goddesses to the sixteenth-century saints, and the love they had for the beautiful year-long cycle of sacred rituals already in place for centuries.

The missionaries' religion looked so dry and unappealing that most people felt sorry for them. As a matter of fact, we used to invite them out of pity to our "pagan" feasts to bless them and feed them.

This, of course, was before they began threatening us with their hell.

Wherever these missionaries came from was already culturally bankrupt, so they needed to tap into the Indians' centuries-old spiritual exuberance in order to revitalize their dried-up imaginations and boring religion. In their narrow-mindedness they branded all shamans and the Scat Mulaj as archenemies of their God. Having mistaken us for some opposing organized religion, they were sure we were barring their way to successfully missionize the village. The people were taught that they must denounce us shamans and get rid of the Scat Mulaj in order to get to heaven, or they would all burn in their version of hell with us village officials.

This worried the women in particular, who, like a flock of waterbirds, chattered nervously about it when they gathered to wash their clothes at the lake's edge. The shamans and Scat Mulaj, however, were more like quiet old trees and shy ocelots who sat watching from afar as the missionaries made themselves frantic by the same fear they peddled, running in senseless circles, out of their element, like nervous machine-dependent mice, insisting we be like them and exchange our rich heritage and real beauty for the superficial values, simple-mindedness, and panic of their grumpy God. To become friends with them meant that we had to stop loving the Sun as our Father, that we could no longer weep into the Lake as our Mother, no longer greet the Fire as our Grandfather, and force ourselves to forget to take our hats off to the rising Moon, the Grandmother of all life and things. The Female had no place in their religion.

At first we didn't pay much attention to their presence. The evangelizers were considered just another mysterious kind of irritation, like those jungle crickets whose incessant whistling won't let you sleep all night, and for which there is no remedy except toleration. So tolerate we did.

But because the shamans and the Scat Mulaj tolerated the foreign invasion and watched without buying into their religion, the traditionals were feared even more by the Christians. Finally the missionaries stepped up their war by setting up film screens in the middle of town and showing horrific scenes of hellfire made with Hollywood special effects. The trauma and panic generated in the villagers, who had never seen a movie or a television, made the missionaries smile as their ranks grew overnight, filled with terrified villagers. These converts were told that they wouldn't have to experience that kind of suffering if they joined the Christians' ranks and denounced their old spiritual way of life. By having actual images of that hard place in their possession, missionaries had proven to the villagers that hellfire existed.

As if that weren't enough, one day, and then on a regular basis for some months to come, we were attacked from the air by other missionaries who began flying low and slowly over the village in little single-engine planes. Loudspeakers were mounted on their wings and they played loud obnoxious foreign Bible tunes on top of which an aerial preacher screamed and crackled his sermons, once again promising heaven to those who converted and eternal hell to those who continued in their "backward" traditions. To show their compliance to his god, the people were asked to run out of their huts and signal the flying preachers by flashing mirrors.

To the Tzutujil, flashing mirrors is an enormous taboo against the Sun, and all those who did so that day would truly have showed that they'd left their respect for their gods behind. That time, however, the only things people were flashing at the airplane were their machetes, angry at the life-disturbing noise.

The people were harassed and harangued as never before, but we never retaliated. This was partly on account of the fact that missionaries were ignorant, having no idea of what they were destroying. But it was also because the politics in that area were so complex and closely intertwined with foreign religion that any negative reaction from the Mayan people would have only served to reinforce the Christians' allegations of "Native" ignorance and a need for these missionaries' God. This would have legitimized their platform and probably inspired them to step up their efforts.

The truth is, we all had work to do feeding our families, and those of us concerned with ritually keeping the Flowering Earth alive were busy doing just that. By keeping the spirits alive we benefited everyone, including the presumptuous preachers, who really had no notion of what gave them life or their complicity with what took it away.

We had no idea of what to do, unaware as we were that the many different missions hated each other and competed for their quota of souls and converts. What they all had in common was a prime initiative to demonize the ancient deities, old saints, and traditional values of the Tzutujil, especially the village initiations and feasts, which needed total village participation, causing a wonderful interdependency between people and calling on their creativity and love of the sacred. This interdependency created by the initiations was the spiritual skeleton of the Tzutujil people, and once it was crushed and disassembled, the missionaries could easily offer the people hope in the resulting despair and confusion that the missionaries helped create. We had no way of imagining how sick these God vendors really were. We figured they were like orphaned children who'd never known a home and just needed a place to play it all out and then they'd settle down or go away.

We were wrong.

My parrot knew all about it and she had her own ideas about what to do. This fat, mischievous, shiny green bird had learned to equate the way a person spoke by the way he dressed and moved. Because of this, she appeared to be able to speak at least three separate languages: Tzutujil, Spanish, and missionary English.

When village people came to visit, they always dressed tribally and addressed Ya Lur in their native Mayan Tzutujil language. When Ladino or non-Mayan Guatemalans visited us, they wore their Western-style clothing and inevitably spoke to my parrot in the animated friendly Spanish of highland Guatemala. For the most part the only English speakers whom we found in our compound were tall American missionaries who wore short-sleeved white shirts, ties, and slacks, had short hair and shiny shoes, and carried their reading materials with them. Ya Lur got to the point where she could distinguish the different types of people and say things to them that other people dressed that way had said to her on a previous occasion. It was very magical how she put it all together.

Whenever a crew of evangelical missionaries forced themselves into our compound, to break the ice they would often go pester my three suspicious parrots, greeting them in English. Then they would turn to whoever was unfortunate enough to be in the compound and proceed to deliver their evangelizing harangue in what can only be described as kind of Tarzanic approximation of some Mayan language.

If you'd seen the look in her wicked little eyes, you could tell Ya Lur, the parrot, had been planning it for months. Finally the day arrived when she decided to have the first word. I remember that day well. Most of the men in our group of huts were still out. My father-in-law and I had just returned sweating and tired and, after hanging up our burden nets, we were about to begin winnowing a large basket of *sip kinaaq* we'd brought from the wilds. *Sip kinaaq* was a very large bean that could not be cultivated. It had a beautiful gigantic red-orange flower, and when you first harvested them, different beans were spotted with different colors, some red, others purple, some yellow, others pink, and yet others maroon. When they dried they all had a kind of lovely black-and-white pattern like a paint horse. They were the archaic parents of all domesticated beans and very highly prized by all Mayans, traditionalist or not.

Most of the women in the compound were dyeing thread; my mother-in-law was warping a loom for my sister-in-law; and my wife was washing Jorge's little wiggling bottom. All the ladies had their shawls doubled over their heads for shade.

Right at that moment in the middle of the afternoon, two white-shirted, Bible-toting, soul-hunting, gigantic young missionaries slumped into our compound. Before either of them could manage to get a word out, Ya Lur the parrot oozed a loud, perfectly drawled, west Texas "Ha, haow or yeeoo?" Then without so much as a break to let it sink in that this was a bird speaking, she proceeded to deliver, to their drop-jawed amazement, a comical, spirited rendition of one of the missionaries' own hackneyed sermons in the worst imaginable bad Oklahoma-accented Mayan. She went on and on about us backward Indians, how we shouldn't smoke, dance, drink, or eat corn (it was for the animals, don't you know); how we had the wrong gods and were all going to burn in such-and-such a way in you-know-where if we didn't hurry up and get in line with their program, and so on, all of which was directed at the missionaries, who'd intended to deliver the same sermon.

It was a funny little speech, delivered in the parrot's strange high voice, and the missionaries were disarmed. Anything they tried to say that day was drowned out by shrieks of hilarity issuing from their intended congregation of children, ladies and a few men.

Unfortunately this got to be a habit with the crazy parrot. Every time a missionary began to preach in our compound the parrot would talk even louder about God and hell, stopping when the missionaries stopped, starting up when they started. This eventually put most of the missionaries off, causing them to beat a sensible retreat to some hut without a smart-aleck parrot.

Of course, there was one group of proselytizers who wouldn't be deterred and then it was time for our little dog, Morning Star, to go to work. Morning Star was a hero in our compound and somewhat famous throughout our end of the village, not only because he'd survived the unforgiving fangs of three types of highly venomous serpents, two landslides, a couple of floods, and could swim the lake alongside a fully loaded canoe, but because he'd survived all of that while in the act of saving the lives of many of our clan's menfolk. This he did over and over.

He was a tiny little creature, not ten inches to the shoulder from the dust. Morning Star loved his people and was well loved by us all. Like Ya Lur the parrot, he was very ingenious. If a pack of feral dogs, a couple of opossums, or a pile of raccoons decided to maraud the central cooking hut, Morning Star, being so small, would hide behind a tree trunk covered with orchids between my long hut and my in-laws' and bark loudly and crazily as long as he could. By spinning and sprinting furiously back and forth behind the tree, he created the auditory illusion that there were at least two or three fierce unseen canine guardians. This was usually sufficient to send the hungry pirates packing.

If that didn't get them going, then the parrot would team up with Morning Star, shrieking in a totally believable human voice, "*Haht, haht, haht, kishelila ajmun,*" which means "Out, out, out, all of you greedy things, leave at once." Between the parrot scolding and the loyal little dog, we rarely lost any hard-earned tortillas to the hordes of poor homeless street mutts that roamed our then-doorless village.

With the same loyalty, if a missionary refused to be outdone by Ya Lur's sermon, then Morning Star would come to the rescue, growling, spinning, barking and hissing madly, his miniature ferocity faking a loss of control.

Inevitably, the soul-hunting preacher would ask us if the little dog would bite a man of God, and somebody would have to warn him, usually one of the ladies: "You're fine as long as you don't start reading from the Bible!" Which was true, strange as it was. If Morning Star heard the Bible being read out loud in Maya or Spanish, he'd bite those guys right on the ankle, run back, then spin on a dime barking, gallop forward and bite him again, the parrot preaching fire and brimstone all the while.

All the missionaries finally left our family alone after a while, spreading rumors of the great presence of the devil in our compound. But we knew the animals were only defending the flowering heart of our ancestral village and what gave them life.

Having named the parrot after her daughter, my mother-in-law continued her mischievous pattern by naming our orange-feathered rooster after me. Everyone called him Martín. That fierce old cock ran the place, at least at ground level. You could hear him hit the ground with a thud when he dropped out of his perch in our *anona* tree in the rear of our compound. His long ivory-colored spurs sharp and dragging in the dust, his feathers quaking, orange eyes glaring, he'd bound out from behind Grandfather's hut to protect his hens, get more of them and fight anything big, small, or imaginary.

His fame was built on his mysterious origins and from his seeming ability to impart invincible health to his offspring. When I first came to Atitlan, before I was initiated or married, a notorious and highly feared sorcerer whom everyone called Kchimbp, Burned-out Pipe, augmented his income by sidelining as a chicken thief. He'd been one of old Chiv's students years back, but he'd begun to use what he'd learned for evil, and nothing could be done to stop him. Though generally pitied and shamed by the Atitecos, he was nevertheless in great demand by non-Mayan Guatemalan politicians, who were well known for hiring witches to magically kill or disable their opponents.

After losing seven chickens, one turkey, and a pair of wild *trish cum cum* doves I laid an ambush for two nights in a row. I expected to catch a possum but I caught Kchimbp instead with one of my turkeys flapping wildly in his hands.

Naively, I gave him the choice of voluntarily marching around the village announcing his crime in daylight or having me turn him over to the village guards. Always a good talker, a magical talker, he convinced me that he would pay me back in full by bringing me a magic rooster and hen.

I was unable to turn down such an offer, and it wasn't two days later when a strange cross-eyed man showed up holding the two promised birds and cordially handed them over.

A year later a terrible chicken plague raged through the highlands, killing every single rooster and hen in our village of over one hundred thousand chickens. Only my rooster, Martín, and his little black hen survived unscathed, while thousands of chickens began running backward for days, feverish, not eating and finally dying in monstrous piles of birds covered in horrible warts and lesions.

Everybody was helpless as we looked on at the gigantic bonfires of burning birds. When new hens were gradually brought in, the villagers invariably petitioned me to have their hens serviced by my stuck-up red rooster to ensure the survivability of the forthcoming clutch of chicks. This worked, and, after a couple of years, all the village chickens were the work of old Martín the rooster. And he acted like he knew it.

At first it was difficult for some of the young ladies because Ya Lur, my wife, was a very jealous, overly possessive woman with whom you had to watch your wording. Often an attractive village girl would wiggle into our compound with an armload of hens, casually exclaiming, "I brought these to have sex with Martín!" referring, of course, to my rooster.

Besides our three parrots, Morning Star, and the rooster, many other animals lived with us because they were orphaned or maimed or couldn't live in the wild alone. There was Francisco the mouse, held in high regard by all the shamans; Tamandua, my golden-bristled anteater, who hung in the rafters; a little woodpecker with one leg; and a one-eyed elf owl who puttered and strutted like Napoleon.

Above all, the closest to my heart was Aq shik the crane hawk. From the waist up he looked like a small harpy eagle, able to raise and curl his little round head feathers when he was irritated or threatened. From his crotch down his yellow water-wading legs looked for all the world like a night heron's.

He'd been crushed under a felled tree during a log-poaching operation somewhere up north in Guatemala's Peten Rain Forest. Recognizing an opportunity, one of the workers, an enterprising Qekchi Mayan, wrapped the poor bird in a cloth and took him to Guatemala City, where he was trying to peddle him for as much as he'd bring, hopefully before the bird died.

During one of my journeys to that city, known to the Tzutujil as part of the underworld, I was accosted by this man. Seeing how the bird suffered, I bought him for three *quetzales* to either heal and release him or bury him properly. Animals have powerful souls, and some people have powerful animal souls. Without each other they live lonely and sick, but when like meets like they revive and take heart.

The hawk's wings were damaged and he wouldn't eat. Having never seen a hawk like this, I failed to find what he would eat, and he went so long without eating or drinking I was sure he would die soon.

One day, one of my little barefooted eight-year-old brothers-in-law who ran wild with all the others of his age came scurrying over the threshold of my dark sacred house with a larger-than-usual toad to show us all. With all the energy he could muster, the ravenous wounded hawk flip-flopped like a slow bat on his damaged wings over to the boy and stole the fat toad right out of his startled hands. Returning to his perch, gripping the toad in the four talons of one foot, he plopped the poor amphibian belly up and proceeded to devour him, belly to back, bones and all, leaving only the toad's head and skin. The toad's milky medicine on its back and head was toxic, and the hawk knew this.

We became fast friends, the hawk and I, after the toad incident. My little male relatives and their associates were more than happy to hunt down frogs, toads, minnows and the like to supply the beautiful raptor with his meals until he healed and could hunt on his own.

He was a solid charcoal black with one wide white stripe on his tail, and he knew things. The Scat Mulaj were very fond of him, and whenever one of the old fellows would come to visit, he would meet me in my sacred house where the old hawk lived. If someone entered in whose heart resided an impetus to destroy the old traditionalists, the hawk could tell and would turn and shoot them with his messy droppings, driving them away, never missing and never hitting the wrong person.

Though the hawk only ate amphibians and fish, the rooster had no use for the hawk and gave him a wide berth. My bourgeois, group-oriented parrots must have felt a certain kinship with the frogs he ate through their greenness and noisy communal way of life, and were also intimidated by the gentle, unassuming hawk's intense focus and solitary majesty.

When he had fully healed, the big black hawk would soar out of the village, searching the shallows of the surrounding waters for frogs and toads, wading like a crane by day. Then at dusk he'd cruise eaglelike back to my sacred hut where, in his own safe corner of my flower-studded altar, hidden in the aromatic holy fog of copal incense and the smoke of the women's evening cooking fires, he would sleep with the stately gatherings of wood and stone figures of our ancestors, Gods and Saints, head under wing, immune to the bubbling chatter of all the people, the barking of the dogs, the crowing of the rooster, and oblivious to the raucous hysteria of the screaming crew of opinionated parrots who bobbed on their long marimba wood perch outside the short doorway of Grandfather's one-man hut.

GUARDING THE SACRED HOLE

In view of that fact that the old sixteenth-century Spanish colonial Catholic church in Santiago Atitlan was built on top of an even older Tzutujil Maya temple, the Scat Mulaj had over the centuries made various bargains with a variety of Catholic priests who presided over the sanctuary. This truce allowed them to pursue their feeding and renewing of the universe, using the infrastructure of the old temple of time and Earth, which was camouflaged inside the trappings of the church, without interruption from the Catholic officials, who hated our dedication to what they called "outdated idol worshiping."

To fulfill their part of the deal, the hierarchy was required to attend mass on Sunday mornings as well as provide the priest with a royal escort as he walked down the center aisle. Though not one of the old creatures had been baptized, confirmed, or had even received the wafer or the wine, nor was able to repeat the Lord's Prayer, all of them, including myself, now had to attend the weekly mass. Dressed in our finest tailored blankets, tied headcloths, sashes, fancy sandals, and handwoven shirts, we shouldered majestic solid silver staffs, large silver banners, and crosiers, and held a silver-mounted canopy over the priest, arriving at the altar like a medieval procession. In keeping with the Catholic traditions of the times, the old men and women were required to split side to side, into two groups, the men sitting on the left half of the church and the women to the right. Though in all appearances the Scat Mulaj were given the most privileged seats in the old colonial church, the first rows right up near the altar, the Catholics had seated them in front of everyone to verify their attendance, which otherwise would have been pretty thin.

This was all somewhat absurd, as the Scat Mulaj had actually owned the title to the church since the Spanish departed and were sole keepers of the keys to all the little cloisters, rooms, and the iron-barred baptismal in which all the church's silver accoutrements were stored.

But in the interests of preserving the sacred and keeping the village peace, every Sunday we'd poke each other to keep awake during Father Stanley Rother's enormously boring masses, his Oklahoma-accented Latin and un-intelligible Mayan.

Invariably, ten or fifteen of the old hierarchy would doze off. The jazzlike din of their combined snoring and wheezing, echoing off the vaults of the big, crowded, stone church, resembled a whole shoreline of mating bullfrogs and late-night crickets.

During one of those Sunday mornings, just as Ma Xcai, Kindling, that year's headman, was dozing off to Stanley's comforting drone, a commotion echoed up to us from the back of the monstrous old church, tumbling over the congregation and rising up to where we all sat.

After a moment a great yelling and whooping arose from the rear. This was the familiar "*Aj Hai Hai*," the signature war cry of old Chiv. This got everyone standing and turning, moving their heads from side to side to get a little glimpse of wild old Chiviliu climbing the four-story back of the colonial wall like a giant spider monkey.

Stanley was just offering up the wine and the hosts when Chiv made everyone forget what they were there for.

Little children playing in the plaza came running, holding their loosely tied pants and skirts, and every villager in the church scurried to the base of the wall where Chiv, still yelling, scaled the vault by means of small hand-forged iron handles.

"*A Plas, A Plas, kin peta anen ta'*." Francisco, Francisco, I am coming up, he bellowed. He almost slipped off a rung now and then, and the crowd would cry out. But finally, dangling like an old anteater, he managed to pull his ninety-five-year-old body up the sparse ladder and roll out of sight and into the sixteenth-century belfry tower. Everybody began breathing again, their heartbeats back to normal.

No one knew what he was up to, but finally a little girl outside yelled up to him in a sweet singsong voice, "*Ta nak nakanouj chila?*" Grandfather, what are you searching for up there?

"The Prophet, Francisco Sojuel, he gave me a message (in a dream) that I should meet him here in the bell tower for lunch. He said there's a lot of trouble coming our way and he wants to talk directly to me about it."

The old hierarchy smiled knowingly as one. Some of them gazed away toward the altar while others looked at the ground, pretending to be giving attention to mass, amazed at Chiv's divinely inspired interruption. Meanwhile the priest continued unheeded, plowing through mass like the Oklahoma wheat farmers he was descended from.

As there were no more sounds issuing forth from the belfry, the crowd, now calmed, had turned back to face the altar when all at once the bells began swinging and clanking like mad, with Chiv yelling out in between. Chiv's head must have been aching because the force of those bells point-blank could have knocked the molars out of a cow's head.

Nothing could be heard over the roar and jangle Chiv had started up there above us, and pretty soon even Stanley had to give in and stop his service. Chiv, smiling to himself, climbed down the wall, this time for sure almost slipping to his death. But he made it to the slick old stone floor where we grabbed him so he wouldn't teeter over. All he said was, "I guess something important came up and the Prophet couldn't make it for lunch."

Throwing his red headcloth regally around his neck and shoulders, adjusting his fine wide-brimmed black felt hat, Chiv said good-bye and thanks to all and stalked nobly off down the front steps, where he turned and knelt outside, praying back to the Hole inside the church, and then disappeared into the thick clouds of boiling dust that rode the dry season wind that day. There would be no meeting of the Scat Mulaj after mass, as the north wind was too fierce and held the land that day. You could hardly stand up in the gale, never mind hear what anyone had to say.

Once the mass was over, in love with pomp and spirit, we usually marched the priest back to the baptismal, locked up the silver and handed the keys to Ma Xcai. On regular days we repaired outside the church to the old stone benches where we held court. Here decisions were made, arguments were settled, problems discussed, and whatever had to be done to keep the Earth alive was considered and put into action. Sitting lined up against the white-washed stone at the summit of the fanned-out delta of temple stairs, the old people of the Scat Mulaj smoked and waited for the first order of business.

The Tzutujil elders weren't undemocratic. They listened to each villager's complaint or questions one at a time. A large part of what the old Scat Mulaj chiefs and Tixelí did with their time during the many intermediate meetings they held in front of this old temple was simply to listen. If you added it all up, they listened a great deal more than they spoke because they knew that most people's problems were just part of life and would never be finished or solved by human invention.

When living simply, most people's problems were part of the breathing and functioning of the Big Picture of life, for which few humans, if any, had a large enough vision or imagination to comprehend. By trying to fix or remedy what people envisioned as the injustices and setbacks in their lives, they usually compounded the situation, making a bigger problem for somebody else in the future.

The Scat Mulaj in their initiated calm knew that there was no cure for the unfairness and hardship in any human's life. To the Tzutujil, people were not put into this world to have a good time; they were put here to be beautiful. In our esoteric prayers humans were called *ruq'op ruchiuleu,* the "earspools, the jewels of the Earth." Our happiness fed the Gods, but our suffering did as well. The Gods were not interested in alleviating our pain but they were interested in furthering our existence if we made life shine with our human creativity.

This is not to say that the zany old people didn't have ways of dealing with village problems, because they certainly did, but whatever they came up with was masterfully engineered to keep suffering from escalating into mass depression and violence by making sure the village grieved for any person's difficulties. Being heard by the elders and the village at large didn't fix anything, but it made life bearable because we were together, in love with the adventure of our tiny collective relevance to the hungry universe.

Being allowed to grieve in a public way and have the sympathy of your village insured that the hungry ghosts of past transgressions could not take over the lives of the villagers. This prevented feuds that would otherwise escalate into war, and sadness that could become life-threatening sickness.

However, when people had a serious difficulty that threatened the safety of the village as a whole, then all the council would leap to their feet, blankets flapping, eyeballs rolling, eyes bulging and squinting, faces wrinkling, some cocked to one side, jaws moving and tongues clucking. Everyone had an opinion, and they all talked at once to everybody they could see to the front, side, back, or far away. Miraculously, everyone listened to everybody else simultaneously, pointing and gesticulating, pouncing forward, pacing, jumping up and down, yelling, laughing, or preaching in a low oratory.

Amazing and insane, the roar of such a meeting was like a plane taking off. Just as quickly as it began, it stopped, everyone having understood and been heard simultaneously. And in the second of silence it took everybody to sit back down, and calmly go back to smoking and waiting for the next issue, the headman would state matter-of-factly, "That's decided then," and the royal crowd would grunt in affirmation. Then the next issue would be presented.

At first I couldn't understand how anything got heard or what plan had been adopted. Sometimes I was not even aware of what was being argued about, and I never comprehended the outcome. Gradually, however, I too became a participant in the word orgy of the decision making and learned to hear as I was being heard. It was a most gratifying experience to merge into the oneness of diversity of the village mind where all opinions and ideas mattered and all went into a distillation process run by chaos, humor, and God, from which a strong policy emerged that was understood by most. Those who didn't understand soon did, as the policy passed into action.

There was an inner-sanctum aspect to this form of decision making, and anyone not initiated into it could not hope to participate, though the meetings were open to the village. Tourists and anthropologists who witnessed these uproars mistook them for feuds or arguments but were mystified when the hubub stopped on a dime and took up again at different times and intensities.

I loved flapping and yelling and listening all at once, then stopping and starting again. It was a difficult, ancient art developed by an undepressed people who were not so impressed with human needs, but in love with the need to be human.

Sometimes when two warring families brought an old serious quarrel to the old council of the Scat Mulaj, the Scat would take arbitrary sides and argue with great conviction about absurd subjects of which they had little or no interest. Once a furious old lady and an angry man presented their case in regard to a decrepit avocado tree. The Mayans invented the eating of avocados and the Tzutujil alone grew over thirty varieties, not to mention uncountable varieties of delicious wild types.

This lady had an old avocado tree planted by her grandfather that over the years had branched over her neighbor's jumbled stone wall. Oddly, the tree made fruit only on the branches that drooped onto the old man's land. The old man harvested all the avocados and claimed that since the land where they were collected was his, the buttery product of the tree had favored him and belonged to him alone.

The old lady objected, saying that the tree grew on her land, was planted by her grandfather, and therefore the avocados were hers.

The old people listened patiently as each side of the argument was presented and then, like a band of wild howler monkeys meeting a large flock of parrots, they began to scream and argue among themselves regarding these two people's avocados. The crazy argument raged on and on. It incremented beyond loud discussion to the verge of mass violence where almost two hundred barely interested hierarchy officials were at each other's throats over a bushel of avocados. Finally the originators of the fight tried to calm the hierarchy, some of whom had sent for their axes to cut down the tree!

When the old lady and old man finally succeeded in getting the council back onto their stone benches, the whole village started to roar with laughter at how stupid it all was and then the leaders spoke: "I fine you a turkey, Grandmother, give it to your neighbor. You, Father, cook that turkey and feed that old woman half and give the rest to your children. Then both of you sweat in your *touj* to remake you as neighbors again. Find out what ghost has made you enemies."

Though stubbornly hopeful, the traditionalists of Canyon Village were beleaguered by numerous forces that came in upon them to suckle the cultural richness of Atitlan. Many of these outside forces came plowing in like slow penetrating winds, winds of rationalism and spiritual doubt that left the people feeling increasingly unsure of who they were, and left the youth more and more sure that their elders were simple and ignorant.

Besides the constant pressure of certain political entities and missionaries, whose policies were obvious and potentially the most powerful dismantlers of Tzutujil culture and spiritual intelligence, there were other dangers. The deep effects of the daily swarms of tourists who inundated the village like hungry locusts can never be underestimated. There was an implied curse in being looked at as a dead object by unknown people who never really wanted to know you. Most tourists regarded our village as an interesting prop in a world observed externally—like a TV program. Mayans, like other peoples and places throughout the world, were there as curious entertainment, something simple and lesser than the tourist's strange, synthetic, machine-made way of life.

All people understand well the difference between being visited and being "touristed." After having been visited by people who want to know you, you feel good about yourself when they leave to go home. However, after having been touristed by outsiders, you feel hollow and spiritually robbed.

Every day, just before midday, a loud blast from a large tourist boat would echo off the compound walls, church buttresses, and through the crowds in the open market. The boat would dock at the bottom of Chinimya', the great gate would open, and up they'd surge, huffing and puffing their way up to the entrance hill behind their guides, straight to the huge colonial stone church. Often the Scat Mulaj would be in session out front, seated on our stone benches and making decisions about one ritual or the next. Mostly Americans and Northern Europeans, these tourists looked like strange, gigantic pink shrews covered with hanging cameras and Gore-Tex. Their small pale eyes were scary and sometimes friendly, but always powerful and incomprehensible. Babbling and cackling, they usually marched straight into our meeting as if we were some kind of furniture, maybe part of the walls, a distant landscape put there on the set for their viewing enjoyment.

The tourists were completely unaware that what to them was just a pile of poor wrinkled Indians was, in fact, a whole magnificent gathering of queens and kings, a knowledgeable royalty who actually knew holiness and God personally as one knew a neighbor.

The Scat Mulaj would not be convinced that every tourist didn't come from a single nation of tourists, who all spoke the same language called Tourist. To them English, German, Japanese, Arabic, Italian, and Finnish were all mutually intelligible dialects of Tourist. I, unfortunately, had shown my ability to speak Tourist when some years back I was asked by the headman to talk a shouting, abusive couple from New Jersey into not taking pictures of a ritual with Holy Boy, which in those times was never allowed to be photographed.

From then on I was the official interpreter and go-between for the Scat Mulaj when dealing with anybody not from Atitlan. It was so obvious to them that Atitlan was the only real place in the world. Everywhere else was Tourist Land and all Tourists, of course, wanted to visit the Center of the World, which is where we lived.

It's strange how modern cultures spend so much trying to make the rest of the world look and act as they do. When they go touristing they consider everything that looks like them, but acts differently, as an insult to their narrow-minded image of purity, a purity their very presence tends to destroy. The Tzutujil didn't care what color my hair was, just how well I could play the flute, joke, translate Tourist, and feed God.

Many tourists were fine until they saw me in my finely embroidered, bird-covered knee pants and hand-woven shirt. The self-hatred that many tourists brought with them became visible when they scolded the old people of the village for allowing me, who sort of looked like the tourists, to adulterate the integrity of their tribal look. The Tzutujil Maya, however, were not concerned about how they looked to each other, but rather how they looked to the Gods. The Gods are fed by our true contents, that inner kernel of regularness that prepared its flower hidden under the beautiful husklike clothing of our village identity.

By taking pictures of themselves standing next to what their own culture had shunned and forgotten, the tourists tried to fill their own hollowness. Their people had long ago traded their ability to live square on the earth for the coddled comfort of the uninitiated. Throwing away what they now tried to steal from us, the price paid for their tribeless unconnectedness and personal freedom was depression and neurosis. The old people would huddle up around the tourists to convince them of how honored they should be to have a Tourist talker like me to help them keep the whole world alive, in the umbilicus village of the universe, which was the only reason any of the tourists were actually alive. Of course, since I was both the interpreter and the criminal on trial, it all ended up as a typical Tzutujil shouting match, what the old people thought was a good decision session. All the black-blanketed old guys, who only came up to the tall terrified tourists' chests, mobbed them. Everyone talked at once, gesticulating and poking the tourists on their chests, nodding their heads and inviting them to come drink and discuss. But all of this scared the tourists, who couldn't understand a word, and probably thought we were preparing to eat them anyway. At this point the tourists usually ran away with their guide, anxious to board their big old boat and get to a more relaxed village where the natives weren't as interesting or weren't as interested in the tourists.

But there were always more and more tourists every day and more opportunities for the village to develop theories on who these tourists really were. One man, Ma Sicoy, The Finder, one of the greatest Tzutujil thinkers of our day, seemed to have figured it out.

A sacred house chief in charge of all the powers of Little—little children, little animals, little plants, everything small and young—Ma Sicoy would become a great headman two years later. Atypically, he was also a fine shaman and a repentant sorcerer, and tall for a Tzutujil man.

All Mayans are curious philosophers, but Ma Sicoy was a very focused folk logician. He was our Bertrand Russell. His littlest grandson Chat, Bed, was a husky nine-year-old who always sat at the chiefs' knees during all the meetings. It was common for little children to come with their grandparents to the sessions. Though we didn't believe all of what Sicoy thought up, we always listened to every morsel because he was so brilliant.

This time he'd stolen an idea that had become a very common belief among all the women of Santiago. The women, as everyone knows, were always more logical than the men because they tended to deduce their answers from a question rather than enforce a conclusion from an unquestioned fact as we men generally did.

For a whole generation now, the women had thought that the tourists who came on the boats were not people at all but were really the Spirits of the Dead. Being dead to the Maya people was not a disgrace but a very holy thing, and being dead was an eventuality we all had to look forward to. The Maya, who had no term for absolute nothingness or vacuum, considered living to be constituted of at least 50 percent death. Therefore, being alive couldn't be assumed or taken for granted; it had to be worked at.

Anyway, one day when Ma Sicoy was expounding on his new deductions in a meeting in front of the old Temple, he asked all of the gathered hierarchy, "Have you ever seen a Tourist die?"

A lot of grunts to the negative went around the crowd, who all leaned forward on their canes, craning to hear our great theoretician.

"No, that's because they're already dead," Ma Sicoy said. "So, why would the dead die?"

That was true, we all had to agree.

"Now, how many of you have ever seen a Tourist eat, even a crumb of one corn cake, a soup of soaked peppers, or a piece of poor dried fish?"

Everyone grunted in amazed agreement, myself included, because the tourists were so afraid of eating anything from the hands of these Indians and getting sick that they never really ate, except in their hotels somewhere.

"Listen, don't you see how pale they are? Even their eyes are paler than Martín's, and the dead are a pale bunch, right?"

"*Jie,*" we all yelled in agreement, starting to see his point.

"What about this, did you ever see one of them get cold? You know perfectly well a lot of them take off all of their clothing in the middle of the cold season, jump in the lake, and swim, laughing, while the rest of our people shiver wrapped in blankets against the cold by their cooking fires. This means it must be true what the old women say, that the Tourists don't have blood like the rest of us, but have ice blood!"

A general commotion ran though the collected officials, who were now pretty convinced.

"Besides which, how many of us have ever seen a tourist work or do anything to support himself, and yet they never run out of money. We all know that the metallic wealth of the world comes from the other worlds where the dead were, and these creatures have an endless supply. Did you hear them say that they come from the other side of the water, the ocean, on the backs of flying iron? And, like the dead, they disappear every day before dark. We all know that the dead must return to their world by dark."

On and on Ma Sicoy went, proving to us beyond a doubt how all these herds of irritating, interesting tourists were really beings from the next layer of existence who were dead and now came back to visit the real Earth here in Santiago Atitlan. Never mind that the tourists worked the rest of the year to have enough money to visit or that their boat only allowed them two hours in the village in fear of the Tzutujils' notorious reputation for having a fickle attitude toward outsiders. Nobody knew that people from Minnesota or Denmark thought Guatemala was a tropical country, or realized that the water was warm to them compared to the icebergs and subzero weather of their homeland. When I tried to explain all this, however, it did nothing but reinforce the idea that where these people came from really was the land of the dead, because who else would or could live in a place covered in frozen water in such cold?

That was it. Everyone was convinced. Tourists were dead people.

The word spread throughout the village and was tasted and savored, and, like a new crop of corn, everyone added and developed his or her own variations on the main concept. But the question that was uppermost in everybody's minds was, "Whose dead are these people?"

Chat, Ma Sicoy's chubby grandson who'd sat through the whole exposé and who'd become as much a thinker as his inspired grandfather, came up with his own theory. It wasn't long before, holding his own important meetings with little tykes his own age in imitation of his grandfather, he began to explain how not only were the tourists dead beings from the other world, but that they were actually the Mayans' own ancestors. Everybody knew that when you died you went to the next layer of life, where you were given a new body and a different look. There, everything was the opposite of this world.

So, these Tourists were really our own people who had lived here before us. And like us who, when we are born, forget where we come from and are blessed with a natural amnesia of our origins, they had to go about trying to remember spiritually who they were and where they came from. Therefore, Chat reasoned, these tourists must be born forgetful just like the people living in the village. Because their form had changed, no one recognized them, but something inside them drove them to come back to us to visit their origins. To them we must be a dream, and like us when we dreamt and went to visit the worlds before us where we used to live, these dead came into our world in a dream.

If, as everyone always said, the dead were the opposite of those living here, wouldn't that mean that the Tourists' language would be Mayan spoken in reverse?

It had long been thought that those tourists who spoke English were really speaking Mayan backwards because of the similarities of sounds. With these new deductions it all began to make great sense. Soon it was declared a fact and spread throughout the children's gossip grapevine like a taste for sugar.

All over the village and under trees in the various compounds, little bush colleges came together in which older girls and boys would concentrate on teaching their younger siblings how to talk Tourist by speaking backwards.

In Maya there was no real word for "tourist," so they used the Spanish word, *Turista*. Most of the kids who were interested were of the age where they were missing their front teeth and so the word *Turista* came out *Choriza,* which in Spanish means sausage. The little kids practiced speaking "sausage" every day for weeks until a group constituting the cream of the most adept at backwards-talking emerged from the crowds of little people who had applied themselves to the challenge. It was bizarre and dreamlike to see whole tight lines of little potbellied youngsters talking Tourist as they walked the village streets. Some of them could tell whole stories backwards, and the most impressive part was that the rest of the kids could understand them. Stranger still was the fact that they did sort of sound like someone talking English in a Romanian accent with his mouth full.

When the tourists came to town, the little kids with their spinning tops and beeswax discs would be sent by the older kids, like scouts, to creep within earshot of the tourists and listen to what they said. After memorizing a line they'd run back from the lake and report their findings to the most professional speaker who, in all his or her great knowledge, would figure out the meaning by running the sounds forward again into Tzutujil.

During one of these reconnaissance missions, a small girl heard a tourist lady speaking to her husband while trying to buy something from the village women selling their weaving: "Gosh dang, hun, it's a shame!"

The girl child ran back like a little quail, her copper face sweating, and, out of breath, blurted it out to the waiting crowd of young experts before she forgot. Her twelve-year-old elders determined that if they turned it around and said the words backwards they came out roughly as *"Mash stina' ajni at chaq,"* which means in Tzutujil, "Tomás will feel how fat you've become!"

Amazed and utterly convinced now, the lakeside classes of tykes began planning an earnest conversation with the tourists. They practiced for weeks until a day was chosen, D day, on which several of the bravest and best backwards-Tourist talkers were hand-picked by their ten- and twelve-year-old speech captains. After a great deal of Mayan-style chaotic discussion, it was decided that the chosen commandos would, at a signal, run up to a group of disembarking tourists and yell very clearly a certain phrase in backwards Mayan to see if they could begin to communicate with their strange pink ancestors.

When The Day arrived, the urchins gathered together sitting on their haunches in a jumbled row, their tattered handwoven shirts, patched frizzy blouses, baggy knee pants and skirts flapping in the brisk morning breeze. With running noses, their big brown eyes fixed at a distance over the lake, they waited at the top of the hill at whose base the tourist boats were known to land. To control their nervousness they practiced talking backwards over and over, whispering under their breaths.

After what seemed like a whole season, the motorized tub could be heard percolating toward the village out of the steam of the Mother Lake. Terror sank its dull teeth into their tiny brave hearts. One said, "I feel goose bumps." Another stated, "Cold is coming all over me" and "Fright is walking on my back." Another said, "I have to vomit." But they held the line and waited like scared soldiers before a scheduled ambush.

When the boat had gone through its ritual tie-up and the planks went down at the homemade pier, the tourists started waddling up the stone cobbles. The signal was given and down charged two little shave-headed raggedy boys and a fast-trotting, red-skirted girl.

They ran up to the first tourist they met, huge and terrifying, held out their funny little hands, and together yelled in backwards Mayan, *"Kashi halir gab acab ayit,"* which meant when spoken forward, "Give us some of your metal (money), old lady!"

The tourists, delighted by what they took to be a formal Mayan greeting ceremony, pulled out coins and stuck them into the kids' tiny palms, saying, "Thanks," which, when rendered backward into Tzutujil, was "*Sqat*," meaning "We're even," which was always spoken at the conclusion of a business dealing.

The triumphant kids ran back up the hill to their anxious waiting ranks. Jumping up and down, holding their loose pants with one hand and the money in the other, they shrieked with delight, "It works, it works. It's true, they gave us the money and said '*Sqat*'!"

After that every kid in town took turns running up to the tourists and yelling a little backwards Mayan. They all came back with a coin. More ambitious children began laying more extravagant ambushes on whole tour groups, and soon different schools of tourist talking developed.

The tour guides who did speak English, German, French, and so on, and especially those who themselves were Mayans from neighboring villages and spoke a dialect of the same language we did, were really stumped by the children. When their foreign charges asked them what the kids were saying, their eyes would dart anxiously from side to side. They were stunned by the fact that they could still understand the adult Tzutujil but not the kids, who were all of a sudden speaking a whole other language.

"It's all an ancient Tzutujil greeting language," they replied with the alacrity of all tour guides who made up a lot of well-accepted facts. Or they would say, "The kids here are hard to understand, but if we ask their parents they might tell us," and so on.

Highly alarmed, some of the older village women, knowing full well that shamans actually did speak certain incantations backwards to call powerful spiritual beings into this world, beings too strong for little children to handle, petitioned the officials to put a stop to the Tourist talking to keep their children safe.

To the Tzutujil, communication was a powerful ability and oral literacy was a serious study, and the children had gotten ahead of themselves. The talking of Tourist persisted as entertainment in certain households where it was tolerated, and the tourists certainly missed their greeting ritual.

◈

This Tzutujil love of speaking to other worlds was the reason behind their shrines and temples. Mayan temples were not monuments to their Gods;

they were faces where the mouth was a doorway through which humans could feed and give the ritually sacrificed words and human creations of this world back to the spirit; the world that, in turn, fed them.

The Tzutujil people did not concern themselves with building large wooden and stone structures dedicated to their greatness or to the greatness of God, which would still be standing and proclaiming these things when they died. What monuments they did try to leave were a race of descendants who could continue feeding life. Culture was not measured by who had the biggest buildings but by the happiness of its people, and that came from their ability to make ornate gifts for the other world, gifts that decayed and disappeared, consumed by the spirits. There were many places on the earth where these powers of life and these deities could be fed. Extending in every direction out over the earth, in the Inner Bigness of the Universe they formed a huge net of holy places, a net of mouths. Each knot in this net was an actual spot on the earth that we considered to be hollow and hungry, little mouths through which ritual food could be pushed to nourish the universe. This kept the interconnecting lines between each of them, which were time and the bubbling life of the creations, from grinding to a halt of oblivion, truly keeping the whole world fertile and in live movement.

The whole world's net of holy mouths was represented in a smaller, more concrete form, which was spread out through the village like a maze. Each of these sacred hungry knots had been originally marked on the village streets with both wood and stone shafts, and then later, after the Spanish, with stone crosses. By the time I got to the village, the locations of these hungry life-maintaining shrines were known only to certain shamans and the older generations.

When shamans went to the other world or the Scat Mulaj processed through Santiago as a group, we had to maintain a mazelike pattern, stopping at each of the angles in the maze where the old stones had stood, lighting candles and leaving flowers in order to continue to the other worlds.

At the center of the net of sacred mouths was a Hole through which all of creation as we knew it had originally gushed, spreading and growing the mighty net like vines of the far-reaching universe on whose stems the buds and flowers of this creation blossomed into all the lands, plants, weathers, waters, animals, and winds, the veritable tangible reality of this existence.

Out of this Hole had grown and flowered a magnificent vine, and a tree and vine on whose summit perched a gigantic eagle, which some said had two heads, one male and the other female. This original mother tree had flowered and then fruited, covering herself first in diversity. She gave birth and made fruit, of which there were no two alike. Then each fruit of that first flowering seeded itself in the surrounding earth and grew its own vine shoot, or umbilical cord.

Now avocado trees bear only avocados; deer don't give birth to falcons; birds don't hatch avocados. All things exclusively reproduce their own kind. Having achieved diversity, the old vine died back, the old tree dried up, and, over thousands of years, died and rotted into a humus that became the Earth. The vegetal memory of the old tree in its humus continued to fertilize the old tree's dream of diversity through its decay.

The places on this network of vines—the mountains and valleys, springs, oceans, and volcanoes where the first seeds took root, dawned, and sprouted this world into life—were the locations of those hollow knots in the maze of sacred places in the village streets.

Having died back, the vines and trees that bore all life left us with hollow places, mouths that had to be nourished, where trunks had once stood. This nourishment was ritual itself, and ritual fed the deified earth and the network of time carried from each of these old places as spiritual humus, allowing the ancestral roots of all things to absorb enough ritual nutrients to keep the earth alive in the diversified and motion-oriented forms we live in today.

When the Original Trunk and Vine had died back, she left us with the most powerful Hole, mouth, hollow knot of all, right in the center of the universe. Out of this Hole our lives still flow. We the Scat Mulaj fed the world there, and began and ended all our rituals there.

It was a place that made you weep to see. Like the footprint of a God, the nostalgia of the malice-free beauty of the powerful thing that had so exuberantly lived there, and to whom we owed our ability to be here and feel the pain of her loss so deeply, was overwhelming. Most initiated people who understood the enormity of it all simply shed tears there, very adult tears, right into the Hole. Tears of realization and gratitude, the eternal grief of losing the original Mother of all life, made these tears worth a great deal. These kinds of tears were jade beads that she wore in that other world. Our grief at missing the old tree was the shine that the Goddess wore on her neck. That shine was the shine in leaves, the shine on piled-up fruit, the glittering in a puppy's eye, the shine of a young girl's hair in the wind, and the shine of humans understanding such things. A hollow place we had to fill with grief and gifts is all she left of her original place. She was a life-giving memory.

This Hole of the original tree was in the middle of the village around which a small temple had been raised long ago. When the Spaniards built their monument to their God, they built it right over that temple. The Hole was now right in the middle of that church and had miraculously survived there for over four and a half centuries.

Ironically, once a year on Good Friday the old-time Catholics had used the Hole to brace a heavy timber cross two stories tall on which they reenacted the crucifixion of their God-man Christ, with a well-articulated image of Jesus killed. The Mayans saw the cross as the original tree and Jesus as the diverse fruit of that tree, so they covered the dead Jesus at Easter with millions of beautiful flowers so that he was entirely hidden in beauty. When the Catholics lifted him nailed to his tree, the Mayans saw a flowering tree whose fruit was God's-gift-son crucified, whose blood ran down the tree into the Hole to feed the roots of creation.

It was not the original Tzutujil method, but since the Hole was left undisturbed the rest of the year there was no conflict. When the Franciscan fathers saw the hierarchy weeping, praying, placing fire, flowers, liquor, and incense into the Hole throughout the year, they assumed the Indians were venerating the Passion of Christ.

The sacred Hole was about words coming together and about longing, remembrance, and feeding what needed to live. Ma Um, Spider, was the official in charge of this portal. He would hold this position for life or as long as he wanted until he chose to pass the role of guarding and maintaining this Hole onto a shaman with the desire and knowledge. Ritually, we called this Hole the Umbilical Stump of the Earth Fruit and, like the navel on an orange, this spot was the memory of the ancient flowering.

Ma Um told me that anciently four women had been the original custodians of the Hole. Placing their grinding stones flush up against the Hole, each woman would grind amaranth, cacao, chia, and squash seeds to make a fat that was fed to the great beings in the other world. Some of this holy rich fat was then fed to the fire God who distributed it to the other Gods of this world through the Hole. The women also gave the liver and fat of animals to the guardian eagle who lived high up in the temple rafters right above the Hole.

This constant feeding kept the earth and everything female rich and fertile. In those days, the temple had been full of chattering animals and evergreen trees, which all disappeared when the women were forbidden to grind at the Hole by the Spanish Christians. The immortal two-headed eagle that had lived first in the tree and then the temple had been seen personally by a couple of old people I knew, but it mostly kept its distance now.

No one was allowed to look inside the Hole without being initiated. Children, uninitiated youth, and pregnant women (they carried uninitiated children) were kept at a distance, because looking into the Hole was the same as pondering infinity or being struck by a grief at an age when you weren't strong enough to bear it. An uninitiated realization of infinity could cause depression or craziness and could even pull you back into the other world. After all, it was at this same Hole that shamans and the Scat Mulaj came to see, feed, and talk to the other worlds before us, worlds that had unfolded here before we were invented.

Many prophesies were made at the Hole by its priests and these were very much heeded. Most of them have come true in my lifetime. This was accomplished in difficult times by feeding the Hole, weeping into it, and praying the words it wanted to hear after walking the maze of the village satellite mouths, then peering into the Hole. The other worlds would reveal themselves and one could even visit them in all their great beauty.

The Hole churned and blossomed fast because the immensity of all things had their origination concentrated in such a little place, the belly button stump of our world. This is why the Tzutujil call the world Fruit Made of Earth, because all form was considered the fruit of the other world's creation-layered tree.

Once a year, after leaving a gift for the Hole, every family rekindled its snuffed cooking fires and had a candle or a torch lit inside the Hole by the Hole's official. The family would kneel and the official of the Hole would grab all their hands regardless of age and put them under his headcloth, which he had stretched across the opening of the Hole. When their hands emerged, their candle would be on fire. It was a fine thing to have your hands blessed in that old hollow place left by the old tree of life, and to be magically holding in your hands a flame that came from the other world. This flame was called the Fire Flower.

The Spirits saw the fires of such ritual candles and bonfires as the flowers on the original vines. The burning fats, chocolates, candles, and tobaccos we fed these flowers of fire allowed our own lives to burst into fire flowers.

The old Spanish Catholics may have been fooled and possibly even impressed by the sincere faith shown to the Hole but the "New Catholics" of our time understood it as a pagan ritual. These recent Catholic converts, under the direction of an order of modern priests from the U.S., were scandalized by the swelling congregations of their competition, the Protestant Evangelists. Protestantism had become the religion of money, coming in as it did on the backs of foreign interests and a merchandising mentality from the modern world. Catholicism, on the other hand, had been the religion of colonialism, tribute, hierarchy, and farming. Catholicism had already been categorized as unprogressive by the Evangelists, and, not wanting to be left out of the religion race, the New Catholics took it upon themselves to aggressively eradicate every sign of Mayan traditionalism, Catholic image worship, colonial Spanish customs, and anything they saw as an enemy of their new starkly pared-down religion. They killed every ornateness they could find, including the old language of the mass, the cryptically beautiful Latin that none of the Indians understood but loved for its magical sounds.

Because of their misguided zeal and their inability to comprehend the beauty, if not the reality, to which the Scat Mulaj dedicated their lives, these New Catholics in a fit of rage came one day and filled in the Hole to the other world. They filled the emptiness that created longing in us for the old mother tree, the place where we could speak directly to the other world, the place we were still plugged into, receiving spiritual sap.

They filled it to the level of the church floor with hardened American concrete, smoothed it, polished it, and left it the same color as the floor so as to render its location invisible.

When the official in charge of the Hole found out the next morning that the connection between this world and the others had disappeared, every compound in the village knew it before we'd had time to fully awaken.

By the time I'd heard the news, the Catholics had proudly confessed. Infuriated, with tears in my eyes, I marched straight to the church, pushed my way through the teeming throngs around the place where the wonderful Hole had rested and saw for myself the damage done. Returning to the front of the church, I was hysterical with frustration and anger over the death of such a magnificent and ancient uninterrupted connection with the other world. This presumptuous invasion of the Female, the rape of the Mother Hole, had me hopping mad and humiliated and, like the brother of a raped sister, I wanted revenge.

I blurted out my hatreds, fears, and observations to the seated members of the Scat Mulaj, both men and women, who sympathetically nodded and responded quietly, letting my anger run its course as they smoked, squinting, wrinkling their foreheads, sucking in air in horror, grimacing and looking quite concerned.

When I'd run out of breath, realizing that no one was volunteering any more hatred to feed my revenge-oriented thinking, I sat down to catch my breath and waited to see what everybody else thought. The headman Ma Xcai went first: "We sympathize with you and feel bad about it all too. We have all been young before. But the truth is, those Catholics are implacable literalists, and very primitive on top of it all. They're uninitiated; what can you expect of people who won't have their eyes opened? They're little children trying to help their mother's cooking by dropping dust and gravel into the corn dough. You have to be primitive to think you can destroy spirits by burning their images or stopping up the other world with a little mud! Anyway, it's a hole that needs to be dug again and we have chisels and sledgehammers. So, Brothers and Mothers, let's get to work!"

It was amazing to see that with no more than a minimum of attention to what had caused the Hole to plug up, the hierarchy went to it, parading into the big echoing church, their incense pots smoking, their digging bars over their shoulders, hammers and chisels in hand. The women carried buckets and tin cups for the chunks and dust that would come tumbling out of the Hole; the Scat Mulaj, young and old, took off their fancy blankets and head ribbons, rolled up their sleeves, and began praying that they do a good job.

We all helped and, in a little over two hours, the square Hole was back again. The top of the old stone temple beneath the floor was also visible again with its ancient, round, stone, hooplike Hole extending down into the bowels of the other worlds whose singing made our life out of its gurgling symphony.

The Scat Mulaj knew their job on earth was to keep all the avenues of giving and receiving gifts open. This stopping up of the magnificent Hole could just as easily have been caused by a landslide, an earthquake, or a flood. The main thing was to keep it open.

Two weeks later the Hole was again filled with concrete, and again we dug it out, only making it a little bigger this time. Then a week later it had been filled yet again. On and on we went, and back and forth in a battle of determination and wills until a young man had the idea of making a cover for the Hole.

At first there were misgivings on both sides but, in the end, it was decided in the normal way that his idea would be the best way. A cover of old stone was carved by a traditionalist and two little finger-sized holes were drilled in the middle so that it could be lifted out like a bowling ball.

The cover was fitted to set flush with the church floor and looked like a medieval stone drain.

The Scat Mulaj surrounded the Hole cover with flowers every day and kept candles burning on it day and night. When a ritual dictated that we get into the Hole, we simply removed the stone cover with great reverence and prayer, replacing it when we were finished. And with that the Catholics let it all go, as now they could pretend it wasn't there.

ELEVEN

HUSBAND OF THE VILLAGE
BECOMING CHIEF

Anyone visiting Atitlan that afternoon would have heard the raucous beeps and whistles of the male grackles and the deafening chatter of treeloads of birds in whose midst rose an abstract cacophonous barrage of thuds and pops from a mob of small two-sided drums being clubbed in an unholy exuberance by roving bands of *Aguaciles* yelling out messages at the top of their lungs. The insignia of their service hung over one of their shoulders, a shin-length *anona* stick topped with a thick bullwhip affair of old braided leather, which formed a loop that hung away from the wooden staff while its tail and wicked popper coiled around its handle. The whole staff was polished from centuries of use by these young men's parents' ancestors.

At first look, the young men seemed like a combination of well-dressed town criers, a gang of Spanish colonial sheriffs, and a warrior society. They were really the previous year's Tzutujil initiates, young men trying to become men eligible for marriage and a life independent from their parents and childhood. Called the *Aguaciles,* or Auxiliaries, in Spanish, who and what they really were, like all truly Mayan things, was craftily hidden away inside an institution superimposed upon the village during the crush of the power-hungry regimes of Spain and the various permutations of the Guatemalan Republic.

Over the din of their tiny drums, the young men called out in all directions, each in his own way simultaneously announcing an all-important meeting that would be held the next morning in front of the old temple in conjunction with the Scat Mulaj. Over the sound of their rattling drums, the boys' messages were hard to make out. Never ones to be too thoroughly informative, these teenage initiates only hinted at the subject of the town gathering.

> *"Kix jona, nkiwaj ibanic*
> *Ix conjilaal*
> *Ruman, xinbin,*
> *Xintinea*
> *Jie Najbey Mam."*

All of you come, they desire the contents
of your thoughts, all of you.
On account of they have said the office
of the First Grandchild will end.

There were four groups of whip-cracking, well-dressed youth beating drums and announcing this tumultuous news to each of the four major divisions of the village that radiated out from the center plaza, where the boys' thirteen village leaders and overseers, the *Mayori,* sat in an row. Each of these young chiefs was regally attired in the long blankets of his office. Their luxurious headcloths neatly draped over both shoulders, each of the thirteen brandished a long white *anona* fighting staff. In appearance these *Mayori* were similar to the Scat Mulaj, but they were much younger and fiercer looking and of slightly lower rank.

When this year's whip-carrying, noisy *Aguaciles* had finished with their startling proclamation, they returned to the center of the village, to these *Mayori* chiefs whose leader was called the *Najbey Mam,* or First Grandchild.

Normally the *Aguaciles* carried out their required year-long village service as guards and criers in rotating daily shifts so that every one of them had a chance to go home and make a living. This evening, however, the news they were carrying concerned their future and the future of the initiations, so every one of them had been put into service.

It seemed that the village initiations of the youth were under fire and to-morrow a full village meeting would be held. This is what the young men had been called upon to announce to the whole village.

On this evening, like every other before, when the *Aguaciles* arrived back in front of the old colonial government building, they made a huddle. Yelling and whooping, they pulled their reluctant, smiling chiefs into their midst; and off they moved as a group, howling like guard dogs, walking to the cadence of their peccary-skinned drums, chasing off any evil that might hurt the village with their animal beauty, parading down to Panul where the First Chief had his hut, wondering if this would be the last time.

◇

The next morning was sultry, but you could tell a storm was brewing. Two thousand people congregated in front of the church. Those in front relayed back what was being said to those in the rear and, occasionally, someone from the back would elbow his way to the front to make a point.

Sitting off to the left of center with the Scat Mulaj, I tried to keep my seat but found myself jumping up to pace with the rest of the hierarchy, who were in a bind concerning the banishment of the office of *Primer Mayor,* called *Najbey Mam* in Mayan, along with his subchiefs, and the Auxiliaries.

Every Atiteco over the age of twelve knew the history of this controversy, not just the traditionalists. Centuries ago, the Tzutujil people had their complex ceremonialism saved by the *Nawal Achi* and *Nawal Exqui* in a brilliant coup of fierce spiritualism and adaptation. These prophetlike holy Tzutujil men and women of the sixteenth century divined clever ways to hide all their people's ancient rituals, pomp, feasts, and theocracy right inside certain foreign institutions put in place by the various Spanish colonial governments and the successive waves of equally harsh independent non-Indian Guatemalan governments.

Just as the system of ritually feeding time as a place carried by the village Gods, and the feeding of the spirit layers, had been hidden and incorporated into old sixteenth-century Spanish Catholic image worship, so had the two years of initiation tasks and the six weeks of ritual rites of passage for the youth survived fairly intact inside the imposed Spanish civilian military society of the *Primer Mayor.*

Installed during the old colonial period and originally intended to enforce Spanish policy in the region, jail offenders of Spanish law, and secure tribute and taxes due to the king and clergy, the *Aguaciles,* or Auxiliaries, were supposed to be comprised of one male member of each household. The Tzutujil men were drafted to stand guard over the village under the jurisdiction of the *Mayori,* or "Majors," who stood ready to be pulled into the ranks of a regional colonial army in service to the viceroy of Spain in the event of a war.

The Auxiliaries were very rarely called into national service, and most villagers Mayanized the office of the *Mayori* beyond recognition. By the seventeenth century, when the Spanish population in the highlands was in a great decline, the Atitecos had steadily implemented and hidden all their ancient youth initiations under the guise of the village militia. The Auxiliaries and Majors had never been under the jurisdiction of the Church, anyway, and all the Spanish government officials really cared about was that the Auxiliaries guard the *cabildo* where non-Mayan officials sent by the royal government were housed during their occasional inspections. The rest of the time, they were left to their own devices.

Later, after independence from Spain, the Auxiliaries were required to be a constant presence with their Majors, standing well dressed at attention in front of the *cabildo.* This was because the government by then had permanently installed a couple of non-Indian officials in the village. The Auxiliaries were required to serve these officials as escorts, bailiffs, etc. By then the Auxiliaries were made up entirely of initiates, and therefore it was only the young men who were required to fulfill every whim of their would-be overlords in mandatory year-long stints.

The only reason the village lowered itself to this rare instance of obvious servitude and abuse was because, according to the national law, young men who had proof of having served in the Auxiliaries would be exempted from the national conscription, which involved two years in the Guatemalan army. Nobody wanted his child in that particular army. So by going through initiations and serving a stint at guard duty with your nest mates in your own hometown, you avoided leaving your home, family, and sweetheart and entering the soul-destroying experience of being stripped, kicked, and whipped into an anonymous soldier in the service of white officers who themselves served rich landowners.

For this reason even Christian converts and progressive factions in the village stopped short at denouncing the "pagan" rituals of the *Najbey Mam (Mayori),* and the Auxiliary initiates, even when they were hard at work gnawing at the foundations of all other spiritual traditions. Converts even allowed their own boys to participate. All the people could agree on this, that they didn't want their children hauled away from the village into the army.

In the 1960s and 1970s large canvas-covered trucks descended upon Santiago and out of them would leap civilian thugs in the pay of certain military factions. Armed with lead-weighted, two-foot-long rubber hoses, they chased, wrestled, roped, handcuffed, bullied, and beat as many young men under the age of twenty as they could into the trucks, packing them in tighter than cattle. These recruiters always hit the village in the evenings while young men were out dressed up for courting where they could be hunted and more easily snatched. The young men were ransomed off on the spot to their parents and relatives, who often handed over the family's land deeds in return for their son's freedom, thereby further impoverishing the village and the family.

This procedure was entirely unlawful but rampant, and though it was not officially sanctioned, no one was ever punished for it. The fact that young men who'd been initiated and served as *Aguaciles* were exempted from military service was utterly disregarded, though the law remained on the books. Often underage boys of thirteen whose families couldn't afford to ransom them ended up in the ranks, heads shaved, identities removed, given guns, and pointed toward the sinister and sick whims of their overseers.

For a couple of years I succeeded in securing the freedom of many illegally shanghaied boys by having health documents drawn up that showed how many of them had been "diagnosed" with active cases of tuberculosis. This usually got them out of boot camp instantly, as the officers and sergeants didn't want to catch that dreaded disease.

Finally, the Christians, in their incessant need to rid the world of paganism, and now seeing no value in their ancestors' rituals of initiations so painstakingly hidden behind the position of *Aguaciles* and *Mayori,* began to petition the Scat Mulaj and the national government to ban the whole ritual since participation no longer guaranteed their sons' exemption from military services.

Despite this and the dwindling participation in both the *Mayori* and the Scat Mulaj, initiations continued to creep along in their slow, romantic ornateness because traditionalist villagers knew that the world itself would die without the initiation rituals. The ecstatic, collective vision was too precious to give up without a fight.

The village depended on it, the youth depended on it, the Gods depended on it, the world depended on it. The converts and missionaries wanted initiations eradicated because, until they disappeared, the missionaries' God would never be a priority in the village. He would continue to be just another God, a plain, severe God buried in a crowd of noble, brightly colored, mysterious dancing Gods and Goddesses who lived, died, gave birth, made mistakes, and favored living instead of being correct.

Then yesterday an official communiqué was telegraphed to the village by government representatives. One of the three hierarchy scribes read the edict out loud, translating it to the villagers, who rippled out beyond him below the steep, fanlike temple staircase. The telegram stated that "the contents of a petition received by the government asking for the dissolution of the institution of *Primer Mayor* and the *Aguaciles,* a petition submitted by the students of Santiago Atitlan and the members of the such-and-so liberation group had convinced the bureaucrats in whose jurisdiction it pertained, to officially impose an ordinance specifically prohibiting the rituals, offices, privileges, and procedures of the *Mayor* and *Aguaciles.*"

You could hear the paper the edict was printed on rustling in the wind, so stunned was the silence that followed; but it didn't hold for long. In the few quiet seconds it took for the village to build up a critical mass of grief and indignation, even the croaking voices of the waterbirds returning to the lake could be heard a mile away. Then two thousand voices exploded into the air in riot proportions, as every one in the crowd, shaking their fists, pressed forward to yell different opinions all at once.

To the side, standing on the wall between the whitewashed pillars above where the *Xuoja'* always sat, twelve youth recently returned from school in Guatemala City, dressed in white-man's clothing, smiled without speaking, peacefully observing the uproar around them. Five of them were members of my old music band from years back.

What the Christians couldn't do and what four and a half centuries of oppressive government policies had failed to accomplish, these youths, Atitecos by birth, had joyfully toppled in less than a month. It was unheard of and unbelievable that uninitiated young men, the sons and daughters of well-known village families, would want to and be able to do away with a beloved and archaic institution—one the old people believed the students themselves needed to go through.

Rotating their deeply carved countenances and pirate-tied red headcloths to face the students, the Scat Mulaj headman addressed the youth directly. Quieting a little, the crowd strained to hear what the old people were thinking:

"Why don't you want to go through initiation?" he loudly inquired.

Aquel, the son of a Christian pharmacist, chirped up, "Father, what use is it for us to spend our early years as lackeys and gofers to that drunken Ladino government official? Don't you know he sends the *Aguaciles* to ask his wife what it is they should buy for her in the market for his dinner? What's good about being a conscripted slave to our oppressors?"

The gathered village shouted in utter agreement, myself included, as this was all true. Ladinos were Guatemalans who conformed to a non-Indian lifestyle and spoke Spanish. It had nothing really to do with a person's race. It was a cultural delineation. Ladinos in general considered themselves a caste higher than the native Mayan people and treated them accordingly. But because the Atitecos were so numerous, had such noble bearing and royal image of themselves, and had so little truck with the outside world, arrogant Ladinos posed fewer problems in our village than they did in other places. This was not to say that all Ladinos were hard cases, in fact there existed Mestizos and Ladinos who were conscious and proud of that fact that many of their forebears had been Mayans. But the government syndics, bureaucrats, and police sent to make sure the Mayans didn't get any ideas about self-rule were quite abusive to the *Mayori* and *Aguaciles* who were Mayans. They used them as their personal servants, gofers, and whipping boys. In recent years even the initiating chiefs, the *Mayori,* complained bitterly about the situation. Nonetheless, they tolerated the injustice of it all in order to keep the initiations going.

"Yes, son," the old men continued, "we understand and sympathize with you in regard to that. But what about the bringing of the fruit from under the mountain and the ceremonies of the youth?"

"It will be better now without any of these old outdated things. The whole thing is just a bad worn-out version of religious lies and superstitious customs imposed upon us when we were still ignorant in the old days. We've been taken advantage of. There is no God in these rocks and trees that you revere. What we need is a good economy and to quit wasting our food, energy, and resources on these old rotting customs. They only make us poor and more ignorant, more easily manipulated and enslaved."

The old men and half the village stood with their mouths gaping, incredulous and astounded that these youth didn't see what needed to be fed in the world. They were acting just like the individualist tourists who came to stare at the village unable to see anything but ignorance and squalor. The old men loved the people and tried to understand, but they couldn't entirely comprehend what the youth were alluding to. And before they could make a rebuttal, the old women of the Scat Mulaj, the *Xuoja'* and Tixelí, jumped to their feet, which was a rare and serious thing, and began their speech. After all, these were everybody's mothers, and we always listened.

"Young Lords, you're getting more altitude from standing on that wall doing nothing, serving no person or God, without jobs and no eloquence abilities with our language. And yet you insist on judging something you are unwilling to accomplish: your initiations. Instead of accepting them, you, with your newfound school ways, have decided to cut down what you are too lazy to cultivate, all the while trying to make your laziness look like you are doing us all a favor. You're willing to kill what gives us life though you are killing what gives you life as well. If you don't want to be initiated, why didn't you let the rest of the village decide for itself? Who made you our deciders, our leaders? You are acting like the uninitiated children you are, but you are armed with weapons that need initiated wisdom beyond your years to work them properly, a wisdom you could've properly attained by rescuing the Earth during your initiations. But now look at what you've accomplished. You've made nothing, created, rescued, or returned nothing. To cut down a cornfield is easy, lazy, and means nothing to us; to grow one up by hand with sweat and worry is hard enough, but you boys are just cutting. . . ."

And then the youth turned their backs on the women and, laughing, jumped down from their wall and stiffly walked away from us, pushing their tongue-lashed pride through the crowds and out of view, while the rest of the village milled around dazed and frustrated.

After another hour of Mayan discussion, I volunteered an idea to my elders: "Why don't you just make the initiations voluntary? Make it so the chiefs and the initiates, the *Mayori* and *Aguaciles,* don't do any civil duty. No more slaving for the bureaucrats, just spiritual patrols to keep the village safe from evil as they already do. That way the initiations could be held voluntarily without the government service. Youth who were ready for initiations could do so at their own discretion."

I was proud of my idea, thinking, like many others, that we would have to accomplish something quickly to save the sacred aspect of the initiations. We knew that, as time lapsed, it would become harder and harder to regain that delicate comprehension of the whole that was being washed farther and farther away from us by a swelling flood of literalism and ignorant deconstruction.

"It couldn't be done, Father, because initiation is not a thing desired, it is a thing that is mandatory and imposed. Its imposition takes the guilt away from the parents and the child. No one would voluntarily go through all the hardship involved in initiation. Worse yet, anybody who thought they would at the beginning would pull out in the middle when it got tough, which is worse than no initiations at all, because that would endanger the person and the village as a whole."

Irritated, tired, and in despair they shot down my idea as an impractical and hopeless compromise to comfort and free choice, two enemies of initiations.

We spent a full day talking and arguing, trying to assimilate it all and failing to adapt what was happening to what we knew from previous experience. We knew full well that the whole culture was beginning to crumble before our eyes. By the time we wandered to our homes in the dark, some of us took along a friend because we didn't want to go alone toward the end of our world. For the first time in their history, the chiefs and ladies of the Scat Mulaj felt like a society, a separate entity, a body of its own instead of the heart in the body of the village that pumped life into the rest. The leaders felt alone and the last of their kind.

◇

People began having hard and strange dreams. The shamans were overrun with clients disturbed by what they saw in their dreams, and with people who were *xibein,* or infected with fright. As one of the shamans, my compound was crowded with people demanding ceremonies to restore what the shock of the recent events had stolen from their souls. People were ill, and the village depressed. People stopped going places, arguments were put off, children cried, and the air got colder every day.

The dusty North winds of *Qiq'* were again sanding the waters of his sister, the Mother Lake, driving grit into every crack in every hut, and turning his brother-in-law, our Father the Sun, into a deep honey-colored disc. Our faces were hot from the polishing volcanic cinder and our insides froze at night. This season was always hard. Called *Bis* by the Canyon Village, or the "time of sadness," every year at this time all that was female was kidnapped by the Lords of Death and hidden in the Underworld, leaving our earth cold, dry, and unsure of its future.

Because the Tzutujil didn't have a literal future tense in their language, what stood for the future was never taken for granted. Every year they dedicated themselves to the spiritual planting of the following year in hopes that the future might sprout into the Nowness we could once again live in. To the Tzutujil the future was essentially the same as the past, living in the same invisible concentric rings of the other world's spirit layers whose fruit was the daily life we lived. The past became the future, redone with the uniqueness of now.

This year's particular time of sadness was worse; the village as a whole was apathetic, depressed, and without direction, resigned to sinking into an uninspired future of ritualless subsistence. The dust and wind kept up for a week, until everyone was coughing. The birds were silent, making the streets no good even for courting.

Ya Lur, myself, and old A Sisay were sitting and shivering by our corner cooking fire, trying to keep Jorge from falling and teetering over into the flames, when we heard the single raspy sound of a hierarchy chief calling out to one of his equals.

"At kol Tdtali."

"Jie en kola nen Tdta," I replied, and in rolled one of our least favorite Scat people, the head of one of the most prominent sacred houses, called the House of Santiago, where the Center of the Year and the Morning Star resided. A fat, nosy merchant, he had ended up as a chief by default and had little of the medieval eloquence of a normal Scat member. But he was dedicated to his job and did the best he could.

Ya Lur hated him for other well-founded reasons. But before I could run all of these through my mind, he'd been seated by the fire and given some hot chocolate to drink. Then, in his normal noisy fashion, he began to blurt out his reason for coming without the customary florid circumspection.

"Ctzijwa, is it true that you would loan us your very long stone hut to house the shrine fruit if we found a way to bring it, *Tdta,* Brother Parent?"

Telling him that this was so, I repeated what I'd told the council two days before: that anyone who would somehow make this year's initiation ceremony come back to life would be welcome to use the old long house that sat next to my mother-in-law's compound, just off our long traditional *pach jai,* hut.

Then, without two words or a nod, he slipped out a small eighteenth-century blue glass carafe, a small glass, from somewhere in his bulk, the glass hissing smoothly against his *manqash* black blanket tunic as it appeared in his chubby fingers.

Pouring out a tiny cup of what turned out to be better than normal *psi-wanya,* he forced me to promise to the earth and to the fire that I'd keep my word if anything came of it all. Dropping some of the liquor in the fire where it blazed up blue, I promised, and sprinkled the remaining drops on the earth.

Shaking hands with us all and yelling his farewell, he donned his fancy Italian hat, bent his head into the sandy wind, and was gone.

Innumerable meetings continued to rage on before the winds calmed down, forcing the Scat Mulaj indoors to private huts where more spontaneous smaller sessions were held out of public view. Because of the wind some of the gatherings took on the air of secret meetings, where I again reiterated my idea of voluntary initiation, in which every aspect of the ceremonialism could be kept alive and intact while all the controversial civil duties of the *Mayori* and *Aguaciles* could be discarded and allowed to pass into history. After all, the edict against the offices of *Mayori* and *Aguaciles* came from the government, whose non-Indian predecessors were the originators of the institutions in the first place. What was good about it didn't come from them. What was obvious was that the government was trying to please the Christians and politically active people in the area. If we acquiesced to what was obvious in the ordinance and removed the initiations unseen into the jurisdiction of the Scat Mulaj and the initiating officials—who would then report only to the *Ajaua,* the Scat chiefs, and not to the civil government—then we wouldn't be breaking the law. If the people would volunteer, then maybe the initiations could go on.

The complications of such a switchover were so complex and of such a mind-boggling dimension that none of us could figure out how it would all work. The circumstances surrounding initiation had been an adaptation to begin with; and now it would be an adaptation of an adaptation.

The ramifications of even attempting such a move in those times was serious in view of the recent revelations: Most if not all of the students in the village were in contact with, or already members of, the many political groups who saw themselves as liberators of the country. Lumping Mayans, Mestizos, poor factory workers, and indentured plantation servants into one oppressed category, their idea of the revolution did not include the Mayan vision of the universe, nor did they understand that by sacrificing that vision the people would cease to be Mayan.

The status quo, progovernment people, the rich landowners and their relatives, from whose rank the military dictators and bosses emerged, fought among themselves as well. In Guatemala these kinds of people had been the enemy of everything Mayan, ritual and otherwise, for four and a half centuries. The tribal elders of every generation had danced a waltz of cultural survival on the edge of these people's swords.

To the revolutionary Left the human being was still the center of the universe—all people should have a share in what the other had. But they believed only in *human* effort and ability, not in the sacred or the Gods. All else was dead matter to be used by humans to build a world with no suffering for humans.

The opposing Right wing was the decadent power of the status quo. This incumbent caste of rich landowners and their associates divided the country up into a series of unofficial feudal territories, each with its own military in its employ. These powerful families considered all the people residing inside each of these districts as their personal workforce, Mayan or not.

To the Right, their kind of human was the only kind that mattered, and all the others were families of poor serfs who worked on their plantations, or in their coffee operations, factories, or businesses. If these elitists believed in a God, the God they believed in was on their side and this God said that they were the only real humans and that the universe, including the rest of the people in it, were theirs. And just like the Left, whom they hated and oppressed, they believed all else was dead matter to be used by their people to build a world with everything and everyone in its place so as not to cause any discomfort or suffering to this Right-wing elite.

The Tzutujil were not trying to build a nonsuffering world. The world they were part of was not run by humans, and it had only live things residing in it. There were no dead things. Instead of eradicating all the misery of the world, the Tzutujil were trying to suffer together creatively in a beautiful way to keep their world of delicately balanced live things more vital by feeding it the grief of their human failures and stupidity. These failures were made beautiful by the ornate and graceful way the people dedicated their suffering to the earth and to that which made life live, in a proven ritual attitude of great antiquity.

So the Tzutujil stood dangerously between two powerful forces, the Right and the Left, neither of which could understand the nonliteral intelligence and finesse of these Mayans' mythologically oriented lives. The Tzutujil elders surmised that neither the Left not the Right could "see" because none of their people had gone through initiation. Now both sides wanted it banned, and by disobeying one, ironically, we would be defying both. How could our elders dance with that? In the past it had been dangerous and difficult to keep what they did alive, but still there had been only one wall of oppression to cajole. Now there were two opposing walls, one claiming to be our liberators, the other our parents.

The old people knew that they were keeping the beautiful universe alive for everyone, including these unhappy and militarily powerful opponents. Patronized and disregarded by both sides, the village elders were like the fine smoked duck meat caught between the eager teeth of the upper and lower jaws of a monster of modernity. This heartless creation of polarization would soon bite down and devour the Tzutujil culture to feed the bottomless hunger of its need to feel more powerful and to be in charge of what it couldn't comprehend.

◇

The lake waves split on the rocks all night, dragging off beached canoes and parts of people's terraced gardens. Everyone was snug under their covers beneath the stale fumes in their huts made smoky by cindery winds whistling through the double-thick upper walls of cornstalks.

Because of the wind, my clan went to bed down in the long old ceremonial stone house, whose antique walls made of old temple stones smoothed centuries ago with jade axes blocked a great deal of the choking powdery breeze. None of us could sleep, our minds turning in the wind and our hearts moored tightly to our uncertainties to keep them from drifting into deep despair. Finally, a little before the first dusty light of dawn began to paw its way into day, the angry wind returned to his home in the North. A feeling like warm water, the warm amniotic ocean of sleep, gushed through our limbs and thoughts until all of us had drifted into sleep in the dusty red dawn.

Covered in orchids from head to toe she came walking, long legged and yellow skinned. Covered in yellow orchids, tiny yellow irises, jungle roses, and dahlias, her skin was a woman-shaped orchid petal. Her amber nipples peeking through the orchid storm of her hair leaked a milk of yellow light or amber pollen whose smell resembled the smell of food roasting on the wind to a starving man. Things were seen in the milk of that woman: an umbilical rope made of a thousand brightly colored baby birds who burst streaming from her navel suckled there screaming for milk with open beaks, somehow nesting in her smooth yellow thighs and feet. It was then that I noticed how she pulled her sister, all blue and jade green, behind her, and behind her stood yet a younger sister. This third woman was all white paved in sea foam and sun-colored mouse ear orchids, and armored with the smooth part of whales' teeth and mouse ivory.

Holding her head sideways, the blue sister spun backwards in slow motion until she faced me in line with the yellow woman and her milk-eyed sister. When Blue Woman spoke you could see that her sensual mouth held a sea green row of translucent polished jade teeth, out of which words made of iridescent green hummingbirds plunged in all direction like waterfalls. Her breasts were lakes, and when she spoke her tule reed hair rustled and ducks flew out. Her breath smelled of waters, foul waters and sweet waters, the water at the edge of a marsh, then water in the pool-like eyes of deers and otters, the milky water of the grinding tooth that smelt like delicious corn water when women ground and dipped their hands. Her breath was the smell of floods and the muddy dust of grinding boulders.

Caressing me, her shy blue hands grabbed my shoulders, she began to make love to me as only a goddess might and we did so, for a year. . . .

Her eyes had changed, and, looking down, I realized she was gone. In her place her yellow sister of the birds was my lover and she whispered to me, her voice like her eyes made of the fat parts of every seed on earth, and I felt the strength in my body swell effortlessly as she whispered in a voice like bees, "We've come to be with you, Husband of the Village," filling me until the milk-eyed sister began filling my bed, the very bed I slept on, with every color flowers, flowers and more flowers, just the flowers' heads, no stems, not just petals but many feet deep of flowers.

Then over them she hovered and dropped like a great kingfisher into a lake of flowers, herself bursting into a billion white bees and I became a flowering tree, no longer a man, but a man made entirely of flowers, in whose middle a hive of wild bees was filling with honey from the milk-eyed sister, the ivory-skin woman, making love to me like a billion white bees filling me with sweet honey guarded by bees whose humming said, "We've come to be with you, Husband of the Village."

And in that instant a loud, thunderous pop and crashing din resounded in my middle. And then far off a weeping of a million eyes and a billion cries of all the world's things missing their mothers and lovers. Then the women were gone, far away into the dry and unhappy dust of a rutted road.

Three women came walking toward me. First as small as the thoughts of ants, but slowly and timidly they arrived, very large. Each wore an ample single-colored shawl over her head and body. One wore white, another yellow, and the third a beautiful dark blue. In their hands each bore a jewel-like ear of husked dried corn the same color as their shawls. Placing this corn into my hands, each of them opened their luxurious shawls to reveal bodies and faces made of solid flowers. These fell into the piles of petals they now became, their voices fading into the sound of a singing breeze: "Bring us home, Father. Bring us home, Husband. Bring us back, bring us . . ."

The smell of Goddesses still on me, the smell of waterbirds, dawn seeds, pollen, flowers, and corn still in the air, my body almost my own again, I could barely make out the crying. It took me a while to realize that it was Jorge. It took even longer to realize that it was Jorge whining over the loud and plaintive voice of an adult village woman and the polite salutation of a chief layered over the beelike murmur of a crowd of Tzutujil villagers. Staggering from the weight of too much meaning, deliciousness, and fright, I made my way to the hut's doorway. There I leaned against the old doorpost gaping and blinking into the cloud-free, windless, bird-singing day, until I could escape a bit more of the powerful spell of the dream. Slowly my eyes focused enough to realize that the entire village hierarchy, two hundred strong, stood there in full dress. Through the abundance of fresh orchids and lilies tied to the ends of their staffs of office, their old eyes, glazed blue by time and service, both scared and kind, met mine in a hopeful gaze of triumph, resolution, and the certainty of failure. Like warriors of the heart who now faced impossible odds, they'd come to fulfill their vow to feed to the last the Gods with the beauty of their final struggle. I loved them and they must have loved me, as they were going to appoint me the head young man's chief, the chief initiator of the youth, the *Najbey Mam,* the Husband of the Village. They knew that I knew it. The Goddesses had told me. The dreams had told me and they had also told them. Together we would try to retrieve her back to the village. Together we would, with knowing looks, a lot of sweat, and no certainty, try to bring the earth back from the grips of the Lords of Death.

The hierarchy would still have to carry out the ritual of trying to convince me, using powerful images from their archaic "delicious words." Like the courting speeches made by word warriors to beguile parents into allowing their daughters to marry a boy, the village was required to court its new "husband" and to beguile his family into allowing him to accept the position.

Then out of the crowd, carrying the flowering staff of the Lord of Obsidian Blades, A Clash, stepped Aqel QoQuix, son of the drummer, a chief now.

He'd been the initiate who'd called me out of Chiv's house long ago to become flute player.

Now in a position of knowledge, he stood behind two younger men who held the holy liquor, supervising them while they began to speak the delicious ancient cotton of old-time thoughts spun into threads of today's words, the speech prayer of the *Najbey Mam:*

"Yesterday and the day before
When we came walking
When we came limping
Carrying the Foot of Dawn
Bearing the Foot of Day
Like our Grandmothers
As our Grandfathers
Who taught us to remember
Not to forget
Whose faces have now
Gone into the house of loss
Into the house of death now
Whose faces, the fruit of their own
Ancestors' trunks
Seem now invisible to us, the walking
Little blind beings
Whose words no longer seem to
Hum and buzz in our deaf little ears
Who have become dry dust
Who have become dry earth
Yet still today their way of going yet in
Some faint footprint isn't refused
But matched with ours
As we come walking
The eight hundred shimmering
As we came searching
The eight hundred glistening
Yet still under our Sun Father's face
And in our Mothers' Lake breeze

Their old fluid words stiffen from amnesia
Growing into a hard currency, a hard gold
The solidity of excellence
Their overabundance
Their too-heavy-to-carry yellow greatness
Sits hard in our indebted throats
Sits hard in our indebted bellies
Like our manhood
Like our motherhood
And only a little finds its road to
Spill out toward you the owner of
This house (Moon)
With your own little
Father (Sun)
Because yesterday and the day before
Our Grandmothers
Our Grandfathers
Burned their shinbones
Spilled their layers of fat
To buy back from Holy Death
A day or two of indebted sparkling
Life for us
Like the big trees
And big vines they were
Who spend seasons of leaves
To buy their children space
On this earth
Who spend falling leaves
And fruit of delicious words
To pay our rent to Death
To buy this day
While we the forgetful eaters of the Earth
Go around peeing and eating
Shitting and dreaming
Complaining, while asking for more,
Go around

Not feeling
The high price paid
The deep heavy carrying of
The weight of this sparkling life
That deepened the footprints
On the trail of our remembering but
Gone-away ancestors having tread in the sandlike
Dust of their own ancestors' excellence
Till now
When like toyless orphans
Noticing better what he/she
Doesn't have, finds what others think is already
Dead
And watered by our tears of
Desperate remembering
And watered by our tears of longing to see her face again
The little orphan
Cultivates the
Lost seed in the dusty footprint where
Our ancestors carried the seeds in a more
Seeded time
In this way the Canyon Village Heart was found
Fished from the dust, from the comfort of its invisibility
To burst forth into a flame of flowers
Of the very location of its original loss
In the hollowness filled with the flower
A flower of longing, whose fragrance
Might draw back she whose
Throne is in that Hole
Which would now go
To dryness
To death
If you little Brother Parent
If you little Mother of the Village
Don't pick up this flowering footprint

Or don't choose to grab tightly the treelike staff
Or the first Grandchild
The openness of roads
And the openness of eyes
And lead our Flowers
And coax our Sprouts
Who could carry the Fruited Face
Bent under the Seeded Fruit
Whose wild forested hearts
Bearing spears tipped with irresistible eloquence
Causes the return of She who is the water of the earth's thirsty face
Returning the Village Heart to her body
So that which had been done
Yesterday and the day before
To buy us one or two days of life
Will be done again today and again
To buy back our faces from invisibility
To steal back our fertility from the dust
To coax a little of the delicious original
Flowering Mountain Earth Water Navel
Of the jumping of birds and confusing density
Of nature that inebriates
Out of the wept-on seed heart
To purchase back from Death
Our children's lives
To carry what we carry so our faces will not
Be lost or forgotten
In honor to the Gods and Goddesses
Please receive a little of Warmer of the Earth
Don't push us into canyons
Don't push us into big holes
Don't refuse us as if we were people with no thanks in them
Please receive a little of the smell of
The Original Flowering Mountain Earth
Please receive a little smell of rain on dust,

Please receive a little of the smell of corn
Being toasted and ground before a feast by chattering, joking women
Please receive a little bit of our Poverty."

And with that, every chief's third officer poured out a small shot glass full of the worst-tasting liquor ever invented. It tasted sweet, though, as Ya Lur and I accepted it, signifying our mutual acceptance of stepping into the hard and controversial position of *Najbey Mam,* Venerable Grandchild, the chiefs in charge of initiating the adolescents and bringing the seeds, fruit, and branches back from the annually dying village.

Their words devastated us with their conquering beauty, and I accepted without consulting my compound or wife. Though this was an unforgivable oversight, I was quickly absolved by them, in view of the desperate nature of the task.

TWELVE

COURTING THE CHIEFS
MENTORS, LORDS, LADIES,
AND WIDOWS

The Scat Mulaj had waited and waited for them through two meetings and this was the third. A week later, at the sympathetic beckoning of their own initiates, these last year's initiating chiefs felt honored enough to finally come in to relinquish their positions, thereby allowing me to take over. We watched them until finally, rising up at a distance into the clear area in front of the elevated church, last year's proud young men's chiefs, the *Mayori,* the *Najbey Mam,* came striding toward the stairs beneath us with the air of a grudge. What were once fine new blankets had now lost their fuzzy pile and were visibly worn and covered in a year's worth of candle wax. Their thick staffs over their shoulders or cradled in their hands had once been as white as bone, but had been handled and polished to the color of old teeth from months and months of standing, marching, handling, pushing, pulling, and leaning in copal smoke and the village wind.

Arriving up over the last step, they strode into the atrium to where I sat with the Scat Mulaj on benches. Though a little peeved, they graciously shook hands and gave their greeting in esoteric terms peculiar to their office, most of which I didn't understand, because I had not yet gone through a year of being a chief.

After all had been spoken, and each chief had addressed all the elders and myself, we blessed and praised them for jobs well done. Only then did the *Mayori* hand the next year over to me in a well-worn tradition used by all sacred houses when changing officials. Each of the sad thirteen men begged me to take good care of her, the village.

They were sad and resentful of the recent dishonoring of their positions, but more skeptical of my plan, and resentful of that as well. The *Mayori* hated me in a kind of friendly way for my stealing from them what they'd come to covet and love, but they were still happy that the initiation wouldn't die.

The village was an initiating chief's "bride." After a year of metaphorical marriage to her, deep roots of understanding and love had grown into the chiefs' hearts until that love had taken over their entire lives. To hand her over to another man was as hard as it sounds, and in no way was anyone unsympathetic. But these ex-chiefs were now asked to give up being chiefs and graduate into a more exalted and adult civilian status where they were expected to transfer all this affection for the village and the initiation ceremony onto their wives and children, solidifying themselves into village men who would eventually become ritual advisors for other new chiefs in years to come.

In the middle of the last praising, the thirteen proud and tired broke down weeping. Everyone understood their exhaustion and grief. Pulling them down to sit with them, the old wrinkled Scat Mulaj chiefs and their ladies held them and kept company with them for a long time, telling them things which at that time were none of my business and seemed to comfort them.

◇

For years after his oldest daughter had regained her health, Ma Tec Sisay had brought gigantic wild calla lilies and intoxicating white lilies to my shamanic altar as gifts and offerings to my deities. Though what she suffered from looked like a combination of endometriosis and tuberculosis, A Sisay, a committed traditionalist, was convinced that his daughter had been witched out of envy to punish him for his successful life and ability in the Scat Mulaj. I removed the deadly thing shot into her and she recovered well. A Sisay and I became very close friends during her illness. Nobody knew exactly where he came up with all the hundreds of pounds of flowers he brought into the village every week, but his ability as a diligent farmer and a short-distance merchant were recognized all around the village.

His face was a lot like Holy Boy's, both old and young at the same time. A gentle dapper man of sixty years or so, he walked straight, wore his little fedora cocked to the side, and had a sense of humor about everything. Chiv and he were friends but Chiv always thought of A Sisay as a boy, as he was almost thirty years younger.

Chiv was a celebrity, a shaman, and a mischievous kind of hero. When he came around it was like a herd of teeth-gnashing peccaries crashing in on you. Ma Tec Sisay, on the other hand, was more like a tree, a steady canoe, or the sparkle in a rock. That's the kind of man we needed as a leader to teach me to become a chief.

A *teonel* was like a ritual coach, a mentor. All the leaders had them, and they had to come from the body of men and women who had served in the same position one was trying to fulfill.

A Sisay had served as chief initiator in the late 1940s. After hours and hours of forcing me to checkmate all his doubts, thereby pushing my eloquence into action and testing my sense of reality and firmness of resolution, he finally allowed himself to be *bojchijn,* cotton-mouthed, talked into, becoming my *teonel.*

Inasmuch as I was now the *Najbey Mam,* Ya Lur, at the tender age of eighteen, was now the *Najbey Ixoc,* the First Woman, the Mother in charge of initiating the young unmarried women. While I was cotton-mouthing old A Sisay, simultaneously in another hut Ya Lur was courting his wife to become her *teonel.* Ya Piskát, a woman of great bearing, much grief, and generous years of knowledge, would have to accept for Ma Tec to give me his final word. Just as Ya Lur and I had to accept our position together, our teachers also had to be a couple. Except for a very few celibate officers and the shamans, everything in public ritual had to be done with male and female representations.

Lucky for me, the slim woman accepted Ya Lur's words. They both joined us in a feast of wild tree greens and square bean-speckled corn cakes called *shep suban,* cooked by their daughter. Each of us dedicated a portion of our food to Old Man Fire, asking him to contact all the Deities and let them know that we needed their help to somehow keep this ceremony alive. Praying for good luck, all four of us ate together, two generations hoping to bring a third to where we sat.

As Ya Lur and I had position but no knowledge, we two men and our two ladies would go searching the village, courting as we went, for old valuable men and women of substance. These would form two separate personal councils of ex-chiefs and Tixelí to mentor us on our journey of initiating the young.

Every day for over three weeks in a row, dressed like kings and queens and loaded up with flowers, tobacco, liquor, and fruit, A Sisay and I made at least a hundred excursions to the huts and compounds of retired hierarchy members, courting them with word gifts, a procedure taught to me by A Sisay. This very much resembled the words and procedures I used as a shaman when addressing the spirits. Anyone unaware of the village customs might also have mistaken A Sisay and me, or Ya Lur and Ya Piskát, for marriage brokers.

The Christians scoffed, the Catholics fumed, the government didn't even know about it, and the village at large began to glow again as people laid aside foodstuffs and resources we might need later for the youth during the next year.

The first four or five men were the hardest to convince into joining, but after gathering seven it became increasingly easy because each man we convinced was added into the courting party. As we went along, each day gathering force and increasing our numbers, the next old man we courted with gifts and delicious words would be even more likely to desire to be a member of such an exalted company of community-endorsed duffers.

In the end, my personal council consisted of thirty-eight old men, including A Sisay and me. Every one of the thirty-eight had been initiators at one time, and most were retired from various years of carrying their loads in the Sacred Houses as members of the Scat Mulaj.

Ya Lur had almost as many women, but she and Ya Piskát had also been able to gather eighteen *Melcani,* as well. Melcani were husbandless women with young children whose husbands had been recently killed in the mountains, died of sickness, or drowned in storms or in the lake, not women who were divorced or abandoned.

Tzutujil women widowed during their childbearing years often had a difficult time feeding themselves and their children. Traditionally, they became a very important part of the rituals of the *Najbey Mam* during the initiations. They were allowed to live in his compound and worked straight through the initiations, grinding, cooking, and doing other ceremonial duties. This way they didn't starve and were given a home, usefulness, and a visibility that did not include pity.

I was chief over my council of dignitaries and A Sisay was my teacher. Together we worked, old and young, and now we had to court men like me to be subchiefs, the initiators under my direction. These men were a little older than myself, married with young children whose wives would be willing to serve as women chiefs and initiators to the village girls under the direction of Ya Lur and Ya Piskát.

This would be much harder than raising a council because these people would be in active service with me. We would be chiefs, with the backbreaking responsibility for the lives and rites of passage of the youth. Since we'd all been through initiation, we knew how dangerous and involved it would be, and our task was made that much more uncertain by the present political animosity.

To initiate the youth you had to be raising youngsters of your own, but under no circumstances were you allowed to initiate your own children. In those times the willingness of a couple to work a whole year without compensation to serve the community in this difficult responsible position was understood as a sacrifice and a gift of the most generous sort. That meant, also, that they had to leave their own compounds and families without their help for a lot of the time, returning home exhausted at the end of the day.

Still, the old men had some ideas of who might accept, and the old women had still more. So, once again loaded up with gifts of chocolate, flowers, honey, candles, tobacco, liquor, and a barrage of finely tuned words in the bellies of our counselors, we moved en masse into the streets, the women and men all together this time, Ya Lur, myself, Ya Piskát, and A Sisay in the middle of this surging party.

I wished those moments could have lasted for centuries, bathing in the honey of the evening sun, carried along in a crowd of flowers and wrinkles, all of us proud to be together. The people who stood and saluted us by the road were comforted by the mysterious usefulness of the old men and women, who looked noble and handsome as they meandered through the streets in a florid knot on a mission to bring the village back alive on the backs of the youth.

Standing and shifting from leg to leg, we crowded in front of the compounds and huts of the candidates for my subchiefs. Though I did most of the actual talking, A Sisay whispered it all into my ear. It came pouring out of my mouth only a second after he'd spoken, as if he were my mind and I were his mouth.

If it looked as if I was faltering or losing the attention of the couple I was courting, the old people would gang up on the couple and chime in with even more irresistible charm. It was hard work, but we found three strong couples from traditionalist families who were willing to become chiefs and chieftesses. These, in turn, had some others in mind. Joining our ranks after dressing as well as we, all of us marched off together into nine other compounds, where we achieved six more couples. The final three would come along in a month.

As I needed twelve subchiefs, thirteen counting myself, we'd done well—much, much better than we had expected. Every night we gathered, every night we planned and mapped the year. Every night I learned, finding as I went a more profound intelligence in this ritual than I'd recognized there before. The greatness of the ritual was not to be found in what we said about it or in what it was supposed to address. The mind of the ritual would only appear through the doing of the ritual, in the moments of its days. The meeting began in prayers specific to the initiation and rituals of offering and incense that I'd never witnessed before. Now I was the one being taught how to do them.

My hawk was happy. He turned and flapped and turned at the description of each stage of the year's endeavors as expounded on by an old woman or a man. The rest would add forgotten bits and parts, supporting each concept presented to us new initiators. Each old-timer helped build in our minds a kind of house. Some of the ideas were the poles and beams, others the roof or walls. Every counselor added the mud of experience, wetted with our hopeful idealism, to fill in the gaps left in the verbal blueprints made by the others until a palace, a temple, a strange hut comprised of a year's time stood bristling in our expectant hearts in the form of an invisible house, now with a soul of its own, immersed in possibility, longing to come into view at the end of the year-long ritual initiations.

Among my subchiefs and Ya Lur's ladies, there were three "climate chiefs" for each "altitude" in Tzutujil ritual thought. These in turn each presided over three subchiefs.

Ma Shar, or Cup, would be in charge of the coastal lowlands, the wide trees and rain forest, the ocean, the underworld of the earth, and the night. The oldest of the young chiefs, he had a voice like Skip James, and a face yellowed from farming on the wild forest side of Atitlan, toward to the coast.

A fine loyal man, and a notorious ceremonial musician, he was full of jokes. He kind of cheated me because he had already been an initiating chief ten years before. But people seemed to have forgotten because, instead of acting his part as a subchief, he'd ended up playing the music for the boys, leading their return from the underworld. We were only allowed one turn at initiating but, in this case, everyone looked the other way, which turned out to be a good thing. Ma Shar's unkillable will, constant rested awareness, and his ability to sleep standing propped against his staff in one-minute stints would save us from disaster. No one ever really noticed him coming in and out of sleep, which made him a vigilant leader.

A Cwa, Hot Spring, was the thirty-year-old grandson of one of our best counselors, and was named after him, as is the custom. Little Cwa was a ceremonial dancer like his old grandfather, and could retain long lines of liturgy in his head, reciting them with emotion, even while starving and unrested during the ceremonial fasts that go along with the dances. He had the bearing of a noble person and was loved and admired for his handsome appearance and his total affection for his wife and three little children. I put him in charge of the earth's surface, flat places, roads, the palms, the flowers, the sun, the daylight, the village, and human existence.

Though I'd absorbed a great deal from the days of my own initiation and this ritual was no stranger to me, I'd never been on the other side of the ritual with the chiefs and the planners. Through the counselor's jadelike words I was given a priceless widening of understanding to add to my overwhelming love of the ceremonies.

Ma Bai, or Gopher, as he was called, was a tall, slim, talkative Tzutujil man whose little toddlers went with him everywhere he went. Younger than he looked, he had a huge bulbous nose and small close-set funny eyes, a bent thin-lipped smile, and ears so prominent and batlike that he could have heard what his unborn grandchildren were thinking if he'd only stop announcing his every move with his slurry mumbling charm.

Some people had to hold back their laughing gossip when they heard that Gopher was our man, but he too loved the initiations and, despite his name, he was a powerful climber of trees and cliffs and had no peer out in the bush. Untrustworthy in some ways and lazy when it came to speech, he was still loyal to the beauty of the rituals. In public he could teach the youth to walk like him, to give them that attitude of self-worth that is so necessary for the young. Ma Bai never forgot that our ancestors were watching.

His wife had long arms and fingers like the tapering wings of diving birds. Her face, worn by work, glowed from the royalness of having been chosen to join in keeping alive what was royal in the village. When the world saw Gopher and Vine together, they could see that each made the other complete. Though young, both were as in love with living as any old Tzutujil couple, in love with being useful to what made people alive, and in love with each other inside of that.

To Gopher I gave the Mountains, the Sky, the tall trees, the pines, the spruce, and the cedars, the moon, the lake, ropes, wood, and canoes.

Though the wives of these three weather chiefs were given positions, theirs were not altitudes or climates or manlike understandings but something that we called "depths" and different "densities." These were women things, and men couldn't understand them until they got too old to need to. This wasn't true, of course, because many of us men did understand but, like lovemaking, menstruation, childbirth, and death, we left these private things to those who needed to know them and, in this case, it was the women. Instead of claiming knowledge, we stood there admiring the women in their uniqueness, as they admired us in ours.

When we finally did gather up the youth, if there were to be any, the women and girls and men and boys would be separated during ritual times, doing different things in different places.

It would eventually become apparent that we would have separate meetings according to gender in different places at simultaneous times. Though off limits to each other for the first part of the year, we men were not working for the males, nor were the women chiefs working for the women, but separately both camps aimed toward "cooking" the boys into manlike beings and the girls into womanlike beings. At the end of the year, both groups would come together in relief and longing to make a third villagelike thing, without losing the solidarity of themselves or their differences.

But it was not yet time to break off according to gender. So, for a few more delicious weeks the old ladies, the old men, and we younger chiefs and ladies met together, over and over, to be harangued and gently harassed into becoming the tall-walking, semiarrogant, finely dressed, well-spoken, heroic royalty the village needed to inspire its youth into desiring to become like us.

Poverty was ever present in Atitlan. Most families had to share one egg with five people once or twice a week. To be able to farm enough corn to feed one's family for a year took enormous dedication, strength and health. People died regularly from malnutrition and diseases made lethal from weakness due to parasites and lack of protein.

Initiation was a dangerous ritual, spiritually precarious and physically hazardous. Chiefs and Ladies as well as initiates had died doing it in years before. The old folks spent weeks explaining what to say and not to say, what to do and what to avoid in many given situations. It was against these very real stakes of Death and difficulty that the initiates would be forced to dig up the deepest and most powerfully useful aspects of themselves to effect their mutual survival. Outside experts were brought in for a day to explain what had happened to them. As head chief, I, like those who had come before me, had to be a man of some wealth because I had to supply the resources necessary to make the long, extravagant, unbelievably expensive ceremonies. Especially expensive were the ritual feasts that occurred in spring when the young people's relatives, the whole village, and visiting Indians came in massive flocks to eat for days at the house of the *Najbey Mam*. As many as five to six thousand people a day could show up, and never less than eight hundred. No one starved during the initiations of the *Najbey Mam* except the initiates and the initiators.

Happily, the rest of the initiating chiefs and their Ladies, though required to put something in for the private feasts and rituals of the chiefs, were not burdened with much more than the contribution of their physical and spiritual efforts. Because of this the poorest man or woman could become "royalty" in the village. The regalness of the initiating Lords and Ladies came from their willingness, eloquence, and courtly excellence, not from how much money, land, or resources they had.

In this way the village gave everybody who had royal qualities a chance to reign. This was not just a metaphoric royal status, like that given to parade queens or Miss America, but a truly powerful position of spiritual and village responsibility in whose cradled arms and vigilant care the spiritual health of the village was protected. The maturation of the village youth was understood as a serious life-or-death issue.

This way, a woman whose everyday blouse was ragged and whose husband's sash was shredded, found, upon the acceptance of the position of subchief, that distant relatives, friends, or the *Najbey Mam* himself would struggle to provide them with handwoven headcloths, clothing, and other garments of royal significance. Becoming holy chiefs, these poor people earned the right to be regal by their full service to the village as initiators.

Initiations raised the honor of all things, peoples, and Gods. This was one of the elusive aspects of our ritual that the Marxists, right-wingers, and missionaries couldn't seem to comprehend, that it truly freed and ennobled the people by infusing their world with a sense of spiritual usefulness and village grandness.

When a Tzutujil made a true commitment to do something, his promise was called *Nya ru chitzrij,* meaning to "give your mouth over to it." This kind of promise meant the spirits would take you at your word and from that moment on, every one of your actions had a significance beyond your own life. Initiation was about sacrifice. All the little and large taboos we observed were the operating rules of this ritual. We did not follow them because they were morally good or would bring us any reward. We observed the taboos because, by doing so, we might be able to bring the year-long ceremony to fruition and pass our royal positions on to new candidates. Then we would have made the Earth live one year more and our people with it.

These rules were to help us get through without being damaged as people. An odd and bizarre assortment of incantations, taboos, and objects that were gifts from the old people, they were given to us to insure our survival as it had insured theirs. Just as in old European fairy tales there are always old people giving away objects and special words to the heroes so that they can pass through monsters and trials, so we were magically tutored by our mentors.

When the rituals got hard, expensive, and exhausting, we were not to say anything bad about it or the Gods would be insulted and our children would suffer or die. An initiate might even career to his death in the mountains. Every person's life would be endangered if the chief spoke ill of what was done. We had to be careful, because our focus kept the village safe. People knew we were focusing for them and didn't interrupt us.

As part of this focus, the *Najbey Mam* and his wife, myself and Ya Lur, were never to argue about anything large or small for one whole year. This was a very difficult sacrifice. If we failed in this sacrifice our children might be sacrificed by dying, getting sick with fevers, or a house could burn down or one of the initiates be badly burned.

As chiefs, once the actual initiation began for its duration, we were never to speak to anyone in the village directly, with the exception of our immediate family members, our ritual companions, and the initiates. During this almost intolerable exile, our initiates would have to serve as our ears and voices. This is why we chiefs would never be seen in the village unaccompanied by an initiate who would speak for his initiator as his leader whispered what he had to say into the young person's ear.

There were rules about food, walking, dressing, sleeping, treatment of animals, word taboos, and so on. The elders or the village would never punish us if we broke a taboo; the spirits were in charge of that.

We and our initiates were to be on call for the Scat Mulaj to build any ritual structures they needed; to bring ritual materials like flowers, branches, reeds, water, or rope; to break up any fights or mediate any arguments in the village that might threaten to ruin one of their rituals, even to the point of detaining or jailing people to keep others from getting hurt. We were not to arrest people for trials, but to always try and help people see reason, calming them down by understanding them, while at the same time slowly removing them from the ritual they were interrupting, and then only if asked to do so by a Scat Mulaj member.

Each of my subchiefs had four minor chiefs attending him, and all of them had to have an old mentor chosen from the gathering of elders A Sisay and I had courted. The same went for the Ladies.

The ritual year officially started when all the chiefs, separately in their own houses, with their spouses and their ritual mentors, both men and women, took a *touj*, a sweat bath, together, feasting together afterwards with their relatives. Made by the women of stone and timber, the sweathouse had stones inside that are heated in a two-foot-tall pyramidal pile until they crackled in a white-hot heat. When bathing, these rocks were doused with cold water, which released steam inside the *touj*. Every traditional compound had at least one. Rich villagers' compounds had one huge *touj* that could hold up to ten people plus a small one for the family.

Our compound only had one, and it held six people. My mother-in-law had built it with Ya Lur and one of her aunts had blessed and stacked the rocks. Jorge's placenta had been planted deep beneath the old Womb of the Moon, as the sweathouse was called in shaman's language.

Sweat baths were hot and the women were required to run them. Men didn't get a sweat going or even build one. They just brought the wood and waited. If a woman didn't build the fire, clear out the ashes, insure that the heat was strong, and go in to bathe with the crowd, then men couldn't take a sweat bath. That's the old rule.

That night all the ladies of the compound lit the oak fire and scraped out all the ash they could when the rocks were glowing inside. They placed four thick shocks of wild avocado leaves inside the entrance beside the rocks, a large clay pot of heated water and another of cold water with a dipping gourd. Stretching a blanket over the tiny thick stone doorway, they announced its readiness.

It was close to midnight when we entered, taking off our clothing outside and ducking into the ovenlike heat of the *touj*, lit by the glow of the porous volcanic basaltic boulders in whose heads we all knew our mutual ancestors resided. If you looked hard you could see their eyes and mouths in the glare. After the first prayers were said and Ya Piskát had spilled the first dipperful of cold water onto their glowing faces, they spoke in hisses, whistles, and moans, filling the *touj* with a glorious and delicious blast of well-deserved heat that drove the aching stress of the weeks of politics, courting, and doubt right out of our bodies.

The instant anyone felt the effects of the heat they would begin to fan their backs and feet with the branches of leaves in a rhythmic way. The heat would normally rise to a point where you'd feel you were going to faint, but by saying a magic phrase, you would be made whole again. Anyone hearing that phrase would help you by acknowledging you with a man or woman word. They would do this even if they were just passing by you in the street and didn't really know you.

But tonight, after all the beauty and admonishments from the mentors about no swearing, expressing of bad thoughts, or arguing, Ya Lur accidentally knocked the biggest white-hot boulder, weighing about fifteen pounds, straight onto my naked foot. It sizzled as it burned into me in an instant, and the smell of my burning skin rose fast in the steamy air. Without a word, I took the little crook stick for moving stones and rolled it off my broken and burnt foot onto the ground by the pyramid of its relatives hissing in the corner. I left the *touj* without a word and began walking as best I could, pushing my roasted foot into the cool mud whenever I found some, wandering the village paths in front of our compound with only a very tiny *stoy* cloth over my "bird." The villagers were astounded to see me so unregally attired, drifting up and down the street naked with a limp. But the old people knew I was trying to avoid arguing, swearing, and the thinking of bad thoughts. People had to laugh at the irony of it.

By the time I'd made it back home, A Sisay, Ya Piskát, and Ya Lur were out of the sweat, leaning back flushed and panting, trying to catch their breath after forty minutes of baking heat. They were scattered next to our compound's cooking fires where a previously cooked bass sat cooling in a clay cooking tray in its juicy bath of *coban* chiles, limes, and *miltomates.*

Faint from the *touj,* all of them started quaking with laughter when they saw me, and pretty soon I was shaking in hysteria myself to think how funny the spirits were to test my grandiosity and my pride the very first night. I'd retained my temper; I hadn't argued. All was well; I was a shaman and I had good plants for burns. I cooked some and, within the week, I was walking easily again.

THIRTEEN

RAINBOYS AND SHIMMERING GIRLS
GATHERING THE INITIATES

Aq Shik, my crane hawk, took to flying into the belfry every time the young chiefs visited the sacred Hole at the center of the universe to pray and feed the other world, as we did every evening. The strange hawk always made it there before we did and was sitting excited on the altar in our initiate hall when we arrived.

Every morning we gathered together and examined our dreams, then off we'd go to whatever sacred house was indicated in the dream, starting our daily tour at the flowering Hole where we left luxurious offerings in keeping with the knightly positions we'd agreed to uphold.

It was here over this Hole that the original House of the World shrine had been annually built and dismantled by initiates for millennia before. Now at Easter we would attempt once again to make the world live by constructing the world in effigy. We'd have to raise it back a bit from the Hole, as the old-time Catholics used it for Christ's crucifixion.

Spending our words like coins, we gave the rough gold of our untrained tongues to the Goddess who was lost down the Hole, somewhere in the many other worlds therein.

Kneeling in a horseshoe around the Hole, wearing our black blankets over our shoulders, our hats in our hand, we prayed to whatever we'd dreamt, placing our offerings at the invisible foundation of the shrine house we hoped to build. In this way we fed the deities of the house's form, those who lived invisible in its corners, in eternal possibility. After making the motions of Mayan genuflection, off we sauntered in the slow and rolling warrior walk taught to us by our mentors, donning our hats when we hit the deserted sun-filled meeting atrium of the Scat Mulaj and proceeded down the steps to the chosen Sacred House of the day.

This morning was different from all the others. Later today all the Scat Mulaj, we young men and women chiefs, and all of our bantering crew of experts and elders would follow the old drummer house to house, pulling in the young men and women whose day had come to begin their initiation out of childhood into adolescence.

Ma Stev Tzapalu, his big old bulldog head bristling with little silver hairs like an ant bear's back, led the men to a group of *Quash* trees, the *anona*. Whipping the trees so they would flower, we asked the trees for help in the release of the Goddess. Then we young chiefs ceremonially cut thirteen straight staffs, each chief's staff equaling his height. Because the moon was right the bark peeled so luxuriously that it came off in a thick tube. The exposed wood was full of the Goddess's body, water that melted away within the hour leaving a smooth knotless bar that looked like polished bone the color of fresh hail.

Blunting the ends somewhat, the old men bound all thirteen staffs together into one heavy trunk. A candle was fed to them and then, incensing them, we left them to lie in state as a sign of the chief's deity. The women were occupied somewhere else with a similar rite involving some large clay pots.

By midmorning, our Jcamel Bey, Road Opener, had passed over our initiation house threshold, first kneeling at the doorway, then addressing the bundle of staffs as the "old trunk's branches" from the Hole, kissing them as he did so.

The Road Opener, a hired shaman, metaphorically cut away psychic poison, thorns, arrows, blow gun pellets, shot cow molars, death dust, traps, snares, witchcraft, envy attacks, dream sickness, generation ghosts, and any other thing that might hurt the young chiefs, the counselors, and especially the young men and women we had to gather for initiation.

Called Diez Peso, or Ten Bucks, by the village, this particular Road Opener was a married-in uncle of my father-in-law's mother. Outside of Chiv and Mlvish, he was the most sought-after shaman on this side of the lake. In his midthirties, he was the hope of shamanism in the village. Not only knowledgeable but creative, his prayers outdid anyone else's as he wept; and he could see so well who and what he addressed that he used the names for the Gods and Saints given him by the Gods themselves. When he prayed and sang, the Earth's Layers listened and stepped up their own life-giving songs. He was a very shy and quiet man, unlike Chiv and some of the other shamans, but when he was on the job, he spoke loud and meaningfully.

When the women had returned, we rose amidst the smoke and headed for the church to address the Hole. Two men shouldered the bundle of staffs, while the rest of us swung incense pots and cradled in our arms the normal loads of liquor, candles, tobacco, incense packages, and flowers. Ma Diez showed us how to walk the maze of the village, stopping at each invisible Hole, spirit branch, and crossroad to pray, leaving little offerings behind. Like Hänsel and Gretel, we made our way, dropping crumbs of sweet smells and beauty behind us as we journeyed into the center of the other worlds, finally arriving at the old church.

We stopped and knelt at every holy angle and piece of deified time, some represented as saints and others as building stones, waking them again. Then we entered another maze that only shamans could see and the Scat understand, until we finally arrived at the Hole, the center of the universe.

Here, after the prayers and offerings had been given, Ma Diez made a prayer of unforgettable content, spreading it like spiritual honey over all the flowers and smoke, through whose lusciousness the old counselors pushed the trunk of the gathered staffs into the Hole, along with our hands and feet, thereby blessing us. Then pulling the loose knot on the handmade rope that bound the staffs into one, they broke the trunk apart, and each staff fell outward like long spokes on a wheel. Every young chief was presented with one of these bone-white *chmai* by his chosen mentor. A Sisay handed me my staff, which still hangs over my altar. The old men were the trunk whose roots were in the Hole. We, the chiefs, were their branches, the chiefs on whose branchlike arms the youth would flower. It was all a flowering tree.

Keeping our staffs in front of us, we backed up and turned away from the Hole, all in a row. With our hands over the top of our staffs holding us up, from the ground to our chests, we became branches off the old trunk who'd grown into visibility here.

Leaning on the blessed wood, with our backs to the women, we looked out and away when they began their ritual at the Hole. It had its own beauty and procedure whose secrecy kept the uninitiated world from trespassing the delicate mysteries of the holy womb, thereby keeping the Female in the universe alive. Although this time of year what was Female was held prisoner in the world of Death, this evening we would go and gather up the initiates whom we hoped might be able to go into that world and bring the Bride of Life back to our Earth, to the women and to the village. If the Goddess returned, her child, the Flowering Fruited Earth, would be riding pregnant in her belly, put there by Death itself.

Finishing up, we made the Mayan genuflection: Mother-Father-Parent Male Child-Maker, Female Child-Maker, Face of the Fruited Earth and, kissing the ground when we'd finished, we moved off like finely dressed dancers leaving the ballroom in a solid graceful mass, and returned "home."

It was midday by the time we arrived back in our nest, as the initiation huts were called. Filing into the long dark room, the men took off their hats, and the old ladies, happy and chattering, twisted back their head ribbons. Then we all settled onto the pine needles, stools, benches, and reed mats to await the widows who had prepared a feast of turkey broth, *qixtan* greens, and paper-thin *wej*, white tortillas. We were hungry.

No sooner had we eaten than a runner from the Scat called us to present ourselves at the columns and steps to face A Cuxtin and the student youth. Something was wrong again.

We sat the messenger down and fed him, which is what kings, queens, chiefs, and initiators do, after which he filled us in, gesticulating in great perturbation. After learning how I'd been appointed as chief to find a way to continue the initiations without the inclusion of any of the degrading enforced service to the bureaucrats, the "progressive" youth had laughed at the idea, calling it an utter fraud. Underestimating my love of the village and the village's love of the ritual, they disregarded it all as the last-ditch attempt of a doomed and dying thing that was trying to lift its head one last time before it succumbed to what they saw as the inevitable justice of the educated mind.

After a month of our ritual preparations, however, they began to feel forgotten. No one was paying any attention to them, as their political platform had been made somewhat irrelevant when the village adopted a purely spiritual initiation. The majority of the village began to prepare in great enthusiasm for what it always prepared for every year: the initiations of the youth and the regeneration of the Earth.

As children of Christian converts who'd raised them to disrespect their own village's spiritual ways, these young men and women had spent their childhood without the stories, admonishments of the taboos, and attendance at the ceremonial feasts where the village learned the details of the beauty and ritual eloquence that kept the village alive. The youth could not desire what they hadn't been exposed to. This left the students utterly unknowledgeable of the very system they were attacking. What they knew of the traditionalists' life was based on the demonizing propaganda of the Christians, the right-wing rationalist thinking of their schoolteachers in the capital, and the soon-to-be armed, antigovernment Marxist student groups who were anti-traditionalist.

After hearing about the successful beginnings of our ritual, not of course to thwart the students but to keep the Earth alive, the ignored students held meetings with their guerrilla associates and superiors who suggested that, in this case, they themselves volunteer to "bring the fruit." This referred to the most visible part of the initiation, the return of the initiates on foot from the hot coastal plains with orchid-decorated closed boxes filled with sacred types of fruit from the Underworld.

In their further ignorance, instead of approaching the headmen and headwomen of the Scat Mulaj, the students made friends with a despondent chief named Ma Cuxtin. They did this because he was a Sacred House chief in charge of Holy Boy, a deity, who played an enormous part in the initiations and in the Tzutujuil's version of Easter.

Ma Cuxtin, who was a New Catholic, ended up chief of Holy Boy by default. He'd loaned the former appointed Scat chief his long stone house to shelter the God, but when illness killed the real chief, Ma Cuxtin slipped into the vacant position without the endorsement of the Scat Mulaj. The third official who was actually in charge of the hands-on ritual feeding of Holy Boy was aghast and asked the hierarchy to find a new chief before the initiation, but Ma Cuxtin wouldn't allow anyone in.

Almost as ignorant as the students about the reasons and teaching behind the annual village rituals, Ma Cuxtin, who dressed in slacks, white shirt, and a pullover sweater, now agreed to let the students become the bringer of the fruit, housing it next to Holy Boy.

To the old folks this was a disgustingly ignorant case of world wrecking. The fruit, which represented the Goddess and the initiates' own souls, had to be kept totally out of view of Holy Boy until the crucial day and moment when the Goddess could be brought together with Holy Boy's Male Force to fertilize the Earth. If this part of the ritual were endangered by bringing it to a precipitory climax before the young initiates themselves were "ripe," the Goddess would flee. Then the Earth would become porous and sterile, the people would fall into a chaos of flatness and paranoid depression, and the youth would remain in a kind of hopeless limbo.

Ma Cuxtin was trying to run his own show, and the priests of Holy Boy and all the sacred house members had left him and begun to frequent my house to show their support of the initiations.

A meeting had been called by the head men and women to hold a face-to-face discussion with Ma Cuxtin and the students in hopes of disentangling the problem and explaining to them why what they were suggesting would not work. These elders even suggested to the student youth that they were welcome to enter my ranks and be initiated like all the men before them.

Ashamed and recognizing that the students and Ma Cuxtin wanted me removed at all costs, albeit rationalizing it all in an entirely hypocritical premise, I decided to attend the meeting alone as a civilian without my robes, headcloth, staff, or subchiefs. If the meeting went badly I wanted it to go against me personally. I didn't want to jeopardize the whole ritual by having it implicated in some strange political complications.

By the time I arrived, the villagers had been arguing with the students for an hour already. It was clear to everyone that these young men wanted to be chiefs, not initiates. The students' plan was to pick up just any kind of fruits on the coast, bring them up on trucks, stop a couple hundred yards outside the village, and then march in with the fruit on their backs as if they'd carried it the entire round trip of sixty miles.

Ma Cuxtin had not altered his position and had been hiding inside the church. The students fled when they saw how the old men pulled me into their midst and sat me down next to the headman and a hundred furious old Scat Mulaj members.

A crowd of six thousand raging people roamed out front below the steps. Up in the atrium a couple hundred more stood mumbling and discussing the possibilities with each other. Many ex-*Mayori* were there, at least thirty years' worth of former initiating chiefs, none of whom I'd ever seen gathered in one place before. Now that I'd shown up, the Scat directed them to go looking for Ma Cuxtin. In five minutes they had succeeded in pulling him out of the old church. He was wearing his unearned black blanket, red-tinseled headcloth, and brandishing the short flowering staff of his assumed office. When he tried to flee down the front steps, the men barred his way.

His gold teeth showing though his Ladino mustache, this would-be chief blurted out, "No, I'll be the young man's chief, the students will bring the fruit. What more is there to it? Holy Boy is already there. It's all together as it should be. Just get rid of that over there." With that, he pointed at me with his staff.

My face went red with humiliation and hurt pride. I had truly thought, in the most naive, idiotic way, that the magnificent start we'd given the ritual had charmed the hard hearts of everyone in the village, that by now they could see how it could be saved authentically, not just in appearances. But at that point there was no time for philosophizing. The old chiefs shrieked and yelled at Ma Cuxtin, asking him to listen to sense. Instead, yelling at the top of his lungs, he unexpectedly wheeled around and in the crowded tension managed to strike one of the seated sacred women in the teeth with his flailing staff.

The crowd almost rioted as the chieftess of the Sacred House of Ya Chon grabbed her bleeding mouth and wept, her head ribbon tumbling over her head and down around her neck. Ma Tun Ratzam, our second headman, the distinguished old canoe mogul, grabbed Ma Cuxtin by the shoulders, ostensibly to calm him down, but Ma Cuxtin whacked him squarely across the face with his staff, knocking him back against the wall.

Looking on from some thirty feet away I saw the headman's wife, Shell, stand in her long white robes with a face so fierce that it could have curdled steel, and, without a word, in half an instant, her jaw jutting, she flicked her index finger above her head. The ex-*Mayori,* obeying her rarely used but well-understood gesture, grabbed the punching and wheeling Ma Cuxtin and threw him bodily down the front of the church steps to the village women and children below. The old chieftess tottered over to the edge of the stairs and ordered the village to stone Ma Cuxtin. The villagers commenced to do exactly that as he tried to run away toward his house half a mile to the south. I made a move to stop the people from killing him, but the old chiefs, their faces even fiercer than their wives', grabbed me in a grip as firm as a giant anteater. "This is not your business. You didn't start it and you won't stop it. Your business is to make the Earth come back to life and to get our youth through it in one piece."

Luckily Ma Cuxtin's head caught only one small stone on the side by his right ear, but his body was beaten with sticks and rocks, and dust was rubbed into his hair and forced down his pants. His blanket and staff lay torn and cracked in the cindery dust. He struggled from wall to wall alone and damaged, back to his house, bruised like a melon having been mashed on the unforgiving ground of the Canyon Village.

I hated this. I hated this thoroughly and started to lose my taste for ritual, for humans, and for the village altogether.

There was something about the unabashed medievalness and the village's uncomplicated reaction that made me feel as if some part of me had always lived here. At the same time I knew that I'd been in this way of being so long and so deeply that I could now afford to not like the village without the fear of losing it, as I had for so long.

When I looked up from my disgust, the whole village was staring at me in silence. The old men's faces had not changed their expression much since Ma Cuxtin's punishment.

The headman spoke fiercely, "The stakes are high now, Brother Parent, First Grandchild. So you had better get to work." Shocked and frozen to the spot, I could barely move. But when I did and had finished kissing all the old hands and rings of the old serious ladies and righteous old men, Ma Ajtujal, the leader of the sacred house of the Underworld, spoke. "The next time you and your chiefs show up here, we want you wearing your *qu',* blanket, your *xcajcoj,* headcloth, and carrying your *chmai,* staff. We're over here throwing our own people down stairs and hitting them with firewood to save you, and you show up looking like a boy who couldn't bother to be proud enough of us to look like us and be one of us. Get to work, Brother Parent. It's time to gather up the youth."

And they let me go. The crowds disappeared, nothing was solved, but all was made clear. Rattled and stunned, I padded home in the cindery dust of Atitlan where my roots sank another five centuries deep into layers of life and ways of seeing that had nothing to do with my comfort, my happiness, my enjoyment, or my own opinions, all of which, freely held, were only by-products of my responsibility to bring home and reassemble the House of the World in a village that would beat a man for trying to subvert it.

Shuffling along like an old man's overworked knees, moving just enough to keep them from seizing up, even supernatural events in the village creaked along in a pretty regular and gradual sway. Then one day everything bursts out like rock salt on a bed of coals, snapping, whistling, zinging, exploding into action, people everywhere get things done all at once on different fronts, one occurrence after the next, like a million flowers of possibility opening in unison while a million buzzing bees bury their funny heads in the thick pollen of tradition.

I returned to our initiation house where all my council sat waiting for the news. Of course they had already heard, but out of courtesy and the Tzutujil love of small details, they listened attentively with horrified interjections and piteous looks on their faces. As soon as I'd finished my account, the courteous A Sisay jumped up and, shaking with frustration, reminded me that it was now time to go gather up our initiates.

Having planned for this moment for two months, now it was here and I was straggling!

The *Mayori* and I marched back to the church with the drummer and a new flute player, a fisherman named Sweet who had been a member of my old band. I'd taught him everything I'd been taught, and now he was the new flute man. We'd all come to invite the Scat Mulaj to come with us and bring in the new initiates. They were out in full force and considerably calmed down. Cheerful as ever, shaking hands and hugging us as if this was the first they'd seen us all in a month, they barely allowed us enough seriousness to assume our fierce young chief postures. Finally, they lined up, and we chiefs, leaning on our long staffs, our blankets finely arranged, formally asked these old people to help us gather up what they called our Flowers and our Sprouts, the eligible young men and women.

The rolling echo of the drum and the shrill birdlike screams of Sweetboy's flute drowned out our words, but the old folks pretended to hear us ask them in the ancient words they themselves had taught us. Unable to distinguish a word of it, the Scat Mulaj nodded and responded at all the right places knowing full well what we were saying, like a row of deaf Beethovens listening to their own symphonies being played back to them. And when all the nodding, smoking, toasting, incensing, and responses had been made, smoked, and spilled, the old chiefs with the young chiefs and the old chieftesses with the young chieftesses all walked arm in arm, clacking and scuffling down the steps like a bunch of medieval kings and queens, our robes rustling and our staffs clinking. The majestic entourage jammed the entire face of the temple stairs, fanning out into the open like a massive bed of moving flowers. The drummer and flute player thundered and tweeted in front of us, announcing our progress through the village and our mission to fish for teenage boys and girls who had been made eligible for initiation by having fallen in love. We were to pull them into our old flowering ranks, out of their beloved homes and into a new life where they could save the earth, save the Goddess of Water, and save their parents, to save themselves from becoming youth having babies before they had become truly human and eloquent.

Crowding the narrow village corridors and wider thoroughfares, we pushed on with a great sense of purpose. The day had been hot but the afternoon was cool and clear as we arrived at the compound of Axe, a wealthy merchant whose son, Gourd, had been seen courting a girl, Reed Mat. We massed outside as the drum pumped away, playing the Song of the Flowers until someone from the compound ventured out. It was a little seven-year-old girl whose big eyes, filled with the sight of all of us, blurted out, *"Tá ntie Naqniwajo?"* Father, Mother, what do you want? She was obviously being coached by an unseen parent who whispered her lines through the cornstalk walls. We chuckled at the tiny three-and-half-foot girl who was holding back two hundred adults on a mission.

I spoke up, A Sisay also coaching me by whispering into my ear, "Little madam, you, are your grandparents home? We've come to fetch your uncle, the one they call Gourd." At first she didn't respond, biting her lip. Then, whispering to the wall, she asked, "What?" Finally she blurted out to us in the singsong voice of a child repeating her lines in a play, "Fathers, Mothers, there is no one here by that name. You must be mistaken, unless you mean our little Ma Xep, but he is too young to walk with Ladies and Lords."

At this point, the village headmen and women took over the talking as A Sisay and the advisors grabbed my arm and pointed. He told me to take my chiefs and run to the rear of the compound to catch whoever was disappearing over the rock wall there.

Off we bolted holding our hats, our tailored blankets flapping in the wind, just in time to apprehend a shaved-head sixteen-year-old called Gourd, just touching down on an old root at the base of a loose basaltic wall shining from years of rear exits.

We grabbed him gently by the arms like constables arresting a friendly pickpocket, and escorted him back to the front of the compound. Luckily he didn't struggle.

His brave little niece clapped her shawl over her mouth in astonishment when she saw her uncle in our midst and ran to call all her people, about twenty-five in all, including Gourd's father, Axe.

Again whispering in my ear, A Sisay choreographed my words as I directed them to Gourd's parents. With one hand firmly on Gourd's arm and the other on my staff, I began:

"You Lords of this Earth
You Ladies of the Earth
We the eight hundred shimmering
The eight hundred flashing
Come at your feet
Come at your branches
Desiring the company of
Your First Sunlight
Your First Dawnlight
As he our Flower, our Sprout
On the branches of this the trunk of

The Village, the Complete Gathering
Is held alive by the same
Ancestral root
Who yesterday and the day before, and then today
We came searching, shimmering
We came desiring, flashing,
In the presence of all our mutual
Ancestors, to hold him in our branches flowering
So that he may become cooked and ripe
So he may become the carrier
The sacrificer
The bringer of Her
The maker of the House of the Holy."

The parents made replies at each pause, "Yes, Father, yes, that's a true word. Yes, we understand. Yes, it's time," and so on.

Then the young fellow was asked to speak to his parents as he stood buried in chiefs and initiating princes. I whispered my well-practiced phrases into his ear and he repeated them loudly:

"Mother, Father,
Look upon me well
This is the last
You will see of me
Like this
In this form
As the Earth's face is a fruit
On the tree of all ancestral given life
So I am a fruit on your tree
When you see me again
I will have a new face
And different one
Please don't abandon me
Please don't forget me
I won't abandon you

I won't forget you
Long Life, Honey in the Heart,
No Evil, Thirteen Thank-yous."

Most of the women's faces were dripping with tears and Gourd's father held on but finally wept. The whole truth of that hollow place that would be left in the compound and in their hearts by their child's absence crashed in on them in a sudden and honorable way. Though most families had been through this before, and the parents knew full well that their boy was in good hands and was never going more than two hundred yards or a couple of miles away, it never helped them to deal with the reality of children pulling away. The fact that the village helped the youth to disobey the toxic desire of a parent's instinct to keep their children small and friendly was always a hard thing to bear.

We turned Gourd away from his parents and told him not to look back, that his youth was over. I signaled to the drum and flute and they began to thunder and squeal as the crowd of well-dressed old ladies and men surged away from Axe's compound through the copal smoke, Gourd being washed along in the middle of the human flood.

In a frantic, wild-eyed tone A Sisay told me to take my chiefs and stride to the rear of our column, to watch out and keep our staffs up and ready. We were not to hurt anyone or the initiations would be doomed.

I had no idea what he was talking about. The Tzutujil don't train people to do jobs, their rituals are like storms that start happening with or without you. You learned as you went in an immediate kind of on-the-job-training.

We ran to the rear, just barely in time to catch Gourd's mother, his aunt and three sisters coming at us furiously, throwing stones and wielding sticks. They were weeping and shouting evil things about our ancestors and our appearances.

We dodged the missiles all right, but then they ran up to us, trying to break the line, screaming:

"Why do you steal our children,
you pile of buzzard greens? Don't take my boy, my Sunlight,
My Dawn.
I want to die,
you evil chiefs, you dog-hearted, motherless bastards."

Like parade police, we kept them back with our staffs and kept them from getting to Gourd and the elders who were marching away. The women were strong and beat us with their fists and nails until they collapsed in a sad pile, sobbing in deep grief.

We sympathized with them because we had young children too, and saw what we would face when we came to this.

Together the young chiefs gently lifted the ladies up off the volcanic dust and walked them back to their people, who continued to comfort them. The older folks in the compound kissed our rings and thanked us. We turned to the street, adjusted our dusty blankets and hats, and paced, focused and fast, until we caught up with the drum and the Scat Mulaj. We took our place in the center, right next to Gourd and A Sisay. Gourd was teary-eyed too. He'd been told not to look back, but they always do, and see their parents fighting the chiefs to get them back, sometimes very violently. It was a custom and it was very real. The feelings and fighting were all part of the ritual. Knowing you were missed at your house was the most important thing. Knowing that your absence created a vacuum in your parents' home and hearts and that they couldn't bear the pain of your leaving was a necessary understanding for the youth.

To be missed at home and to be carried off by the entire village sacred hierarchy, who desired your presence, made you feel valuable, spiritually and at home, and proud to be a Tzutujil. This way the child couldn't blame the parents and the parents couldn't blame the youth. Parents who didn't fight the chiefs when they took the youth away were a disgrace, but most of the time it was hard going for us chiefs. Now I knew why we had such stout poles. They weren't for looks, they were for keeping angry villagers from killing us and to keep them from taking back their kids, for keeping the youth from falling back into an eternal state of dependency.

The next boy had already made it to the canoes and was paddling madly away. We borrowed two short fishermen dugouts and caught him in a pincer action halfway to Xetuc.

Everyone cheered when we finally came back, out of breath and muddy. But as the afternoon wore on, we had an increasing number of boys tucked safely within the heart of our crowd of nobles, thronging through the dusty village behind the ever-rumbling beacon of Ma QoQuix's drum.

Every time we told the boys not to look back, they all looked back as a group. It did them good to have each other witness that they were all missed a little and to know that they had company on this pilgrimage into the other world brought on by their desire.

It took us a week of evenings to get all the eligible boys gathered up. Though initiation was not mandatory anymore, we went about it as if nothing had changed. It being a well-practiced tradition, it all took place as if it were still enforced.

Nonetheless there were those who refused. We had scouted it all out beforehand and we only went to the houses where the boys were most likely to come. Unknown candidates, boys who volunteered, just showed up at our doors the following week after seeing how well it was going and how grand the other boys were made to be. If they promised to stick it out, we added them to the rest, ending up with over fifty youth between the ages of fourteen and eighteen.

The young women went along more peacefully than the boys, probably because in their ritual there was less isolation from the village and also because they were anxious to get out into the world with their new mentors, away from their jealous or fearful mothers. For whatever reasons, the ladies had a full quota of young women before we did, and started up their initiations separately from the men.

The young chiefs met up often with their wives, the initiators of the girls, but neither saw the inside of the other gender's initiation houses until the end. If all went well, the young men and their sweethearts would be reunited in four or five months.

FOURTEEN

ROBBING MOTHER, DRINKING TO THE GODDESS

You couldn't even say the words much less willingly do such a thing. Everything in your early life said this was the deepest treason. The old people of your compound spent most of the time they had with you drumming the taboos and rules into you: what not to do, and how not to offend the Earth and all the spirits that reside in every place and thing.

And now here you were with a pile of young men whom you might mistake for a nest of eager fox cubs whose strange, preoccupied eyes dreamt about everything in the world except becoming adult foxes.

One of the things taught to these fox kits was that since the beginning of this world, humans were thieves, holy thieves, weak thieving beings who stole every bit of what humans claim as theirs: their abilities, their material wealth, and their territory. It was all stolen from nature, which, in the end, is just a fancy name for the holy Face of the Gods.

Anciently, the Tzutujil had discovered that if humans were forced to steal within the ritual context of initiation, then, after they completed their initiations, men wouldn't be inclined to steal. They would understand that all thieveries are against the Great Mother and that all survival is a direct thieving from she who births and bears all fruit, corn, meat, fiber, and warmth from wood. These were all her children that we humans cut, kill, harvest, butcher, and consume, some of us with no consciousness of where any of it really comes from.

All ritual has to do with this understanding and with making things good again with the Old Woman. The reality of this ran through all Mayan thinking. It didn't cause shame but only the awareness of the shame in it. To enforce the meaning of this on the youth, the initiators' first task was to teach them to rob their mothers. All these old righteous men who'd been telling you for years never to steal were now teaching you how and forcing you to do it.

None of the Rainboys, as the initiated were called, wanted to do that, as it wouldn't bring them any love or honor from the women, which is mostly what boys want. The hatred and disrepute that would be heaped upon a thief who robbed his beloved mother would teach the boys exactly how the spirits viewed humans in general, those men and women who never give anything to the spirit or weep for the huge holes they dig into the heart of the Mother of all Life in the name of human survival and conceit. In order to learn true respect, boys had to first understand the destructiveness of disrespect. For this reason, the boys were sent off to steal a certain type of wide-mouthed heavy cooking tub from their own mother's hut.

The old men made prayers to all the spirits of their boys' ancestors to give them ability and to let them return unharmed without causing physical hurt to anyone in the process.

Then they lit candles and poured liquor, shredded flowers to the Goddess whom they were about to insult, asking her to indulge them in the interest of learning about being the thieves they really were, and whipped their hands with certain plants. Then off they went, trotting like idiots, straight to their mothers' houses where, of course, the women were gathered, armed with switches, logs, and rocks, cursing the chiefs and old men for sending the boys so late and interrupting their normal routine of toil, child rearing, and weaving.

The boys had already forgotten that their mothers and her relatives knew all about this custom. As soon as the women caught sight of them, they set upon their own sons as they would have set upon any kind of thief—raccoon, dog, or human—startling the boy away from his mother's side like a little colt who, after suckling for so long, is no longer welcome as a child because he does not recognize himself for the stallion that the women can see he's becoming. Driven off like a stud colt into the stallion herd, safely away from the little kids and women until he can find a way to live without wanting to be both a son and a lover, ending up as a father and a husband, or at least knowing the difference.

Some of the more naive boys just stood there, stunned by the fact that the women who, only a couple of days before, would have killed his initiator to get him back were now threatening him with an ironwood branch. Even his little siblings were yelling at him to get out of their compound, telling him that he was not a kid anymore, so what did he want here now? Many a boy was driven back to the initiation house empty-handed with a few extra lumps on his head and his soul, and a scared look in his eyes from the little hair of rejection growing in his heart. But the old men knew that, at this point, the boys shouldn't be allowed to sit and mope. They had to be pushed or they'd grow terrified and hard. So we sent them out again and again, sometimes with older initiates from the year past to help their minds find the ancestral stealth necessary to steal these huge old sooty pots that usually sat heaped upside down like a pile of gigantic sleeping turtles right under the thatched eaves out in front of a traditionalist's hut.

These weren't just any old pots that we were asking them to steal but those earned by the adult women in their initiations. These pots represented their services to the sacred and their marriages.

To steal one you had to climb under it because, indeed, they were so ample that a teenager could climb right in. They were delicate things and the slightest jar the wrong way could cause these earthenware tubs to crash into pieces, which was absolutely not part of what we were doing. To ruin your mother's pot was more unthinkable than stealing it.

After hiding under one like a pea in a shell game, you had to judge the right moment to stand up and start walking with your knees bent and your little feet poking out. The old tubs covering your head, back, and bottom made it so you couldn't see much of where you were heading.

The trick in this was knowing that the women, your mother in particular, were not interested in the pot getting damaged. So if you were moving fast enough they wouldn't throw anything at you, protected as you were by their love of this symbol of their womanhood. They also didn't want you to fall and smash it, so they didn't allow the children to whip your bare legs and funny feet that were walking the pot to the initiate hut in a squatting kind of way.

If you made it a hundred yards, you popped the edge of the pot up on your forehead so you could see and started moving. When you passed over the threshold of the initiate hut, your chiefs, old mentors, and peers let out a shout and a cheer for your theft. The old fellows relieved you of your mother's pot, and put it in a pile by the altar with the rest.

It was good to get the pot. Not everybody did, but it was important to have the experience of being driven off so that you could understand the reality of your new life. You couldn't be around your mother anymore until you were fully awake, because it wouldn't be good for you or for her. That separation kept you from being hated by or hating your father. Instead it made you miss him, and he longed for you and prayed for your safe return.

The women called these pots their "navels," and they stood for pregnant bellies. For a boy to separate from his mother, he had to steal the place where his mother wanted him to stay, the place where she had hidden him to keep him safe when he was little, in her navel, her womanness. This is why the ladies received these pots during their own initiations. It was not likely that a woman would crack her own womb, so by stealing it, a boy was not only driven out but also protected by her in a different way—albeit you were being protected from her, mostly. That kind of knowledge was so immense that only a few boys would ever really understand it. But going through it all was more important than understanding it, and you were protected a little by the pot no matter how much of what you'd done had actually sunk in.

Since the initiate hall was off-limits to everyone except the mentors, the initiates, and the initiating chiefs, no women were ever allowed to come even close to it. No immediate relatives were allowed in either, and in particular your father and never your mother.

The girls in their dealings with their initiator had equal rules. The girls lived in their initiation house, and the boys in theirs, sweeping and watering it down, each youth putting up a candle that was kept constantly burning to feed the master of his soul.

In the days following the thefts, certain of the mothers came to ransom their cooking pots, their umbilicus, their womanness.

Standing at a respectful distance, they sent little brothers or cousins of their initiate sons into the big hut with their message, and we chiefs came out to greet them.

With great kindness and weeping for their boys, whom they missed, they offered us special foods that took great effort to prepare to trade to the boy for the return of their pot.

We always accepted these gifts with grace and, lifting the ancient tub, a couple of us would walk it back home to her house.

Other boys, however, were forced to return these big clay pots to their compounds with as much planned stealth and circumspection as when they'd stolen them, and that was very comical. Some pots never got back at all.

◈

The adolescent river of amorous fire that gushed through the young men's longing bodies had an inebriating quality. Overflowing the banks of reason, this delicious flood excavated a young man's mind, washing away all but a smattering of what he'd learned as a child. The hollowness that remained was a painful longing to be filled with more of what had made it hollow.

This hollowness was natural and was meant to be filled with his soul, for it was the young man's soul that had been stolen by Death in the confusion of that flood. That hollow place, like the Hole in the church, was called the Throne of the Goddess. It was here that a man's personal soul was supposed to sit, at home in her regal chair, using the boy as her bench.

Only old chiefs and priestesses knew that the Goddess a boy longed for in his tearful and moody desperation was his first true bride. Old people knew that a flood-hollowed boy saw this first Bride, the Goddess, in the eyes of every deer-eyed girl in the village. He saw Her in every sway, surge, twist, and trot of every tinsel-flashing, copper-skinned girl whose barely parted lips exposed the shell-white knives of her water-speaking mouth. Every girl was a goddess at that point. When a boy finally settled on a particular goddess, if he married her before he learned that the real Goddess was living in the Underworld, he would remain emptied, trying to fill his Goddess place with regular girls, one after the other. In his longing search to rescue the Goddess from the Underworld, he would hopefully find his own Goddess Bride, a smaller Goddesslike being. This Bride we called the soul of a young man.

The hollow place of his desire could receive his soul, but not the over-heavy, overly burdening, too great, too delicious, too powerful Goddess of the Flowering Earth. Only then, with that Goddess part of himself well seated, could his mysterious marriage with his soul Bride, his deified personal spirit, give birth to a child. The child of a boy married to his divine soul Bride was called *Acha*, meaning "man."

Only an initiated man or *Acha* could marry a woman and not be miserable and disappointed. An uninitiated man was one who didn't know that his first love was a divine being, a being that lived and kissed him in nature, as a village, in the landscape of the world. If he tried to find her first in a human woman, he would become angry or depressed because she could not be that Goddess. It was the same for the girls, since the husband of an uninitiated woman would have to be a God or he would be trivialized and discarded as a failure, or, worse yet, start believing that he was one!

Uninitiated men beat women for not being Goddesses. They left women behind who turned out to have thoughts and opinions of their own, or they allowed themselves to be ground to dust, year by year, by women whom they wanted and hoped would miraculously turn into a Goddess later on. Women had the same experiences with their husbands, men who disappointed them when they refused to be the Gods the women longed to be loved by.

Therefore, the old people knew that when men in their youth lose their souls, their hearts, their *Rukux*, to the Lords of Death, who cruelly take them to the Underworld, the world too in the dry season loses its Goddess, the soul Bride of all collective existence. She is abducted and taken to live in the Underworld with the Great Kings and Queens of Death.

The Goddess's heart contained all possibility of growth and flowering, while her body holds all liquids, waters, and tears of grief. This secret knowledge of initiation did not come right away; and in no way was it given over to the boys as I have written it down here, in a literal transmission. It would have to be discovered slowly by each young man, through experience, as he was pushed through the tubelike roots of initiation into retrieving the Goddess from the underworld. The magical and delicious consciousness that occurred as a result of this experience gave them a vision that can only be remotely, and never accurately, transmitted to the uninitiated.

What we did tell each other as we discovered these delicate details of a true man's way of being was that each man's personal soul Bride was also a particle of the Bride Soul Goddess of all life. In other words, every man of the same age set was ripe for love because his heart had been stolen by Death. By facing Death in a ritual struggle, he might retrieve his own soul. By then putting all their retrieved soul Brides together, the Goddess of the Earth could be reassembled from these different individual souls. The peculiarity and uniqueness of each man's personal soul, his Bride, was equally a different organic aspect of the Great Goddess, whose heart was held in a mutual trust in the form of a very well protected, powerful bundle that other rituals succeeded in retrieving from the Holy Death.

For this reason, the personal initiation of young people into adulthood brought the Earth back to life, and themselves back to sanity and life. The madness of youth was enormously useful and was honored as the necessary magical consciousness needed by the culture to save its existence from disintegrating into a flat nothing. It kept the world flowering, but it needed the spiritual intelligence left by the ancestors and directed by the elders. The byproduct, of course, was that each man got his own heart back. When his hollowness had been filled with the small Goddess of his own heart, then when he married a woman, she could see that he could see her seeing him seeing her, and both looking at the little piece of God and Goddess that resided in the other's "Heart Throne" and they were free to love each other properly, as themselves. Having understood and risked one's life for the delicate survival of the divine, one would not readily or willingly destroy it, especially in the heart of the human being who really can love you.

Before initiation, most men try to fill that young hollowness, that empty place carved by the fire flood of desire, with something that will continue the flood, trying to fill the hole with more of what made it hollow. That hollowness is Death itself, and it is in Death's kingdom that the root of all possibility and beauty resides.

Desire is Death's shovel, and digs the hole where one's heart once beat. Stolen by Death, it is this hole, this hollowness, where the heart—transformed by its visit to the Underworld and its rescue made possible by the courting of an eloquent, weeping man—will be replanted, giving it a home. It is in this very hollowness where life will burst forth into a fire of flowers as it takes root once again, finally at home. That is the Home all things search for.

If this hollow place that occurs in adolescence is not negotiated with great guidance by the mentors and chiefs, then a boy could grow uninitiated into the physical size of man, but not yet be a man spiritually. If he should attempt to fill that holy hollowness with alcohol, food, women, fighting, war, ruthlessness, business, or anything else that resembles the delicious inebriating quality of that first hole dug into his life by desire and Death, then he will always be courting Death. He will probably either find his death or begin destroying things.

One becomes a drunk, trying to stay drunk in that first overwhelming delicious hollowness of desire at fourteen. Where, the old chiefs asked, would the men's Soul Bride Goddess sit if he's filled the hole up with liquor, food, women, or money? To keep his hollowness open and his throne available and holy, a boy had to be sent on the journey to retrieve his heart with great finesse, humor, and stories, armed with all the little tricks of men who'd made the Underworld journey before and returned home as cooked boys, ready to grow into men.

Because of this—to the great consternation of the Christians and the literal minds of certain modern people who watched in horror from their smug seats way in the back—our elegant and strange old mentors not only instructed the boys how to rob their mothers, but then, after this was accomplished, they moved on to teaching the boys how to be drunk. They taught them how to be drunk on the alcohol made from the Flowering Earth itself while longing for the love of the Goddess, how to be drunk without filling the hole. In this way, one kept from becoming a drunk.

❖

As in the past, and as would ever be as long as the Flowering Earth had lovers of her watery, divine face hidden deep in this wallowing, windy earth, we young chiefs, our Rainboys, and a few old mentors moved along behind the musicians, striding together as one. We leapt over stumps, straddled roots, bent under lumpy, hairy vines, slushing through leaf litter, sidling, rocking, ducking and dueling the thorn trees and loose granite cliffs, up and down the side of the cloud forest jungle. Finally, lowering ourselves down and down, we landed at the scant, leaf-choked entrance hole to the Underworld at the base of *Xejuyu'*, the mountains beneath. A grove of sky-bound corozo palms called the Throne of Clouds grew in such a close way as to hide this opening from where the Lords of Death and Disease came and went from their world to ours.

The trees that surrounded this entrance hole were over six feet in diameter where their trunks appeared, thrusting out of the ground. They rippled with rings of stony armor under which long stalks of springy wood ran the length. From these stalks old Tzutujil warriors made their hunting and fishing bows and throwing darts. *Chich,* as the corozo wood was called, was so hard that when the Mayans first saw Spanish steel, they began calling it *chich*. To the Tzutujil, everything made of hard metal is still known as *chich*.

With its roots stretching deep under this lowland canyon earth, the corozo tree knew the Underworld well. Pulling water when every other plant was sad and dry, its fibrous stalks pumped the Underworld water straight up to the sky, forcing this juice into the seven-foot-long, torpedo-shaped flower pods that hung below the corozo's hublike convergence of rustling fronds. These were the flowers of the Umbilicus of Heaven. They hung out of the sky above the granite cliff beneath where we men and boys stood sweating, our heads thrown back, our thirsty mouths open. We stared and commented in wonder as we unloaded our axes, machetes, string bags, and black blankets. We knelt at the entrance to a world that only the older of us had ever seen.

Some twenty miles from our homes, this place had been used for initiations for hundreds of years. For this reason the sad skeletal remains of the gigantic toppled palms lay everywhere for miles, their trunks jutting through the forest here and there forever.

In some sixty days my nestlings, our initiates, would enter the Underworld here. After a long, long walk, they would meet up with the enemies of

Life, the Lords of Death themselves, in whose possession the secret of all growth and life resided. If they were successful in retrieving their souls and the Goddess of Water, it was through here at this hole that they would pass on their return journey to the village, through this world of wild living things, the wilderness mansion of the Gods where the Mother jungle wept for the loss of our little Mother, the sister, daughter, wife, and mother to the Gods.

Centuries ago, before the Europeans came, Tzutujil society was still divided into mobile castes of hierarchical theocrats, warriors, and farmers. Each of these divisions conducted its youth initiations separately at different places, all coming together in the end. All that time, the warrior caste would bring a captive warrior they had procured in a raid on a neighboring tribe the previous year. Although this captive was well-treated throughout the year, it was known to all that he would be killed here during a sacrificial dance in which he would be strapped to one of the Cloud Thrones. At a certain point in the dance, long wooden trumpets would have been heard blaring off the mountain tops. For this reason, we still called thunder the trumpets of the Rainwarriors. When this horn blast was heard, the old-time warriors during their initiations would riddle the captive with arrows, killing him on the tree. The bows and shafts of these arrows were made from the wood of the *chich* from the previous year's tree of sacrifice.

But in our day we simply divided our initiates into temporary divisions. The whole village was seen as a little centralized version of the whole world, and each person in the village had an ancestral soul that corresponded to a different part of nature's landscape. Some souls corresponded to trees, some to animals or weather, water, coastal plains or mountains, and so on, ad infinitum. As in ancient times, each division of the village was spiritually in charge of a different part of the sacred geography of the world.

The warriors were in charge of the Underworld and the Underwater. The workers and farmers were in charge of the Earth. The hierarchy was in charge of the trees, the mountains, and the sky.

Each of my subchiefs held one of these divisions, and from then on, for a year, he was called by the name of his altitude in the sacred geography, Lord Mountains, Lord Underworld, Lord Earth, and so forth.

A fourth division, called the Village Home, was created by the combination of the other three. As *Najbey Mam* this was the group I was in charge of.

Together, all four groups of boys would be called the Horses of Clouds, Bringers of Steam, the Little Bringers of Flowers, or the Slaves of Moisture. There were a hundred names for them because, though they were divided into the different parts of the holy landscape, all the altitudes gathered together would build the House of the World in which every possible thing, climate, and altitude existing in the Inner Bigness of the Tzutujil world would be represented. Annually the village initiates brought all the pieces of the world on their backs to the center of the universe, to the center of the village inside the church, all in an organized and ceremonial way.

The killing of the captive in ancient times was not only a sacrificial payment to the Throne of the Clouds, the trunk of the Tree of Life that we in our survival and the pursuit of human culture destroy on a yearly basis. The death of this one beautiful man was meant to be a gift to the other world. The vacancy of his allotted space in this world made by his ornate death would make it possible for a new crop of young initiates to possibly be allowed to survive their adolescence. It was thought that if a sacrifice were not made, a youth's adolescent years could kill him, literally or spiritually. Tzutujil thinking had not changed much over the years. When anything was taken from nature and given to humans to cause their survival, small sacrifices and offerings had to be given to fill in the void we had created. The things we take from the earth, no matter how inanimate they seem to modern folks, are the "children" of parent deities. Those deities don't like us killing their children any more than we liked them killing our own. All great human inventions are made by sophisticated methods that alter and destroy the original form of the source of their components. The youth of those great inventing societies often have their lives sacrificed arbitrarily when they are not given any visible usefulness for their teenage shine and amorous madness.

When things are taken from Nature and the Gods that are huge and are used to cause human ease, comfort, recreation, or excess—the definition of which is not determined by humans but by the spirits of those things—then huge deliberate sacrifice has to be made to the deified Earth. Without these sacrifices, large wars, diseases, and depression would take over the Earth to create enough death to pay for our comfort. Our comfort is not the Gods' prime cause for having humans on the Earth.

The Hole in the church was used by the Catholics to dramatize the death of Spanish Christ on a tree. To the Tzutujil, Jesus' yearly effigial death at that

Hole on a tree looked a whole lot like the old-time death by impalement of their exalted captive who'd been dressed, fed, and treated as a God of Youth called the White Painted Dawn for a year before being killed on a tree. The blood of both deities watered the sad old trunks and holes of the life-giving Earth.

Today in the secret jungle, bird-twittering hollow in front of the holelike doorway to the wealthy realm of the Kings and Queens of Death, Diez Peso spoke sweetly to a firmly held, unblemished young male turkey, newly named White Dawn Youth.

His feathers were shingled in iridescent layers of gold, bronze, glittery reds, and sparkling blues. His sweet open eyes and warm downy body shifted each time he was held to the tree and offered to the world in all its directions—not four, six, or seven but two hundred sixty.

Each man in turn held the poor little beast, telling him how much they appreciated his dying for us, making prayers for all our families and for our village, for themselves and the chiefs. With great emotion in our voices for the sincerely felt truth of what we were doing, we chiefs raised the worth of the fat village bird by counting his attributes over and over to the deities in loud weeping voices. We transformed the beautiful beast into the White Painted Youth in a bath of rich and regal words taught to us by those old image keepers, our mentors. He became

> The graceful walking
> Child of jade
> Child of dawn
> Who lived to play
> And dream,
> And fly
> And run
> And walk
> And sing
> And defend the Flowering Mountain Jade Water Earth
> Whose feathers were Dawn's light
> Whose scratching feet planted seeds of things not yet invented
> Whose eyes sparkled because some

Stars got drunk and lost and couldn't remember
How to get back to the sky, deciding to live
Here in a turkey eye of White Dawn Youth.

On and on we went as chiefs, priests, fathers, and men do when they are in love with life and can understand that beauty and tragedy are the thumb and forefinger on the same hand of that Goddess who spins the story of our lives into this reality in which we learn, step by step, how to live.

The turkey died flapping his robust wings, raising a breeze that blessed all our reverent faces. Diez Peso held the White Painted Youth by his scaly gray legs, so the turkey's blood spattered the trunk, the leaves, and blessed the Hole to the Underworld.

We were silent as his soul took all our messages to the other world. When he lay inert, our shaman ordered a fire to be built into which the liver, back fat, and a little meat was given as a food to the God of stories and the village, the Grandfather Fire. The head of the White Painted Youth was buried under next year's *chich* tree, while the feet, heart, and meat from each part of the body was buried at the entrance to the Underworld.

The remainder of that beautiful bird was roasted and eaten by us with tortillas made earlier by the widows.

We felled that enormous beauty of a palm. When its tons of wood-bound water, bark, pods, and fronds crashed into the hungry Earth, our old men were reported to have privately mumbled in a prayerlike way, "Thus we go cracking and rustling, raising dust in a cloudy thud, thundering to the Earth. Could I be so full and worthy as to leave such sounds echoing behind me when this thickly barked old man hits the ground in death?"

Three feet of the wavy trunk remained protruding into the dusty air, and men and boys pitched in to dig out the watery pith and netlike cells that made the core of the tree a juicy place.

As we dug out the trunk some three feet down into the roots, it became a hollow barrel of sorts that filled, moment by moment, with a root-fed liquid thicker than water and thinner than sap. We capped our barrel with sheets of woven fronds to keep debris from falling in.

We separated and seated our initiates into four groups, the mountains, the earth, the underworld coast, and home.

Each chief picked his "dog." A dog was the name given to an initiate who ran in front of each chief when he was traveling. Each dog got to perform tasks for his chief, often guarding or escorting his wife and children to and from market. Being a dog meant that you got to be less isolated from and more immersed into the village, though you only did what you were asked to do and then returned to the initiation house immediately. A dog was a scout, and for a scout eloquence was of the utmost importance.

We did not elect our dogs or choose which boy went with which group. We gambled for them, relying on the method used by the Gods whose lives are as relegated to "Holy Chance" as our own. The Gods didn't choose where one sprout came up or another didn't, or why one man died or another lived. It was chance, the roll of the knuckle-bone dice, that decided.

We used corn dice and, by the end of an hour, all had been decided by the divine.

To my great dismay I ended up with shave-headed Gourd, the son of Axe, as my dog. Strong-willed, born into what Tzutujil viewed as a wealthy family, Gourd was a stuck-up, hard-headed bully who now assumed that even the Gods recognized how important he was, since they'd chosen him to be the First Chief's First Dog.

The mentors took me aside and told me that I had to remove him to a different position because only the most loyal and invisible boys should have this position. A spoiled boy like Gourd would be better off given a lot of strenuous work to which he was not accustomed. We had to do our best to cause Gourd to learn without constant preaching. While not doing any disservice to his initiation, we chiefs had to protect the integrity of the ritual as well as the other initiates.

I couldn't decide what to do because, on the one hand, I knew that the spirits had their reasons for having Gourd end up being awarded a role that corroborated his conceit and his assumptions of immortality. And yet, as the old guys said, any energy wasted on his elitism would hold us up enormously. Night was coming on early in this canyon here at the Underworld entrance. We expected to be out here in the bush for three days, listening to the old mentors relate ancient stories in front of the Old Grandfather Fire, the Lord of Stories, the God of Eternity who is the only deity that actually likes human beings.

These stories have never been told outside of ritual context or written down, but in them lies the secret of all that we did during the initiation. Their content was so well planted in our memories that, for the remainder of our lives, not one small feather of them ever escaped into amnesia.

For every part of our lives, a story had been there before we had. Much of what we learned from these stories literally caused us to avoid dangerous situations, making it possible for some of us to live to old age.

These stories were living treasures that transformed into greater and more expansive meanings that men returned to and examined over and over. We understood more and more about these stories as our own increasing experience made their richness burst forth into the leaf and flower of a more complete comprehension. Their meaning was rooted in these original days when, together in the bush, we men studied them by remembering them. Here we learned the making of ancient tools, ancient foods, and old-time ways of doing things before the advent of the top-heavy, settled existence of the village.

Boys struggled through every stage of their people's history by living an abbreviated form of what they'd heard in the stories. Many of these stories and mythologies had taken place in the very landscapes we lived in and over which we traveled. During initiation the events and places in the stories were not explained and learned but secretly and magically experienced, when through initiation the boys became their own ancestors.

Our first night in the bush was just beginning when we heard a voice far off beyond the granite cliffs. No one else was allowed to come here, and we had guards watching to keep unsuspecting travelers away, even though it was unlikely that they could find us. This place had been made magically invisible by our shaman, Diez Peso, who had the spiritual key to the invisible lock that made it so only we could enter.

The small river of sky we could see above us ran purple and silver like an abalone shell as the impending darkness and stars began to close in. To whom did this funny voice belong? We chiefs with our dogs scrambled up the hill and searched around, cutting our bare ankles on the thorn palms, encountering no one.

Quietly we stood and searched the darkening closeness of the jungle with our glaring eyes, listening, our mouths a little open with our heart beating in our ears. We saw no one, heard nothing other than the snapping of the fire below us around which sat the rest of our nest mates.

With great reverberation the voice spoke again, *"Esh kola ta, jie aii?"* Am I welcome? Are you there, you fathers and boys?

It yelled out echoing, echoing, *"Naq vinaaq at atet?"* What people are you?

"n A Clash." I'm A Clash, the voice replied.

"Which A Clash?"

"A Pioum." Chicken Louse.

The canyon filled with choruses of initiates' laughter, while repeating, *"A Pioum?"* Chicken Louse? *"Pinaq oka?"* What's he doing here? and so on, echoing up and down the little ravine.

The strange boy was already standing at our fire by the time we were able to get back down to the rest. Somehow he'd slipped past us unobserved. Barely thirteen years old, Chicken Louse stood warming himself in his normal unassuming way, slouching a little, his bony arms tucked into his raggedy but well-tied sash knot. His hat was of the cheapest sort and had been twisted into such an abstract unhatlike shape that it resembled a gigantic piece of dirty popcorn screwed onto his head.

Squatting there in the flickering of our story fire against the deep dark of the wilds, Chicken Louse, his body slimmer than a mouse tail, dressed in the frizzy handwoven rags of his extreme poverty, looked like a tiny jungle orchid, with his hat as the blossom. His eyes were huge like a baby kinkajou with hardly any whites, his cheeks sunken and his lips thick, but the voice he spoke with had the firm unafraid quality of a grown man, but with the pitch of a boy.

His father, all of his brothers and sisters, his father's brother, his aunt, and his cousins had all died when their canoes capsized in a storm as they were returning overloaded with firewood and food from the fields. Chicken Louse was the last born and, besides his aged mother, he had no living relatives. His mother had a large incapacitating growth in her belly, which was all she ever talked about when she wasn't in excruciating pain. In the predictable cruelty of village life, she had ended up with the nickname Big Round Ball, by which she was known throughout the Canyon Village

Chicken Louse loved his mother. She would have starved to death had he not, from the age of ten, rowed a borrowed canoe to his family's land every day and cleared, turned, and planted it with corn, squashes, cotton, and beans.

By age twelve, he was made of pure sinew with no fat. He'd lost most of his childhood. Chicken Louse had seen more of life than most adults and was more adept at farming, firewood making, fishing, and harvesting wild plants and fruit. His tiny malnutritioned frame strained and shook under the full-sized loads of neatly split firewood he expertly tied with the right knots. Chicken Louse was admired by all the men and women but mercilessly teased by boys and girls of his own age. His mother was too sick to weave so he was forced to trade his hard-earned food and firewood for the weaving of other women. He kept his mother clothed. Between them they had one blanket, which was Big Round's skirt, and Chicken Louse had only one set of semi-new clothing, that he never touched. The rest of the time he worked patched, frizzy, and poor.

No one of any age was his equal in the woods, on the land, or in a canoe, but he knew nothing of a life in a compound where one could just be young. For him to walk the twenty miles from here to the village alone, without his tools and with no weight on his back, was no strain whatsoever to him. While the rest of the boys thought they were suffering, to Chicken Louse this was a vacation. He was one of my heroes. We all wondered what had brought him out here to the mouth of the Underworld.

"*La' narumaq at pinaq waviera?*" Son, what reason do you have for coming here with us?

"The situation you are in means you need all the help you can find to keep the world alive," he answered. "I've come to help you bring home the fruit and all the rest."

He wanted to join our ranks, not so much to get initiated, because in some ways he was overly initiated and mature, but to make sure that we succeeded. He also came because his mother wanted to make sure he really did get initiated before she died, because she hoped that he could marry someday. Chicken Louse looked deceptively innocuous, but to him, going to face Death in the Underworld with no food or water and carrying the Goddess back to the village with all of your friends was like going to watch a ballgame compared to the suffering of his everyday life.

I wanted Chicken Louse as my dog. Gourd, with his typical cruelty, had been deriding and kicking Chicken Louse from the moment he'd arrived. The old mentors and I had to pull him down a couple of times.

Finally, I had them gamble against each other with corn dice, to see who'd be my dog and who'd go where I put him. Chicken Louse didn't even know how to handle the dice but he won anyway. Gourd was furious and went off to brood. I put him in the Underworld clan attached to the tenth chief.

All night the stories raged on, "The Tobacco Boy," "The Toe Bone and the Tooth," "The Story of the Deerboy." Some two hours before dawn a loud puff and pop shot out of the hole of the Underworld, startling us to our feet. Leaves and dust settled all around us in the firelit dark as we watched the hole come alive with rushing air shooting up into the sky, a deity about to appear at any moment.

The boys were scared and one even ran. The old men said that it was the Lords of Death coming to look us over. Soon they would return back into the ground, covering up the hole when they returned.

Sure enough, just at dawn the air in the hole reversed, now sucking in where before it had been blowing. The leaves and debris from all around re-arranged themselves back over the hole, as if magically pulled there by some invisible hand until it was again plugged up, almost unnoticeable.

❖

The initiates slept with their heads to the *chich* trunk, their bodies radiating out from it like wagon spokes, each representing a branch of his lineage off the old tree. Every night after the stories, they slept this way to the gurgle and foaming of the palm liquid in the trunk, cooking itself into wine.

After three days I was instructed to open the old trunk. Having been "cooked" by the story-filled fire and our youthful heat, the trunk was now full of the Goddess's spirit and her big story.

Pouring a little as an offering into the hole and some into the fire, the old men showed the boys how to receive the holy liquor, teaching them the words used by grown men and women when addressing men and women of different ages. They demonstrated how to pray not only *to* the Gods but *for* the Gods, so that the sun could succeed, so that the Goddess of the Moon, Water, and Ocean could succeed, and so that the Rainwarriors could succeed. Each time they prayed, they sacrificed a little to the trunk, the hole, and the fire.

Only one gourd was used and each man drank one at a time. As each gourdful was drained, the boys sat in front of the trunk, saluting the sacrificed tree, each of their chiefs and the mentors, the Underworld, the setting Father Sun, and the Goddess. Instead of making them drunk, the cool, thick, spicy, foamy liquid, both sweet and soapy at the same time, filled their bellies with endurance and the overwhelming power of the Gods.

After all had drunk, the chiefs filled a bottle with the liquor and gave one of the young men a small cup. They told him to give each and every person there the same amount of liquor by estimating the amount, being sure not to forget himself. This meant a small swallow each. Every initiate was given this opportunity to learn how to measure because, in the end, what made you useful on the Earth was developing the confidence to try something and see how it worked by trusting the spirits and the spirit of chance.

We forced our nestlings to pray as they got drunker, never letting them speak to anyone except the Divine or the Spirits, keeping them ecstatically focused at that point. If one seemed sleepy, we woke him up. If one seemed to be sobering, we sent my dog to get him another gourdful, keeping them all the while praying. Continuing in this way, they eventually broke into blessing, weeping, blessing, singing old prayers, blessing, weeping, and praising. Young men need to bless.

They wept and wept for life, for the grief of being a person destined to die, a person whose friends and relatives died, a person who suffered in so many ways. They wept for any of the many griefs that men and women knew and began to speak it all out loud in a way that began to sound holy.

Two hours before dawn when the winds came rushing out of the ground and the blowing began, jumping up out of the deep earth, out of the hole where the road begins to the great realm of the Holy Lords of Death and sickness, some beings stood there listening to us. I could tell they were there, some of the others could too. But most just got scared because they could feel Death's strange cold wind around them. It was down that seed hole, that planting hole, that old hole where their souls had fled, where their soul Brides had been taken, where the Goddess had been dragged, far away into that other world.

We poured offerings to these beings and spoke to them in our best archaic speeches. Some of the boys spoke hoarsely, others with voices like loud kazoos, drunken and sincere. Whether or not they could see Death, they addressed these wardens of their hearts in full poetic voices, speaking of their empty places, trying to convince them of their desire to have their souls back, their willingness to carry the watery clouds back to their village to moisten the sad thirsty earth there.

But the spirits were gone as quickly as they'd come, and in their place stood a *xiwaan,* a ring-tailed cat with big red glowing eyes, who moved off into the starless cloud forest night, carrying their words into that world invisible to humans.

FIFTEEN

THE ENFORCEMENT OF ELOQUENCE
THE HEART OF INITIATION

Singing to the Goddess, to the Gods, to God, to Life, everybody had passed out by the time the mysterious wind had run back down its hole and closed itself again.

Ruch'ab Qij, the Sun's Spear, came gleaming into the dry leafy canyon. It cut itself on the vines and thicket into smaller arrows of robust, dusty light, pushing its way over the granite cliff down to us, the thirteen chiefs, where we sat swollen-eyed as we kept our sleepless vigil, guarding the snoring old men and Rainboys. Sleep was a vulnerable time for the boys and we the thirteen chiefs had to make certain that they didn't get lost in their dreams where Death could easily kill them here so close to its lair. At the same time we didn't want this particular sleep to be disturbed so their dreams would not be interrupted as the boys wrestled in the other world with their fates.

During initiations, sleeping was an infrequent but energetic part of the ritual. In the dream world each youth lived out his life in a special altered way, strengthening his spirit mind, little by little, lifting at least one layer of the amnesia given to humans at birth, which had caused them to forget their true origins. If we chiefs did things right each boy would meet the challenges of his life in dreams before he got to them in the waking world. He could fail over and over in the dream world at endeavors of great difficulty and danger, as much as he needed, without having to die or suffer much. The dream world in a well-made initiation was the spiritual gymnasium where the young could scrimmage with life and God, flexing spiritual muscles they'd never used, learning by failure to form the ingenuity of their souls necessary to negotiate the waking world of an adult when they got there. To be startled awake during such dreams could mean death to the dreamer and, at the very least, the loss of a good lesson. In these bush dreams, the Spirits were the teachers. We guarded the Rainboys and kept them from harm during their classes in the other worlds.

Down here this morning, in this canyon at the base of the hollow trunk in front of the hole of Death, these boys were filled with a particular kind of dream given to them by the spirit of the sacrificed palm. Through its death, its spirit had been freed to enter the liquor, which, when the boys drank it into their hollowness, had begun to speak to them in their dreams. Something always had to die to make other things live.

The old tree's blood ran alongside the boys' blood like a friend in a slow race, showing them secrets they'd remember forever. The Tzutujil knew that men without such secrets, given to them by natural beings such as plants, the weather, or animals, didn't have much chance of becoming human. By receiving the gift of nature's speech in dreams, a boy's nature found its own voice, the voice of a man whose true naturalness would grow to become what he had dreamed in those days of initiation.

Nature is the symphonic imagination of the Deities, who make it tangible with their collective voices. They sing and speak this world into life in a constant way. Their eloquence is the world we live in. All life is a story well told by deities who hunger for the delicious speech, rooted poetry of grief, richness and surprise of our God-Feeding rituals. This keeps them vital, and their vitality is the health of the world, which makes our lives possible.

Without an old-world-style written language, the legs the village ran on was its speech. There was woman speech, man speech, silent speech, delicious speech, unknown speech, sparkling speech, noisy speech, angry speech, senseless speech, child speech, chief speech, baby speech, misleading speech, story speech, in pain speech, gratitude speech, old person speech, shaman's speech, God's speech, speech of the Dead, Sacred Speech, grief speech, praise speech, hurts speech, attacking speech, devastating speech, hello and good-bye speech, every speech. The memory of how to do anything, like making reed mats and houses or how to farm a field, carve a canoe, weave a blouse, or raise a child was all in the speech, without which the village would cease.

Having robbed their mothers, gambled, killed, knocked down trees, gotten drunk, slept away the day in class and vomited, the boys were now ready to learn to speak as men, women, humans, and villagers.

We herded our boys—pale, grumpy, dazed, and some wishing they were already dead—back to the village. We left good offerings behind, said our ritual good-byes, and stopped at every shrine along the way to feed the beings that lived there.

Diez Peso stayed behind to lock up the canyon, closing the spirit road and entrances and making this place invisible until the boys returned to descend into the Underworld.

To rescue their lost souls, their first loves, the Earth's Bride, the Goddess of Water, the youth would have to learn to court the Gods and the Lords of Death and Disease. Like the courting of a girl with the word warriors, the boys would launch a siege of devastating beauty against Death who, if suitably intoxicated by their barrage, would release their souls and the Goddess into their charge. It was only this ritual ability of eloquence that gave them any power with Death. Of course, they would have to understand that their deaths at the end of their lives would be the agreed-upon payment for having lived at all.

In this kind of initiation this way of talking was like a furious bath of boiling village sounds, inside of which the young folk were immersed and blanched to loosen and peel away their undersized childhood husks. We kept them cooking there in this irritating flood of archaic speech and learning until their unique fresh hides, the strong skins of potential adults, began to toughen and glow with signs of a mature beauty, resilient enough to withstand the rigors of their strange new lives as adults.

From this steaming pool of story, speech, and vision, clumsy and shiny be-ings would stumble forth whose deeper voices would not only be able to feed the life-speaking Gods with words of great spiritual nutrition but would also be able to speak about the longing vacancy in their hearts with words that filled the hearts of those who listened.

To learn the exalted speech of adults, the boys would first have to learn the speech of women. Tzutujil men and women have different words for different things and different sentence structure.

At one time men and women had utterly separate languages. In the mod-ern world people are fond of saying that men and women don't understand each other, that they are speaking different languages. The trouble is, how-ever, these people insist on using the same words for different things. For the Tzutujil, each gender uses different words for the same thing. This way, the things that are truly different for men and women show up clearly.

The speech used in rituals was definitely gender oriented. Only by great exposure to it could a person gradually learn how to function in a ceremony, how to address the Deities in their own language and the Chiefs and Ladies in their own special hierarchical eloquence.

The youth were exposed to a certain amount of those archaic royal tongues in their initiations but now their main challenge was learning to speak the Exalted language of a man and to learn to listen to and understand the Exalted speech of women. Most boys understood women's regular lan-guage, as they had spent the first half of their lives up till now at their mother's and sister's sides, actually speaking like a girl until they were eight or ten. Then they began to accompany their fathers and brothers and even-tually figured out how to speak as young men. Exalted Speech, or *Nimlaj Tzij,* was not really taught in the family, as it was the speech of courting and elders.

To "cook" the youth into fine speakers of this Exalted Speech, an ancient institution was imposed upon both the chiefs and initiates that required great diligence and personal sacrifice on the parts of both. None of us thirteen Chiefs were allowed to speak directly to anyone in the village, including the Scat Mulaj and our extended family, with our own voices. The only exceptions, of course, were the initiates, our mentors, our wives, and our young children.

By the same tradition, none of the villagers could speak to the Chiefs di-rectly either. This constituted a form of almost intolerable exile that could last as long as a year and no less that five months. After a while, the chiefs' inaccessibility gave them an air of solemn grandness that went with the job. Also, it gave the initiates great access to them, making their experience with the chiefs and elders into a closeness that, for the time being, was even greater than the one they had with their fathers.

It soon became apparent to me that initiation was taking place on many levels. Not only were the young men passing into the next layer of society but the young chiefs who had already been through that experience were themselves passing into a different type of adult initiation. This stage of becoming an adult Tzutujil, a human being, was an even deeper layer of the heartwood of the village trunk.

Simultaneously, the mentors were being initiated into what the Tzutujil call the realm of the echo. These old men had already done what we young chiefs were doing and, by helping us, they were forcing themselves to dig into their much freer, zany souls and pools of experience to fish out the necessary ingenuity and eloquence to get us through. Every year, everybody in the village was somehow getting a rite of passage simultaneously in different groups at different levels; but every size person, man or woman, was doing it to save the Earth, not to become initiated. Initiation was necessary to keep the Earth alive, which is why traditional people kept coming back to help the "New Ones" get through, because if these nestlings did not get through, the Earth would die and everybody with it.

We Chiefs could speak to anybody we needed to if we used an initiate as our mouthpiece. For this reason, anytime a Chief went anywhere during his year of service, he was accompanied by at least two initiates.

When walking in the streets of the Canyon Village on a mission to invite some expert to the sacred house, or to borrow an article necessary for a ritual, I, for instance, would take my dog Chicken Louse and a few other of my nestlings. The boys always guarded me on the sides and my dog ran in front, sometimes actually howling to let people know that the warriors were in the streets.

If the boys walked too shyly I would stop them and, putting my staff over my shoulder, I would teach them to walk with a conceited elegance and a pompous manly grace. The old men had told me when I was a young initiate that if men didn't walk with the attitudes of young warriors, then when asked to be fathers and village men, they would still act like young pompous idiots with attitude. To avoid that, the boys were required to carry themselves with an erect attitude of appropriate disdain and a kind of grandiosity hopefully without contempt. This proud bearing is hated in modern people, who would rather have hate-filled soldiers made of beaten-down, unhappy men than a culture of erect, relaxed men, proud of who they are because they are admired for who they are.

It was comical and naively beautiful to see the boys' willingness to help me look fierce and capable with my escort of dogs and warrior boys. There were those, of course, to whom we could teach nothing regarding pride, such as Gourd to whom we did better to teach prudence and kindness.

When we struck out onto the village paths and trails, people ran to take a look at us, as if they were sighting a whale or seeing a family of jaguars from a distance. It was here that the Rainboys began to be admired for their shine. They were regarded differently now as they went about their focused missions with some austere Chief, doing a mysterious task to which the village as a whole owed its welfare.

Whenever we arrived at our destination, I would turn my back, lean on my shiny bone-colored staff, and whisper into the ear of one of my escorts the words I needed to speak to the person who stood there listening patiently. Chicken Louse, or Skunk, or Red Jumping, whichever I chose, began to relate my speech, word for word, out loud in the same rhythm, intonation, and syntax to whomever we were addressing.

Whenever we were out on tasks, every boy got a chance many times over to speak a chief's words for him. When the person we'd been talking to replied, knowing the need for young men and women to learn to speak well, that person most often made a fine speech of it too.

As I was not to be addressed by anyone except my initiates, I pretended not to listen to the reply, and once again my initiate transferred the person's words back to me, loudly and directly. At first, as everyone knew, it could take quite a while to complete a conversation. But after a couple of weeks, most of the boys could respond so quickly in both directions that they were like little loudspeakers, accurately blurting out whatever was said in the same moment it was said.

Because the boys were learning and the Chiefs had become holy representatives of something other than people, we never spoke in everyday speech. Life became very rich and elevated, taking on magical, larger-than-life proportions.

The young women were involved in an identical way with their initiating priestesses and old mentors. Some of the greatest learning came to the boys and young men when one of us chiefs had to deal with a woman chieftess who, under the same restrictions as we men, had to relate everything through her initiates.

In this case Chicken Louse or some other boy might reiterate one of my finely phrased orations to the sacred women through her initiate. The girl then related the speech in Exalted Male words, exactly as spoken, to her initiating mother.

The initiating Mother would then address the subject, speaking back to her initiate in the High Form of the women's language. Her initiate then repeated this exactly to my initiate who, in the Exalted Woman's language, related it verbatim, loud and clear, into my patient ear.

Our missions and tasks took us everywhere. At one point we had to gather up some of the netted boxes traditionally used by the boys to bring their souls from the Underworld. Kneeling at the threshold of the compound courtyard of Ya Chéywí, Stirring Stick, my dog Chicken Louse, and I spoke to the ground there, addressing all the ancestral souls who for hundreds of years had lived and crossed over the polished temple stone where the spirits who guarded it lived. This is how the boys learned to do the same.

Like shadows of each other, we both rose up gesticulating in the fashion of Chiefs. Taking a little of the doorway dust we both kissed a pinch of the Flowering Earth and let it rain back to its home.

Turning my back to the compound, and leaving Chicken Louse facing it, I whispered into his rarely washed, crinkly, mushroomlike ears a prayer speech, couched in the couplets in which Exalted Speach is always spoken, pausing at the end of each couplet to allow Chicken Louse time to repeat it:

"Is the owner of this realm present?
Is the Moon whose sweat is silver here making the Earth wealthy?
I the Chief of the eight hundred shimmering boys
Desire to see her, the fruited face on her ancestor's trunk
I the husband of the village, a chip off the trunk of the eight hundred
    starving boys
Desire to see her mouth, where our Father Sun rises in the morning."

At this point Stirring Stick's initiate, Roundness, padded down, much covered with her tinseled shawl. Her initiating mother looked off behind her as she transferred each couplet to her. We continued as each phrase was once whispered and twice repeated out loud.

"We the eight hundred hummingbird water boys
Come rowing on dry land in canoes made of tears with oars made of
    old songs
To the foot of your tree
To the base of your branch
You who well rooted in the tear-watered dust of your ancestors' bones,
Let us flower in your arms and in your branches
Let us sprout at your feet and at your roots
You, grandmother:
    Eyebrows of sea foam
    Teeth of translucent white corn
    Breath of white butterflies
    Hands of fish and rivers
    Clothing of reeds
    Voice of waterbirds
    We remember you
    We don't forget you
    We the eight hundred intestine road boys
    We the walkers of the Milky Way the cold road of heroes
    Please don't forget us
    Please don't abandon us
For Mother we remember you
How a woman like you was forgotten once and ever again over
    and over
And on account of our forgetting, She, the Waters of the Earth
The Birther of Food
Was lost to us
Was dispersed into infinite fragments
And now to remember you
And now in order to put Her back together again, She
Lost in the dust

Lost in the depths
We had hoped that you might loan us
We had hoped that you might give us
The ancient netted boxes of your unforgotten grandfather
The ancient netted containers of your ancient people
Who never to be forgotten by us the eight hundred shimmering boys
Who always to be remembered by us the eight hundred dust-raising
    boys
Could live again somehow walking
    Somehow jumping again,
    Somehow struggling again,
    Somehow tolerating again
    The hail, the wind
    Facing death
    And hardship,
    Somehow your old gone-away grandfather
    Will be remembered and
    Walk with us again
    With his old netted boxes
    Firmly set upon
    The backs of us the eight hundred
    Shimmering boys.
    Please may we borrow
    Your netted boxes?
    Long Life, Honey in the Heart,
    No Evil, Thirteen Thank-yous."

And with that, we left off and kissed the earth in front of the two teary-eyed women. It was Stirring Stick's turn now, and she began her retaliatory barrage of beauty by whispering into little Round's mouselike ear her untranslatable responses in the Exalted woman's speech. Round started to repeat the substantial intelligent woman's words in a coy girl's voice. But Stirring Stick didn't like the pretended weakness in her sounds and began firmly thumping the girl's shoulder blades with the bottom of her fist as a sign for her to put more volume and backbone into her fine old-time phrases, and Round tried. Chicken Louse then repeated, in a babylike way, the same woman phrases. I too had to elbow him into greater conviction. We continued in this manner until both the boy and girl were speaking like old Chiefs and Priestesses.

"In just this way with this very sound
Those who first felt the delicious aroma of the newborn Earth
Those first people who wept themselves into adults
In just this way
They came walking
With this very sound
They came limping
To their jade thresholds
To their flowering doorway
To behold our Father the Sun
To behold his little brother the Morning Star
Who rises born there above the Cliffs of Talc
Above the Cooking Pot Mountain
 Our Father whose eyes are bees
Whose eyes weep honey
Whose tears
Fill the hive of my heart
Whose hundred tears are amber
And collected and worn as necklaces
By widows and the Moon who miss their men
Whose days are guarded
By the rainbow monster whose tusks are mist
Whose road is made safe
By the water monster who guards the sun
Whose tusks are made of steam
Steam from the meeting of male fire and female water
Whose scales sprout flowers
On whose back stands the sun who carries day
From hill to mountain
From valley to canyon
We his Flowers
His Sprouts
See you, the guardians of the road, which brings back the Water

Goddess from

The land of which, we with wombs, the well-fitted, patched-blouse
  beings

Cannot mention

On whose back, our faces shall be avenged.

You who need the netted boxes

Whose nets are made of stars

Whose nets are made of rope of the

Milky Way the cold road of heroes,

Over which the unfortunate Rainboys

The Shimmering-of-the-Lake boys

Must always travel cold and unfed to save the warmth

Please do me the goodness

Do not forget us

Do not abandon us

We who remember you

We who never abandon you

Want only to be remembered

As each of your footsteps with my Grandfather's netted boxes on your

Back brings home that

Woman who births us all

Please receive this gift

  Like we've seen forever before and want to

  See forever again that is how it's done

  Today, and well done it is, thank you."

And Stirring Stick and Round kissed the Sun. They stood aside and
there, in a long row, stood the old netted boxes, placed behind the old woman
by people we never saw as the women were speaking.

In this old laborious, delicious way, we in the Canyon Village wrestled
each other's beauty, using the young as our mouths to raise their worth in the
eyes of life and to insure that their abilities as speakers of delicious words
would not die out but continue to be taught to the generations we would not
see.

We didn't speak this way for its own sake. We were always on a mission of
true relevance, to ask a question or borrow a ritual item traditionally held by

someone who needed to be courted annually in a certain way to convince them to willingly surrender to us whatever we needed.

A great deal of patience was needed by all parties for this to succeed. But this was the only context in which a young woman would even be able to speak in the fancy male language. This was even more true for the boy who would have only this opportunity to learn how to make his mouth move in the female tones of a matron's sacred language. Also, this gave both shy young women and shy young men an opportunity to speak to each other in a context of sacred poetry, discarding their timidity to serve a higher power.

By serving as our mouthpieces, the youth were able to see how we grown men and women preferred to court everyone, including the Gods, instead of commandeering and ordering people around. We *inspired* cooperation by our worthy missions and the honor bestowed upon the people we spoke to. They also began to see how the hordes and hordes of ancient verbal images kept sacred by the old folks and generously taught to them through their Chiefs were in fact an oral dictionary of holy concepts that could be fit together in many creative ways with some freedom and still be true to the ancient traditional form where the speech had sprouted.

And for months that's all they did. They built shrines for the Scat Mulaj; brought logs, netloads of pine needles, flowers, axes, ropes, buckets, and canoes; gathered things they needed to do the ceremonies, but always accompanied by us chiefs, speaking our words for us and transferring them to us. Until one day the old mentors decided that the boys had learned enough and should be sent out on tasks alone, without us chiefs.

One of the major responsibilities of a fully matured adult Tzutujil man or woman was the Enforcement of Eloquence upon the village, and in particular upon the teenage youth.

At some point three or four months into the initiations, a boy would be sent on an errand to fetch some small but necessary item we needed to complete a particular part of our rituals, perhaps an especially thick length of handmade rope. Probably there was only one very old fellow who had this kind of rope, which was used every year for the same purpose for centuries. At the direction of the mentors, we chiefs would then talk to one of our nestlings in the same way we spoke to other chiefs. We would ask his Lordship if he would do us the goodness of approaching the Great old tree, old vine Ma Mixit, the Little Cat, and ask him if we could borrow his thick old cord.

Off went Red Jumping, the chosen initiate, to call at the threshold of the tiny house of Ma Mixit. The old man invited him to come sit in his miniature house, big enough only for two. "Are you doing well, son?"

"Yes, Father, thank you. The chief says we need the thick old rope you always give to the initiates."

The old man with skin more like dehydrated *jocote* plums lit his half-cent cigar, blowing the smoke toward the ember of his almost-dead cooking fire.

"*Jie*," offering the boy his own half-cent cigar, "*nix nawaj?*" Would you like to smoke?

"Thank you, Father. The chief asks if you could loan us the thick rope you like to give to the initiates."

Sitting smoking and enjoying his cigar, Ma Mixit finally spoke. "Son, you know I knew your great-grandfather. He married my brother's wife's aunt, and she had a lot of cows on the coast. In those days women didn't ride horses, but she did, you know, your grandmother, I mean. It's too bad how your grandfather got beat up by those men sent here by the government, he never really recovered, you know? But, in those faraway days, what could we . . ."

And on and on he went, nonstop, for at least an hour without ever once giving the poor boy a chance to speak again, and never mentioning anything whatsoever about any kind of thick rope!

Disgusted and forcing himself to interrupt, Red Jumping said his formal farewells and marched back, kicking dust all the way, to the initiate chambers where, empty-handed, he had to present himself in front of the row of chiefs who were seated against the far wall, perpendicular to the much-adorned altar made ready for the return of the initiates' soul-filled netted boxes, when and if ever that happened.

The room was dark but full of wonderful grass and pine smells, which hung thickly in the air. The ceiling was completely studded with green plants hiding the secret Heart of the Sky, and the floor was a carpet of soft pine needles. A million of A Sisay's wild lilies covered the altar.

"You didn't touch his heart, did you," I called out to the boy.

"That old man is crazy. He just kept talking about my sandals and my grandparents. He never even mentioned the rope."

We had to laugh a little bit, but the sad boy didn't, feeling like he'd failed somehow, and he had. But then, every man in this room had failed to touch hearts somewhere and, like us, he had to try again. A Sisay took over, telling the boy, "You must make him feel your sincerity. Speak as you've been speaking in the streets with your Chiefs. Go try again."

And off he shuffled, the poor tired boy, trying to grasp it all. Once more, only an hour after he'd left, Red Jumping arrived again at Ma Maxit's hut, but this time bearing gifts. He was again admitted into the little hut of Ma Mixit, who happily received his gifts and once again offered him a smoke, and this time even a cup of coffee.

The boy began as Ma Mixit, oblivious to it all, continued to drink coffee, still trying to get his half-lit, funnel-shaped cigar to work, sucking in his wrinkly cheeks, his eyes crossing at each hard-earned puff.

"Father with eyebrows of sea foam
Teeth of white corn
Yesterday and the day before
When we come walking the
Eight hundred shimmering boys
We—"

The old man interrupted him. "You know, I really like your sandals. Your grandfather had fancy sandals from Totonicopan with thirty rivets on each foot. We'd never seen such things in our . . ."

Once again Ma Mixit went on forever, never mentioning any rope. Fleeing in frustration, Red Jumping returned to the initiation hut angry and ashamed, his heart bit hard with dull teeth, as the villagers called that special feeling of humiliation, doubt, and heartbreak.

But there in our midst sat a famous First Chief's dog from the previous year called Honey Puncher whom we'd called in to help the boy. This tall nineteen-year-old fellow took Red Jumping outside and talked to him alone about trying to speak real words—not just any words to con people into getting what you wanted, not just words to conform to tradition. "Try using the old-time forms with your own words, and say what is in your heart. Touch the old man's heart too, and maybe you'll come home with the ropes."

Red Jumping thought about it all for a long time. He wasn't the only one out on a task. At least ten boys were missing and, unbeknownst to him, all of them had failed too, but none of them could sleep until they'd succeeded.

Once again Red Jumping sauntered over to Ma Mixit's tiny hut. This time he began to speak, head bowed to the threshold, never allowing Ma Mixit to answer him until he'd finished.

"Father, Ma Mixit, you are the fine thick rope that binds me to my
Grandfather, whom I never saw.
My sandals must be his, their every creak is a prayer
In his remembrance,
As I try to walk as excellently as you
Old men did,
Unfortunately stumbling but never stopping
In our struggle, however clumsy, to
Inspire the Earth to jump up and live again.
That rope will outlive both of us, Father
As it outlived my grandparents but somehow
Each of our lives, a twist in its holy length promising
From generation to generation to pull
Into life each time again as before
What it is we here hope to bring into visibility.
Long Life, Honey in the Heart,
No Evil, Thirteen Thank-yous."

Red Jumping's eyes were wet. He was still staring at the flat stones marked with his tears when he saw two dusty feet with round cracked toes like palm fruit hanging over the ends of some very plain old *xoy* sandals. Looking up, he saw Ma Mixit standing speechless, the old thick rope crisscrossed over his chest, his hands held out to pull the grief-soaked boy to his feet.

Together they walked to the chief's house, discussing Red Jumping's grandfather. And when they entered the reed-framed door to the initiation house, a cheer like thunder and howling dogs went up that lasted five minutes, and many boys wept for the joy of having been forced to find the grief-spiced eloquence of their beautiful young souls.

Initiated old people didn't casually make presents of knowledge to the young until they were convinced that the youth understood the subtle immensity of the gift. Without the custodianship of cultural substance, the elders knew that the world would become filled with meaninglessness. The mysterious spirit-made richness of the world would become filled with people with no stories, soulless objects with no substance, and a life of intolerable and efficiently maintained boredom, the modern world's constant need to be entertained. Any culture whose adults would not take the time to enforce eloquence upon their young people was killing them, rewarding ignorance by ignoring excellence.

In those days of chiefs, initiations, and feasts, true Tzutujil elders like Ma Maxit were called Echo People, not because they had a lot of knowledge but because their vision and creativity caused a lot of knowledge to be learnt. An Echo Person never enforced eloquence with slaps, violence, or scolding but by simply ignoring everything that wasn't eloquent or heartfelt. The effects of this kind of inspiration echoed on the Earth long after his or her tired old heart gave out, and for this they were never forgotten. Their echoing sound merged like a memory spoken with the sounds the Gods made as they perpetually sang the world alive.

SIXTEEN

FEMALE EARTH, MALE EARTH

THE BOYS GO DOWN TO FIGHT DEATH

The Tzutujil Earth was divided up into Male Earth and Female Earth. Up in the highland mountains, the Canyon Village, Santiago Atitlan, lay the Male Earth. Green and stretching out forever straight to the Pacific, the humid coastal plains were called the Female Earth. Just this side of that hot flat land was an intermediate piedmont zone of mysterious, thickly forested hills and mist called *Xejuyu'*. Tradition held that the peoples who lived there had once been a parallel tribe of southern Tzutujil and some non-Mayan peoples called the Pipil.

Living separately from the Tzutujil, though totally related, the Hill Bottom people—as the royal families who held sway there in the olden days were called—were courted annually by the Canyon Village people during their initiations. The Canyon Village was, in turn, courted by them.

Because the hierarchy in both areas was anciently dedicated to ritually feeding and keeping healthy the deities that gave life to their respective mountains and valleys, the courting and ritual gift giving that went on between the two tribal divisions was thought of as the literal courting and marriage of the Male and Female Earths. The Female Earth and Male Earth needed each other. The lowland dominion of chocolate, honey, salt, parrots, bananas, and cotton had all the rain clouds that the highland realm of lake fish, tomatoes, avocados, hard jeweled corn, rope, and reed mats needed to water their pine mountains and fields.

Without this massive, intertribal Earth courting, peace between these two peoples would surely have been forfeit. Wars in the old days were understood as blood sacrifices to a gender problem among the Gods and Goddesses, between the Female Earth and the Male Earth. If the people of the Male Earth stopped their elaborate courting of the Female Earth, the two Earths would fight, with the human inhabitants as their warriors. After a suitable amount of sacrifice had occurred through the arbitrary bloodshed of both sides, the war would cease and life would go on.

If courting was not resumed between the two Earths, then another war would flare up. These courtings of the Earths by the chiefs were seen as what warriors should be doing, because this kind of ritual courting fed the hungry Male and Female Earth that would otherwise need blood to survive. This was another reason why initiations were so important, and why banning them meant for certain that a lot of people were going to die. The continuous desecration of the Female Earth by corporate farming, logging, and mining meant that continual violence would plague the country's inhabitants.

The Spanish interruption of the Mayan culture, their unscrupulous enslavement policies, and the illegal rezoning of tribal lands by the independent nineteenth-century Guatemalan Republic and the foreign, corporation-pandering governments of the twentieth century had seriously damaged and insulted the Female Earth on most of the coastal lands. But for all that, the courting relationship between the highland Male Earth and the exuberant and luscious lowland Female Earth had been continuously carried out without break for all these centuries as part of the Tzutujil initiations of their young people.

This intertribal courting was a form of peaceful warfare in which the men's instinct for heroism, pride, honor through competition, struggle, and territorialism were made into useful attributes that could make beauty and therefore keep the Earth alive. In the same way both the adversarial Mayan kings of the past and the initiating chiefs of today sent their troops to conquer the other with friendship, using gifts of fish, flowers, and archaic tear-inspiring discourse as their weapons.

Known only to the Scat Mulaj and the appointed royalty of the initiating Chiefs, the descendants of the original royal families of the Female Earth still kept vigil over secret sections of wild lowland forest, keeping them spiritually alive with their own quietly held ceremonies, distinct from our own.

It was to these families of hereditary Chiefs and Ladies, some thirty-five miles away from us, that we sent small warriorlike courting parties of male initiates bearing traditional time-honored gifts of a particular type and number, packed exactly as had been anciently specified in the first days of the original truce some seven hundred years ago.

Each chief sent his all-star initiate, so there were thirteen boys. It was a great honor to be chosen, as no chiefs or adults accompanied these boys on their journey. They had to trot each way with some twenty-five pounds on their backs, stopping only to place offerings at the several mountain summits and valley bottoms where there were shrines, thereby opening and blessing the road for the entire body of initiates who would descend through there on their way to the coast into the Underworld in seven weeks.

Many of the boys didn't know where the shrines were and could have gotten lost looking. The old pre-Spanish trade routes they used as they cut their way through the confusing hills, as their ancestors had done before them, could only be ascertained if the boys could remember the myths they had learned in the last three months. Those myths referred to the very landscape they were moving through today.

Each boy carried a type of fresh fish packed in leaves that had to make it through the coastal heat before it rotted so that it could be delivered into the hands of the coastal chiefs. Besides the fish, there were many other perishable gifts and products that could only be obtained here in the Male Earth.

If the initiates' gifts were accepted by these faraway families that most Tzutujil had never seen or met, it would be because the exalted speech and ritual procedures the boys had been practicing for months had thoroughly touched the hearts of the coastal spiritual Chiefs and Ladies. This courting of the people of the Female Earth by the boys from the Male Earth was the same as a young man sending his Word Warriors with gifts to his prospective in-laws. Only this time I, as chief, was the courter, and the boys were my Holy Word Warriors, who went between the chiefs of the Male Earth and the royalty of the Female Earth.

If the boys had learned it all well and did everything right, then all thirteen of them, tuckered and proud, would bring back to us a load of gifts from the Female Earth's chief in even greater quantity than the ones we'd sent down. We all hoped they would soon be seen rising up over the ridge at Xekisis some four miles away. I'd posted a couple of dogs closer in as scouts and runners to warn us of their impending return. This way the food prepared by the widows could be already laid out for them when they arrived, as they would have neither eaten nor drunk the entire way.

My scouts, Leaf Velvet and Dog's Tortilla, trotted in out of breath, each holding his little short-handled whip symbolizing his initiate station.

"Xiula', i elnaq chiq xejuyu' ta." Fathers, they are coming, we saw them rising out of the other Earth.

Like a fretful parent, I'd been pacing for two days, thinking of all the canyons the boys could have fallen into, the kinds of poisonous snakes that could have bitten them, the bandits and soldiers that could have shot them or beat them or hauled them away, the landslides that could have buried them, and the heat that could have melted them, all the while praying for their deliverance with the old fellows and my subchiefs. The time they were gone seemed to stretch on forever, but then, all too quickly, they thudded into our courtyard like wind-driven boulders.

Standing in a panting row outside, they yelled, *"Ex kola ndta?"* Our Fathers, are you present?

"Jie oq kola aii." Yes, we are here, young lords. And rushing out of the doorway, each chief unloaded his initiate, pulling off his back box and head strap while the other boys mopped the sweat off their brothers' faces.

Each of them had been loaded with a gigantic torpedolike palm flower and enormous lusty-smelling jungle melons called *kixlan kum* that looked like big red-brown salamis. This meant they'd been successful.

As custom dictated, we sat the boys on the chiefs' bench and the chiefs brought in the big tortilla basket and bowls of ritual soup, proud to serve the boys as returning heroes. We gave each boy a cup of canyon water, and, after our shaman Diez Peso had blessed the food, the boys ate every last crumb.

One never talked before eating, so we waited until they were fed and settled before we debriefed them. Mile by mile, the all-stars described what had happened on their mission inside the maps that lived in the highly developed mental geography of the Tzutujil. We chiefs urged them on. Miraculously, Gourd had ended up as their leader, and it was he who did most of the talking. The others corroborated when they could, having become more confident since passing the hard test of two thirty-five-mile hikes without food or water. The details of the journey went on for two hours.

The coastal chief was a man called Augustin Q'aq'. He and his wife had not been there when the boys arrived, but when the neighbors heard the effervescent birdlike speech of the highland Tzutujil, they and all their people converged for miles around to get a look at our all-stars. The boys' words were well accepted and their gifts sorted and registered. The fish was cooked and fed to all the coastal royalty, the boys included.

Augustin Q'aq' told them how relieved and inspired everyone was to see them because some young men and a fellow named A Cuxtin had come there by bus to warn them that under no circumstance were there going to be any more of these courtings, fruit bringings, and initiations. The coastal people were told that the initiations had been ended.

Taking the all-stars into the wild land, Augustin Q'aq' and his wife showed them the well-hidden corozo palms, cacao trees, jungle melons, plantains and other sacred Mayan trees and vines where the initiates had, for generations, always found holy fruit. They were assured by Augustin Q'aq' that when the entire crew of Rainboys came to fetch the Goddess six weeks later, they would not be hindered and would be welcomed in this place.

Loading the boys up with some of each ripe fruit, the couple fed them again and sent them on their way back up the steep mountains and canyons, out of the Female Earth and back to their beloved Canyon Village up on the Male Earth.

Now two subchiefs, Nettles and Gopher, began to unroll some reeds to tie the oversized palm flowers onto our overhead beams. When we cut open the flowers' six-foot, longitudinally ribbed, torpedolike shell, out popped an ever-expanding white treelike profusion of branching stems, each supporting thousands upon thousands of tiny sticky, narcotic-smelling blossoms that made every person who'd ever smelled them wonder, with a great nostalgia, in what other world they'd experienced this Godlike heady aroma.

Just as the young men were assisting the chiefs to lift and hang the heavy flowers on the ceiling, a tiny potbellied, self-assured, barefoot, five-year-old boy swaggered in as if he belonged there. Nonchalantly strolling like a king, with his hands tucked into his finely woven little sash, he inspected all the initiates, looking them up and down, and then the flowering altar, the ceiling, and the corners. Then, with great familiarity, he plopped himself down in my seat, presiding like a chief on the bench next to the recently returned all-star initiates.

Everybody was looking at him because little children were not allowed into the initiation rituals. It was considered spiritually risky for them to see things that their young minds shouldn't have to deal with just yet. But this little fellow was so mature and imperial, like a knowledgeable elder, that it didn't occur to any one of us to remove him. Unabashedly and in a strong little man's voice he trumpeted out: "My father is very happy with what you all are doing here."

The room went silent as all of us stared humbly at this child who spoke beyond his years like a deity.

"You're doing well. Don't stop, keep it going. We thank you."

Gourd, with his usual loudness and lack of tact, interrogated the boy, not yet comprehending who he really was: "What's your name?"

"Alko'." I'm not sure, the child replied.

"Then who's your mother?"

"Alko'."

"What's your father's name?"

"Alko'."

Many of the boys began to chuckle and look at each other, touched by the oddness of it all. When they turned back to view the child, he was gone, disappeared. I ran outside to catch him, and the other chiefs ran past me to see which way he had gone, but there was no sign of him anywhere.

The mentors didn't go chasing anybody. Ma Sisay had lit the copal burners and the old men were busy praying and putting up candles, lighting fires, and dropping liquor as offerings.

They knew who the boy was and so did I. He was not a person but a God turned into a little boy to speak to us. He was the spirit of the corozo palm and the sacrificed child of the Sun Father. His endorsement made us all fall to our knees, praying and weeping for the luck and the blessing of it. That's why we were always slow to chase away derelicts, animals, or children, because we knew, as we'd been taught in these initiations and seen with our own eyes this day, that most often they were deities come in human guise to inspect the goodness in our hearts. It wasn't uncommon in those days for Gods to visit. The luckiest of us got to eat with them and visit for a while before they went back to work, disappearing into the singing layers of the other world.

We sent boys to the coastal chiefs six more times, every seven days or so. The other initiates continued learning, preparing, speaking, and dreaming themselves into life while serving the village at the hands of their initiating chiefs and mentors, looking forward with excitement to beginning their descent into the coastal Underworld to retrieve their soul Brides and the Goddess of Earth's moisture.

Ya Piskát, Ya Lur, her subchiefs, and her group of hardworking widows were allowed to come and bless and encourage the young men each week as their major challenge neared. Entering for only a moment, the women looked so much like Goddesses that it made the boys understand how much all women were really part of Her, and that no one woman was all of Her any more than we men were all of God.

It was then that Gourd truly began to buck, rebelling at the idea of calling my wife by her ceremonial title, unwilling to call her "My Mother," as the rest of us called all the sacred women, no matter what age they were. Most of his unwillingness was due to the fact that Ya Lur was a mortal enemy of Gourd's family on account of a feud that had existed between them before I was even born. Another reason was the well-established fact of Gourd's fierce jealousy of Ya Lur's extreme youth and poor caste in such a high position. She was younger than he, an enemy, and poor. He would not bow to her or refer to her with respect as the wife of his chief, even though the protocols of his initiation said that he had to receive her blessing and encourage her with his thoughts and actions. He was doing neither.

Both Ya Lur and I would have let it all take its course but the other initiates hated Gourd for his self-centered interruptions. Most important, the old men said that some of the boys could die in the Underworld if the Chieftesses were not addressed properly, because the Goddess would not come home after having been insulted as such. Never ones to scold or yell, besides which we weren't allowed to argue for the entire year, we simply called on the body of the previous year's initiates, formerly known as the *Aguaciles,* to help us with our problem.

Before the great violence came to our village, the *Aguaciles* had very little to guard against and couldn't wait for something interesting to do. Over fifty initiated youth responded to our call, dressed in their fancy clothes with the staffs, drums, and whips of their position of office. We informed them about Gourd's misgivings.

They in turn surrounded the poor rock-headed fool. Their First Dog asked Gourd about his problem and all the boys listened intently, agreeing with him, of course, but reminding him that his actions in here had nothing much to do with his whims or opinions but with the general survival of the creation.

Having nothing better to do, they sat with him for a full thirty-four hours, sweating him with their discourses on initiation, threatening him as only young men can, and not letting him sleep until, finally, he acquiesced, not out of terror or agreement but out of a desire to be seen as important and because, by then, he was hungry. The *Aguaciles* whooped and screamed, kissed our rings, and shook our hands with great pomp and respect. Then off they ran, feeling victorious, tired, and useful, back to a village that didn't assume that its youth was disruptive but initiated them so that they could be called upon to break up fights and mediate feuds. The youth and the elders were our peacemaking people.

Of course, Gourd wasn't cured, but he plugged along with the rest of the exuberant nestlings, saying what he had to say, doing what he was supposed to do. He would have a hard time in the Underworld, I was sure of it.

I wasn't as worried about him, though, as I was about a more silent, unseen boy of sixteen who, a couple of years before, had stolen all my thatching straw. His people were Evangelical Christians, and it was odd that he should want to go through with this ritual, seeing that the Christians were so opposed to all the old customs. The mentors said I shouldn't have allowed him to participate, but I knew I had to give him a chance and us a chance to show him what we were really doing. I suspected he wasn't completely sincere in his reasons for being here and probably didn't have much faith in our rituals. That could make it spiritually very dangerous for him and for the rest of the boys later.

Turning back, however, would have been even more dangerous for him.

There was nothing that could be done about it, and the time to descend into the other world had come.

◇

The morning of the boys' departure the chiefs and I, along with our old mentors, the women chiefs, the widows, and Diez Peso, interrupted mass to pray at the old Hole and to the different saints and parts of the church to help the young men survive their upcoming ordeal.

Over twenty-seven copal burners raised a billow of choking, luscious fumes. The smoke was like a summer storm cloud climbing up off the Female Earth over the ridge called Molar, at the bottom of our Mother the Lake, over which our initiates would soon climb to descend to that coast. Father Stanley was outnumbered and, having seen the likes of our ceremony before, retreated to his sacristy.

Earnest and worried, dressed finely in the robes of the Lords and Ladies we'd become, we put up eight hundred candles and spilled a lot of canyon water to feed the journey of the boys. We raised a din of pleading, grief, and hope that resembled more the sounds of those who'd done this centuries before than the small people we would have been had we not been loaded with such majestic responsibility and the otherwise unattainable magical vision inherent in our positions.

Afterward, as we rounded the last corner in our homeward trek through the early morning streets, back to our reed-covered doorways, pine-needled floors, and flowering altars, the sound of Old Chiv singing out a flashy harangue of encouragement in his unmistakable hornlike voice enveloped us like the copal smoke that billowed over us as we walked.

Striding into our compound, we found that our initiates, in their nervousness, had, at Chiv's instigation, gone ahead and arranged themselves outside the initiation hut in a well-formed line, shaking as they waited like well-trained colts overready for their first real race. Each boy stood behind his netted *kahsh* while Chiv blessed and smoked out every corner of the emptiness of each boy's box by dipping his surging copal burner into them, speaking a well-polished stream of shamanic words of protection as only Chiv could do.

The netted box, or *kahsh,* represented each boy's ancestral body, the body we all inherited from our parents' people. The net around it stood for their personal form, their unique faces and the particular way of being everybody had. These nets would be adorned in the Underworld according to the initiates' whim if the spirit gave the boys the wherewithal and grace to return to us.

The hollowness of their boxes was the most significant part of the ceremony, because this hollowness was what was calling out for the boys' soul to fill it up. The hollowness of the ancestral body's container, caught in a net of tangible form, would house the delicious and inebriating burden of the young men's unripened souls like a little mansion, if all went well. It was here that he would carry home his spirit Bride, his particle of the Goddess seated in the strong throne of his netted box.

The head strap that went over the boy's forehead and supported the *kahsh* and its cargo firmly on his back and shoulders was called *ruq'a ejqan,* the hand of the burden. This tumpline was the universal insignia of a village man's life, a life of carrying heavy loads to and from the mountains on his back. It was on these men's shoulders that the whole village depended for food and fuel.

This forehead strap that would be used to carry the boys' boxes from the Underworld was treasured and eventually buried with each boy when he got old and melted back into the ground. But for today it would attach them to their youth and to their emptiness as they descended into the coastal Female, into the bowels of the Earth in search of their souls. They went to confront and fight Death, trading their brittle eternal youth and notions of immortality for their souls.

In their longing for the Goddess in a girl's eyes, in their longing to live well fed in the village and well loved by a woman, they sought the magical woman, their soul Bride. They would exchange a life with no death and no failure for a life with a soul, and with their new found souls they would be able to love a woman whose soul was her own. By giving Death the deed to their existence, boys and girls became men and women and could together give birth to more Flowers and Sprouts, their little boys and little girls who, in turn would carry the netted boxes of the ancestral hearts, remembering their parents' agreement with Death as they too descended into the Underworld, hoping to fill their forms with their own fruited souls.

We chiefs spoke about all of these things to our boys, who may or may not have been ready to hear such discourse from men scarred by life who had already made their bargains with Death long ago. Still, if one had to fail, it was better to do so in such a beautiful way. We filled our initiates' bellies and hopeful faces the best we could with food and advice, knowing full well that this was the last of either that they would taste for three days.

Chiv's presence was an unsolicited gift to make sure that we did as well as we could. As even greater insurance, he'd brought along Ma Reant Co who would escort the boys while he played music as they went and returned, marching in front of them.

Chiv was wearing his yellow-and-black checked *jaspeado* handwoven shirt, a brand-new pair of purple striped knee pants, and his black wool coat, making him look like a big spotted bee. Ma Reant Co, who had just been appointed the chief of the sacred house of Axuan, had on a white-and-dark-indigo striped, handwoven shirt and profusely embroidered knee pants, making him look like a friendly potato beetle.

Both men were chiefs and shamans. Ma Reant Co had taught me all the old shaman songs on the five-string, buzzy Atiteco guitar and I was happy that he was going to go with the youth into the Underworld. A real professional, his music would never stop for twenty hours at a time. He'd been to the Underworld as a musician twenty-three times and knew more than most about when to call a rest, when to do this, when to say that.

Any man who'd ever made this journey could tell you that it was the music that got the boys back home. It gave them a beacon to follow, and we believed it, because the song he played all the way down and back was the Song of the Road, the Road of the Sun. The song itself was so strong that it made the boys powerful enough to continue in its rhythm, even when all their strength had been stripped away by the other world and by their superhuman exertion.

I lined up my chiefs in front of the boys and we blessed the youths' bodies by whipping their joints, feet, and hands with their head straps. This gave them strength. We watched each boy tie his head strap on to his *kahsh,* then we loaded up each box with gifts for the coastal chiefs through whose lands they would travel.

We gave each boy a Mayan hug, going down the line one by one, every chief speaking according to his climate and desire the old encouragements in a traditional ancient praise poem whose secrecy kept it special. Simultaneously, each boy spoke his heart, promising to do his best, to fight Death by keeping his mind clear and focused and to bring the Earth back alive. The

chiefs and initiates all spoke and listened at the same time in the best Tzutujil tradition. Then across the jumbled walls of volcanic stone we called to the
Melcani, the holy widows.

In their dirty dresses, their faces, hair, and hands all covered in corn
dough, soot, and calluses, their little toddlers grabbing at their skirts, the
eighteen widowed ladies took their place in front of the young men. Each one
spoke to the initiates as widows always did at this point in the year.

"Young Lords, it's good to see your faces
It's good to feel your breaths
Today, tomorrow, and the next
You must endure cold, hail and whirlwinds
You must tolerate hard rain and foggy mist
Obstacles of Earth and cutting stone
Branches at your eyes and heavy loads
Upon your backs
Down you go to those who
Stole my husband.
Who crash landslides, shake the Earth,
Turn over canoes, cut ropes and
Smash with lightning, cause the bite of the old woman (snakes)
You shimmering youth
You with glistening reflections of our Father (Sun)
In our Mother (Lake)
Carried on your backs, go avenge us, bring us back to life
We the weeping mothers of
Fatherless and hungry children
Who no more hear the thud of firewood
Off our returning husband's back
Who no more see him rowing for the
Waters of Confidence
Who no more see the chips flying
From a stick carved by him
Who made our looms and brought us
Food, fuel and his jokes
Alone his tools sit dreaming of the

Dead while we women
Sweat and singe our hair staring at fires
To feed our fatherless children.
You avenge their deaths, our husbands gone,
Our teary and lonely days.
Go fight Death for the woman who is water,
The well-fitted blouse, skirt of reeds,
Voice of WaterBirds.
Steal away from Death
With your beauty and bring Her back home to us,
She whose absence kills us here,
Like we women far from those whom we love
Ask you to bring back life to your people.
Please don't forget us,
Please don't abandon us.
We don't forget you,
We won't abandon you. . . ."

With the old priestesses joining them, speaking on and on, the widows explained that justice in the hands of humans was impossible and irrelevant to the mission of being human. They explained that the Canyon Village did not want to make young men into hateful makers of war sent to exact revenge on some human enemy in return for the maddening death of the people we'd lost to violence, accidents, or life. It didn't take much talent to do that, and it only created ghosts who made more war.

What the widows asked of our nestlings was a much harder thing. They were now to become young warriors, armed only with their natures, their knowledge of wild nature, and the precious jadelike speech of their ancestors. With these weapons, the widows encouraged the boys to wrestle away from Death and the amnesia of life the blooming woman's heart that had been stolen from each of these grieving widows. For Death had stolen the Goddess out of them too. Their love for their husbands, these widows' souls, were now in the Underworld grips of Death, on the verge of wedding themselves to His eternal amnesia. If these Flowering Warriors could bring the Goddess back to life, back to the village, then the widows' lives could be restored, the Female remembered and restored. Instead of forgetting their husbands and what they had lost, what they had lost would flower into a new face called the Flowering of the Dead. For those who could understand it, this was an initiate's greatest goal, to avenge the loss of the Female soul on the Earth, trading his youth to Death in a vessel of beauty, and bringing Life back to the Earth and to the grieving village. This is what cooked a youth into a village adult.

Chicken Louse was weeping, and the rest of the boys were teary-eyed. Gourd might have wanted to cry. As soon as the boys had spoken their hoarse sincere replies, the widows came forth with *patín,* a food for the royalty on the coast, and placed it into the boys' boxes.

I gave the signal, and the widows came forth with their *stoys.* Every initiate girl, the girls these boys had admired or courted, sent their marriage shawls to keep the boys safe in the Underworld and to protect them from the power of the Goddess too, who was very strong.

The boys hadn't seen their sweethearts for almost five months now. Each girl had woven four of these wide ornate ceremonial towels: one for the boy's father, one for his mother, one for herself, and this one, for her initiate boy, her love. He must wear this towel-like shawl all the time now until his initiation was over. It was a woman's cloth and it was her way of armoring a man from danger.

Like old-time knights with their beloved's dress sleeve tucked onto their helmets as they went to face the struggle and possible death, each boy graciously received his sweetheart's fresh weaving from a widow. Putting it over his shoulders so that it draped down his back and sides, each initiate loaded up his *kahsh* over it onto his back, hanging it there by his tumpline.

Two chiefs, Spotted and Nettles, were going along with the forty-three boys, one at the back, the other at the front. Each carried a string bag full of magic, a big water gourd, a long staff, a black blanket, a hat, and sandals.

We prayed for a while and then Ma Reant Co began his Song of the Road:

"Ctlun tlungun Pa'
Ctlun tlungun Pa'
Ctlungi tlungi Pan
Ctlun tlungun Pan
Ct lungi thungi tlugi tlugi tlugi Pa'."

All of the boys with their boxes on their backs began to dance in place; and when they were all synched up with the music, I gave the signal. We thundered the earth with our yells and whoops. And off they went, a caravan of empty-box warriors, their whips on their shoulders, dancing single file in a graceful line behind the music, up the stony street away from us and closer to Death. We chiefs, mentors, and widows felt sad, hollowed out, proud, and exhausted. We wondered, as we prayed in the strangely quiet initiates' hall, how they could ever make it back with the village's life tucked into their boxes.

SEVENTEEN

EMPTY AGAIN FOR GOD

GOING BROKE AND GETTING FULL

The initiates gone, the initiating mothers and widows began to invade our compound. Bringing with them armloads of clay jars, shieldlike clay griddles, mats, stone grinders, and masses of cooking tools, they moved into a long hut running perpendicular to the men's initiation hall.

When all had been situated and every girl's station assigned, the Young Shimmerers, the girl initiates, began to arrive. They processed through the streets, finely dressed, leaning forward straining, their heads and backs covered as they carried their freshly bestowed clay cooking tubs down the village streets into their new quarters.

Ya Piskát had each pot danced and placed reverently in its place. In front of each pot the initiating mothers placed lit candles. Then their shaman, a midwife called Ya Liien, spilled liquor and incensed each of the new clay pots, addressing the woman's spirit in each in a florid harangue, not unlike the one Chiv had made inside our boys' boxes.

Then each initiating mother "rang" the pots, and out of them issued a warm bell-like earth sound, which, of course, was the voice of the pot's nature. The girls were instructed on how to take care of their wombs, their grinders, and their cooking pots, about all the taboos and many things that are not the business of chiefs or men.

It was not uncommon for such tubs to crack, disintegrate, or even explode when first placed on a fire, no matter how gradually heated or cured they might be. This didn't matter so much in everyday village life, but during this ritual it would signify the girl's failure at some aspect of the initiations. Sometimes if any of the initiates, men or women, had said or conceived an angry thought or had quarreled, one of the pots might explode. The jealous thoughts of slighted sorcerers could bring on the same disastrous crackling and shattering.

Two years before, the chief in charge of the initiation lost his temper after someone in a crowd had yelled an insult at him. That night while the women were performing this cooking ritual, the biggest tub exploded and a flying piece caught his wife's mother in the temple and killed her. Therefore, to keep everyone safe the maturing of these new pots, which stood for the containers of the girls' souls, had to be cured over the fire in a careful and reverent ritual fashion by old women who knew how.

In these tubs, with the coaching of their elder women, the young girls and the widows, side by side, were to prepare two kinds of thick ceremonial drinks. The first was made for them to share with the boys when they returned from the Underworld. The second was for the entire village, especially the Scat Mulaj, who would come in two days if the boys returned in one piece.

The first drink, called *qátouj,* was made from two kinds of chocolate beans from the cacao plants, corn, and the large vaginalike seed of a luscious fruit called *tulul* or the *sapote.* The *qátouj* would help both the boys and the girls at the last stage of initiation, giving them the feeling of the Goddess, whose euphoric deliciousness would cause their lives to loosen, ripen, and become fertilized.

The use of cacao, or chocolate, was invented by the Maya, and its use in the youth initiations was central. But the deep understanding surrounding cacao was secret. There were two kinds of cacao. One, a wild cacao called *peq'* or *pataxte,* was riotously perfumey. Its pod was decorated with deep convoluted veins and designs as complex as the curly grain on its big luxurious beans. The whole fruit caused euphoria just by its smell. Then there was the domesticated cacao with its more prosaic look and modest little beans, the source of the world's chocolate. After the two types of cacao were toasted, ground, and cooked together with particular prayers of fertility from the old women, then the seed of the *tulul* was added. The resulting drink was considered a potent spiritual beverage of desire, whose flowery smell and power promoted a swelling abundance that engendered fat, fertility, romance, and health. It was fed to the boys and girls shortly after the boys had returned with their soul Bride and the Goddess.

The girls would mature their own souls here for the next three days by making these drinks. If the drinks soured or burnt, all was lost. They were not ready or the Gods had refused them. It would be the same for the boys if they failed in their tasks.

The second drink was the same *maatz* made for baby namings, plantings, weddings, and funerals, and especially initiations. Made in two separate consecutive batches in the same tubs, each drink had to be consumed hot within an hour of its completion or it would sour as well and all would be lost.

Therefore, like the boys walking out of the world of Death, judging each step against the fat and energy left to them, the girls had to judge and measure the cooking of the *maatz*. Measurement and timing were so much a part of initiation.

All the girls' efforts in grinding the ingredients, sluicing, straining, and cooking were said to magically help the boys come home in one piece. The same went for the boys. Neither boy nor girl was to allow their mind to wander. The taboos and the focus of their thoughts were given to them by the chiefs, both men and women.

Up till now, most the materials for the initiations had come from Ya Lur and I. And all the money had come from myself. But now an even greater amount of food had to be prepared for the initiation feasts, where every day one or two cows were cooked into stews, and eight hundred pounds of corn ground into tortillas. Although I had a bit stored up from last year's sales of my paintings, when I went to fish out another one hundred *quetzales* to pay the marimba band for the village dance for the boys when they returned, the funds in my little carved box from Nahuala just barely covered it. This was a disaster.

In the intensity and confusion of my desire to make the initiations work, I hadn't given enough attention to my dwindling funds. Now I didn't have enough to last the day! This week was the most crucial part of the ceremonies, and if everything was not provided for, it would all fail. The Goddess would not return, and the village would see how unviable it was to keep these ancient rites of passage alive, as all the Christians and politicians, both Right and Left, were hoping.

What could I do? I was lost. A dull tooth of terror, self-doubt, and frustration came pinching in on my pride and the little that was left of my overtaxed mind.

For the first time in five months, I had six hours to myself, but when they were up what would I do, how could I succeed? Because from here on out it would be twenty-four hours of crowds, executive decisions, danger, constant ritual, and the final acts of my position of responsibility. The verdict on whether initiation could be voluntary would come from the results of this final ecstatic week.

From where I sat, resting and worrying, on a distant rock above the compound, I could barely hear the slushing and crushing sounds of rock on cooked corn on rock, water spilling, women chattering and praying and widows' skirts rustling above the sounds of their thudding feet as they brought jar after jar of water into the long cooking hut, where out from under the eaves smoke curled thick and blue up into the dry April air. All of this rose up to me as one symphonious composition whose old sound had been written by the ancient Tzutujil way of being, which understood that even the earnestness in preparing such beauty kept the starving deities fed and smiling.

Breathing in a big breath of nostalgic air full of expectation and doubt, I rambled in my head about my embarrassment and my unwillingness to expose my dire economic situation to A Sisay and the dedicated elders who'd never abandoned or failed me.

Then I heard a sound of wood and skin clattering up our stony path in a strange cadence like the sound of a three-legged crab, *kleep klunk talap, kleep talap kleep clunk talap.* . . . Closer and closer it rattled until it turned up toward where I sat. Completely bent over at the foot of my rock, an ancient fellow, dressed in patched Tzutujil clothing from the nineteenth century, stared up at me on my perch. His eyes were so blued by age and cataracts that they shone out of his face like hard, tiny scuffed sapphires lost in a dried to-bacco leaf. Banging at my rock with his use-polished ironwood cane, he pleaded with me to drop out of the sky for a moment, come down to earth with him and repair somewhere where his little tired body could sit.

As I leapt down from the rock, I heard him say, *"Inpinnaaq kastaln awxin tdta, A Martín,"* I've come to look in on you, venerable sibling parent, old Martín, mysteriously addressing me as a peer and mutual chief. I helped him to a dried *tzan tzuy* stump with no ants, just his size.

He wore an old-time chief's faded headcloth, red with purple silk stripes from the days when Guatemala was a big silk-producing country. His dried-up legs looked like warped wagon spokes, his hair and eyebrows were sparse and white. Blinking in the sun, his old jaws open, he looked just like a pale opossum about to fall asleep; but he surprised me when he turned with a grin, whispering loudly and breezelike: "I'm A Tec Reanda."

I'd heard of this man, but I never believed he was still alive. Everyone talked about him in the same way that they spoke about a legendary charac-ter from two centuries ago. Like an old sloth he never ventured far from his little hut surrounded by his great-great-great-grandchildren.

"I'm one hundred six years old, and when I was twenty-seven years old, it was your job I did. I was the *Primer Mayor,* the *Najbey Mam.* I've been watching you go up, go down, back and forth, in and out, marching everywhere, worrying about the village, pushing those lovely idiots of yours into becoming humans. We've heard your prayers and felt your Exalted Words against oblivion and ignorance in your struggle to keep the village from crashing into holes and canyons. We've seen your struggle against Death for the young people's hearts. I had a mentor too, he was better than that little boy you have. His name was Ma Plas Sojwel. . . ."

Everyone believed in Sojwel. An orphan prophet, he wasn't born, but found as a baby in an ash pile on the land that I now owned at the edge of the lake. Sojwel himself had personally saved Tzutujil culture several times in the last three hundred years. A combination of Gandhi, Leonardo da Vinci, and the Nez Percé chief Joseph, Sojwel reappeared and disappeared over the space of centuries. The last A Tec had seen of him was in 1903, and that's what Chiv said too. Sojwel was supposed to have walked back into the ocean to visit his parents in the other world.

"Son, you're doing a very good job, the best that has been done since I was chief, and I've seen them all," he said, patting my knee one time with his lizardy paw. My eyes were loosened from my trials of self-doubt and exhaustion, and tears took their tracks down my face, falling into the dry hopeful dust of Atitlan.

It must have taken A Tec hours to amble down here from Xechivoy on the rocky trail, bent over his sickly legs with two arms holding his cane, just to buoy up my flagging spirits. His ancient mind knew full well what we stood to lose and what kind of focus, courage, and endurance of mind and spirit this position required.

Like little children looking for a lost kitten, a pile of dove-eyed youngsters, children of his children's children's children, came searching for old A Tec. And when they found him they giggled and cheered in delight, sliding in around us, listening with their hands on their cheeks to the old man's tales and complaints from the time before anyone else in the whole village had been born. We all listened as he went on and on, teaching us what Sojwel had taught him and how I should proceed from here, giving me ritual secrets from his immense experience. I directed the rest of the initiation from the inspired information he gently hammered into my being on that day.

I was embarrassed that I had no chiefs or initiates to escort him home, as we always did no matter who came to visit, but the old man brushed it off. "I've got my own *Aguaciles,* look," he said, pointing to the valiant, big-eyed kids, half of whom had his face. The happy kids held him on every limb, leaning, pulling, laughing, pushing, lifting, and sort of rolling the old man back up the hill while he grunted like a new puppy, all the way back to his nest, safe in the middle of his compound—where like an old trunk he was buried by the exuberance of the generations of his shoots.

Inspired by the endorsement of the oldest man in the village, I dressed in my chief's armor and dropped into the village path to the compound of Ma Xkin in whose compound my mentor, A Sisay, lived. Once the initiates had left for the Underworld, the ban on speaking directly to the village was lifted. It was wonderful to be able to say hello and good-bye to everyone once again.

A Sisay was finishing his breakfast when I arrived. He seated me in his kitchen granary where he had neatly stacked his corn, using different colored ears to make a mosaic of magical symbols. The walls were made of solid ears of corn, laterally stacked, butts out.

"*Ta,* Father, I've got a terrible, terrible problem."

A Sisay went pale and stood up, his nervous eyes fixated on mine. "*Nale xbanga, xicamjun aii xitzac pisiwan!?*" What happened!? he anxiously conjectured. Did one of our nestlings fall into a ravine? I dreamt it. Did one of the girls get scalded badly?

"No, no, nothing like that," I said. Relieved, his solid congenial face relaxed a little, but he still wasn't breathing.

"It's simply the fact that, and I hate to admit it, but I've run out of money."

Everything went silent as if I'd killed something. Neither of us said anything but stared into the walls of corn until A Sisay finally began to speak. I cringed, waiting to hear what he would say.

"Well, aren't you going to tell me?!"

"I did tell you."

"What did you tell me?"

"That I ran out of money and resources."

"That's your problem?"

"Yes."

The whole compound, who wasn't supposed to be listening through the thin cornstalk walls, burst out in fits of laughter. A Sisay was laughing the hardest.

"You're just now running out of money? We wondered how long it was going to take you! Every other chief has always run out five days after his appointment, and here you've lasted almost six months. Everyone in the village talks about it every day, how you never seem to run out of personal resources. I thought you must have a tail hair from the horse of Santiago tied up in your money box, so you'd never run out! We are much relieved."

Though dumbfounded and mystified, I noticed we were both breathing again.

"What can I do then to pay for the marimba band, or continue feasting the village, or buy all the material things that we need to build the shrine and—"

A Sisay interrupted as he was putting on his fine sash, black blanket coat, and Italian fedora: "I'll show you, let's go."

The two of us could be seen waddling up the village streets, ducking in and out of one compound and into another throughout the morning, visiting chiefs, ex-chiefs, sacred ladies, and past initiates' homes.

At every stop we were invited in to sit and talk a bit, as Mayans do and Tzutujil etiquette dictates. We described everything we were doing, building up slowly to the resource problem, at which time our host would lumber over to an old wooden coffer, or order someone else to bring in an ornate little tin box or an expensive silk scarf where carefully folded, hard-to-come-by bills were neatly hidden. These old-timers handed me fifty or even seventy-five *quetzales* with little ado and with great smiles and encouragement. A Sisay and I made expressions of gratitude and relief and promised to remember them in the ritual prayers.

By midday, going hut to hut in this way, we'd gathered over two thousand dollars. That was four years' wages for a Guatemalan man with a family, and had the equivalent buying power of over sixty thousand American dollars earned at minimum wage in today's world. This would just barely get us through the ceremony.

As we returned to the initiates' house, we could see people coming and going with filled baskets and loads on their backs. As we came closer we heard a gentle murmur issuing from within the loosely piled stone walls that formed the boundary of our compound.

As we strode past the outer threshold into the space before the young men's house, a sight of great beauty and surprise met my groggy eyes.

The *Melcani* were all busy clearing the compound and making room to set the multitudes of baskets containing fresh, bright tomatoes, chiles, squashes, and beans. A ton of dried corn lay in piles of baskets like buckets of jewels— white translucent old Atiteco corn, yellow and blue and striped corn lay un-husked in mounds as tall as a person. The villagers had been waiting for months on end to help us out, gathering and setting things aside for our ritual. It had been hard for them to wait so long for me to announce my emptied-out status. Even a couple of good-looking cattle were tied to the initiates' house to use in the traditional stew made for the returning initiates and their families. The whole courtyard was impassable for the abundance stacked and laid there.

Where six hours before I'd been broke, out of money and food, I now stood custodian over a more than adequate supply of food and funds that had come directly out of this ancestral earth through the sweat and ingenuity of its people. They provided it because they knew that their young men and women must come through well or the possibility of being a village would cease. Beauty, generosity, fatigue, and hope everywhere told its tale, as the village gave its all to bring us through.

◇

We waited for days after that, looking for signs, hoping for words of the initiates far away under the hills. All the old ex-chiefs had shown up to join the vigil with my subchiefs and our mentors. What we had to do was to sit and concentrate, thinking good thoughts, helping each boy through his individual duel with Death for his soul. Everything we did was done to remember the initiates because remembering made certain that the magical umbilical rope we'd ritually tied to them stayed connected through the intense focus of the people remembering them. We were trying to reel them home with our focus. When we ate, we put food into the fires to feed the boys' souls and to give them endurance and guidance. Candles and incense were kept going day and night.

Sitting, eating, praying, dozing, praying, eating, staring, nobody went home. Everybody stayed concentrating, dedicated to the boys, making a hub for them to return to. By the morning of the third day, I sent scouts to the mountains, bearing gifts, liquor, and food, to see if they could find the boys returning. I was breaking the prime rule of not helping them, but every year the chiefs broke this rule. In this way every year the chief shows how much he cares about his initiates by doing so. Breaking such well-laid rules are what mentors are for. They show you what not to do and how to disobey in a meaningful way. Some traditions were traditions of disobeying.

I really was worried and began to pace, but the old men and women who were together again made me sit and concentrate.

The scouts came running in out of breath, with their gifts gone. They'd come up on the initiates some four miles out, resting.

Shaking with nerves and pride, this moment well rehearsed in my mind, I sent messengers to the Scat Mulaj, the village at large, and the parents of the boys. I then ordered the fifty incense burners I had hidden in the corner distributed to the women initiates and their Mother Chiefs, who ran to scrape hot oak embers from the widows' fire to load the copal burners for the meeting with the boys.

Along with two other mentors, I dragged out a hundred-pound sack of the rarest white candy-looking copal with an aroma beyond imagination. I'd been saving it for six months for just this day, using the more common copal up until now.

Lining up to receive sticky lumps of resin the size of a baby's head, each woman official and *Capoj,* Shimmering initiate girl, wrapped the copal in a big jungle leaf, thanking me with an excited smile, knowing we were ready to go meet the boys.

For the girls, this meeting would mark the end of the hard part of their initiations. It was the first time in months and months that they would be able to see and speak to their beloveds.

Everyone was yelling orders, chattering and nervous. The older ladies donned their ceremonial frocks, long white gowns shot through with tiny purple stripes and simple neck adornments, nothing like the closely embroidered, tinseled, shiny complex outfits of the girls, who had already bathed and combed themselves, and donned their belted halos, dragging shawls, their *stoy,* and fancy skirts.

All the women tore off tough sheets of wild banana leaves from a pile Ya Lur had brought and rolled them into a funnel shape around a thick kidney-fat candle, to be lit by myself from a ceremonial fire in the mountains.

People all over the village were running through the streets, getting ready to go together to see the boys, doing last-minute errands, and notifying relatives. But the widows had to stay and watch the pots and fires and show the marimba players where to set up their band.

When we were all in place, dressed and ready, I ordered a powerful skyrocket to be shot and exploded in the sky overhead as a signal of our imminent advance. We knelt as a group, praying for us to do well and for the earth to come alive again, to see her mouth and face, the door and fruit again.

Trying to look fierce but mostly worried and happy, we rose up and walked, the subchiefs, myself, Ya Lur, her initiating Mothers, their initiates, our mentors, men and women together, straight and gracefully to the old church to pick up the entire gathered Scat Mulaj.

After we greeted them with a short eloquent harangue, they agreed to come with us. Over two hundred officials dressed in their most ancient ceremonial headcloths, frocks, blankets, staffs, and shawls, rose up to join our ranks, flanking us on either side.

Ma QoQuix commenced rumbling his drum with Sweet, the flute player, cutting the air again with the Song of the Flowers. I ordered two more rockets to be fired to signal that we were complete, had been joined by the Scat Mulaj, and were advancing to the Edge of the Earth. Like a ship on the water, Ma QoQuix at the bow, we moved through the streets, gathering up the village as we surged toward Pruwachibak, Above the Mud.

Hundreds upon hundreds of villagers fell in behind us. Neighboring Indians from other villages and different tribes always came at this time, but this year instead of hundreds there were thousands who'd come to see what the government had tried to stop, what the students thought must fail. People had come great distances on foot and by bus from the coast and the mountains, because what happened here in this ritual kept their Earths alive too, and the blessing of it made people healthy. Many sick people came just to have the youths and chiefs bless them, some claiming later to have been miraculously cured.

We proceeded through Xechivoy and on out of the village, surging like a big multicolored serpent, gathering increasing numbers of villagers and outsiders, until a teeming riverlike throng over thirty thousand strong was following behind.

We weren't really leading them anymore, but were being pushed to where the villagers needed us to be. When we came into the traditional spot where the boys had for centuries been pulled officially out of the Underworld, the villagers fanned out to the sides of the surrounding hills, and out along the clearing. None crossed in front of the Chiefs and the drum. The people had all come to welcome the boys back into the village after five months of initiation, two weeks of ritual, and three days in the Underworld with no food and hardly any water. Sacred liquor from that world was all they were allowed, but that made them even drier.

At the urging of every person over forty-five years old, enthusiastic and emphatic, we initiating chiefs began to make the Edge of the World. We created a line with our staffs, made offerings and spoke magical words that made the line sacred. No one on this Earth was allowed to go over that line back toward the Underworld, only forward into Life, out of the Underworld, back to the nest and into the welcoming arms of the village.

The entire crowd quieted to a hush after that in the annual attempt to listen for any little signs of the boys coming over the ridge. Ma QoQuix stopped playing. We signaled the initiating Mothers, and they arranged their *Capoja,* the young Shimmering initiate girls, into a long train beside the chiefs. The girls swung copal burners in the pregnant quiet of the waiting crowds. Occasionally a child cried, but it was so silent you could hear the copal resin crackling in the coals.

All in a row, in fancy bird-embroidered purple-and-white blouses, and red wraparound, tinsel-sparkled skirts, the Shimmering girls held their young proud chins up, their exaggerated red halos peeking through the white intoxicating smoke. Their shawls draped over their halos like wide multicolored mantillas hanging long on both sides, they waited for the boys. The old ladies, one hundred of them in their smaller halos and long gowns, asked me to start the fire back a ways from the line, clearing the crowd just enough to allow me to do so. I lit the women's candles that they cradled in their hands in front of their bellies. The leaves wrapped tightly around the candles made the women look like they were holding flowers made of fire.

The old chiefs leaned on their staffs, smoked cigars, tightened their headcloths and waited as they knew well how to do, just as those before them had waited for them, when they'd been initiate boys on the other side of the line.

A little ten-year-old boy yelled from the top of the Deer Hill and a rippling whisper went through the entire crowd, who hushed each other and turned their excited heads to hear better. And there it was—far, far off at first, then louder, the slightly out-of-tune tinkle of Ma Reant Co's little yellow guitar, slowly coming and going on the shifting lake air. And under that sound, another was increasingly audible. The crowd held its breath as they heard the squeak and groan of ropes on wood and the shuffling creak of the boys' sandals as they waltzed out of the Underworld with their souls heavy on their backs, dancing down the mountain trail to the guitar's pulsing rhythm. And then just as we could hear their deep straining breaths . . . it all stopped.

There were no boys and no sounds. The crowd was silent as we waited behind our line, holding our breaths, trembling, staring at the narrow road ahead. What had happened? Why was no one coming?

And then there they were, crowning the last hill, like a caterpillar made of men, bristling with blossoms and flowers bent high over their heads, bouquets of orchids that bobbed and waved in the wind. Dancing and waltzing, their eyes glazed, ecstatically glowing, almost in slow motion, the boys moved as one, as if their feet didn't even touch the ground as the guitar pulled them down to us. The two stocky black-blanketed chiefs, white staffs over their shoulders, hats cocked, exhausted and smoking, danced in with them, right up to us, face to face at the Edge of the World.

We didn't have to imagine what these boys saw when they came over that last hill after so long a journey, and such a long time away from their homes and people. All eyes were wet on both sides of the two Worlds. The whole world on our side of the line wanted to see them; they were not forgotten and they were not abandoned.

Some of the initiates were tall, some had tuberculosis, some were stout and powerful, some tiny. All of their dusty copper limbs streamed in sweat, and their gaunt, panting faces held eyes that were a little older now. Some part of them was like a baby deer, weeping and exhausted, full of visions, understandings, and abilities. Beneath their loads dressed in rare jungle flowers from the Female Earth, their bodies shook and their knees knocked as they stood patiently waiting in their stupor of beauty to be pulled into our world, into the welcoming arms of the village, out of the Underworld and out of their youth.

With the young Shimmering girls to our left along the Earth's Edge, the old ladies to our right, and the old mentors and male chiefs whispering our words to us from behind, we thirteen chiefs, all at the same time, made the welcoming speech to the youth:

"When I saw you coming over the hills
I thought the Moon had gotten drunk
And was wandering the Earth looking for you,
But I was mistaken for
It was you dancing home
To us.

When I saw you, your fruited soul
Was so bright I thought the Sun Father
Was raging here searching for his lost Wife,
But I was mistaken. It was

Your shining eyes and toothy heat
Bringing Her home to us.

When I saw you climbing the last hills
I thought the Milky Way had
Fallen to the Earth, and was struggling to get back to the sky,
But I was mistaken. It was you
The eight hundred shimmering boys,
The Jade Boys,
Rain Warrior Boys with clouds
And steam on their backs,
Dawn Boys, Red Jumping Live Again Dawn Boys,
The playing boys,
Walking boys,
Running fast boys,
Dancing boys,
Flowering boys,
Unknown boys,
Winged boys,
Singing boys,
Dreaming boys,
Defending boys.

You: our Flowers, our Sprouts
Water Bringers, Bringers of Deliciousness,
It's good to see your faces again,
It's good to feel your breath again.

You who yesterday and the day before
Were planted past the snapping toothy jaws
Of Death, and gambling with the gold-belled
Owners of our indebtedness
Shed the currency of your "other" skins
And sprouted out of that on the Earth
Into the face of day, your face returned,

Your mouth returned,
You, Dogs and Rainboys, having
Endured the hills and canyons,
Endured the road of obsidian blades,
Endured the unseen holes and caves,
Endured the traps and snares,
Endured the hail,
Endured the people's words,
Endured the loneliness,
Endured the floods,
Endured the tooth of our Father Sun's heat,
Endured the whirlwind,
Endured the thorns and deep ravines
To retrieve out of the clouds, mist,
The steam and rain
On your backs like a flower
Who rides your stalk
Sprouted from your death-destroyed
Seed, who pokes his head back into
This world well rooted in the ancestral world,
In the other world,
And all this to water the
Flowering Mountain Jade Water Earth Navel.

In this village our indebtedness to you
Is unpayable
And your ability to be seen in our debt
makes you a Human.

Long Life, Honey in the Heart,
White roads paved in the eyebrows of the Moon,
Which is sea foam,
Yellow roads paved with yellow, fat, and abundance,
From the tail of the Morning Star,
No Evil,

Thirteen Thank-yous,
Earth Fruit Face, Thanks."

Signaling all our chiefs, old and young, and all the women and girls, I had my chiefs grab my sash with their hands, and the others grab their sashes in turn, and on and on in a glorious commotion, all the way back, until the whole village had lined up behind me, thirty thousand strong. I lowered my long smooth staff to the first boy, Ma Lush:

"*Tchipa akaslimal la.*" Grab your life, son, I yelled to him.

"Yes, thank you, Father. I've grabbed my life," the tired boy sang back, as he grabbed tight to the old branch.

Then, at a given signal, the whole village pulled on the person in front of them in a huge tug of war with the Underworld. Thirty thousand villagers and visitors pulled four times, and on the fifth we pulled the initiate all the way across the line, like a big beautiful fish, right into a pile of enthusiastic, welcoming chiefs and old ladies who all lined up to give him liquor and talk to him with admiring words. All the girls made a line and, one at a time, gave him exalted woman words of praise and ability, and gave him a drink as well.

We continued to pull each of the boys in. Every time and in the same way they were received with equal enthusiasm, including the musician Ma Reant Co and the two chiefs too. Every boy got to speak to every girl, one at a time, along with the sacred hierarchy of women and men who were all people of such legendary stature that very few young people would have been given the opportunity to meet them, much less in such ecstasy. The parents could not yet talk to their sons, just the hierarchy, but some cheated.

Everyone kissed the boys' bundle boxes of fruits and flowers with the Goddess inside. The initiates were bringing Her home. But, since She was not assembled yet, we had to be careful still not to scare Her away.

The chiefs lined up the beautiful boxes and the boys. The initiate girls took great care not to touch the boxes, as the boys' souls held within were not yet finished. Instead the young women blessed the boys and the boxes with the delicious-smelling copal smoke, raising a cloud so great that it obscured the village in mist.

Then, donning their much-carried orchid-covered packs once again, the boys lined up four across, their two chiefs beside them. All the musicians began playing while the hierarchy of old lady chiefs began to process to the village, walking immediately in front of the flowering boys. My subchiefs and I walked at the very front of the sacred women whose white gowns hung to the ground, and who had their candles going. The villagers crowded into every available space alongside the girls, who kept rocking their incense burners under the boys' packs as we walked. The Goddess and the boys were coming home. We made the boys dance into the village, yet another mile away, where the very old people would be waiting in the center of Santiago to bless them.

We chiefs all locked arms, ecstatic and proud, trying to look as if we could defend the village, but mostly crying and laughing. Our staffs over both shoulders, we formed a solid wall of blanketed young chiefs and one big solid white staff clear across. We too had to dance, and we did so as majestically as we could to give the boys a beacon to follow behind. The old men egged us on so that the Gods could see the Flowering Goddess progressing to the heart of the village, carried along by a jubilant crowd of life-loving humans.

When we came to the village plaza, we were greeted by the sight of a dense congregation of the most bent-over, wrinkled creatures, the great-great-great-grandparents of the village. Some of them had seen a time before glass and money, before pants and buttons, before metal pipes, wire and windows, before tin cans and airplanes, before bottled liquor and lightbulbs. And here they were to tell us we'd done it the same way they'd seen it done before, that we had done well. Each of us chiefs knelt down before these regular people of age who to us were Kings and Queens. After they heard our grandiose eloquence, gained throughout the year, we listened to their quiet, muddy words of blessing roll over their toothless gums like little streams over water-smoothed pebbles and we were devastated by their beauty.

Then came the youths' turn. As they were shaking from too much knowledge, hunger, exhaustion, and deeply-lodged emotions, we steadied them as they knelt with all seventy-five pounds on their backs. Miraculously renewed, the boys gained strength, when the old-timers touched each boy on his head, sending their deep old encouragements straight into every boy's chest. After each of us had received the old people's blessing, we stood the boys up, our chests heaving, and I yelled the old war cry of the Tzutujil youth. All the sacred house members shouted back, proudly whooping like ancient Dogs and Rainmen:

"Ay Ruqansac
Ay Ruqan Qij'
Rumac jajala
Nkaban Waviera
Xin kibean cdta aii
xinkicastaja ctit cmama'."

Oh, the foot of Dawn (white)
Oh, the foot of Day (Sun)
because of what we do here
the Sun keeps walking,
our ancestors jump up and live again.

With that signal, all of last year's initiates rushed in and grabbed one of the new ones to steady him. We showed our admiration to all of them as we lined up in file behind the drum, dancing the last half mile to the reed-covered doorways, pine-needle floors, and flowering altars of our initiation house where the widows waited with a feast.

By the time we arrived, a large pressing crowd of villagers, along with the families of visiting dignitaries from the other villagers who were traditionally allowed to live here for the remainder of the week, had gathered in our court-yard. We had to use our staffs to push the people back quickly to make room for the young bringers of the Goddess, the initiates.

The marimba band began to play the song of reception, and the boys danced in one at a time with their loads. Then, removing their boxes, they lined them up in front of the place where they'd spent the last five months to-gether.

The *Melcani,* the widows, now in magnificent borrowed clothing, poured out of the cooking hut with fresh braziers of smoking copal. Each woman picked a boy and began to dance majestically with him. Then after a minute she'd take another, until all had been danced with. Quieting the pushing crowd and the marimba band, the widows addressed the Rainboys:

"She whom you carried out of that other world
Makes us want

To jump up and live again.

We thank you,

The avengers of the death of our husbands.

You brought our stolen hearts.

It is good to see your faces again.

It is good to see your mouths again.

It is good to feel your breath again."

Then the marimba band blasted a beautiful old Atiteco sōn, and each of us chiefs danced individually with every boy, while one of the Scat initiates poured canyon water to welcome all of us Home.

The world began oozing as if in slow motion now as I danced the beautiful, tired young men, one by one, over the threshold into the waiting line of old mentors inside, who in turn danced with every boy, bouncing as if they were underwater. Outside the compound, every person in the village broke loose and began dancing outside. After a few minutes the young girl initiates stormed into the initiates' hall, which had previously been off-limits to them, fought their way through the whirling ecstatic crowd and tore each of their sweethearts out of the arms of the old men. The boys and girls danced and wept, danced and wept, happy to be in each other's arms again.

After a while Chiv and A Sisay stopped the music and signaled the feast. We separated the boys once again from the widows and the young girls, and sent them to bring in their packs. The marimba band started playing a slow Mayan rhythm and the boys danced their packs, holding them in front of them like a girl. They danced with their Soul Brides, their chunk of the Goddess, rocking beautifully. Drunk for God, for their souls, for Life, for the village, they floated and danced around and around. When all three requisite songs had been finished, we directed the boys to place the souls of our village right in the altar space, where they would all live for the next three days, standing in flowering rows full of concentrated Life.

The boys were led to seats along the walls and fed by the widows. With the floor now cleared, the famous Dance of the First Chief started. A Sisay and I danced as a pair, as did the other chiefs with their *teonel*. With our staffs over our shoulders, we hopped and swayed, ecstatic and in love with life.

For A Sisay and me, this was how we toasted the Gods and Goddesses and showed our admiration for each other for having managed to bring the boys home in one piece. For that we danced and laughed, wept, shuffled, and slid in a kind of medieval courtly majesty, leaping high off one leg, then the other. All the mentors' wives came and danced with us, and then our own wives. The village craned to see us, joyously commenting, cheering, and admiring, until nobody could hold them back. The whole world started dancing like a camp of crazed gypsies crossed on whirlwinds, everyone with everybody for the rest of the night. When the Sun Father was once again deep in the bowels of the Earth, most of us were lying on the pine needles passed out, asleep in front of the Goddess still in the boys' box hearts.

EIGHTEEN

RETURN FROM THE UNDERWORLD
REASSEMBLING THE GODDESS

Like animals getting ready to molt, the boys were put into a collective isolation where they worked on ripening and maturing their souls for three days. For this reason, on the following morning the initiating hall was closed up tight and dark. No one except the chiefs and mentors was allowed in, and the boys were not allowed out except to relieve themselves, and even then they were escorted.

All of the boxes that had become the containers of their souls sat like a stately row of rectangular eggs, golden and alive, that had to be warmed constantly. Inside these packs were five types of holy fruits that had been picked long before maturity and placed between layers of other magical materials to keep them separated and unbruised on the journey home. The manner in which they had been picked, packed, and combined with other elements made them engender a spirit. This deeply held secret caused the maturation of the boxes and the Goddess, if carried out properly.

The fruit in each package had to be matured in three days. This was considered to be the final test of the boys' graduation. If the fruit was judged not green, not overripe but perfectly ripened, then the boys had passed their initiation.

Nobody was allowed to open the net-bound, orchid-studded boxes to check the fruit at any time. That way, when the Scat Mulaj came in three days and opened each box for the first time outside in front of the whole village, the maturity of each boy would be determined according to how his fruit had ripened. The headmen would open the box and simply hold up the fruit for the people to see. If it wasn't ripe, the boy had failed. Perhaps he had not been focused and had begun thinking mean thoughts or perhaps he had committed some other infraction of the rules. Most of the time it would be because he had not worked hard enough to mature himself. When one's fruit came out green and unripened it was considered quite a failure. We all feared it, and worked hard to avoid it.

If the fruit ripened in three days, however, this was considered nothing short of a miracle by the village, thereby proving the literal presence of spirit, which was assumed to be the boy's soul and the returned Goddess. Her beautiful smell permeated our hall even now. The steam building up in the pack was a secret, but it meant that she was coming alive. The walls were covered in cedar branches and *kip* palm leaves, and another six inches of pine needles had been added to the floor, layered on top of the first six. The ceiling was solid cacao, palm flower, jungle melons, *coyol* palm fruit, portulaca, and mouse-ear orchids. This was the womb of the Goddess and its smell was otherworldly.

For three days the boys burned over two hundred pounds of copal resin, saturating our lungs, our clothing, the building, the earth, and their boxes with its heady, delicious smell. All the initiates swung their burners lifting clouds upon clouds of warm holy aromatic smoke to cook their souls and fruit into maturation. Day and night they worked at this, six or even seven at a time. Then they would lie down in the pine needles and rest, allowing a few others a turn, on and on until their shift arrived again. Each boy's chief monitored his initiate's package, trying to judge from experience how much heat and smoke each boy's fruit might need to be made holy and mature.

The boys had their food brought in once a day by the chiefs. They hadn't been allowed to change clothing or wash since coming from the Underworld. Their baby skin, all they had been and all they'd had to be, was being literally cooked away while they were maturing their souls and the Goddess.

Whereas most of the initiates looked very haggard and were suffering, Chicken Louse, who was busy energetically smoking the devil out of his fruit in a very even way, seemed happier than he'd ever been and more physically relaxed. This was a very hard time for some of the boys, and they eased some of their suffering by relating what happened on their journey in greater detail.

The journey back home had not been without its problems, we learned. After leaving the Underworld, having convinced Death to return their souls and the Goddess, the boys had begun their dancing trek back to the male Earth in the moonlight. It was much cooler than on their way out and they had made good progress, but when they'd come to the edge of the canyon before the cliffs of Tuq, the young Christian boy began babbling to himself. The chiefs watched him closely as they marched to the pumping guitar music. Suddenly, they saw him drop his pack and commence sprinting toward a cliff, intending to throw himself off into the deep rocky ravine. He was screaming all the while about a woman he saw there who was calling him to sleep with her and into whose arms he was running. Of course, he was running to his death. Death was not going to let him have his soul.

Chicken Louse had been watching all along and, without saying a word, chased him and succeeded in tackling him just before he would have plummeted a thousand feet. Ma Reant Co, who always knew what to do, told the boys they'd have to carry him, kicking and screaming if necessary, back to the village.

Chicken Louse wasn't going to have anybody on his team failing. He tied the Christian up, trussing him up like a killed peccary. Removing the very strong netting from his own pack, Chicken Louse put the crazed Christian boy right inside it, face out so he could breathe, and tied his head strap to it. Giving his pack to one of the chiefs, and the Christian's pack to the other chief, Chicken Louse loaded the screaming, tranced-out boy onto his back and carried him up and down mountains all the way.

While they were still hidden by the forest, just before they came to the village edge, the returning column had gone silent because Chicken Louse had stopped the procession and untied the Christian, who'd recovered somewhat. Then he had rearranged his fruit for him, put it on his back, took his own box from the other chief—and the entire body of initiates marched to the line as if nothing unusual had happened! Chicken Louse saved our initiation and the life of the poor Christian whose faith was not in the ritual, who'd almost lost his life on account of his negative thoughts.

About one in the morning on the third and last night, while all the boys took a well-deserved nap, A Sisay and Ma Um woke me, motioning for me to follow them. Barefoot on tiptoes, the three of us silently edged our way over to the fruit brides, whose overwhelming smell was now a special alchemy that was so definitely divine that no one could have doubted the presence of the Goddess and the boys' souls.

A Sisay began to open Gourd's box, lifting up the wild leaves under the orchids and net, fishing around in the hot steaming bulk of the contents. I grabbed his hand to stop him, whispering, "We can't do this, it will ruin the ceremony!"

"We always do this," Ma Um said.

"This in my hand could ruin the ritual," A Sisay hissed in a kind of sandy hoarseness as he held out a totally cold green cacao pod, weeks away from maturation.

I was aghast. How did they know Gourd's fruit would be cold and unripe? No one could tell by simply looking at the packs.

"Go wake him up and show him," the two old men commanded. Gourd's big sunburned, dirt-glazed head popped up with a start. I covered his mouth. "Come on, son, I have to show you something, don't wake your nest mates."

When Gourd saw the violated pack and his green unripe fruits, he fell to his knees, grabbed me around my legs, and began weeping in terror of his failure, asking for forgiveness for bad-mouthing me, for thinking only of women in compromising situations, and for making lewd jokes about the Goddess as he marched home.

Ma Um elbowed him solidly in the ribs, telling him, "Boy, this isn't going to help you. Only the spirits you've insulted can help you now. Let's get going."

Throwing my chief's blanket over him, and still barefoot, the four of us struck out onto the starlit streets of early morning, turning and striding for a mile and a half till we came to the sacred house of Holy Boy. The reed-covered doorway glowed from within, and when we entered and cried out our greetings, more than twenty voices responded in kind. "How come you came so late, Brother Father Martín?" they asked. I was confused.

"How did you know we were coming? How did you know someone's fruit wasn't ripening?"

The whole room started to rumble with laughter as the Teleniel, the priest of Holy Boy, and the third official in charge of the deity clunked down the ladders from Holy Boy's home in the rafters. Taking terrified Gourd, they made him kneel in the front of Holy Boy.

Gourd began to pray fervently to Holy Boy, asking him to forgive him and mature his fruit, his soul, by dawn when the old men and women of the village would come to inspect his box in front of the village and all his relatives.

Gourd and I, with A Sisay and the Teleniel, prayed for a long while too. We lit our candle and distributed liquor, offerings, and copal.

Then, saying our good-byes, we marched poor shivering Gourd back to the initiation house and made him swing the copal burner all night without sleep, with the rest of the youth who were back at it again. Miraculously, after an hour steam began to rise from the folds of the outside leaves and Gourd's box, but we couldn't risk looking to see if Gourd's fruit was actually maturing. We could only wait like the rest.

The following morning, we opened the hut doorway cover for the first time in three days. Dawn flooded into the house of vegetation where we men had been living with our maturing souls. A great gust of strange steam and fumes escaped visibly into the world, like the smell on a pond after frogs' eggs have made tadpoles.

The boys' female relatives had been standing respectfully in the streets for a while or sitting on the rock walls all about, their tied shawls filled with newly woven clothing for the New Men.

I gathered up the precious clothing from the mothers and sisters, and they trotted back to their compounds to ready themselves for the village inspection of the boys' maturity. Even I received gifts, three brand-new headcloths befitting my newly earned position, which, like the boys' souls, would hopefully come to maturity today as well, but only if I'd succeeded in leading them into theirs. That remained to be seen.

Keeping the people away, we herded the grateful youth down to the lake to wash off their husk of childhood and, for the first time in eight days, to bathe. They were so happy in the water that we chiefs joined them, joking about how skinny everyone had become.

All new and dressed, we returned, readorning our chambers and our boxes with flowers. Then I sent five patrols of last year's initiates to bring in the Scat Mulaj, the government officials, the Catholic priest, the evangelical preachers, and the village itself. Traditionally, on this day the new men and new women had to bless every living thing, and the people had to come here to receive their benediction. I personally caught two evangelical preachers trying to skip out of town in a boat to avoid our insistence on their getting blessed by us "pagans," but the other seventeen got away. Stanley, the Catholic priest, came along peacefully, only pretending to balk in order to keep up a decent appearance in front of the New Catholic converts. In reality he was fond of our ceremonies but couldn't admit to it in public.

When everybody in the village had arrived, the Scat Mulaj officials took the bundles outside, lined them up, and asked each boy to kneel behind his package. The headman of our village and his two side chiefs came and began opening the tops of the bundles. We young chiefs were all in a row, holding our staffs in two fists held low over our thighs. In the village, the way you hold your staff and wear your clothes is a language that all understood.

Each initiate, all clean and beautiful, knelt in front of his Fruit Bride. Each time a bundle box was inspected, old Ma Tun Ratzam, the second headman, unlaced the net and pushed aside the green leaves now gone brown. Then with a little puffing sound a big cloud of delicious steam would visibly rush out into the clear morning air. Everyone hummed in admiration and the whole village inhaled all at once, ceremonially breathing in this luscious musk believed by all to be a powerful, restorative medicine because it signified the complete return of our Mother Waters, the Goddess of Life, as she rushed back into the village and the World of Life. We in the sacred house called this steam "a little bit of the aroma of the original Flowering Mountain Earth." This was the smell of the flowering of a young man's heart. It was a delicious smell. No one ever forgets it.

We chiefs were really on trial today. If any boy should fail, we were the ones who had failed him. As the youth fruit matured, so our lives advanced toward adulthood. As each package was opened, the fruit was pulled out and one example of each kind was held up high for parents, compound relatives, the entire village, and visitors to examine. The terrified boys stared, waiting and hoping for the words *"Qán Chiq,"* yellow already, (meaning matured). When their young ears heard the sound, each boy would breathe again, pray, stand and smile, having passed his initiation. When they got to Gourd's box the whole village held its breath because everyone knew he had very little chance of having matured. When they opened his bundle, however, steam came hissing out like a sweatlodge, and a hummingbird actually came and hovered in the steam cloud of Gourd's soul. A little rainbow held itself there until the strong-smelling mist cleared. Ma Tun Ratzam held up two large ripe cacao, squealing the words *"Qán Chiq"* while shaking his head. Gourd began praying and then weeping as the old fellow laughed and the surprised village cheered at the very perfectly ripened fruit of a once-insolent boy that, six hours before, had been totally green and cold.

Every one of my boys came through matured. My chiefs and I just pursed our lips and looked at each other knowingly, bonded for life, water welling up in our eyes. We raised our staffs over our shoulders, adjusted our blankets, and called for the widows to call the women chiefs to bring out their initiate girls and the *maatz* for their test.

We seated the old women chiefs and the old man chiefs in the places of honor in the initiation hall, along with the white political officials and the missionaries. But the latter were uncomfortable in such richness, confusing happiness, and massive accord, and tried to escape; but we caught them and wouldn't let them leave. I still retained the right given me by the Head Man to jail people. I hadn't exercised it yet, but my young men were aching for an opportunity to guard the integrity of the village, which they loved now more than their freedom.

The drink came in breastlike gourds served by the initiate girls. If any of the hundreds of old-timers drinking the liquid found his or hers "soured," then that girl who made it had been thinking bad thoughts or had transgressed a taboo, and would have failed her initiation, so distinct from the boys'. I drank mine, and the thick pastelike, nutty-tasting liquid filled my parched worried belly like a welcome rain on dust. It was perfect. I signaled this by placing my empty gourd upside down inside the circulating basket, which was soon filled with more of the same. The official verdict was positive.

All the drinks were fine except those received by the government officers. The old women were horrified, but no one knew whose *maatz* their gourds had come from. Mysteriously, nobody could determine which girl had failed. After tasting every girl's huge tub, they found that not one was soured. They served them up again. But again, when the government officials drank, their drink was soured. This time I jumped up and the village Head Man too. We tested the officials' drinks and, by God, they were soured.

For a third time, we were all given new gourds filled from yet another tub. But when the white men got theirs, they were again soured, whereas ours were as perfect as ever. The politicians were scared, realizing that something more powerful than a simple tradition was alive here.

Staring at each other, the old ladies, old men, chiefs, and the *Melcani* started to laugh. All of us began to comprehend what had happened, and we were much relieved. The officials, however, were unable to comprehend. They got up and exited to the freedom of their impatient ignorance, along with the preachers, and this time we let them go. Stanley stuck it out, of course, hoping that the earth warmer, the homemade liquor, was coming along soon, which it was.

Many stories tell of the souring of this ceremonial drink when the spirits of the ceremony reject someone they don't like. Since these missionaries and government officials were involved in the attempt to stop these initiations, the spirit must have refused to have them drink.

All the girls passed. Sweetly euphoric and relieved, they delivered hundreds upon hundreds of cups and gourds full of *maatz* to the rest of the waiting village as a blessing, everyone drinking the girls' excellence into the collective belly of the village.

The boys gave steam and fruit and the girls gave liquid and food, and between the two the village came back to life.

❖

The canoe makers built the bottom layers because they were the owners of the ancient beams and supports that went into it. The rope makers brought the rope, the basket makers brought the canes, the high-altitude initiates had brought the branches last night, and the palm-flower initiates had returned this morning. Piece by piece the House of the World was coming together.

Called New Men now, our initiates did all the climbing, swaying themselves up the rigging like old clipper ship sailors, working like ants, swinging the struts and cross pieces into their position in the Tzutujil Universe. The Sky, the Earth, the inside, outside, all sides, the doorway where the Sun came up; everything was represented.

Our shaman Diez Peso blessed every knot, and we chiefs supervised the materials and the raising of the house.

The complexities of this shrine were an institution. It was an ephemeral manifestation of time fed by its own form as a house, which was called Pot Mountain. Pot Mountain was the ceremonial name for the volcano immediately behind the village, the place where the Father Sun marked the spring equinox by rising directly over its caldera at the dawn of that day. Ideally, adolescent initiates crossed the line into early adulthood on the equinox. The House of the World shrine was also called Pot Mountain because it was being assembled by the New Men as an offering to feed Time as an adolescent. The equinox was the year's adolescence and it too could mature into a fully grown year. Because every bit of the House of the World was some part of the living Earth in miniature, the offerings that were hung on it fed those particular places, and the whole then became an offering in itself. Built the day after the maturation inspection, it was located just behind the Sacred Hole in the old Catholic church.

The major offerings that hung on this beautiful house were the initiates' fruits of maturity: the cacao, the sacrificial palm flowers, the jungle melons, and the wild bananas. At this very moment these offerings were being further adorned and fitted with *zibaque* reeds so that the initiates could tie them onto the House of the World where they would hang free to form the walls of the sacrificial edifice.

The fruit had been already fertilized by Holy Boy during the same ceremony I had witnessed the first day of my flute playing years ago. After the fruits' deliciousness had been eaten by the Deity and its seeds fertilized by him, they became the holiest offerings in the world. For a whole week the initiates would have to guard the fruit from evil and keep incensing the House as well, as they had in their isolation. Candles were lit all along the height of the House, and wild animals in cages were brought in alive and hung in the matrix of the House, as they had been for centuries. We released them back into the wild at the end of the rituals, to take our messages and report what we had done back to their Gods.

The New Catholics, who had stepped up their efforts to appear as civilized and advanced as possible, were required to hate everything that was native and natural. They were outraged by the presence of the House of the World in their church, even though it had been reduced in size to only two and a half stories over the last four centuries.

But when the animals appeared, that was the last straw. The zealous converts confronted us chiefs, formally ordering us to remove the "dirty beasts" immediately. I sent for Father Stanley who, after hearing all sides of the argument, looked over the beautiful shrine, examining the cacomistle, the parrots, the squirrels, the ocelot, the wild doves, the rabbits, and so on. Coming to a decision, he spoke in bad Mayan in a great pontifical voice, "Martín, can I have a squirrel and a dove when it's over?" and walked away. The Catholics stomped off, mad and plotting, and we continued to guard the Flowering Mountain Jade Water Earth House of the World, Pot Mountain.

When we'd almost finished putting the World back together again, remembering it back to life, the drummer and flute played the plaintive Song of the Sacrifice while we knelt and wept for the House of the World. Behind us a big crowd of our boys' mothers moved slowly toward the center of the church, some with their backs to us, others facing us, carrying something in their midst, which they incensed over the Sacred Hole.

They called for me and the subchiefs. Then, lining up, the mothers addressed us:

"Here, freely given, is the
pot you wanted to steal,
to roof the Umbilicus of the
Sky. Young men, you are free to
return home when your chiefs
let you, please receive this gift."

And with that the Mothers whom the initiates had robbed so long ago, now gave to them the biggest lime-painted, clay cooking tub they'd ever seen, weighing more than two initiates.

It was the woman's choice as to who would climb the dangerous two stories to the crown of this House of fruit, cedar branches, fires, animals, and flowers, and place the heavy pot right on the apex of its pyramidal point. For his initial disrespect of the women, and his sudden popularity among them for his heroic realization of the beauty and magic of being a man who could serve his own Soul Bride, the Earth, instead of being a self-serving bully, they picked Gourd, who was only too willing to try.

After putting the extremely heavy oversized earthen tub up over his big box head and massive neckless shoulders, the brave fool couldn't see a thing. As he crawled up the struts and riggings, offerings, and branches, he shook and strained. The animals panicked. But, climbing like an ant bear, slowly and with great strength, he made the summit, although it took him three tries to leave the pot on top evenly so that it wouldn't drop and kill someone. But finally Gourd ducked out from under the tub after managing to situate it firmly into its primordial home at the very point where the Sun begins its new life and young boys become humans.

This was what we men always had to do: carry the containers of the Female's umbilical remembrance over the beautiful and living earth without damaging the offerings of one's soul, and then return home again to be a regular person.

❖

Holy Boy had been hung in his dahlia tree and the village shamans were pouring into his grotto to make their annual gifts to him on a personal level, just as the boys had done for the village as a whole. For years I'd been involved with that ceremony, but this year my every waking moment was absorbed in the initiations.

After the House of the World had been built, and the initiates had successfully restarted the village heart, a whole burst of simultaneous ceremonies was carried out by several sacred houses, all hidden under the guise of the celebrations of Easter.

Called Loqlaj Qij, or Magnificent Sun, these village rituals were in the hands of the Scat Mulaj. The initiated youth were now charged with making sure that their shrine was safe and patrolling the village against any force that would try to disturb its spiritual integrity for the seven months that followed. While our young men were building the House of the World, the very oldest male members of the Scat Mulaj disappeared into a little stone house where they spent the better part of two days preparing a meal for the shimmering initiate girls and certain little children.

Puttering around, so earnest and sincere, bickering about cooking methods though none of them knew a thing about it, they singed their eyebrows in the cooking fires, burned the beans, and dropped their crooked tortillas into the dust so that they had to be fed to the dogs. It took forty old geezers forever to get together a questionable feast that three women could have accomplished in five hours.

That, of course, was not the point. The purpose was for the old men to carry on the best they could at a task that the women did on a regular basis in order to make a gift to the New Women, a blessing from honorable men who were neither husband, brother, or father to the girls. When all the food was made ready, the *Capoja,* the girls, the Shimmerers, were sent for. After seating them against the wall in a long row of sparkling teenage girls dressed in their best, and placing their initiating mothers to the side, the old fellows, now dressed in ceremonial robes, having doctored their burns and washed off the soot and corn dough, blessed the young ladies with an old prayer.

Then each man took a bowl and placed in each one a different cooked or uncooked food, all of which had been brought by the Rainboys, the male initiates, from the altitude or climate to which their group pertained.

There were fish and crabs from the Mother Lake; corn, beans, deer meat and wild honey from the mountains; tomatoes, chilies, and greens from the village gardens; and chocolate and myriad types of fruits from the hot coastal Female Earth. From each of their bowls, the old tottering, toothless chiefs took a little bit of each food from every part of the world and fed it delicately into the mouths of each young girl, going down the row, one after the next.

This took quite a while, until a little of the returned Goddess was inside each young woman. Their mouths became Her mouth, and through them the dried old men could nourish the newly returned Goddess of Water. The girls giggled, but tried to be serious. This was part of the ritual of the House of the World.

The girls fed by these lovely old fellows cold not vouch for the old men's cooking abilities, but this marked the formal end to their initiation ritual. And they would swear ten years later that this food had been magical to them and would keep them healthy for the rest of their lives.

The subchiefs and I were witnesses to this feeding of the young by the old, of the Female by the Male, along with all the initiating matrons. When the old chiefs released us all to the streets, our duties as far as the initiation rituals were concerned were also concluded.

❖

The roads in the central part of Atitlan were paved with a thick carpet of green fragrant pine needles called the Sun's Road, the Road of our Father. Throughout the village, every hundred yards or so, tall, lavishly adorned thresholds had been created over these roads standing like square goal posts covered in evergreens, flowers, and small cages with live animals. Each of these monuments had a palm flower hung from the middle of its one cross-beam.

We young chiefs walked the village as a team, patrolling from sacred house to sacred house on this flower and pine needle road, delirious in the balmy air of well-being that saturated the village as our Sun Father went to rest behind the Earth Elbow, the volcano of San Pedro.

We felt like little savoring tongues made into fish as we floated through that delicious scented honey of village happiness. All twenty-six of us bathed in the praise showered upon us by every passerby and the tremendous welcoming embraces bestowed on us in every hut.

Tradition said we should wander, walking beautifully together clockwise until dawn rose over the pine-covered Sun Road, as a visual gift to the gods and to energize the village. On this particular night every year, the initiating chiefs and ladies always checked in on all the older men and women Scat Mulaj officials in the diversity of public ceremonies that were happening all at once in different parts of the village. We encouraged the officials and made certain they had everything they required, sending our initiates to help if needed.

Having encompassed our fifth orbit of the village, we left the grotto of Holy Boy and his shamans and proceeded through the central threshold, heading toward the initiates' shrine, the World House, to visit the Sacred Hole in the church. Then all around us we heard a strange rushing, rumbling sound. A feeling like warm water came over all of us at once.

We looked at each other in surprise, but before we could speak the sensation intensified, carrying with it a euphoric set of emotions far beyond the collective ecstasy of the evening. Then, all of a sudden, we were walking but not moving, and even stranger was the fact that we didn't care. The village we patrolled became the world and the world became a mansion, a jungle house, a water house, a windy house, a flowering house, a mountain house, in whose doorway we stood, away from which we continued walking beautifully, but were unable to leave. We were at home walking in our Home, never leaving the spiritual Home, walking beautifully at Home.

A strong smell of animal birth rose up through all of us, the warm buoyant water rushed out away from us somewhere, and the gravity that accompanied this mammalian musk had so much weight and power that it crushed us to our knees.

When we turned our heads up to see, our twenty-six hearts began to beat in one rhythm with a cadence inside of which we were held, shoulder to shoulder, both distinct and gloriously homogenized into each other's uniqueness, a heart that beat for something so immense we could never comprehend it.

The village was gone, but everywhere, somehow, having spun and spun, the village churned itself into this, its inner form.

What had been a birthing smell now became a life-restoring fragrance so saturating that its penetrating hand recarved our hearts from the Gods' pliable jade, licking them smooth and polishing them into health as a mother deer licks her fawn, massaging as well our tired bodies with paws made of windy leaves and rushing waters.

That's when we saw Her, returned to Her throne, all thirteen of Her returned to majesty. All of us together saw Her and wept. A smell like rotting reeds in the wind was in her breasts, our hair flailing in that breeze, a smell like nesting waterbirds clucking in descending scales, the rushing foamy waves of her ocean womb whose iridescent surface was made of layered hummingbird backs. And then an even deeper smell came from her belly, her flowering belly, her sad hollowness filled now with every kind of young being.

We saw Her, all of us together at one time. Seeing the divine together, we collapsed onto the pine needles that last day of the initiation, our souls like a litter of once starving fox kits, their bellies finally full of their mother's milk. Having suckled all we could after her long absence, full from the Mother of Life, we the young chiefs and ladies fell asleep on the Road of the Sun.

Many days later, the thresholds were all gone, the Sun Road returned to the earth, the House of the World dismantled. The cacao fruit had been distributed by the youth to their sweethearts, who would now plant the chocolate seeds in their mother's land to see if they would grow. If they did, this was a good omen for marriage. The youth had gone home, the chiefs too. I was alone.

Though the boys would normally have had to stand guard over the government officials, they were reprieved. Instead, one chief at a time, once a week, took the new men to help the old people. Throughout the next year we congregated three more times to build shrines for the old people, but never again would we be together as we had in our old initiation hall, which now stood empty and unadorned except for a couple of rotting palm flowers.

There were signs that the rains would grace us again, but for now the street I headed down was dry dust rolling over the occasional skinny brindle dog. Most of the people had gone back to their fields and regular lives. But for me it was like having been in a lovely dream. I found it hard to wake up and to be alone again without the rich magic of those initiation days. The magic was still there, really. What I truthfully missed was being needed.

Though my suggestion of keeping the initiation ritual alive while discarding the civil duty to the government seemed to have been a success, it remained to be seen if another young Tzutujil married man could or would try to do again what we had done here.

I missed my chiefs and my mentors. I missed the boys, the noble sparkling girls and their beautiful tenderness. But to the Tzutujil, this dusty everydayness was the fruit and blessing of all we'd done, oblivion being the alternative. I missed being needed every minute of the day, when each of my footsteps had been a prayer meaningful to the final outcome.

I was fully aware that nobody could live in ecstasy forever, and that the magic of our rituals was only a place visited, done to maintain this much duller everyday life. I knew that no worthy ritual was done for the experience of the ritual but was carried out to maintain a regular life of work and harvest, raising children and struggle. Nonetheless, the abandoned orphan in me never wanted the beauty of these fine days to come to a close. But they had.

All those thoughts sawed through my tired body and open heart. Dressed as a civilian again, carrying a couple of leftover jungle melons and a drying cacao pod, I padded my way down the hill to our compound to sit one more time alone in the old initiation hall before going in to see my son, wife, and exhausted family at their cooking fires.

The smell of initiation still hung in the air of the dark unlit chamber and it took a while for my eyes to adjust. But when they did, I saw, sitting there in their raggedy, patched old work clothes, the thirty old men and women, the mentors, holding their breath and half-drunk. Then they burst out laughing.

"What are you doing here, Mothers and Fathers?"

"We know how you must feel; we've done that part of it too. We'll just stay here until you feel better."

And they did. It took a long time. Weeks. A part of me is still sitting there waiting for it to all start up again.

NINETEEN

TRYING TO BURY OLD MAN EARS
THE ZANY ELDER

A Sisay lived with his wife, Ya Piskát, in the compound of her family. His father-in-law, like most men, was a regular farming man; not a chief, shaman, or hierarchy member but a quiet old traditionalist named Ma Xkin, meaning Ears.

Because we all knew Ears and genuinely liked him, we felt a loss when he died. His other children had children who were evangelical Christians and merchants. To honor their old grandfather Ears and give him a "proper Christian" burial, they had a thin-sided, black wooden coffin built for him. In those days, for many spiritual reasons the old-timers preferred to be buried sewn into a reed mat like a butterfly in a flexible cocoon. One reason was so that their spirits could easily escape and attach themselves to the Sun Father the day following their death in order to begin their journey to the next layer. Being nailed into a box didn't appeal to most of the older generation.

But Ears was laid into a black box milled from old mountain pines with handmade saws and shaved with wooden block planes and pinned with homemade nails. By modern standards the box looked fairly humble, but to our villagers it was a rare and special way to be buried.

As friends of his son-in-law and daughter, all the initiates and my chiefs came to the wake where the proper amount of weeping, hair pulling, scratching, chest beating, and grief was expressed by most of his family to fuel the journey of his spirit into the next layer of life. Without these things, Ma Xkin would hang around here as a ghost, "eating" the next generations. Nobody wanted this so they felt the loss and cried about it. The Christians abstained to some degree, having been taught that this was all a lot of pagan ignorance.

The mourners and relations leapt and wept all the way to the burial grounds below the old ancestral cave shrine. The initiates shouldered the box to the hole, into which all of Ears's undistributed personal belongings were placed, and then they lowered the long box into the ground. When the box hit the bottom, just as they were getting ready to cover him up, a terrible muffled yelling and knocking ascended out of the hole from the earth. In a desperate instant all the generations of Ears's weeping relations stopped breathing as they saw a wrinkled bony hand punch its way right through the top of the thin box. In the next instant, splinters were flying, half the lid was gone; and there was Ears, sitting straight up in his casket, quivering and bobbing, looking like a startled newly hatched buzzard chick.

The people started yelling and shrieking, reeling and pressing in to see him as the boys raised the coffin out of the hole with the ropes still attached.

Ears refused to leave the coffin, so they had to lift him in his box up to their shoulders again. The boys carried him, alive this time, back to his house. Like a paddler in a kayak, old Ears rode along above a sea of people, pontificating as loud as his old voice could manage. He pointed to different individuals in the growing crowd.

"You Box Head," he said, pointing to his younger brother, "Grandfather is not happy you sold our avocado land to the Catholics!" Holding his two palms out to an older woman, he reported, "I saw your mother, she's fine, she's a fish now." And to another, "Your sister, old Washing Rock, says she's not angry at you anymore for stealing her husband." On and on he went, still in the trance of the other world he'd visited, where he'd spoken with the dead. When he was alive he'd been a shy man, but now after he'd died he'd become a talkative person, generously giving everybody the news. He lectured and explained, waving his arms all the way home.

This was the first time anyone had come back from the dead in a coffin. In Atitlan returning from the dead was not as uncommon as it is in other places, but usually they never made it all the way to the graveyard. Ears became the talk around every family cooking fire in the southern lake region for a full month, until men returning from the fields hungry and impatient pleaded with their families to talk about a new subject.

Some of my younger initiates had heard that old Ears had taken to sleeping in his coffin and wanted to see it for themselves. One morning Red Jumping came to visit me. "We could make up something to ask A Sisay, your advisor, and then once in the hut we could look around and see if Ears is really sleeping in that black box!" he suggested.

"We can't do that, that's deception," I snapped back, but we did it anyway.

When we arrived, A Sisay was out, but one of Ears's unmarried great-granddaughters was there, slapping out tortillas in the smoky hut and dripping the yolks and whites of some big speckled turkey eggs onto the hot clay griddle.

Falling for our ruse, she had us sit while we waited for A Sisay. Finally, after an hour, I asked her, "Is it true that your great-grandfather sleeps in the same coffin he was buried in?" "Watch," was all she said. Then, matter-of-factly, she took the broom handle and began banging on the coffin, which was laid out overhead several feet above us, across three of the hut's roof beams up in the rafters under the thatch, in the constant soot and thick smoke of the cooking fires.

In a shrill cry reminiscent of a macaw, the girl yelled as she banged away, *"Ta', ta', nketa-wa-a'."* Grandfather, grandfather, come down and eat.

A shaky, high-pitched voice came down to us from the black box up there in the smoke: "Am I dead yet?"

"No, come down and eat, Grandpa. You're still here with us."

"I'm not dead?"

"No, come down and eat!"

Then in a sad, dejected little voice, he uttered what he said every morning, *"Utz ga."* Okay.

The girl propped a rickety makeshift ladder up against the rafter. After a while old man Ears crawled out. Looking like a slow, skinny monkey, he crept down the ladder. We grabbed the old man and sat him next to us by the warm cooking fire.

We ate together, but he just pretended, as nothing really got inside him. We watched him in amazement, the man who had returned from the dead in the nick of time, who had come home and kept sleeping in his burial box up in the smoky rafters.

After a while I asked him, "Grandpa, how come you sleep in that box up there?"

"Oh, that. Well, you know, I already died once and my relatives went to a lot of trouble to have that box made. I figured that, since I'd already died, by being up there in the rafters, I'm not in the way down here, just like when I'm dead. And then when I die again I'll already be inside the box and they won't have to spend the energy to put me there again, the poor things!"

Though it hurt us not to, we didn't laugh. He was so frail and sincere, his blue glazed eyes looking straight at us. He couldn't wait to die so that his Christian relatives wouldn't feel secretly angry for wasting their hard-earned funds on an unused coffin.

He sat in the sun a while, went out to urinate, and then climbed back up into his smoky box where he lay mostly awake, waiting to die. Every day was the same.

It was just as the people had said, and we were amazed.

A couple of weeks later, Ears's escape was about to slide into the romantic mash of partial remembrance where all strange village occurrences end their days, distilled into the liquor of legend and mythology in which their memorable highlights become an added flavor in an already strange brew. I was sitting in my own hut playing on my rattlesnake guitar three odd, beautiful, and stirring songs for the underwater dead that my mother-in-law, who was away washing, had banned from the compound. She knew that this group of songs had the power to pull the underwater dead out of the lake right into your house, where they would look for someone to kill by drowning.

I was in the middle of the third song when, in the center of a cloud of dust, in waltzed Ears, looking very strong and sporting a new black *paquan* jacket, a ceremonial headcloth (which he'd done no service to even own), fine embroidered knee pants, and a fancy pair of squeaky new sandals. In he spun, dancing like a drunken adolescent, first on one leg and then on the other, pumping and leaping to my tunes while he urged me on. Yelling and singing along, with a lit cigar in one hand and a bottle of bad liquor in the other, this very same frail old man who lived in a coffin was raising the dust on my end of the village better than anyone a quarter of his age could have done. Only a small crowd had gathered to watch, as most people were out working. For fifteen minutes, Ears danced and yelled, then he sprang out of my hut and danced right back into the village streets. He danced all the way to the edge of the village, whooping and shrieking, dancing harder and faster, until a couple of miles out we couldn't keep up with him any more and he disappeared from sight.

When I returned, his people were gathered in my hut; they harangued me for hours about his whereabouts, since he'd never returned to his box. Some of them thought he might have drowned, so I sent patrols to search the lake and mountains, but they all came in empty-handed. We searched for days, but there was no trace or word of him anywhere. Ears had been heading out of the village, dancing all the way, yelling and singing all by himself until he disappeared from the earth. That strange old fellow had just danced into the other world.

Once again, Ears became the major subject of fireside talk and gossip for weeks on end. Many theories developed about this man named Ears, who died, punched his way out of the coffin, slept in it, and then danced his way into the other world all dressed up. He became a great pillar of possibility, holding up the beleaguered mansion of Tzutujil imagination. Forces of politics, foreign religions, and the modern mentality, with their strange need to trivialize mystery and magic, gnawed at its foundations. But the Tzutujil had a great longing and well-educated taste for being stupefied by the wonder of inexplicable things about which they loved to make complex and beautiful theories. Usually these hypotheses were more mystifying than what had inspired them in the first place. The people saw this delicious, incomprehensible entanglement as irrefutable evidence of the existence of the Divine.

Some people thought the man who came out of the coffin was not Ears at all. Others thought that Ears had disappeared fifty years previously, and that the man we called Ears was a sorcerer from a neighboring village who was famous for magically turning into other people in order to sleep with their wives. According to that theory, when Ears died, this guy was the one who had come out and gone dancing to the next village to do the same thing all over again. Others closer to the situation postulated that since Ears's wife had not really liked him that much in the first place and had mistreated him the last ten years of his life, she had probably witched him. But because she was not very good at it, it had all backfired.

Whatever the real story was, Ears was not finished. Six weeks later while twenty of my initiates and I stood in the plaza, togged out in our fanciest formal attire, cradling our staffs, protecting the village by standing around with defending attitudes and looking sharp, the one old revamped green-colored Blue Bird school bus that connected Santiago to distant villages rolled up in front of us.

Dressed the same as when he'd left, grinning and looking spry, the first person who leapt off the bus was Ears. All heads turned to watch as a young sixteen-year-old Cakchiquel Mayan girl swayed right along behind him, her belongings bundled on top of her head.

The village came running up, market purchases in hand and out of breath, their eyes jumping out in incredulity at the vision of an already dead man who'd lived in a coffin and had left the village dancing, now returning on a bus, in less than six weeks, with a full-figured, underaged beauty from a foreign tribe, a woman who wouldn't even look twice at our young men!

Walking past us on his way back home, he introduced us to this new wife from a village miles away. Ears was beautiful, waving to everyone and parading to his old son-in-law's house to install his attractive new wife—where he dodged rocks thrown at him by his jealous ex-wife, who'd been happy when he died the first time.

My initiates said, "When I get old I want to be just like Ears."

Ears died very happy two weeks later. We waited for a long time to bury him, wondering if he'd jump back to life again and show us more about how to be old.

This was the youths' endorsement of their initiates: of wanting to live past twenty with the zany playfulness and courageous ingenuity of their elders running before them. It was this delicious possibility of being old and inspiring that made the village love itself and continue wanting to be a village.

TWENTY

BULLETS AND BUTTERFLIES

THE BEGINNING OF THE VIOLENCE

Initiation was a choreographed war against warfare, where the instinct for battle and heroism was used to fight Death, to bring things back to life in a struggle for life instead of fighting against an enemy. Though my initiates and subchiefs and I were regular people again, the prestige and the story of what we'd accomplished was written all over us and because the village knew this, we were treated accordingly. We remained bound to each other in eternal friendship, unwilling to refuse anything to the other, and careful not to ask for anything impossible.

The year had come and gone. I'd let Ma Yel, Nettles, fight me for my position, as reluctant to hand it over to him as those before me had been when I took over. Now I joined them as a principal in the council of ex-chiefs.

The initiations continued on for a couple of years, fitfully, but at least, for the time being, they hadn't disappeared. I could now dedicate my days to my family, to my painting, and to doctoring once again as a shaman.

The country of Guatemala, however, had not gone through our initiation ritual, nor had the modern world. Their young people had not descended into their underworlds to retrieve their lost souls by giving gifts, sacrifices, and bargaining with Death. Because of this, Death came up to them, into their lands and their worlds, taking up residence and turning the earth around us into the Underworld, Death's kingdom. News of shootings, massacres, rapes, kidnappings, assassinations of union leaders by the Right and the heroic antics of antigovernment guerrillas came into Santiago Atitlan with the cattle walkers and merchants.

Cattle walkers were the village butchers who also herded their cows to Atitlan on foot overland from faraway villages. Because of their dealings with the world outside Santiago most of these men were semiliterate in Spanish. They were famous for gathering up news from the faraway places they passed on their slow journeys home. One such man, Ma Leen, always read the newspapers, which he also collected along the way, and then used them to wrap up the meat he sold to the villagers. Other cattle walkers used big leaves instead.

He'd been a *Primer Mayor* once and, because of the initiations, I became a favorite of his. He showed me favor by always sending me the best cut of the tenderloin, thickly bound in the most recent newspapers, which I also read. Unbeknownst to me, a series of favorable articles had begun to appear in Guatemala City, featuring my presence in Atitlan, and the cattle walker always sent me these articles wrapped around the meat. But when articles calling for my death showed up later in right-wing newspapers, Ma Leen also made sure that I got every one of them wrapped around our meat in order to keep me fully informed about the dangers the outside world posed to our existence.

In the Canyon Village the people had developed a language of survival. In that code, the word for rain now meant oppression and war. And the rain was certainly coming down.

After one of our famous two-week downpours that had turned the whole village to mud and mold had lifted, a man named Karl Hertz came to the threshold of our compound. He was wearing a white polyester short-sleeved shirt and white shoes. His white hair was combed and slicked back and his trim little mustache covered a lack of lips. Tucked under his bare hairy arms he had a loaf of big-city bread.

Hertz claimed to be a friend of an environmentalist acquaintance of mine. Sitting on our balsa bed, he chatted with us, out of place, patronizing and overfriendly, like a fellow buying drinks in a bar. The compound paid little attention to my conversation in Spanish with this visitor, but proceeded along in its normal bustle of pregnant dogs, bickering turkeys, curious toddlers, and busy barefoot mothers. Our world was a little scarier now, but it moved along as always.

Mr. Hertz turned very serious after a while and at some point in our conversation he asked me if I knew who the Communists were in the village, as he'd heard that they hated me and had tried to stop my "laudable efforts at maintaining the great old traditions." This strange man went on to say that the country was at great risk and that we had to stop the Communist guerrilla threat in its infancy. As an ex-Nazi, he could guarantee that his friends would rid our village of all my enemies if I would only tell him who they were.

"What do Communists look like?" I asked. "Do they wear some sort of insignia, do they walk funny or speak a different language? All we have here are villagers with varying ideas about life, all of them struggling to live hand to mouth by coaxing their food out of the earth with very hard labor. I have no idea what you are talking about."

After about ten more minutes of innuendo and confusing talk, Karl Hertz lost his stirrups with me. Bullying his way out of the compound, he yelled in Spanish, "If you're not supporting us, then we must assume that you are working against us, and that you will regret." I never saw him again.

The next day a young village man was killed by two white men in masks after being forced to drink poison. He was the grandson of my mother-in-law's midwife.

Karl Hertz had left the loaf of bread in our hut and nobody had tried it out yet, so our dog Morning Star stole it. Tearing into it, he managed to swallow a small chunk. The poor little beast died howling and was stiffer than an ax handle in twenty minutes. The bread had been poisoned. Little Morning Star had saved my family's life in this last big heroic act.

◇

My hawk had been acting strangely. I was doctoring him in my old initiation hall at my altar when two huge figures crowded the doorway behind me, blocking all the afternoon light from the room.

Whirling around, my hawk flapping in my hands, I turn to see two massive white men in white shirts and ties, carrying attaché cases, so tall that the top of the doorway obscured their heads.

I invited them in and sat them on our old chiefs' bench. The bench was so narrow under them that they looked like a couple of cows backed into a fence. I'd forgotten how big Americans got to be, and these two were from Indiana, which made them bigger still.

English sounded so astringent to me, having hardly heard it spoken at all for years, especially this Indiana version. Speaking it felt odd, like talking with a bunch of old pennies in your mouth.

They introduced themselves as Barry Smyth and John Jeeders, representatives of a U.S. government program attached to the American diplomatic mission in charge of funding agricultural projects that aided American business interests. Since I was an American and, in their judgment, a powerful force in the village of Atitlan, they had come to get me to enforce an avocado-growing program to supply some American supermarket chain.

I told them that chiefs and public officials like myself were spiritual leaders who *served* their village's ritual needs and that we had no desire or power to go around ordering people to do anything. If they wanted their project to work, then they should lease some land here, plant avocados, and wait the seven years for the first harvest. If the supermarket still wanted avocados by then, they could sell them to the company in question. If the project made them fatter and richer, then I was sure some of the Tzutujil would come to ask them about joining it.

This irritated them but they took it in stride. Eventually, as the Sun Father went down and the room faded into a dim evening light, they began to quiz me on the political climate of Atitlan and how I was dealing with the "Communists and guerrilla threat."

I couldn't believe it. One more time, only this time in English, I explained to them how I spent all my time keeping people healed by rebuilding the House of the World in the people's souls and in the village. I told them that the villagers, by and large, knew nothing about politics and that those who did lived and farmed hoping for better days.

But now the room was pitch dark. One of them said, "Leaders like you who stick out and don't help the status quo have been known to be assassinated." Then he gave me some examples.

Luckily no one's faces could be seen, because mine wore an expression of disappointment and defeat. In all these years since I'd left, America had obviously not grown or changed. Its officials were still unconscious, uninitiated men and women who didn't or wouldn't dance with nature or life. I couldn't hope that anything I'd done here in the village would make any difference in what the Mayans called the Land of the Dead.

In the dark silence that followed, Red Banana, my sister-in-law's stout traditionalist husband, yelled a greeting at the threshold. I yelled back, and in a second the room was invaded by a strange swaying, curly purple-green glow that bounced all over the place.

The two big officials fled in terror. With a deep clunking sound they bumped their small neckless heads on the low cross beams of our big hut as they dashed away into the darkness.

Red Banana had just come back from walking down the volcano at night, his path lit up by this backload of beautiful glowing firewood filled with a phosphorescent fungi. He'd proudly brought it to me as a traditional gift since I had been one of his marriage brokers.

I never saw the foreign aid officers again.

◇

Chiv had died the spring before. Before he died, he'd made me promise that I would leave the Canyon Village, the Umbilicus of the World, and head straight back to where I had come from. I was to take the Village Heart with me, which is what he called the complex knowledge of the chief and the vision of the shaman that I'd become, and try to plant it all in the strange forgetful ground of the cold North.

It was impossible to refuse the fine old man's last wish, and even more impossible to keep it. Replanting such excellent and delicate comprehensions as these necessitated the reinvention of culture where the divine is real and not oriented to human-centered activity. Initiation was even more impossible in the U.S. than it was now in the village, and the technologically armed, war-like results of its lack were general and everywhere visible. There were whole sections of some civilizations that were proud of their shrunken hearts and ungenerous policies. Neither the Right wing nor the Marxists were interested in understanding the first thing about village life, and this put all Native traditionalists in a precarious position. But I would do what I could to carry what I'd been loaded down with, even though I would be roundly hated and misunderstood by uninitiated people who feared my folly and courage.

It wasn't long after Chiv had passed on that sixteen of the same angry students who tried to derail the initiations visited me, bringing eight guerrilla leaders with them.

Since they had seen men they considered to be "representatives of the right-wing oppressors" leaving my house while making threats against me, they assumed, as did Karl Hertz, Barry Smyth, and John Jeeders, that I was actually a left-wing guerrilla sympathizer.

They wanted me to help them blow up a Guatemalan army colonel who had a house just outside the village on the edge of our Mother the Lake. I was to invite him to visit me in my capacity as a leader while they mined his house with explosives set to kill him on his return.

"Do you know this man?" I sensitively asked.

"No, but he's a member of the oppressing class and he must die," one of the boy-faced guerrillas replied.

"Still, I would only resort to violence if I was being actively attacked, and this man has not hurt anybody."

"Everything he does hurts the people. Who knows what he's ordered or supported, or if his family are plantation owners who exploit the masses."

"If you kill him," I said, " the Guatemalan National Army will invade Atitlan instantly. By then you fellows will have fled to higher ground. You and I both know the army will then indiscriminately kill a lot of people who know absolutely nothing about your politics."

"This is precisely what we hope for, Brother Martín, because when the people see the stupidity and carnage the army exacts on the poor with no regard for the truth, they will flock to our ranks, and we will eventually be victorious. Many are those who must be sacrificed."

"I'm not willing to sacrifice any of our people for a cause that thinks villagers are expendable and whose final goal is to homogenize the culture and rid us of our old ways of being for the good of the Liberation," I said.

"You, Brother Martín, don't know that these old ways you serve are expensive superstitions that were taught to the poor untutored peasants and the proletariat by the rich bourgeois in the past to keep them ignorant and in their place, doing what they are told, making the rich richer. But now in the glory of the future Liberation, they can become educated and receive a life of common good and equality."

"I'm not against humans treating each other fairly or against the alleviation of suffering. But without the spirit it's all empty rhetoric designed to make human invention superior to what actually gives us life: the Spirit. This Spirit is not represented in political movements, hierarchies, religions, or economic structures. What gives us life takes time and culture to comprehend."

Then, like Karl Hertz, Barry Smyth, and John Jeeders, the students, half of whom had been members of my old musical band from years ago, stated, "If you're not for the Liberation, then you are against it. Help us or the next time we see you, we'll kill you."

"I spend most of my time curing people, doctoring them to alleviate suffering, not creating more suffering," I said. "I want—" But it was too late. These Marxist literalists were striding out the door in their uniforms of crumpled hats, work boots, torn T-shirts, bandanas, and slacks, to make them feel closer to the "oppressed farmer," though some of these liberators had never even touched a hoe.

◇

One night as we were dropping off to sleep, listening to an ancient tale told by Red Banana, Chicken Louse, his hair all burned off in front, and his eyebrows gone, slid into our peaceful hut smelling like a sleepy dog that had left his tail in the embers of a cooking fire without knowing.

Panting and speaking between gasps, Chicken Louse exploded with the words, *"Xin kikat ijuku', jat alnaq kix oqto o', tibij conjilaal."* Hurry, help us, your canoes are on fire, tell everyone.

Up we jumped and out we ran, onto the road, merging into the whole population of our end of the village, all heading together toward the shore at Panaj. Dressed or half-dressed, pressing streams of anxious villagers with buckets, pots, and ropes were filling the dark streets. Once we got to the edge of our Mother the Lake, the people slowed down in realization of the hopelessness of the situation. Fanning out into one mighty throng, they stood stunned and horrified, looking at the vision before them.

The edge of our Mother the Lake was filled for half a mile in both directions with people whose faces were lit by the towering twenty-foot flames of the sabotaged canoes and their reflection in the water as they floated leisurely away from the village in long strings and knots a hundred yards off the shore. Other men in canoes couldn't get within fifty feet of them without their own log canoes catching on fire.

The air whistled and sucked wind eerily as the villagers went silent, noting at once that, on the opposite shore across the bay, three miles off, every outsider's house had been set ablaze too.

Crackling and sizzling, the canoes burned all night as, family by family, the people dropped away from the tragedy and dragged themselves back to their huts and compounds despairing and bewildered. Who would have filled everyone's canoes with pitch and set them to burn? Anyone from the village would know that almost every family would need them to work, to bring home their wood, food, and fish. Besides that, these canoes were carved by hand by only seven families in the whole village, and it could take twenty years to replace them all.

That night, as the villagers tried to sleep, they could hear the sad groans, thuds, pops, and sizzling of the canoes echoing off the lake as they cracked into pieces from the devastating heat. The government said it was the guerrillas. Nobody believed that, but we did believe it marked the beginning of a long, hard time.

◇

A month later my mentor, A Sisay, and four other Scat Mulaj were brought into my compound. They had been beaten up and robbed by several military men wearing civilian clothing who had driven into the village on a spree with an armored jeep.

The neighboring village, which had an armed militia and no traditionalists, caught the culprits after they'd raped a woman and received permission from the government to execute them and did so. Over a decade of horror and killing would follow.

I healed the old men of their wounds and, after a few days, they returned to their compounds.

That night all was silent. By then many people had "disappeared" and no one ventured out anymore at night. Suddenly, we heard a loud *kapop* that sounded like a muffled explosion. The following morning, Gourd came into our hut cradling an untidy armful of leaflets that contained nineteen paragraphs denouncing the activity of various prominent people in the village, myself included, and demanding that the villagers rid themselves of our presence. What was written about me took up the major portion of the leaflet. What we had heard in the night was the sound of propaganda bombs, shooting these papers everywhere.

Gourd and the many others who were gathering them up couldn't figure out why there was paper everywhere.

"Father, what are all these papers for?"

The propagandists hadn't remembered that only a couple of the people in the village knew how to read, so villagers just went around using the leaflets to start fires and as toilet paper, thankful to have both.

✦

A butterfly kept landing on my left shoulder as I leaned, smoking my cigar and resting after a hard ceremony to cure the fright of a child whose mother had been killed by the death squads.

The eye of day, my Father the Sun, percolated through the leaves of my avocado trees, *jocotes,* rock orchids, and papaya plants. At the base of the cliff where our two small houses hung, the wife of A Lip Petzai, up to her knees in the water, slapped and scrubbed her family's wash. Out a ways in the lake below, Sweet the flute player was pulling up his night-laid nets and dropping the sparkling fish into his little dugout canoe.

The Mother Lake stretched out twinkling all the way to the ridge of Tuq, over which, years back, my initiates had returned home from the other world. From where I quietly leaned against my painting hut, I could barely make out the entrance to the flat area across the water at Xechivoy to Prwachabac, where we'd pulled the boys back into the Village Earth.

The butterfly rose again, fluttering off to my left a little, when I heard my name being called from behind the orchid-covered pillars of porous basalt. As I turned my head to look, a barrage of bullets careened into where I stood.

A mist of plaster dust and grit hung in the air as three gunmen emptied their weapons. Two had little revolvers, a third had an automatic paint gun. I watched the butterfly cut to dust in the fusillade, and I was sure I was dead. It had all happened in a split second.

Chiv always said that the other world picked you up as you were when you died. Beginning to sag against the wall, I continued to smoke my cigar, praying and thinking of the beauty of all we'd done here, of my little children, Chiv, the village, and my youth on the reservation. I kept smoking to let the killers know that the spirit cannot be slain with lead.

A little blood trickled out of my chest and I slid to the ground onto my bottom, watching the killers flee until they had gone. Looking down at the lake, I saw the wife of A Lip Petzai, holding a piece of her hair that had been shot off her head, mystified as to how it had happened. Sweet was examining the side of his dugout canoe where a couple of bullets had thudded into the hull.

My knees were weak, but the gunmen had completely missed me, at point-blank range. Only a small chip of curled, ricocheted lead had sunk its whining claw under my hide, embedding itself into my sternum a quarter of an inch.

On my account, Sweet and the woman had almost been shot by hired killers. It was time for me to leave.

◇

Old Ma Ratzan, Ya Lur's grandfather, had been ailing ever since they'd torn down his thatched house. Like the House of the World, that beautiful hut represented his life and his generation. As long as it continued to grace the skyline of our end of the village, Grandpa's body wouldn't give in to death. The hut represented the memories of his wife long gone, taken from him back in the forties during an epidemic of cholera, and it had remained central in his family compound. But when his son, Ya Lur's father, had ruthlessly torn it down, the old man began to melt away from life.

In the middle of all this demolition, nineteen of my friends, three of my initiates, and two cousins of Ya Lur were all killed on the same day that I'd been attacked. The gunmen had failed with me but, knowing they'd be back, Ya Lur and I fled.

To avoid having the entire family murdered along with us, we isolated ourselves in another part of the country. Ya Lur, who was pregnant with our son Santiago, our older son Jorge, who was a bit uncooperative, and I all moved "under the bushes, under the vines."

I was hunted like a deer now, on all sides as promised. The Right put a bounty on my head that rose monthly until I headed the list of those still uncaught.

Ya Lur and I knew that old Grandpa was dying when we left. I was a shaman and I had divined it. The divination bundle said he was still alive, suffering, waiting to say good-bye to us before he could die. He'd been a good and funny friend to us, and we cared so much for him. It wasn't right to let him die without one last good-bye and without our giving one last good-bye to the village. This so-called war didn't look like it was going to end too soon; we'd have to be very careful about seeing him.

The village was now full of soldiers who were permanently bivouacked at both entrances in campaign tents. Somebody was killed or disappeared every day. Sneaking in was not going to be easy, but knowing the land and the village as well as we did, we arrived about midnight at our old compound. Everyone was both delighted and horrified, knowing that in all likelihood we'd never make it out of the village alive. In our absence they had already grieved for us, reckoning that we'd already been killed.

Mayans are an expressive, boisterous people, and it was very difficult to keep our presence in the village a secret. Though he hadn't moved for days, and looked like one of those skinny old twisted jungle roots that stretched out, looking for the solid earth under the leaf litter, Grandpa Ratzan still had a very faint heartbeat. Someone from the family had stayed next to him day and night, keeping a smoky diesel oil lamp going at all times. When I entered the hut, the old man sat up straight, startling everyone. He was blind as always but he knew we were there.

"*Ta*, Father how are you doing? It's Martín and Ya Lur."

"How am I doing?" he said. "How the hell do you think I'm doing? How do I look?"

"You look awful. It's good to see your face again, Grandfather."

"I feel awful, but I've got to go now. Thank you for the gifts, A Martín. Keep telling the children not to fight." And with that the old farmer lay down and died. He'd waited and we'd come.

The old ladies came to bind up his waist and genitals to turn him into a seed so that his soul could rise tomorrow at noon and catch a ride with the Sun Father to the next world. Ya Lur and I couldn't go to the graveyard because the soldiers haunted the place, especially during funerals, and had killed several people as they were burying their relatives.

They'd be waiting for me.

The wake was hard for me because to grieve properly your village has to be a safe place. But at the direction of my mother-in-law, I drank Ya Mry's grief medicine made of twenty-four flowers and began to weep beautifully for hours. I wept for everything on earth, for the old man, for Chiv, for my life, for all I was about to lose that was already gone, for the initiations that would never happen again, for my children who wouldn't get to struggle and laugh as I had in a village that knew me and liked me, for all my friends killed. I grieved for Grandpa Ratzan and more.

When they picked him up to take him to the graveyard, I couldn't stay alone in the abandoned compound, so I snuck out over to the edge of the Mother Lake, to my old painting house. The bullet holes were still there. But from a place in the middle of the cliff, hidden by vegetation, I could lie down and see the funeral party struggling into the burial grounds to the tree under which we'd buried our little son born after Jorge. I couldn't see much as it was two miles away.

Then I heard my name called again. Terrified, I turned and was getting ready to run, when I felt a gentle hand on my back. Looking up, I saw two handsome old Tzutujil women, who asked me to stand.

Coming to my feet, I searched my mind but could not remember who these two ladies were. In a village this is rare.

Dressed in brand-new handwoven blouses, red wraparound, skirts, shawls, and halo head ribbons, they wore no shoes. Their clothing was all from the nineteenth century, a simpler style with very narrow purple stripes, narrow silk head ribbons and so forth.

One of them held a small cream-colored clay water jar and the other a finely made grass basket. Though both were white-haired, their faces were like polished bronze, and each wore ten silver rings, on both hands.

"My father, my son, my brother, my cousin," one of them began, "it's good to see your face again, it's good to feel your breath again. Don't be afraid, we just came to say thank you and good-bye." The other, her big, kind, unblinking eyes reflecting my face, said, "You have done very well for us. We women of the lake don't forget you or abandon you. Please don't forget us or abandon us. But you must leave today or you'll be killed. We don't want that. What makes the world live cannot be killed by the stupidity of humans, but what gives them the ability to live with that power can be destroyed by humans.

"Let these warring beings fight and finish each other off. You must carry the 'baby,' the spirit that they can't see, to safety like a big seed so the world can be replanted again when the smoke settles."

The other lady took a turn. "We'll wait for you to come home, but don't ever try to come here again unless we call you. Long Life, Honey in the Heart, No Evil, Thirteen Thank-yous."

And with that, they disappeared into the verdant exuberance, flowers, and jumbled boulders of that end of the Canyon Village.

MY FATHER'S EYES ARE BEES

BECOMING A VILLAGE MAN

In centuries past, the Canyon Village, like a great ancient tree, had died, flowered again, and fruited many hundred of times. Most of the aggression wreaked upon it by neighboring tribes, the Aztecs, the Spaniards, and other outside predatory missions had been limited to stealing the fruit of that tree but had left the tree standing.

After physically surviving the violent horror and culture-crushing outrages of the 1980s, the tree had been cut down, its trunk and roots torn out, and the Hole filled in. The village where I had become a human being had disappeared. The Canyon Village that understood how to initiate its people, and to feed the Gods that fed them, had been effectively dismantled. Though the population of the town of Santiago Atitlan continues to grow, it is a population that no longer remembers how to reinvent a human being. This new town is now 100 percent missionized. It has been "liberated" from any accountability to the earth of its ancestors. It has become modern and forgetful. The culture of initiated people has disappeared from view. It has fled back down the old Hole to the other worlds and is held there in the form of a seed. There its indigenous spiritual DNA lives on, concealed in a mist of amnesia inside every human heart, waiting for a day or a millennium where the climate will be favorable enough to lift the fog and sprout again the old language in new voices, and the old voices in new language.

Though the ancestral parent tree has been killed, there are still a few seeds of the old violated tree around. As long as a few of us continue to keep them safe, well fed, and viable, the day will come when they can once again jump back to life, their faces returned to day, and from that ancient seed Hole retrieve the modern world from Death's Amnesia, bursting into the flowered fruit of life well married to the Earth.

People ask me how I could be happy or go on living, having known and lived the beauty of those days in the village only to see it all disrupted, dishonored, violated, demolished, and finally erased. How could I go on, having to carry all the excruciatingly painful memories of the death and torture inflicted upon the village during the 1980s?

A Leep had been tortured by soldiers for three months in a hole, until mercifully he died. A Maash and A Xep were dead. Father Stanley had been crucified to death; A Culen and his young bride were killed and mutilated in their new hut. A Quin was shot off his bicycle; Maxar was shot in his house; A Mirez was shot in his store. The list of friends lost in a violence beyond human imagining rolls on and on in my memory to more than eighteen hundred villagers, friends, colleagues, and relatives, all killed and gone in less than a decade. How could I have continued after hiding in hair-raising danger for over a year with two children and an unhappy wife, while being hunted with a price on my head, only to escape terrified to a land where people didn't say hello or know that they were staring at two initiators, and then finally to end up living in a modern culture, as I do now, which has nothing to compare with the village?

My reply to those questions would be as long as my life. Maybe some of the answer lies in the nature of initiation itself. I was rewired by seeing the divine with my chiefs, cooked by Death and aged by the elders until that vision of divine possibility that comes with initiation was residing right in my bones, not in my brain. In my very essence I became a big seed capsule of that vision; therefore, the beauty has not been erased, just secreted away for better times.

The exact things that people imagine I must miss so terribly are what give me the capacity to love, to live. It is the soul-changing experience of the village that inspires me to use these images to reseed the territory of people's souls when they have been razed and scorched by literalism, the rationalist lack of imagination, and badly remembered history.

Mostly failing, but willing to fail, like an incorrigible pirate of the heart, armed with what I earned and learned in my initiations, I ambush complacency, spiritual laziness, and mean-heartedness whenever I can.

Unlike the village, where we had no doors, where we had the freedom to fail and to be imperfect and the freedom to tell stories and exaggerate together, the souls of people in the modern world look like prisoners of their own oppressive mentalities. My hope is that some of the beauty and integrity of that excellent village may yet sprout into these modern times, that others may be inspired by the possibility of such beauty and take courage enough to stage their own rebellion against the obliviousness of this age by blessing it with a sincere search for an authentic flowering of their own, an initiation.

I think that instead of pitying the Maya or myself, concerned people should ask themselves and their own souls the same question they ask me. If people were as worried about the heart of their own villages, their own cultures, and their own souls as they are about something that took place three thousand miles away from them, they might really begin to see that my books are actually about them. What should concern us is the ongoing fact that somewhere, deep in the memory of their own souls, no matter of what ancestry, a deep understanding and capacity for wonderment sits weeping and waiting.

This capacity is not unlike the beauty of the village; I call this capacity the "indigenousity of the human soul." In *Secrets of the Talking Jaguar*, this indigenous soul is described as our soul's memory of the mysterious and natural humans, animals, plants, earths, and deities from which we descend. Although this soul resides in all of us somewhere, most of us have minds like the missionaries and the soldiers who came to Santiago Atitlan who were more concerned with being right and in charge than with helping our souls to have their ancient understandings or the blessing of imagination in our lives.

The knowledge, beauty, and wonderment of our indigenous souls does not usually make it to the modern consciousness. Instead, it is banished into the realm of the deepest recesses of the mind's Underworld, along with the rest of people's ancestral Gods, tribal stories, and the ancestors themselves.

Our souls wait there, held hostage deep inside the underworld of rationalism and bad religion, swimming in generations of grief and frustration, waiting to be courted and rescued, clumsily or expertly, by the eloquence and courage of our hearts. Our indigenous souls hope for the day when, adorned with orchids and lilies, they too can arrive tired and unique out of this Underworld to be welcomed back into some kind of village. Only then will our spirits be able to marry our lives, and only then will we, with our hearts intact, be able to truly love our spouses. Modern people seem to be proud of their despair, entirely imprisoned by their complacent respect for the overwhelming power of meaninglessness so popular today. The only thing that seems to have meaning is no meaning. Modern people are proud of it, and to them everything besides meaninglessness is meaningless.

It is too much to ask, I know. After all, modern culture refuses to spend any of its vast resources to crown the queen of our souls, much less initiate its youth or dig out the concrete it poured into that sacred Hole. Like uninitiated children, modern people like depression better. Depression doesn't take any effort and you don't owe anybody anything. But what modern people do not understand anymore is that by making gifts for the Spirit from their personal resources and by sharing with one another, they can feed life and keep their hearts alive.

A Sisay said it better one day right after my year-long service as an initiating chief had come to a close. Right from the beginning the *teoneli,* teachers of chiefs, the ex-chiefs, advisors, and ex-initiating chiefs and ladies would always remain talking long after the numerous preparatory meetings that the hierarchy held for all of us who were involved during the year-long ritual of initiation.

They would banter on and on about how much good luck the spirits had accorded them the year following their service: "Make sure you never say anything bad about the ceremony for one year, no matter how hard it gets.

Then you'll see later, when you're not in charge anymore, they'll send a gift to you," they said, referring to the Gods.

One ex-chief had received special tomato seeds from an unknown man in the village market. When he planted them, the plants that came up were miraculously abundant and long-producing, making him very financially secure to that day, ten years later.

Another had found a special corn seed spilled in his granary, which, when he planted it, grew plants that produced five immense ears per stalk, making him one of the richest corn farmers in the village.

One woman found stacks of skirt material tied up in her load, enough to start her off in a cloth-selling business, which she'd been managing for twenty years.

These stories never ended. Old men and middle-aged men and women chiefs, everyone who'd held my position before, told of how they'd been compensated for having been flattened financially and exhausted physically. To me, these were the loyal testimonials of faith from those in love with the beauty of the ritual, but I never thought of them much in reference to myself until after I'd given over my old position to the new chief.

About two days after the end of the initiations, I was once again as financially broke as I'd ever been. I was trying to conjure up a way to make a living again, when, miraculously and unsolicited, outsiders started showing up to buy paintings from me. Down by the lake in an old hut, I had forty forgotten paintings accumulated from years before. And, just like the old chiefs said, the spirits had not forgotten me.

Crowds of ambassadors and international counsels started appearing at my hut to see which of my works of art they could get. By the end of a week, I had thousands of dollars. Certain individuals actually took unfinished, unsigned paintings without my knowledge, and just left money in their place. That irritated me. But I had a lot of money now, enough to pay off my debts with plenty left to live on.

I too hadn't forgotten all the ex-chiefs and their wives, and chieftesses who'd pitched in to help me when I was flattened economically. I decided to pay them back first with my new money. I'd give them a little extra to show my appreciation for their having come to my rescue.

I went from house to house during the day while most of the men were still out in their fields or down by the lake, leaving the money with a younger daughter or son-in-law. By the time I reached the seventh hut, one of the older hierarchy ladies who'd loaned me fifty *quetzales* was actually home. I began a flowery speech in the tone of a chief to express to her my great appreciation for the loan, but was interrupted by her bitter scolding, pushed bodily out of her house and chased out of her compound into the street by her and all her livid female relatives who chattered hateful insults as they did so.

Soon some of the women in the other huts got wind of what was happening and, within two minutes, a rain of pebbles and wood whistled past my ears and I had to run to dodge them, perplexed by the inexplicable anger and humiliation of my assailants.

About then, another group of old ladies returning from the market, all of whom had graciously loaned me money and goods during my time of need, joined the first group, continuing to chase me down the street, kicking at me, slapping their hands and throwing whatever they could. Normally noble and kind women, they'd turned into a crazed, tearful mob of screaming, rock-tossing lunatics.

Running now in earnest, they came at me like a herd of enraged tusk-gnashing peccaries. I ran all the way to the bottom of the village, turned the corner and ducked into my *teonel*'s hut. Luckily for me, A Sisay was home. Observing the sanctuary of his house, the yelling women didn't enter, though it seemed they might invade any minute, as they continued to yell angry threats at me from without.

"What did you do to these poor women, Brother Parent?" A Sisay asked me, scowling, almost ready to smile.

"I've done nothing, Brother Parent. I was simply going house to house returning the money I had to borrow from them to complete the initiation ritual properly, plus—" And I was roundly interrupted by old A Sisay himself, who began chewing me out in the same tone as the ladies. Everyone joined in. The resolute nature of the onslaught was impossible to counter for its fierce loudness and sheer numbers. Bewildered and unwilling to fight, I hung my head and covered it with my arms.

Finally, A Sisay silenced everyone. He turned and addressed me, lifting my face, "What's wrong with you, anyway? Don't you want to be one of us? All of a sudden you want to be alone, an orphan again?!"

Almost crying, his eyebrows brushing the air, a very indignant old A Sisay, my loyal advisor, went on to explain. All the others looked on, quietly listening to his words, which I shall never forget: "Yesterday and the days before, when you came here as an orphan huddled against the cold at dawn, we saw your face and sat you with us at the mouth of the fire.

"But now you push us away, you refuse us. There's not one thorn at your face. Shamelessly, you pretend to forget us. Why are you doing this?

"*Kas-limaal,* that's what we call it, *kas-limaal,* mutual indebtedness, mutual insparkedness.

"Everything comes into this Earth hungry and interdependent on all other things, animals, and people, so they can eat, be warmed, not be lonely, and survive. I know you know this, but why do you push it all away now? We don't have a word for that kind of death, that isolation of not belonging to all life.

"You see, every young man's chief, every initiator, every first grandchild chief has to watch his money dwindle away, has to watch the corn in his granaries empty to the bare ground until even the mice and crickets move out. He has to watch the people in his compound holding their tongues and keeping their worried eyes averted, waiting quietly. His relatives are terrified of starving and losing prestige, but they say nothing for fear of ruining the initiation for the village by complaining. The initiation which is bigger than any one of us, upon which the whole village survives, brings us rain and food and more children.

"The young chief you've been watches and wrestles with his imminent poverty and his doubts, keeping focused on the bigger needs of the village, while the patient people and the women in his own compound show their honor for him by not complaining.

"Your initiation into an adult begins with this sacrifice, which you know full well and have done admirably."

The crowd, somewhat mollified, nodded and hummed in agreement, some through hot tears. Then A Sisay gathered himself together to continue. "Every year as the young initiates struggle and pull and gasp for air, as their hides loosen and their loads grow heavier, as they ripen their desire into seeds for food and ripen our seeds for planting, the chief further ripens his own initiated soul into a well-rooted, strong tree to which the youth can tether their hearts as they thrash in the painful and stormy changes they must go through.

"The young initiates must learn to stop being those who are fed, and become feeders of the village. They must cease suckling the village breast and begin to be the breast. The chiefs like you are chosen because they know how to be milk, they know how to give away to the point of having nothing. That is why a man and woman always serve together, each understanding and in agreement with the fact that they will be economically leveled by the challenge of bringing the youth to fruition. This is the initiation of the chiefs.

"But at this point, the village men and women who have served as chiefs and are already elders come secretly to fill the initiation courtyard to the top with meat, corn, tomatoes, chili, firewood, and money. The young chiefs, in the interests of the village heart, must swallow their pride and accept this wealth. That is why in our language we call our wealth 'our poverty.' True wealth lies in being loved enough for giving, being humble enough to be filled by the older people in the village, and by being smart enough to know it must all go to the youths' fruition. It also means being old enough to know that all you get to keep in this village life that won't rot away or be eaten by insects is the prestige the village accords you for having the caring and courage to be flattened economically in order to lead the Flowers and Sprouts, the youth, into life. That is what a true warrior, a true village man, a true chief does and is remembered for. Not for getting what he wants or hoarding or being secure, not for being a good businessman or plundering the neighboring tribe but for being willing to be wounded, willing to fail and to live insecurely so that others can live, so that the village can survive.

"Always the Spirits, the Gods, the Saints, the Many and the One will come through the people to help you. When you learn to trust in this, you realize how all true survival relies on this mutual indebtedness, and then you have become an adult. By hoarding, you kill the village and so you must be made to distribute. The regular man and woman go with their pride to mound up corn and firewood, wealth and clothing, to warm and feed their children. The extraordinary man and woman distribute all they have to feed the village, as if it were their own family, and that's why they called you the Husband of the village.

"After the ceremonies and struggles have ceased, and your service is finished, the spirits almost always give the chief mysterious good luck, often replacing what you've spent and distributed uncomplainingly, ten- or a hundred-fold, so that ex-chiefs have plenty again and then some. But this only happens if they went about their business honorably and were willing to give all.

"So here you are, having had everything you exhausted replaced a hundred times more than you expected by the good graces of the spirits, the Gods, the Saints, the Many, the One, and you go around trying to give back to what fed you in your time of need. But that's no good, you see. Not because you don't owe us, which you do, but because you must remain in our debt, keeping the Hole open, the wound unhealed, to be a fully initiated chief! You have to be indebted to as many ex-chiefs as possible to be part of our village. The knowledge that every animal, plant, person, wind, and season is indebted to the fruit of everything else is an adult knowledge. To get out of debt means you don't want to be part of life, and you don't want to grow into an adult.

"Initiated youth are only half-cooked. They make babies, feed families, and struggle for air, maybe succeeding at rising above others with mounds of goods, in debt to no one, giving to no one outside their own.

"But a further-initiated man and woman become struck with spiritual lightning, their tree full of honey cracked open by the sharp tooth of the needs of the village. And then the Honey in their Hearts can run freely into the greater Village Heart. When you owe every chief in the village and do not pay it back, this means that every chief in the village has conspired to be closer to you than a blood relative. In this way, he and his wife feel perfectly comfortable calling on you again in the future to serve the Village Heart in some deeper sacred position, having obligated you to do so by your debt. They too were put deep into each other's debt by the chiefs before them. You can only properly buy your way out of village indebtedness by more service, which alleviates the initial debt but sets you deeper and deeper into debt with the village itself and to other heavier chiefs and spirits.

"The idea is to get so entangled in debt that no normal human can possibly remember who owes whom what, and how much. In our business dealings, we keep close tabs on all exchanges, but in sacred dealings we think just like nature, where all is entangled and deliciously confused, dedicated to making the Earth flower in a bigger plan of spirit beyond our minds and understandings.

"So here you are trying to ruin the system by returning what you owe to the old chiefs and chieftesses, which says to them, 'I want out. I don't want to be obligated to you.' That voids the young men's initiation, your initiation, and the village flowering! The whole initiation would mean nothing if you had succeeded in giving everything back. Everything would have been voided.

"At the same time, as an ex-chief, don't forget that the new chiefs will soon be economically flattened. Because the spirits have rewarded you for your service, you now will have the means to fatten their ceremonies as these old ones did for you. Then these new chiefs will become hopelessly obligated to you. And when you get appointed to another position and need sacred helpers, you can feel free to call on them, as we want to feel free to call on you to help us again. Be one of us, hopelessly indebted to us, and we to you, each to the other. Do not buy your way back into being a cold little orphan with a big pile of money, unindebted but friendless. Please!? The Sun's eyes are bees that weep honey; the Honey in our Heart comes from the tears of village indebtedness."

The women had calmed down and were weeping and smiling now. Turning to me with their hands outstretched, their palms up, showing their corn-grinding calluses, they beseeched me not to kill their lives with my arrogance and modern independence. With tears streaming down my face, I fell sitting onto the little bench with the dog's head carved on it, and quietly expressed my understanding. Laughing and relieved, all of us were filled with hope and the good feeling of belonging to each other. They hadn't thrown me away. They had forced me to be their friend and relative. Finally I understood something that made the scary, bitter storms of my life turn to Honey in my Heart, and in that instant I became a true village man.

During the course of writing both the *Secrets of the Talking Jaguar* and *Long Life, Honey in the Heart,* I found myself having to come to terms with the problem of writing publicly about what is sacred while still maintaing the secrecy and integrity of all the deities, bundles, shrine locations, and the lives of spiritual officials safe from desecration.

Often ethnographic researchers and anthropologists disregard the prohibitions and taboos attached to the use of the names of specific Deities and holy objects outside of ritual context. This is because of the rationalist nature of academic research, which has no belief in spirit and therefore can talk in objective formulas about living Gods, Goddesses, sacred concepts, and rituals as if these were props dried and stuffed in a museum arranged for their perusal.

The Gods and sacred contexts I refer to in these two books are very real and powerful to me and to those traditionalist Mayans left on this earth who know them. In the interest of my respect for these deity forms, I have chosen to refer to them by the English translation of terms used by traditionalist Tzutujil themselves when alluding to them outside of a ritual. If a true and sacred name is called out or written down, the spiritual force that it belongs to is summoned, ready to be "feasted" by the person who conjured them. If the appropriate feast or ritual is not provided, the deity is desecrated and insulted and, depending on its nature, either begins to wither or to consume the life of the wanton speaker. I have been very careful of this; others have not.

This is not to mention also that many of the names of Tzutujil Holy Beings obtained in academic field research—and subsequently employed in the books of those investigators—come from sources outside the village, or from unsympathetic religious converts who function as translators. In several cases these names are in and of themselves deprecatory and untraditional nicknames originally intended to trivialize the God. They would never be used in reference to a deity by a traditional Mayan in any context.

Another dilemma presented itself when I began translating important

Tzutujil words into English, especially those referring to social and spiritual institutions.

Most of what has been written about Mayan people comes from academic investigation, which has established a standardized code when referring to Mayan institutions and their functionaries. Once again, most of these terms are bad translations of rudimentary understandings made by unsympathetic or unknowledgeable translators. Like the names of deities, the Tzutujil nomenclature for the officials that serve them are often inadequately approximated by those outdated anthropological usages.

For this reason, and in the interest of allowing all people access to the subtleties of the Tzutujil vision of life without compromising any respect to the Gods and their gift of Life to us all, I have chosen to translate Mayan terms in such a way as to show their relevance to concepts already understood by readers everywhere, at least wherever possible. For instance the word *Ajau* is usually translated by anthropologists as a "principal." Principal is an antiquated Spanish term left over from the colonial period that referred to someone who was a member of the town council established by the Spanish bureaucracy. The word *Ajau*, however, is more closely approximated in modern English by the word "lord" or "chief," which I have used throughout, or *ixoc ajau* meaning literally "woman lord," which I translate as "chieftess."

I have also refused to include any photographic representation of holy objects or deities because when I lived in Atitlan the old people never allowed any photography—knowing that to be observed casually in such a frozen state destroys the mystery and sanctity of these spirits, who would never give their permission.

Though Tzutujil is really an unwritten language, for the sake of this book, the Mayan words in both *Secrets of the Talking Jaguar* and *Long Life, Honey in the Heart* are simple phonetic approximations that I have standardized throughout. Some of the sounds correspond in the following way:

x = *sh* as in *she*

tz' = explosive *t* sound, no English equivalent

ts = *ts* like *ruts*

st' = explosive *st,* no English equivalent

ch = *ch* as in *chow*

ch' = explosive *ch,* no English equivalent

t = *t* as in *Tom*

t' = explosive *t*, no English equivalent

c = *c* as in *cut*

c' = hard, hissy *k* sound, no English equivalent

q = *ch* as in the German word *achtung*

q' = back throat pop, no English equivalent

td = no English equivalent

a = like *a* in *mama*

ä = like u in *up*

i = like *i* in *it*

e = *e* as in *exit*

o = like *o* in *note*

u = like *oo* in *loose*

' = glottal stop

j = hissy *h*, like Spanish *j*

and many, many extended vowels, diphthongs, whispered vowels, and accents.

All Mayan male names are preceded by A or Ma like A Martín or Ma Martín. Similarly all ladies' names have Ya in front of them.

A TADPOLE'S TAIL
AN ESSAY ON INITIATION
VERSUS TRIBALISM

A great deal has been said about the possibility of making initiations and rites of passage for non-Native, noncommunity, nonvillage, modern people. Tribal-type initiations have been touted as a remedy for the frustration that modern people feel concerning the desperate lives of their young people. In a nihilistic age filled with weapons, drugs, insolence, and depression, the parents of such children may be powerfully drawn to the wild, elegant lack of complication that can be seen in the eyes of a truly indigenous person. Perhaps they think that by simply obtaining a tribal initiation, the same way one buys a medicine, they will achieve that look of wholeness and belonging in their eyes, thereby avoiding the whole frightening landscape of the alienated synthetic existence of modern life.

What is in some modern people that desires once again to have the nature of a wild wolf usually looks more like an overdomesticated beagle when that wildness tries to surface. We can all remember a little of our ancestral indigenousity but very few people remember anything of how to be truly natural. That beautiful wild look does belong to all of us but it has been energetically and purposefully whipped out of most people's ancestors. You cannot hope to reclaim for your soul in a single year what two thousand years of spiritual oppression has banished into the furthest reaches of your inner bigness.

To have initiations again we'd have to find a way to bring this banished indigenous soul back home to us and we would have to have communities worth coming home to. To do so we have to go very, very slowly. A great deal of study, struggle, sacrifice, and love would have to be expended to make a real initiation for modern folk, one that wouldn't ring hollow. This cannot be accomplished by simply superimposing other cultures' rituals upon a modern people. Initiation has to come from the place where a people lives.

After sorting through the confusing amalgamation of ideas and approaches, the central question in regard to a true and authentic initiation remains, "How do you initiate young people when there are no initiated adults, or anybody around who knows what that looks like?" For me, true initiations would be impossible until the modern world surrenders to the grief of its origins and seeks a true comprehension of the sacred. A tangible relationship with the divine must be found: a relationship to ritual that actively feeds the invisible forces behind all this visible life. Initiation is about sacrifice and education; it must be a learning of the deepest source and yet governed by a wide consciousness of the historical reality of our ancestors' suffering as well as their stupidity. Only then can a useful spiritual vision emerge from what is most ancient in us all that goes beyond the ancestral response and brings us into relationship with our true natures.

Initiations that are attempted without the spirit or a comprehension of the sacredness of the commonplace only serve to placate an uninitiated hunger for entertainment that hopes to fill the spiritual void of individuals and a whole culture with talk shows, corn chips, movies, dope, fast cars, and the like. That hunger is an emptiness that should be wept into, grieved about, instead of blocked and filled up. The Spirit I'm talking about is not human spirit or a churchy God, an elevated concept, an idea, or a metaphor but is something bigger, older, and more dimensional than maybe some scientists could even understand. Initiations with no spiritual root that are only engineered to make people into better people always fail because they are horrible travesties of what initiation really should be. Worse yet are rituals designed by psychologists to address psychological needs through mythological metaphors with no real encounter with the butt-kicking bigness and beauty of Deities, because then humans, not the Spirit, are still at the center of that kind of Universe.

Most of what has been presented up to now as initiation in modern society, such as school ceremonies, corporate inductions, military presentations and training, fraternity hazing, and boot camps, the secret rituals of clubs and societies, fragmentary New Age adaptations of Native institutions, and so on, are not what I call initiations. These are representations of what happens when you don't have initiation or any true remembering adults.

There are also people who hear the word "warrior" and cringe when they think about the confusing issue surrounding initiation, particularly in reference to men. To me and to the Maya, becoming a warrior was not as necessary as was graduating out of warriorhood into adulthood. Being a warrior did not equal being a man. Nevertheless, most if not all men and some women had to pass through some form of warriorhood to become eligible for their journey on to manhood and womanhood.

The strong instinct young people have to be enamored of magnificent chieflike heroes, to follow political movements, to imitate celebrities or to espouse big ideas, comes from all people's natural gravitation toward a confrontation with the divine in this world. However amateurish, the young long for the spirit, for the deliciousness of living life beyond the calculated humdrum and safety of their parents' world.

In their idealism, some youths want to "fix" everything. In a frustrated disillusionment other teenagers want to destroy everything that has gone awry in a world that was handed to them, a world already ruined by "stupid" adults. In either case, the youth want to charge up a hill at the enemy.

Their main enemy, though, is the realization of getting old and of having to die. It is the consciousness of human mortality that makes initiation imperative. The main reason adults seem so inept and stupid to kids is because after protecting them in their childhood, parents can no longer guarantee a teenager's immunity to death. If everybody has to die, then why live at all? Such youth become heroic or despairing as they wrestle with this tragic realization. This is the time for initiation. Someone outside the family has to help the youth survive their despair and fright.

The heroic instinct of some youth has been horrendously manipulated for millennia by uninitiated older people in high positions and exploited to supply soldiers for their idiotic wars, while screaming for Father, God, their Mothers, or their Mother Country. This is the activity of people with only two sections of the telescope: The child and the teenage warrior hero.

Though these horrible military events are not really full initiations, in the sense that this book talks about initiation, the camaraderie that people experience during abnormal times of crisis does have some of the heartwarming elements of true ritual initiations. Most village rituals are basically finely tuned and deliberately choreographed disasters aimed at avoiding arbitrary catastrophe and loss of soul.

Recently, the business world in modern cultures has begun to remember the traditional and ancient relationship of warfare with trading, and raiding with slaving. Trading was considered to be what warriors did in peacetime. Well, it's all war, and war is violence, no matter how you dress it up. The notion promoted by corporations that their ladder-climbing executives are actually warriors in a samurailike elitist society of individuals who skillfully use competitive numbers and appearances as a sword to kill and outmaneuver the army of opposing companies, seems to me like an attempt to make gray into a legitimate color.

If these corporate executives are warriors, they are anonymous warriors, and in the end they are just as faceless as soldiers. They are given meaningless medals and promotions, to reward them for some soon-to-be-forgotten struggle for having gained the top of some imaginary corporate hill for their company and their superiors who care nothing about them personally. Having been awarded hollow honors, increased comfort, and money by their feudal lords, they continue to live synthetically, unauthentically, and uninitiated, with no true village belonging. They are most certainly removed from their organic nature and their human need to be part of the world of people, earth, water, animals, plants, and to be able to die a good death.

It is not the heroic warrior who is the culprit here; it is the lack of graduates in the study of adulthood that is to blame.

If the hero is suppressed by his or her elders or thrown away by the culture, then it reemerges in a sinister subversive form as vicious corporate soldiers, the "sensitive" killer, the passive-aggressive betrayer, the sociopath, the neighborhood gang member or neo-Nazi skinhead depending on what neighborhood the person was neglected in. This heroic warrior stage has a real use but must have the guidance of life-loving adults who have developed through and beyond the warrior to keep this powerful being out of his own hands and the designs of the unscrupulous. By employing warriorness he or she can fight her way out of an overextended youth into becoming a mortal human on the long useful road to adulthood where a person can cease being only a warrior.

This stage of a teenager's ability to fall deeply in love and desire to fight heroically for a worthy cause was known by my initiated Tzutujil elders as the very force that had saved their entire internal Earth from annual cyclic destruction at the hands of us humans as we cut, burned, farmed, and mined the world to feed ourselves.

The main difference between the cultures who send their youth to war or corporations and the culture of a Mayan village lay in the fact that the village elders did not send their youth off to war armed with computers, swords, rocket launchers, or tanks to kill and raid, creating more Death. Very significantly, they sent their Rainwarriors to fight against the Deity of Death, to fight Death itself, not to make more death but to coax Death into releasing life back to us.

By employing the very same instinct of heroism, romantic moodiness, patriotic tribalism, competitiveness, and the need for physical confrontation that has repeatedly destroyed cultures and worlds and threatens this one even as I speak, the Tzutujil elders sent their Mayan warriors down into the Underworld to ritually confront Death. This was not a fake Disney-like event or a mock battle. Men had died doing it, but no human enemy was ever attacked, no other race or tribe was demonized as the enemy.

Armed with an acute oral literacy of courting, poetry, history, and above all a well-developed relationship with nature as a divine female being, these "spiritual warriors" attempted to fight Death, to convince Death to release the Female principle of the Universe, the Woman Earth, as well as the boy's very own soul, which was a Female too; his "Spirit Bride." What those spiritual warriors saw and experienced in their dangerous wrestling match with Death was not what they expected. A soldier's training was of no use in the underworld. Shooting, cutting, bullets, bombs, explosives, trapping, piercing, deception and the like were tools and weapons of Death itself and you cannot kill Death with Death.

Men who didn't fight Death in adolescence were destined to live in a walking death. Already killed, depressed, and dangerous they become wreakers of violence, makers of death, corporate soldiers, and, more importantly, they become the destroyers of all that is Female. Because they had not fought Death, Death still had their souls, their Female Spirit Brides. Because these uninitiated men have no souls, they begin to "steal" women, to "rob" the Female Earth of its minerals, trees, and wealth, in a vain attempt to fill that hollow place in them where the Female soul should have been sitting, trying to steal a soul, just as Death had stolen the Goddess from life to fill his emptiness. In their attempt to obtain position, respect, and fulfillment by raiding, pillaging and dominating, they only create ghosts. Instead of finding their souls, they create hungry phantoms that demand more violence to keep them fed.

Let it be clearly stated that the Goddess was in no way a human woman's soul and a human woman's spirit was not being rescued. To become an adult meant a man had to marry his own soul, his Spirit Bride, before he could truly love a flesh-and-blood woman. He had to use his young spirit warrior to rescue "Her" from the literalist Underworld of Death, whose overriding characteristics were its lack of images, eloquence, and meaning, and its inability to remember anything besides who had to die next to feed its emptiness. This was Death's amnesia.

The young spiritual warrior could not conquer this Underworld Enemy, this Death. He could only wrestle it and weaken it as much as he could with his teenage imagination, idealism, his recently trained and blossomed eloquence, and his youthful memory, filled now through initiation with his people's spiritual histories and mythologies, which are the life-tethering roots of any peoples.

Nonetheless, after considerable weakening, the only thing eloquence wrestling accomplished was a stalemate with Death. The Goddess of life and the boy's Spirit Bride were released to the boy only when he made an agreement with Death to trade his youth and immortality for his Soul Bride. In this way the boy returned to life with his soul knowing, as all initiated people do, that this full feeling in his heart meant he'd signed a lease agreement with Death to die of old age later on. Part of the fine print in that contract was his promise to continue "feeding" Life, the Goddess, his soul, and that by doing so, he agreed to move out of being only a warrior into the pursuit of adulthood by marrying and feeding children. He stopped following an empty longing and began carrying a worthy fullness, dedicated to feeding the spirit with his worthy mortality of being a regular man.

He didn't lose the warrior ability, of course, but its qualities were absorbed into him and distilled into something even more useful. If our parents were like frogs who laid eggs, and we as teenagers were their tadpoles, then our long beautiful tails were our youth, which went into feeding our enormous swollen heads. At least that's how I was. Both the little ingenious child and the heroic warrior are in that swishing tail we dragged behind us in our youth until it was slowly absorbed and incorporated into a fine jumping body that leaped out of our parents' pond into the dangerous outer world of infinite fresh air, beauty, and fascination.

We don't have to cut off the tails of our youth when we become initiated adults because without it we could never have become adults. The greatest terror of today is that people who have never been initiated, who have never wrestled Death with their beauty, art, poetry, or their will to find what they love, are often found leading whole cultures and generations of uninitiated people who mistake tribalism for culture, fundamentalism for indigenousity.

The exclusivity and racism inherent in tribalism is dissolved by a true initiation. For this reason the old-time Tzutujil put their teenagers from opposing village divisions, economic levels, and classes side by side in the rituals, so they could, little by little, work together to form a new generation of villagers who were aware that Gods, Nature, and their destiny were greater than the destructive prejudices of the families, clans, races, and tribes.

Indigenousity happens when a people are at home with who they are and are unafraid of losing their identity. Once initiations are dead, village memory collapses, respect for the old evaporates, and the people melt into adult adolescents with an amorphous identity attached only to their personal wants. If you have a lot of money you could be a yuppie, imagining yourself to be what the TV says you should be. But if there is no food and no resources and there are many of you, tribalism sets in with the most disturbing soul-destroying results.

When there are no true initiations and the people lose their land, entire country, or purpose, their relationship with the Earth evaporates. One of the most common ways groups of destroyed people try to reinvent themselves is by pointing to some others and saying "We are not that" instead of being able to say "We are this." What they "are" in this scenario remains unformed. This sometimes escalates to the point where a tribalizing people will build fortressed societies, countries, or subdivisions, and in the worst cases, everything that is not "us" is destroyed in pitiless civil wars, or political imprisonments, mass incarcerations, "final solutions," and the senseless massacres of ethnic cleansing. What these lost people call initiation into their violent tribalist despair is not initiation at all. They need to be braver and grieve, face Death, with art and spirituality. But not create death, otherwise this is tribalism at its worst. The Tzutujil were not tribal in this sense.

Fundamentalism is just another form of tribalism. Fundamentalist Christians, Jews, and Muslims are certainly not the only peoples tribalizing themselves into fortress mentalities out of fear. When cultural amnesia is imposed upon any group by other violent uninitiated forces from without, the hollow shame they are left with is a pile of devouring ghosts who thrive on fear and narrow-minded thinking. There are tribalist fundamentalist movements in every nation of the world now, peoples who had their original relationship with their stories, music, ancestral histories, and customs destroyed or trivialized by the heavy tread of some other traumatized people whose ancestors' souls are still waiting in the Underworld. All of these people need someone who will bargain with Death in the Underworld for the release of the Goddess, their cultural and individual identities, and their indigenous souls. It would take a lot of grief rituals and some very brave, unarmored, highly initiated poetic shamans to do that.

Tribalism is not good, fundamentalism is not good, but the freedom of individualism can be only as good as there are a waiting village of well-cooked, open-armed, laughing elders who know worldly compassion personally and the complexities of the spirit world well enough to catch us, hold us down on the earth, and protect us from ourselves.

If initiation is about culture and the modern world desires initiation it will have to redefine itself. A new culture would have to develop where humans and their inventions are not at the center of the universe, and where God too is not at the center. What could be at the center is a hollow place, an empty place, where both God and we humans could sing and weep together as a team pushing magical words into that sacred Hole. Maybe together, the diverse and combined excellence of all cultures could court the Tree of Life back out of its frightened and fugitive existence in the previous layers where it was banished into the invisible by our scared literalist minds, dogmatic religiosities, and forgetfulness.

Martín Prechtel was raised on an Indian reservation in New Mexico before moving to Santiago Atitlan in Guatemala, where he apprenticed to Nicolas Chiviliu Tacaxoy, a Tzutujil Mayan shaman. Martín eventually rose to the office of *Najbey Mam,* First Chief. Returning to the United States, Martín began working in New Mexico as a medicine man. He is now a nationally recognized healer, speaker, and artist who writes frequently for anthropological journals and university publications and is constantly on the road speaking and lecturing.

ALSO BY MARTÍN PRECHTEL

Secrets of the Talking Jaguar